Helmut Puff

Miniature Monuments

Media and Cultural Memory/ Medien und kulturelle Erinnerung

Edited by
Astrid Erll · Ansgar Nünning

Volume 17

Helmut Puff

Miniature Monuments

Modeling German History

DE GRUYTER

ISBN 978-3-11-030385-8
e-ISBN 978-3-11-030409-1
ISSN 1613-8961

Library of Congress Cataloging-in-Publication Data
A CIP catalog record for this book has been applied for at the Library of Congress.

Bibliographic information published by the Deutsche Nationalbibliothek
The Deutsche Nationalbibliothek lists this publication in the Deutsche Nationalbibliografie; detailed bibliographic data are available on the internet at http://dnb.dnb.de.

Cover illustration: Model of Hannover 1945, detail, City Hall (Photo: Helmut Puff)
Typesetting: Johanna Boy DTP, Brennberg
Printing and binding: CPI books GmbH, Leck
♾ Printed on acid-free paper
Printed in Germany

www.degruyter.com

Acknowledgments

This book would not have been written were it not for a conversation over coffee I had many years ago with my colleague in the Department of Germanic Languages and Literatures at the University of Michigan, Julia Hell. Returning from Germany, I mentioned in passing a strange object I had come across in a local history museum, a three-dimensional miniature rendering of an urban district damaged in the aerial bombing. My description sparked her curiosity. Her surprised reaction sent me on a journey. Her encouragement and critical engagement have deeply shaped its path. The result is this book – a book equally strange in some aspects as the object it occasioned.

It is a testament to Julia Hell's brilliance as an interlocutor that Andreas Schoenle, a friend and former colleague at Michigan's Department of Slavic Languages and Literatures (now at Queen Mary University of London), opens his *Architecture of Oblivion: Ruins and Historical Consciousness in Modern Russia* (2011) with an almost identical tribute to Julia Hell. I owe a great deal to the venues for discussion the two of them sponsored. They invited me to participate in graduate seminars, workshops, and conferences. Their joint efforts resulted in the anthology *The Ruins of Modernity*, to which I contributed an essay.

For reasons I sketch in the concluding pages, this is a personal book. I feel fortunate in that this project has allowed me to better understand the place and time where I came of age, and connect my interests in European early modern history, literature, and culture to the upheavals of twentieth-century history that have left such profound traces on the generations born after World War II. That both my departments – History as well as German – and the university have supported me on this adventurous path through paid leaves, research support, and, most importantly, words of appreciation fills me with gratitude for the unique academic milieu in which I am fortunate to work.

The interactions with historians of art at Michigan have probably been my most profound intellectual pleasure of the past decade. I learned the ropes of how to talk about things visual in a graduate seminar Celeste Brusati and I co-taught – one of my most exhilarating teaching experiences to date. Her colleague, my neighbor and friend, Betsy Sears, has been a source of encouragement over many years. Tom Willette and others in the department have contributed their wisdom. Will Glover (Architecture/History) generously offered a most insightful response when I presented a talk at the Eisenberg Institute for Historical Studies.

Working for a half a year as a fellow at the Herzog August Bibliothek in Wolfenbüttel, Germany, allowed me to finish a first draft of this book. I thank Jill Bepler, the librarians, and my research companions for their patience, as I was balancing several tasks at the same time. While there, I became close friends with

Gundula Boveland, whose help and enthusiasm have fueled my completion of this project.

David M. Lobenstine, New York, and Michelle Miller, Ann Arbor, were expert editors whose feedback made this an infinitely better book than it would otherwise have become. Cristian Capotescu has been of great assistance in gathering bibliographical information.

I was extremely fortunate in that Kathleen Canning, Celeste Brusati, and Katherine French were tasked with evaluating my academic work when I was up for promotion. I also want to thank the anonymous reviewers at the press for their input. My gratitude goes to Astrid Erll and Ansgar Nünning for having agreed to publish *Miniature Monuments* in the series they edit, *Media and Cultural Memory*. Manuela Gerlof and her co-workers at de Gruyter were models of efficiency.

In the process of writing this book, I have accrued many debts – more than I can acquit myself of in these paragraphs. Here, I can only express a summary gratitude to the many people at libraries, archives, museums, and universities where I worked over the years in the US, Germany, and Japan. Their expert support made all the difference in advancing my thinking and writing.

Some sections of this book have been published before. An earlier version of Chapter Three appeared as "The City as Model: Three-Dimensional Representations of Urban Space in Early Modern Europe" in *Topographies of the Early Modern City* (Göttingen: Vandenhoeck & Ruprecht, 2008), edited by Art Groos, Hans-Jochen Schiewer, and Markus Stock (pages 193–217). I first worked out my perspectives on rubble models in "Ruins as Models: Displaying Destruction in Postwar Germany" (*Ruins of Modernity*, ed. Julia Hell and Andreas Schoenle, Durham: Duke University Press, 2010, 253–269). Some of my thinking on ruins was first published in a piece entitled "Self-Portrait with Ruins: Maerten van Heemskerck, 1553" in *Germanic Review*, vol. 86, 2011, pages 262–276.

Models are objects whose practicality resides not least in their preliminary nature. May my "model studies" (Thomas Demand) serve others to model their own.

Contents

Chapter Five

Epilogue

List of Illustrations

Chapter One

Introduction

Some years ago I stepped into the local museum of a mid-sized German town. At the entrance to the museum's exhibition – rooms filled with traces of urban life from the city's medieval and early modern past – visitors were greeted with a large relief model of the nineteenth-century city. This comprehensive urban sculpture, an exuberant overture to the museum's galleries, sat in conversation with a smaller counterpart across the aisle; the city's cathedral district, at the end of World War II, in a state of destruction. The model was sterile and grey, with neatly caved-in roofs and clean ground. It was, in other words, a figment of the historical imagination. The sanitized display of war left me wanting, if not bewildered: dereliction that had been rid of dust, rubble, pain, and death: war as an architectural abstraction. What is more, aside from a short caption that explained what there was to see ("Cathedral District during the Winter of 1944"), no information on what had happened, who had caused the war, and the destruction, and who died.

That urban model, war on tidy display, along with my inability to comprehend it, led me to embark on this book. I stared at this vehicle of the historical imagination, a tool seemingly for our edification that nonetheless was unable to function as a conduit between a painful past and our own present. I was baffled and fascinated. I went on a quest for models of urban destruction; I sought to comprehend the political aesthetics behind these objects. The 2001-model I have mentioned above is, as I came to realize, a latecomer to a series of similar objects that have been exhibited all over Germany since 1946. These images of urban destruction model the devastating effects of the air raids on German cities during World War II in modeled form. The oldest one is of Frankfurt am Main and came into being not long after the city's destruction (1946). The most recent one is a meticulous reconstruction of a devastated Pforzheim shortly after the attacks that razed the city in February of 1945. It is finished only in parts; one can make a donation to help its completion. Overall, I identified ten such models currently on display in German city halls, memorials, and local history museums.[1] Like the one that puzzled me initially, some feel bewilderingly, disturbingly banal; others

1 Frankfurt am Main, Historisches Museum (1946); Hamburg, Hamburgmuseum (1950); Hannover, Rathaus (1951ff); Kassel, Stadtmuseum (1955); Heilbronn, Rathaus (1960); Münster, Stadtmuseum (1966); Bielefeld, Historisches Museum (approximately 1985); Würzburg, Mainfränkisches Museum and Würzburg, Grafeneckart (Rathaus) (1989); Trier, Stadtmuseum Simeonstift (2001); and Pforzheim, Stadtmuseum (2000-). Exact dates for the make of most of these models are not documented. The Würzburg model in the memorial in city hall is a partial copy of the larger model in the museum.

are far more affecting, and even in their miniaturized form hint at the enormity of war's destruction. Like in the aforementioned museum, however, they are often exhibited together with counterparts that show the city before or after destruction.

Countries across Europe were devastated by the air raids of World War II. These enormous, and lasting, losses have been remembered in multiple ways. However, I know of no European relief models of destruction from countries other than Germany. The only other company these German models have is a group of models on display in the city of Hiroshima in Japan, target of the first nuclear bomb. Why, then, is Germany unique amongst its European neighbors? Why are there no such sculptures of urban destruction in Coventry or Caen, Warsaw or Palermo? The strange place of these German curiosities is one conundrum that this book will explore.

These sculptures bring us to a larger point: the disasters that reached cities from the air have yet to forge and sustain cross-national forms of public commemoration. National borders, in fact, determine how we remember the war as a whole. At present, for instance, there are only vague contours of a pan-European memory culture centered on World War II, so entrenched are national prerogatives.[2]

All urban sculptures of destruction that exist render cities (or central parts thereof) in the Federal Republic of Germany; no such models were made in the German Democratic Republic. As far as I can tell, commemorations in East German cities marshaled the master narrative of socialist struggle, resistance, and international solidarity against fascism. In East Germany, political leaders saw little benefit to commemorating destruction locally; instead, the focus was on connecting locales to a larger story. By contrast, in West Germany, urban communities took the lead in commemorating their destruction, foregrounding the local while de-emphasizing the role of Hitler and German aggression that triggered these urban devastations. What was the appeal of material monuments in miniature for the West German city officials who, as a rule, commissioned them? The rubble models, I believe, functioned (and function still) as a repository of

---

2 Christoph Cornelißen, "Die Nationalität von Erinnerungskulturen als ein gesamteuropäisches Phänomen," *Geschichte in Wissenschaft und Unterricht* 62 (2011): 5–16. See also Konrad H. Jarausch and Thomas Lindenberger, eds., *Conflicted Memories: Europeanizing Contemporary Histories* (New York: Berghahn, 2007); Kirstin Buchinger, Claire Gantet, and Jakob Vogel, eds., *Europäische Erinnerungsräume* (Frankfurt am Main: Campus, 2009); Pim den Boer, Heinz Duchardt, Georg Kreis, and Wolfgang Schmale, eds., *Europäische Erinnerungsorte*, 3 vols. (Munich: Oldenbourg, 2012); and Eric Langenbacher, Bill Niven, and Ruth Wittlinger, eds., *Dynamics of Memory and Identity in Contemporary Europe* (New York: Berghahn, 2012).

temporalities, emotions, and narratives. As we will see, these models were sites where one could and can invoke memories of a past that was lost, the experience of destruction, and a future that never came to be.

This is not to say that the models I have identified are all alike. Their size, scale, and build, the materials used and the use of color all vary to a remarkable degree. If these models are themselves agents in scenarios of commemoration – an idea we will return to – then all physical characteristics, and their differences from other such models, become significant. If these objects goad us to remember, then they also incite responses, dependent on their make, context, and commentary. What is more, their primary function has changed over time; since the 1980s the display of these models has been moved from memorial contexts to historical exhibits. To explore the intertwined realms of memory, history, and representation in this odd world means to study rubble models as material objects in the context of their presentation and their history.

But there is a basic problem with my inquiry. Even in light of the cultural history of the past two or three decades – a historiography much engaged with questions of representation and discourse – studying models goes against the grain of what historians traditionally do. In a recent essay on the historian's craft, entitled *The Landscape of History*, John Lewis Gaddis proposes maps and mapping as analogous to the historian's endeavor of rendering the past legible: "if you think of the past as a landscape, then history is the way we represent it, and it's that act of representation that lifts us above the familiar to let us experience vicariously what we can't experience directly: a wider view."[3] Seeking to survey the past, the historian rises above the clouds – Caspar David Friedrich's 1818-painting "Wanderer above the Sea of Fog" (*Wanderer über dem Nebelmeer*) provides *The Landscape of History*'s visual emblem, a choice tinged with irony. The heroic male figure of the Romantic explorer is said to experience "the simultaneous sense of significance and insignificance, of detachment and engagement, of mastery and humility, of adventure but also of danger."[4] Our own endeavor faces similar contradictions. When the clouds have lifted, what will we be able to see and what will be occluded from view in the landscape spread below our eyes? The tools we use to see, it seems, have an impact on what we are able to find. In the course of Gaddis's plea for the historian's craft, the actual "technologies of virtual transport" disappear from sight.[5] Maps appear

3 John Lewis Gaddis, *The Landscape of History: How Historians Map the Past* (New York: Oxford University Press, 2002), 5.

4 Ibid., 129.

5 Alison Griffiths, "The Revered Gaze: The Medieval Imaginary of Mel Gibson's 'The Passion of the Christ,'" *Cinema Journal* 46 (2007): 7.

mostly as a metaphor for the generalizations in which historians engage: their ability to shift back and forth between micro- and macro-perspectives. But Gaddis actually does not seem to trust the material reality of maps, or other material objects, not unlike many of his colleagues. "Historians are, by profession, suspicious of things," writes Leora Auslander.[6]

Scale models are absent from the growing body of literature on memory and history. "Scholars who focus on images as vehicles of memory contend that from antiquity to modern times," according to Wulf Kansteiner, "the media of memory have been characterized by 'the primacy of the visual.'"[7] Yet practitioners of memory studies have favored particular objects of study in this regard: national monuments, works of art, or documents that bear traces of the authentic, rather than the simulated spectacle – surprising in light of the fact that the field can be said to elaborate the basic insight into the constructedness of the past, and considers visuals as both constructed and construing images of history. Yet relief models are only remote indices of historical trauma, for instance – one of the most prevalent focuses of memory studies. Similarly, in their patent artificiality, these models subvert the emphatic approach that has turned art into one of the preferred objects of memory studies.[8] Removed from traumatic stories by layers of mediation, these models force temporal distance and spatial recalibration onto a scene of devastation, "a wider view."

It is clear that these models pose many problems to the historical endeavor. But the complexity of mapping the past is all the more reason why we must put critical pressure on the media that feed the historical imagination. The present book is an attempt to investigate one of these visual tools, three-dimensional representations of cities, in particular ruined cities. By the nature of their materials, they seem detached; by the nature of their scale, they seem *smaller* than life. They seem to be, for these and many reasons, unsatisfying as objects of historical pursuit, lacking the emotion and the broad swath that we want to read into our history. But these difficulties are, in themselves, revelatory.

Taking inspiration from a number of theorists, Friedrich Nietzsche, Sigmund Freud, and Aby Warburg among them, one of the paragons of memory studies in Germany, Jan Assmann, has issued a plea to break through the presentism of the field. Building on the studies of the French sociologist Maurice Halbwachs (who examined collective memory as a social category), Assmann reaches beyond the

6 Leora Auslander, "Beyond Words," *American Historical Review* 110 (2005): 1015.
7 Wulf Kansteiner, *In Pursuit of German Memory: History, Television, and Politics after Auschwitz* (Athens: Ohio University Press, 2006), 21.
8 Jacques Rancière, *The Future of the Image*, trans. Gregory Elliott (London: Verso, 2007), 137.

connective tissue that binds social groups in the present and toward a richly layered notion of cultural memory. He insists that we must take into account the historical knowledge and media that frame the process of building and undoing memory in both an individual and in groups.[9] Unless we recognize the historical entanglements inherent in various forms of representation, we will in fact fail to unlock the core of the past, in all of its many manifestations, and its multiform presence in the present. I therefore seek to interlace different sites of analysis, connecting the twentieth century with earlier contexts and centuries. In studying this genre of objects, I aim at envisaging the models' deeper history – a history reaching into a past more remote than the horrific events they purport to render.

If we approach rubble models as media of the historical imagination, and as media with a potentially deep history, they emerge as paradoxical objects – and this is, among other reasons, why they merit our engagement. As visual reminders of monumental loss, to be sure, they resemble monuments. But they are monuments in miniature; their size makes both the objects themselves, and our responses, more vexing. As a rule, they are set up with plenty of space about them, allowing visitors to circle around as they look. Wherever they are exhibited, their actual display highlights the semantic charge these objects can have. Put differently, they demand attention from visitors to a site, and have the potential to draw each of us in. Only when we approach them physically and follow their allure will they yield some of the messages they contain. Only when we are at close range can we appreciate their marvelous detail – or be disturbed by their abstraction. In other words, three-dimensional representations of urban spaces issue an invitation. The question then becomes whether, and how, we will answer.

While the meaning of models depends on their manner of display and position, models also *position us*; they usher us into particular visual subjectivities. What distinguishes these miniature monuments from large monuments in public squares is the position they afford us as viewers: as a rule, they give us the sense that we are standing high above the ground, a position of command, and, not accidentally, the sovereign position of the wanderer above the sea of fog in Friedrich's painting. By contrast, conventional monuments of a nation's struggles or victories put the viewer in a subordinate place. The monument typically translates its trenchant symbolism for the community or country into parameters such as size or elevation; as individuals, we are, quite literally, overshadowed. Once we

9 Jan Assmann, *Religion und kulturelles Gedächtnis: Zehn Studien* (Munich: Beck, 2000), 116. In an article cited further below, Alon Confino also refers to Aby Warburg as an inspiration.

recognize the significance of the model's own placement, and its rapport with the body of the beholder, we can start to see these objects as agents.

No matter our position or theirs: visual paradoxes have the power to arrest our gaze. Most models in historical exhibitions – whether of an early version of New York City, for example, or a pastoral scene of the French countryside, seem self-explanatory. As historicist objects par excellence, they are said to render, as perfectly as possible, whatever moment in time they claim as their reference point, even if such a precise point is elusive at best – a tension inherent in any effort committed to recover the fullness of the past. In short, they function as media of spatial and historical verisimilitudes. By modeling a building, a settlement, or a city at a specific moment, they allow beholders to suspend critical disbelief and gain a novel perspective on the past. They make up for what they lack in authenticity with an exuberant material presence.

Rubble models can certainly be approached in the fashion of the historical model; they seek to portray the debris, the hollow facades, the shells of buildings, and the urban organism rendered dysfunctional, and they do so for a particular moment in time. But they are also anti-models. They do not exhibit a vision of architectural or urbanistic fullness as do conventional historical models, for instance. Conventional models invite viewers to imagine a particular locale at its best, most prosperous, or at its architechtural peak. Instead, rubble models depict destruction incurred in war – and in our case, German cities in a war that ended with Germany's defeat. Models of destroyed cities deliver an image of urban forms at a time when they had ceased to function as places of habitation, commerce, and sociability. What they show amounts to a mere chimera of what we associate with a city: we recognize the city that once was and no longer is (in the actual cities destroyed by the raids, inhabitants frequently continued to eke out a living, against all odds).

The temporal scenarios rubble models provoke in the viewer are strikingly complex. For one, as I have just suggested, icons of destruction invoke memories of or questions about what came before – the city on the eve of its demise – and what came after, the city built up again. (Though many at the time doubted whether some of the devastated cities of central Europe could ever be resuscitated, there is, surprisingly, barely a case in which a whole city was re-erected at a different location.)[10] But models cannot show processes; their seductive simplic-

10 This is different from Sicilian towns leveled in a 1693 earthquake that were re-erected at different locations, in the case of Ragusa on an adjacent hill, in the case of Noto at considerable distance to its original place – after nine years of contentious debates over the move; see Andreas Ranft and Stephan Selzer, "Städte aus Trümmern: Einleitende Überlegungen," in *Städte*

ity, and their great power, is that they deny the perpetual passing of time. Instead, they are bent on halting time for the beholders to view, to appreciate, and to let their gaze wander about this static depiction –despite the fact that destruction is unsteady, uneven, and impossible to condense into a stable image.[11]

These tensions – between hints of a temporal expanse on the one hand and an image of impermanent destruction on the other – point to the model's conceptual side. Three-dimensional urban models are, in a way, deictic objects – objects created to show us something about the built environment, be it for pedagogical, artistic, or political purposes. After all, city models are frequently used as an aid in urban planning. Ostensibly, they have something to tell us, even if (or precisely because) they claim their expertise by reducing the complex world to mere shapes and forms. Models thus embody, if not expose, the fictional side of spaces. In other words, they are not exclusively instruments of spatial mimesis; they are instruments of a spatial *concetto* – that is, a mode of imagining space – and of architectural or urbanistic thought.[12] As a result, they allow for exercises in what ultimately is unbuildable. This is why models and drawings acquired a position of prime importance among architects and city-planners in modern times; they allowed for radical visions of built spaces freed from pragmatic constraints. One may think of Étienne-Louis Boullée's (1728–1799) grand memorial architecture on paper or Vladimir Tatlin's (1885–1953) three-dimensional model for the "Monument to the Third International" of 1919 – a building not only never built but also unbuildable. Rubble models thus embody a conceptual as well as perceptual paradox. They are suspended between what we might call the heritage model – the model that promises a truthful image of the built (or in this case the destroyed) past – and the conceptualist model, a model that embodies something far less tangible – a vision, an idea, a memory.

My attention to models is part of a growing awareness that Germans *did* represent and communally memorialize the air raids, although the moral evasiveness of models also points to the fraught nature of such commemoration. To understand rubble models' hesitant message and the many subtle ways in which

aus Trümmern: Katastrophenbewältigung zwischen Antike und Moderne, ed. A. Ranft and St. Selzer (Göttingen: Vandenhoeck & Ruprecht, 2004), 9–25, here p. 23.

11 In his account of the destruction of Hamburg from the air, *Der Untergang*, the German writer Hans-Erich Nossack writes: "we were people without rest. We didn't have a lot of time, we no longer had any time at all, we were outside time" (*The End: Hamburg 1943*, trans. Joel Agee [Chicago: University of Chicago Press, 2004], 48).

12 On models in architecture, see Kenneth Frampton, Silvia Kolbowski, and Richard Pommer, eds., *Idea as Model* (New York: Rizzoli, 1981); Mark Morris, *Models: Architecture and the Miniature* (Chichester: Wiley-Academy, 2006).

they convey meaning, we need to first explore what has kept us (until now) from noticing models' ideological work and community-building among post-war German viewers.

Air War and Representation

In *Air War and Literature*, an essay on the effects of the air raids on post-war German literature, the German writer and critic W. G. Sebald decried "the fact that the images of this horrifying chapter of our history have never really crossed the threshold of the national [German] consciousness."[13] If we follow Sebald's deceptively simple thesis, this chasm between the air raids' profound impact and their absence from representations has had far-reaching consequences for the "stock of emotions" (*Gefühlshaushalt*) of contemporary Germans.[14] The moral obligations that emerged in post-war Germany, the author explicates rather bluntly, imposed severe restrictions on representing Germans as victims of the air raids: "a nation which had murdered and worked to death millions of people in its camps could hardly call on the victorious powers to explore the military and political logic that dictated the destruction of the German cities."[15] Many decades after the end of World War II, the author casts the tending to this absence in Germans' collective memory as an ethical, literary, and historical imperative. This plea for engagement reverberated widely on both sides of the Atlantic when a spate of newspaper articles, reviews, and essays disseminated the book's central conceit to a public eager to discuss a "taboo."[16]

---

13 W. G. Sebald, *On the Natural History of Destruction: With Essays on Alfred Andersch, Jean Améry and Peter Weiss*, trans. Anthea Bell (London: Hamish Hamilton, 2003), 12; id., *Luftkrieg und Literatur: Mit einem Essay zu Alfred Andersch* (Munich: Hanser, 1999), 11.
14 Sebald, *On the Natural History of Destruction*, 11; id., *Luftkrieg und Literatur*, 12.
15 Sebald, *On the Natural History of Destruction*, 13f. On this question see also the following anthologies: Lothar Kettenacker, ed., *Ein Volk von Opfern? Die neue Debatte um den Bombenkrieg 1940–45* (Berlin: Rowohlt, 2003); Bill Niven, ed., *Germans as Victims: Remembering the Past in Contemporary Germany* (New York: Palgrave Macmillan, 2006); Stuart Taberner and Karina Berger, eds. *Germans as Victims in the Literary Fiction of the Berlin Republic* (Rochester, NY: Camden House, 2009). On the term victim itself and its application regarding Germany and World War II in modern criticism, see Mary Cosgrove, "Narrating German Suffering in the Shadow of Holocaust Victimology: W. G. Sebald, Contemporary Trauma Theory, and Dieter Forte's Air Raids Epic," in *Germans as Victims in the Literary Fiction*, 162–175; Aleida Assmann, *Der lange Schatten der Vergangenheit: Erinnerungskultur und Geschichtspolitik* (Munich: Beck, 2006), esp. pp. 72–84.
16 On the reception, see *W. G. Sebald: History – Memory – Trauma*, ed. Scott Denham and Mark McCulloh (New York: de Gruyter, 2006).

While the scarcity of novels on the air war over Germany is his essay's primary focus, Sebald also diagnoses a dearth of adequate histories on the subject.[17] Even though a number of historians *have* devoted studies to the bombings, he states, they have researched the destruction only in individual cities and failed to address the disaster's larger dimensions. What is more, these histories appear untouched by the horrific subject matter they purport to make legible. What we know of the air raids is "inadequate and inhibited," Sebald concludes.[18] The sheer data on lives lost, houses destroyed, or the amount of rubble, figure in Sebald's analysis as an inability to register the multiple losses at stake on a deeper level. At the same time, conventional contextualizations within the confines of military history, a history of state bureaucracy, or a history of the nation are deemed insufficient, if not ethically inappropriate. They risk ridding the experiences of the air war of its monumental suffering. Instead, Sebald searches for an elegiac historical text beyond and outside history, or the historiography on post-war German history as we know it.[19]

Critics have faulted Sebald for this provocative essay – launched, as one suspects, to incite public debate. Some critics have sought to complicate his message by extricating the tensions operative beneath the surface of the essay.[20] Others have unearthed contradicting materials that provide evidence for the persistent presence of the air raids in the individual, familial, and communal remembrances of the war years after 1945. Yet with few exceptions, literary critics, historians, and cultural critics insist that the air raids cannot adequately be understood as tabooed matter.[21] Sebald's flirtation with the term notwithstanding, there was

17 Cf., however, the assessment of Ralf Blank in "Kriegsalltag und Luftkrieg an der 'Heimatfront,'" in *Das Deutsche Reich und der Zweite Weltkrieg*, vol. 9/1: *Die Deutsche Kriegsgesellschaft 1939 bis 1945: Politisierung, Vernichtung, Überleben*, ed. Jörg Echternkamp (Munich: Deutsche Verlags-Anstalt, 2004), 360: "Betrachtet man den Bombenkrieg aus der Perspektive seiner Überlieferung, so läßt sich eine umfassende Quellenlage unterschiedlicher Provenienz sowie eine dichte und frühzeitige Rezeption feststellen."

18 Sebald, *On the Natural History of Destruction*, iii.

19 Cf. Jörg Friedrich, *Der Brand: Deutschland im Bombenkrieg 1940–1945* (Munich: Propyläen, 2002); English as *The Fire: The Bombing of Germany 1940–1945*, trans. Allison Brown (New York: Columbia University Press, 2006). See also Dietmar Süß, "Review Article: Memories of the Air War," *Journal of Contemporary History* 43 (2002): 333–342; Robert G. Moeller, "The Bombing War in Germany, 2005–1940: Back to the Future?" in *Bombing Civilians: A Twentieth-Century History*, ed. Yuki Tanaka and Marilyn B. Young (New York: The New Press, 2009), 46–76, 242–249.

20 Julia Hell, "The Angel's Enigmatic Eyes, or the Gothic Beauty of Catastrophic History in W. G. Sebald's 'Air War and Literature,'" *Criticism* 46 (2004): 361–392.

21 Some of the critical opinions will be cited below; here I cite scholars in agreement with Sebald's argument: Dagmar Barnouw, *War in the Empty Air: Victims, Perpetrators, and Postwar*

no silence, literary or other, regarding the aerial bombings in post-war Germany.[22] His own essay speaks eloquently of the tortured presence of the air raids in novelistic discourse. Sebald's incorporation of images without captions, a much-commented-on characteristic of his novelistic oeuvre, differs markedly from his novels. Of the sixteen photographs included in *Air War and Literature*, half are evidently taken from other publications, as center-folds and captions in the photograph make evident: they resemble quotations whose origins have only partially been erased, pointing back to un-cited post-war literature on the air raids.[23]

At issue in post-war discourses on the air war, therefore, was not so much repression, self-censorship, or public censorship, but the stereotypical patterns of thought and feeling at the heart of these same discourses. After 1945, for instance, German audiences showed a particular disposition toward "rubble poems" with their soothing rhymes and messages – something that has yet to provoke com-

---

Germans (Bloomington: Indiana University Press, 2005); John-Paul Stonard, *Fault Lines: Art in Germany 1945–1955* (London: Ridinghouse, 2007), 33–35. Stephen Brockmann (*German Literary Culture at the Zero Hour* [Rochester, NY: Camden House, 2004], 2f) speaks of "the need for repression" (3), though argues against a taboo.

22 In the following selected contributions to W. G. Sebald's *Air War and Literature* and the debate it unleashed, Ulrich Simon, "Der Provokateur als Literaturhistoriker: Anmerkungen zu Literaturbegriff und Argumentationsverfahren in W. G. Sebalds essayistischen Schriften," in *Sebald: Lektüren*, ed. Marcel Atze and Franz Loquai (Eggingen: Edition Isele, 2005), 78–104; Wilfried Wilms, "Speak no Evil, Write no Evil: In Search of a Usable Language of Destruction," in *W. G. Sebald: History – Memory – Trauma*, ed. Scott Denham and Mark McCulloh (New York: de Gruyter, 2006), 183–204; Susanne Vees-Gulani, "The Experience of Destruction: W. G. Sebald, the Airwar, and Literature," in *W. G. Sebald: History – Memory -- Trauma*, 335–349; Marcel Atze, "' ... und wer spricht über Dresden?' Der Luftkrieg als öffentliches und literarisches Thema in der Zeit des ersten Frankfurter Auschwitz-Prozesses 1963–1965," in *W. G. Sebald: Politische Archäologie und melancholische Bastelei*, ed. Michael Niehaus and Claudia Öhlschläger (Berlin: Erich Schmidt, 2006), 205–217; Ruth Franklin, "Rings of Smoke," in *The Emergence of Memory: Conversations with W. G. Sebald*, ed. Lynne Sharon Schwartz (New York: Seven Stories Press, 2007), 119–143; Ingo Wintermeyer, "'... kaum eine Schmerzensspur hinterlassen ... '? Luftkrieg, Literatur und der 'cordon sanitaire,'" in *Verschiebebahnhöfe der Erinnerung: Zum Werk W. G. Sebalds*, ed. Sigurd Martin and Ingo Wintermeyer (Würzburg: Königshausen & Neumann, 2007), 137–161; Bettina Mosbach, *Figurationen der Katastrophe: Ästhetische Verfahren in W. G. Sebalds 'Die Ringe des Saturn' und 'Austerlitz'* (Bielefeld: Aisthesis, 2008), 89–109.

23 Cf. Lise Patt, "Searching for Sebald: What I Know for Sure," in *Searching for Sebald: Photography after W. G. Sebald*, ed. Lise Patt (Los Angeles: The Institute for Cultural Inquiry, 2007), 62–69; Carolin Duttlinger, "A Lineage of Destruction? Rethinking Photography in 'Luftkrieg und Literatur,'" in *W. G. Sebald and the Writing of History*, ed. Anne Fuchs and J. J. Long (Würzburg: Königshausen & Neumann, 2007), 163–177.

mentary.[24] Also, German photographs of bombed-out cities strongly resonate with religious iconography: crosses as grave-markers on a mound of rubble erected for victims of the February 1945-air raid in Pforzheim, photographed and published repeatedly by different photographers from different angles (one of them included in Sebald's *Air War and Literature* without a hint as to where it was taken, another one in Jörg Friedrich's *The Fire*); Hermann Claasen's *Gesang im Feuerofen* (Song in the Fiery Burning Furnace, 1947) betrays its religious inspiration in the title with its reference to a story in the Old Testament book of Daniel; Richard Peter's famous shot of late 1945 from the Dresden City Hall has a stone sculpture oversee the skeleton of an urban neighborhood: an allegory of charity re-cast by many viewers as an angel.[25] Today's literary critics and historians interested not in approximating "traumatic experiences" through their own writing but the manifestations of the experiences of the air war in post-war society have detected a multitude of mutterings and musings, poetic, religious, and otherwise, about the attacks from the air and their effects on the ground after 1945. What is at issue is therefore less *whether* memories of the air raids could be expressed or not in post-war Germany. Rather, the question is *how* they were channeled, particularly in rapidly changing circumstances. In fact, Sebald became acutely aware of the vigorous, well-rehearsed responses to the bombings. His 1997-lectures triggered a wave of them – an experience he reflects on in a postscript to the published text of the 1999 essay.[26]

Importantly, a solitary focus on suffering (as propagated by Sebald and practiced, though in a different mode, by the historian Jörg Friedrich) fails to do justice to the complex ways in which the war from the air affected and was remembered

---

24 Max Rößler "Meiner Vaterstadt," in *Würzburger Chronik des denkwürdigen Jahres 1945 … im Auftrag der Stadt Würzburg* (Würzburg: Ferdinand Schöningh, 1947; reprint 1995), xii; Wilhelm Fries, "Kleve," in Bernhard Baak, *Zerstörung, Wiederaufbau und Verwaltung der Stadt Kleve: 1944–1957* (Kleve: Boss, 1960), 62; Maria Gindele-Boegl, "Der Drache und der Engel," in *Pforzheim 23. Februar 1945*, 9. In the cathedral of Freiburg im Breisgau, visitors encounter a panel reminding them of the "miracle" that the cathedral survived the aerial attack of November 1944 largely unscathed: a panoramic black and white-photograph of Freiburg with the city's center leveled and the cathedral standing as well as a poem by Reinhold Schneider, "An den Turm des Freiburger Münsters." See also Jörg Friedrich (*Brandstätten: Der Anblick des Bombenkriegs* [Munich: Propyläen, 2003]) who cites a poem as paratext (from Albrecht Hausdorfer's "Moabiter Sonette").

25 Hermann Claasen, *Gesang im Feuerofen: Köln – Überreste einer alten deutschen Stadt* (Düsseldorf: Schwann, 1947); Richard Peter, *Dresden – eine Kamera klagt an* (Dresden: Dresdner Verlagsgesellschaft KG, 1950). See also August Sander, *Die Zerstörung Kölns: Photographien 1945–46* (Munich: Schirmer-Mosel, 1985).

26 Sebald, *Luftkrieg und Literatur*, 75–110; Sebald, *On the Natural History of Destruction*, 69–104.

by "ordinary Germans." We need to work toward a historiography that accounts for the many ways in which the air raids were experienced. The German Jews who continued to live, if only in very small numbers, in German cities were barred from seeking shelter in bunkers, except under exceptional circumstances.[27] The notion of a community based in suffering is at risk of erasing not only distinctions within this community but the pettiness and apathy that shaped life in the bomb shelters – moments of relief, emotional outbursts, and solidarity in terror and distress notwithstanding.[28] In an excellent overview, Ralf Blank demonstrates how life during the air raids was part and parcel of the Nazi state's political structure, with its mobilization policies, competing bureaucracies, and increasingly strained attempts at resolving the basic needs of Germans – strains to which officials responded by stepping up the militarization of everyday life.[29] As we seek to recover historical materials from oblivion or distortion, it is imperative to disentangle the various social formations, mentalities, and temporal layers melded together in enterprises seeking to recover historical experiences from trauma-induced oblivion or distortion. The notion of a collective of suffering, like so much of our understanding of war's realities, is one that emerged retrospectively in the wake of the air raids and after the country's defeat.

In post-war Germany, many families formulated narratives or exchanged stories about their survival and their losses, tales that have found their ways into writings and publications.[30] Moreover, official publications on these urban infernos emerged, in some cases, not long after 1945. Under American military authority, the city of Würzburg issued a commemorative volume as early as 1947 in a time of scarce resources – the first of subsequent volumes dedicated to the same city's destruction.[31] This "chronicle of the memorable year 1945," as the cover

27 Gilad Margalit, *Guilt, Suffering, and Memory: Germany Remembers Its Dead from World War II*, trans. Haim Watzman (Bloomington: Indiana University Press, 2010), 174. Cf. Victor Klemperer, *Ich will Zeugnis ablegen bis zum letzten: Tagebücher 1942–1945*, ed. Walter Nowojski (Berlin: Aufbau, 1995), 661–672. Sebald comments briefly on this description in *On the Natural History of Destruction*, 25.

28 For the case of Hamburg in the wake of the attacks of 1943, Malte Thießen demonstrates how the myth of the "Volksgemeinschaft" united in response to the disaster arose in the Nazi press, see his *Eingebrannt ins Gedächtnis: Hamburgs Gedenken an Luftkrieg und Kriegsende 1943 bis 2005* (Hamburg: Dölling und Galitz, 2007), 45f.

29 Blank, "Kriegsalltag und Luftkrieg an der 'Heimatfront,'" 357–461.

30 See, for instance, Walter Kempowski, *Der rote Hahn: Dresden im Februar 1945* (Munich: btb, 2001).

31 Max Domarus, *Der Untergang des alten Würzburg im Luftkrieg gegen die deutschen Grosstädte* (Gerolzhofen: Franz Teutsch, 1978), first as *Der Untergang des alten Würzburg und seine Vorgeschichte* (1950); reprinted and expanded in 1955; fifth edition in 1982. See also Hermann Knell,

has it with its still life of ruinous matter, reads like a compendium of what would soon be the many standard forms of commemoration: a narrated account of the bombings as well as of the care for the dead; a report of the damages to the built environment (including a map); a description of the city's military defeat, and of the community's gradual re-emergence thereafter, interlaced with contemporary documents; a "rubble poem"; and images of the city before and after the fateful attack of March 16, 1945. Literally at the center of the book, however, is an alphabetical list of all the people lost to the bombs. This decidedly local perspective allowed the author, an archivist, to sidestep a discussion of what role the townspeople played throughout the war and their culpability as agents of their own demise. He took recourse instead to a vaguely defined pacifism in whose shadows many less elevated sentiments have flourished.[32]

In the seven decades since, historians and journalists alike have chronicled the demise of small, mid-size, and large cities in the hail of Allied bombs.[33] The majority of these books have been popular histories, written by amateur historians, focusing on individual military campaigns from the air and offering snippets of eyewitness accounts by civilians who suffered through the raids.[34] More recently, German publishers have produced a spate of books on the destruction from the air of individual cities, often with ample photographic documentation

---

To Destroy a City: Strategic Bombing and in World War II (Cambridge, Mass.: Da Capo, 2003); German as *Untergang in Flammen: Strategische Bombenangriffe und ihre Folgen im Zweiten Weltkrieg* (Würzburg: Veröffentlichungen des Stadtarchivs, 2006).

32 Hans Oppelt, *Würzburger Chronik des denkwürdigen Jahres 1945 ... im Auftrag der Stadt Würzburg* (Würzburg: Ferdinand Schöningh, 1947; reprint 1995). Hans Oppelt (b. 1907) was an archivist. A comparable volume, focused less on the destruction but on the town's re-emergence, is Bernhard Baak, *Zerstörung, Wiederaufbau und Verwaltung der Stadt Kleve: 1944–1957* (Kleve: Boss, 1960) with, among other things, photographs, a poem, and a list of citizens lost to the war. See also Esther Schmalacker-Wyrich, ed., *Pforzheim 23. Februar 1945: Der Untergang einer Stadt in Bildern und Augenzeugenberichten* (Pforzheim: J. Eßlinger, 1980) which contains a drawing, a poem, photographs, and eyewitness accounts.

33 A particularly interesting example in Ralf Blank, "Zerstört und vergessen? Hagen, das Ruhrgebiet und das Gedächtnis des Krieges," in *Luftkrieg: Erinnerungen in Deutschland und Europa*, ed. Jörg Arnold, Dietmar Süß, and Malte Thießen (Göttingen: Wallstein, 2009), 162–182.

34 Fourth expanded edition of *Der Untergang* (1950), see Max Domarus, *Der Untergang des alten Würzburg*. Cf. Ralph Barker, *The Thousand Plan: The Story of the First Thousand Bomber Raid on Cologne* (London: Chatto & Windus, 1965); Martin Middlebrook, *The Berlin Raids: RAF Bomber Command Winter 1943–44* (London: Viking, 1988). With the upsurge of interest in the war from the air, comprehensive historical accounts are increasingly becoming available, see Claudia Baldoli, Andrew Knapp, and Richard Overy, eds., *Bombing, States and Peoples in Western Europe 1940–1945* (London: Continuum, 2011); Richard Overy, *The Bombing War: Europe 1939–1945* (London: Allen Lane, 2013).

and relatively scant texts.[35] What holds most of these reflections together is the fact that they are focused on particular locales – an approach that allows the authors to eschew larger themes, national contexts, and ethical questions of political responsibility. Hans Rumpf's problematic 1961-account of the overall impact of the air war on Germany is an early, and rare, example of an attempt to offer an "introduction into a theme hitherto taboo" (*Einführung in ein Thema, das bisher tabu war*) on a national level.[36]

35 Here a selection of titles: Johannes Korthaus, *Die Zerstörung Freiburgs am 27. November: Augenzeugen berichten 1994*, ed. Stadt Freiburg i. Brsg. (Freiburg i. Br.: Promo, 1994); Uwe Bahnsen and Kerstin von Stürmer, *Die Stadt, die sterben sollte: Hamburg im Bombenkrieg, Juli 1943* (Hamburg: Convent, 2003); Willi Riegert, *Heimat unter Bomben: Der Luftkrieg im Raum Steinfurt und in Münster und Osnabrück 1939–1945* (Dülmen: Laumann-Verlag, 2003); Volker Keller, *Mannheim im Bombenkrieg 1940–1945* (Gudensberg-Gleichen: Wartberg, 2003); Volker Keller, *Mannheim 1945: Kriegsende und Neubeginn* (Gudensberg-Gleichen: Wartberg, 2004); Franz Schreiber, *Augsburg: Die Bombennacht im Februar 1944* (Gudensberg-Gleichen: Wartberg, 2004); Ludwig Faust, *Als die Vernichtungsmaschinerie lief ... Bad Dürkheim im Luftkrieg 1939–1945* (Bad Dürkheim: Ludwig Faust, 2004); *Der 18. März 1945 in Bad Dürkheim: Zeitzeugen berichten über die Bombardierung der Stadt*, ed. Stadtverwaltung Bad Dürkheim (Horb a.N.: Geiger-Verlag, 2006). For reviews of this type of publications with their emphases and elisions in commemorating the air war on the backdrop of historiographical accounts, see Jörg Arnold, "Sammelrez: Bombenkrieg," in H-Soz-u-Kult, June 28, 2004, <http://hsozkult.geschichte.hu-berlin.de/rezensionen/2004-2-062>. To be distinguished from these popular histories are local histories of the air war over German cities such as Martin Heinzelmann, *Göttingen im Luftkrieg 1935–1945* (Göttingen: Die Werkstatt, 2003); Hans-Jörg Kühne, *Zwischen Krieg und Frieden: Bielefeld 1945*, ed. Stadtarchiv, Landesgeschichtliche Bibliothek Bielefeld (Gudensberg-Gleichen: Wartberg, 2004); Michael A. Kanther and Marc Olejniczak, *Bomben auf Duisburg: Der Luftkrieg und die Stadt 1940 bis 1960* (Duisburg: Mercator-Verlag, 2004). On the visual record of the bombings during and after 1945, see Ralf Blank's review of Jörg Friedrich's *Brandstätten* in H-Soz-u-Kult, October 22, 2003, <http://hsozkult.geschichte.hu-berlin.de/rezensionen/2003-4-044>.

36 Hans Rumpf, *Das war der Bombenkrieg: Deutsche Städte im Feuersturm: Ein Dokumentarbericht* (Oldenburg/Hamburg: Gerhard Stalling, 1961), here pp. 9–14. As reasons for this so-called taboo, the author cites people's exhaustion after the war and the inaccessibility of documents in Allied archives; at the same time, he claims, more and more people want to be enlightened. See also his "Luftkrieg über Deutschland," in *Bilanz des Zweiten Weltkrieges: Erkenntnisse und Verpflichtungen für die Zukunft* (Oldenburg/Hamburg: Gerhard Stalling, 1953), 159–175. According to this volume Rumpf was "Generalmajor der Feuerschutzpolizei a.D." On the historiography on the air raids in West and East Germany since the 1950s, see Bas von Benda-Beckmann, "Eine deutsche Katastrophe? Deutungsmuster des Bombenkriegs in der ost- und westdeutschen Geschichtswissenschaft," in *Luftkrieg: Erinnerungen in Deutschland und Europa*, ed. Jörg Arnold, Dietmar Süß, and Malte Thießen (Göttingen: Wallstein, 2009), 297–311; on the notion of taboo and its history in this context, see Thießen, *Eingebrannt ins Gedächtnis*, 328–336. On some limitations in the discussion of the air war's commemoration, see Jörg Arnold, "Beyond Usable Pasts: Rethinking the Memorialization of the Strategic Air War in Germany, 1940 to 1965," in *Memori-*

In the decades between the end of the war and the 1990s, specific urban sites were the most prominent platforms for commemorations. Many communities that suffered destruction during World War II instituted ceremonies to commemorate the various losses, sometimes as early as 1945. Some places erected monuments as mementos to the victims of the air raids.[37] Positioned at an intermediate level between individuals and states, urban memory is enticingly flexible. It is permeable to familial memories, and takes seed and is nurtured by the warmth of nostalgia. At the same time, urban memory can also convey national narratives. With its in-between-ness, its convenient contradictions and appealing flexibility, urban memory has anchored the topography of loss and rebuilding – the task at hand in the wake of the war – in a concrete and experientially accessible space: a startling re-envisioning of *Heimat* as a concept that, in the German context, emerged to mediate "between the immediate local life and the abstract nation."[38]

Only recently have academic historians begun to critique some post-war "truths" about the air war. One 2003 study dispels the veracity of popular accounts that, after the devastating attacks of February of 1945, low-flying aircrafts targeted civilians who sought protection on the meadows of the river Elbe from the fires engulfing Dresden.[39] Frederick Taylor dismantles the notion faithfully recounted by many that the "Florence on the Elbe" had little or no military significance in the Nazi engine of war, but his study does not attempt to answer questions about the ethics of the attacks; he only tackles the assumption that the city was innocent.[40] Similarly, a team of researchers concluded that the numbers

alization in Germany since 1945, ed. Bill Niven and Chloe Paver (New York: Palgrave Macmillan, 2010), 26–36.

37 See, for instance, Bad Dürkheim, Stadtarchiv, 3960 and 3960a.

38 Alon Confino, *The Nation as a Local Metaphor: Württemberg, Imperial Germany, and National Memory, 1871–1918* (Chapel Hill: The University of North Carolina Press, 1997), 97, commenting on Celia Applegate, *A Nation of Provincials: The German Idea of Heimat* (Berkeley: University of California Press, 1990).

39 Helmut Schnatz, *Tiefflieger über Dresden: Legenden und Wirklichkeit* (Vienna: Böhlau, 2003). On the city of Dresden as a symbol in post-war discourses about the air-raids over Germany, see Vees-Gulani, "'Phantomschmerzen,'" 277 and passim. See also Thomas Fache, "Gegenwartsbewältigungen: Dresdens Gedenken an die alliierten Luftangriffe vor und nach 1989," in *Luftkrieg: Erinnerungen in Deutschland und Europa*, ed. Jörg Arnold, Dietmar Süß, and Malte Thießen (Göttingen: Wallstein, 2009), 221–238. The question of low-flying attacks on civilians during the bombing raids in Dresden has again been taken up by the *Historikerkommission* cited below.

40 Frederick Taylor, *Dresden: Tuesday, February 13, 1945* (New York: HarperCollins, 2004). Ursula Moessner-Heckner (*Pforzheim Code Yellowfin: Eine Analyse der Luftangriffe 1944–1945* [Sigmaringen: Thorbecke, 1991]) comes to a different conclusion in discussing the area bombard-

of victims that died in February 1945 in Dresden have frequently been exaggerated. After all available data, archeological records included, were evaluated the committee concluded that the death toll amounted to approximately 25,000 lives. While exact figures will never be known, in the aftermath of the raids, figures up to ten times higher circulated. The notion that the city was crowded with refugees when the attacks started has also become less tenable under critical scrutiny.[41] Needless to say, the horror of the Allied attacks is not in dispute and does not hinge on a count of the dead. The myths that have accrued around the horrific events of February 1945 can be traced to Nazi propaganda and subsequent international press coverage that lent credibility to widely exaggerated numbers of victims. In Dresden as in other cases, historical researchers find themselves often at odds with firmly established "facts" that have been solidified by many retellings.

I invoke these scattered controversies not to insist that we dispense with the vagaries of post-war memories and historical myth-making in favor of some unattainable objective historical truth. Rather, I want to call attention to the persistent presence of narratives about the air raids after 1945. The discourses in the wake of the air raids, whether informal or published, do not lead us away from the past; they are the very stuff from which the past is made. Viewed from this vantage point, *On the Natural History of Destruction* was far less of a turning point than the public uproar on both sides of the Atlantic suggested. Rather the reverse, Sebald's essay reflects and perpetuates the memory-making that started with the raids themselves.

The presence of this painful past and the limits of what could be seen of it in post-war Germany are much in evidence in the rubble models. They muster a familiar form, the city model, with its vast empty spaces devoid of inhabitants. They marshal an aesthetic code – that of ruins (as I will argue in the introduction's next section) – in order to render loss. The models thus potentially operate as nodes of narrative affirmation and, potentially, transformation. Individual viewers, especially those who experienced the raids, were encouraged into thinking back in time. Yet whatever one's personal story, it was or is enlarged by the models' comprehensiveness. Exhibited in construction exhibits and city

ment of Pforzheim and other similar-sized cities (Mainz, Würzburg, etc.) that became the target at a time when many other cities had already been destroyed: "In February 1945, there was no military or arms-industrial necessity to extinguish this city [Pforzheim]" (*Es gab im Februar 1945 keine militärische oder rüstungswirtschaftliche Notwendigkeit, diese Stadt auszulöschen*) (155).

41 *Abschlussbericht der Historikerkommission zu den Luftangriffen auf Dresden zwischen dem 13. und 15. Februar 1945* (Dresden: Landeshauptstadt Dresden, 2010) <http://www.dresden.de/media/pdf/infoblaetter/Historikerkommission_Dresden1945_Abschlussbericht_V1_14a.pd>.

halls – displays that emerged in the decade after the country's defeat – the rubble models encouraged viewers to exchange their pedestrian, lowly perspective and their humdrum experience of time for something more, an impossible clarity on urban space and an apparent freezing of time that took them back to an imagined moment of destruction. This panoramic view is the effect of our ability to walk all the way around a model, and thus gain the illusion that the viewer is elevated to understanding all sides of the story.

What is more, as non-verbal vehicles of the imagination, models allowed viewers to formulate their own narrative of destruction or rehearse something they already know. In post-war West German society, accommodating such narratives and transforming them for the sake of a comprehensive view were useful endeavors in re-energizing communities that based their outlook in recognizing past loss, even if or precisely because the nature of the loss and the reasons for its coming about could not be spelled out within this medium. As Alon Confino points out, a particular memory culture does not necessarily reflect a shared past. Rather, it is the task of the media of history to incite the illusion of such a uniform past: memories of shared experiences, and thus of shared emotions, ideologies, and worldviews, to form a bridge between different social groups and erase the past as a contested territory in order to re-erect it as a communal experience.[42]

Rubble Models and the Ruins Code

In Germany's rubble models, the viewer is not merely invited to insert personal reflections, memories, or thoughts into the cultural processes of signification that occur as we look at the miniature. He or she also is asked to leave behind the rubble and form an image that is comprehensive, reflective, and affective. But more specifically, how would a model do that? In part, the answer lies in what I will call the ruins code. As one may see in a wide range of paintings and other visual media, the West has developed an extensive system of aestheticizing destruction as ruins, a visual form in which damage and decay are made to seem pastoral or at the very least non-threatening. Albeit in ways that are uniquely their own, rubble models draw on this code.

---

42 Confino, *The Nation as A Local Metaphor*; Alon Confino, "Memory Studies and Cultural History: Problems of Method," *American Historical Review* 102 (1997): 1386–1403. See also Jeffrey K. Olick, *In the House of the Hangman: The Agonies of German Defeat, 1943–1949* (Chicago: University of Chicago Press, 2005), 20f.

My project is thus animated by the desire to clarify the kinship between the representation of ruins and of disasters. Wherever we look at how great disasters have been rendered in modern times – the 1755 earthquake of Lisbon, the destruction of Atlanta during the US Civil War, the ongoing violence of global wars, or the attacks of 9/11 – we find that their visual record resonates with the ruins code operative since the Renaissance. By way of example, let us briefly zoom in on the Great Fire of Hamburg of 1842, an urban catastrophe in the course of which roughly a third of the city's downtown vanished – a conflagration that occurred just before daguerreotypes became available. As a result, the disaster's widely disseminated visual commemoration unfolded via paintings, watercolors, lithographs, and similar such media, made commercially available by enterprising artists and publishers.[43]

For example, resonances between the Great Fire and ancient Rome on fire are prominent in Hans Detlef Christian Martens's (1795–1866) evocative oil painting of the disaster. The fire has robbed Hamburg's cityscape of its signature spires, allowing us to see the city with its hollowed out buildings, its waterways, its bridges, its medieval and neoclassical façades, as a double of Rome on the Elbe.[44] What is at stake here are not so much identifiable resonances – though such resonances certainly inform "Fire of St. Nicolai" (*Brand der Nikolaikirche*) – but a pictorial horizon of ancient cities in flames that would have been familiar to a perceptive audience in the mid-nineteenth century.

Let us note also that while urban panoramas and ruined buildings came to encapsulate the catastrophe of the Great Fire in visual memory, scenes of human struggle and survival did not – just like with the rubble models. Tellingly, on Martens's canvas, onlookers and firefighters have a miniature presence set against the disaster's magnitude; and St. Nicolai in the painting's center anchors what is a cityscape on fire. In fact, within the imagistic archive on the fire's aftermath, artists and illustrators seized particularly upon ruins of medieval buildings in order to capture the disaster's synthesis. In many such images, the effects of the fire were translated into a picturesque mode – renditions that invoke Caspar David Fried-

---

43 Claudia Horbas and Museum für Hamburgische Geschichte, eds., *Es brannte an allen Ecken zugleich: Hamburg 1842* (Heide: Boyens, 2002/2003). The Museum für Hamburgische Geschichte (now Hamburg Museum) has a model of the Great Fire in its collection.

44 Ibid., 57. Fireworks were held for Rome-travelers in the Colosseum, events captured by the painter Ippolito Caffi. See Joseph Imorde, "Atmosphärische Landschaft," in *Landschaft, Gehäuse, Orientierung: Territorialisierungs- und Naturalisierungsprozesse in Städten, Wohnen und Körper*, ed. Josch Hoenes and Irene Nierhaus (Berlin: Reimer Verlag, 2010), 149–159. The eighteenth-century German painter Johann Georg Trautmann (1713–1769) painted nightly fires in urban settings (see his two *Nächtliche Feuersbrunst* in Städel Museum, Frankfurt am Main).

rich's church ruins and their forlorn, searching visitors from the early nineteenth century. In other words, artists deployed recognizable codes when documenting a recent disaster – perhaps in an attempt to offer narrative closure to a concerned and curious population. Conversely, the perpetuation of established codes also means that when we see older images, whether the paintings and prints featuring Roman ruins by the Flemish Mannerist Maerten van Heemskerck or the romantic landscapes of Friedrich, they contain echoes of recent disasters.

A rapprochement between representations of ruins and those of disasters may not come as a surprise to us moderns, inundated with photographic and filmic records of war violence and devastation as we are. As Susan Sontag reminds us, "[b]eing a spectator of calamities taking place in another country is a quintessential modern experience."[45] But noticing the resonance between disasters and ruins, it turns out, ruptures much of the canonical criticism on ruins. This criticism has been under the spell of bucolic ruins and an elegiac mode of viewing for its entire life, so much so that ruins' potential to generate poignant echoes with war-related devastation or disasters seems far-fetched.

Georg Simmel, the early twentieth-century German sociologist and author of the classic essay, "The Ruin," epitomizes this view, excluding human destructions outright from the ruin's horizon: "a good many Roman ruins, however interesting they may be otherwise, lack the specific fascination of the ruin – to the extent that is to which one notices in them the destruction *by man*; for this contradicts the contrast between human work and the effect of *nature* on which rests the significance of the ruin as such."[46] Taking his cues from Simmel among others, Jean Starobinski concurs, writing: "... for a ruin to appear beautiful, the act of destruction must be remote enough for its precise circumstances to have been forgotten: it can be imputed to an anonymous power, to a featureless transcendent force – History, Destiny. We do not muse calmly before recent ruins, which smell of bloodshed: we clear them away as quickly as possible and rebuild."[47] In *Pleasure of Ruins*, Rose Macaulay expresses a view similar to Simmel and Starobinski when, shortly after the end of the Second World War, she cordons off "new ruins" from the beauty of the old ones she extols in her seminal book on the matter: "The bombed churches and cathedrals of Europe give us, on the whole, nothing

45 Susan Sontag, *Regarding the Pain of Others* (New York: Farrar, Straus, and Giroux, 2003), 18.
46 Georg Simmel, "Die Ruine," in *Philosophische Kultur: Gesammelte Essays*, 2nd ed. (Leipzig: Alfred Kröner, 1919), 125–133; trans. "The Ruin," in *Essays in Sociology, Philosophy and Aesthetics*, ed. Kurt H. Wolff (New York: Harper and Row, 1965), 259–266, here p. 260.
47 Jean Starobinski, *The Invention of Liberty: 1700–1789*, trans. Bernard C. Swift (Geneva: Skira, 1964), 180.

but resentful sadness, like the bombed cities."[48] Evidently, the same or a similar statement has to be issued again and again, precisely because its persuasiveness relies on reiteration in light of hints to the contrary.

Other post-war observers had a decidedly different response. Hans Sedlmayr, a conservative German art historian whose flamboyant 1948-indictment of aesthetic modernism, *Verlust der Mitte* (Loss of the Center), became a great success with critics and readers alike, stated categorically: "Since today we know exactly what ruins are and mean, it has become impossible to see artificial ruins only as a harmless, painterly motif" (*Heute, da wir zu genau wissen, was Ruinen sind und bedeuten, ist es nicht mehr möglich, die künstliche Ruine nur als ein harmloses 'malerisches Motiv' zu sehen*).[49] In fact, Macaulay seems of two minds about the status of post-war ruins when she notes the beauty of some traces of war in Europe. One could even posit that the devastation of World War II drives her wide-ranging exploration of ruins-gazing across the ages and continents, an essay reflecting on ruins in the midst of the rubble produced by the last European war.[50]

By reading rubble models through the ruins code, we can complicate the notions that cause us to differentiate categories of ruins taxonomically. Instead, we can see the ways old disasters and fresh wounds are in uncomfortable proximity to each other. Similarly, we can see the ways that these scenes of devastation don't just allow for our gaze on the past, but in fact shape our view of it. The forgetting that Starobinski regards as a precondition for our appreciation of devastated buildings as ruins may also be regarded as a potential effect of a ruins gazing scenario. By translating devastation into ruinous matter many viewers of rubble models may learn to distance themselves ever so cautiously from the events that led to ruination. Contemporary critics may fault such viewers for their escapism. Such critics are, like Sebald, in search for the great text or aesthetic

---

48 Rose Macaulay, *Pleasure of Ruins* [1953] (New York: Barnes & Noble, 1996), 454. Interestingly, this statement is followed by a counterexample, Monte Cassino, said to have "put on with wreckage a new dignity, a beauty scarcely in the circumstances bearable; it looked finer than at any time since its last restorations" (ibid.).

49 Hans Sedlmayr, *Verlust der Mitte: Die bildende Kunst des 19. und 20. Jahrhunderts als Symbol der Zeit* (Salzburg: Otto Mueller, 1948), 96.

50 See also Hans Vogel, *Die Ruine in der Darstellung der abendländischen Kunst* (Kassel: Karl Winter, 1948). Vogel traces a history of representations of ruins from the Renaissance leading up to the art of Karl Hofer, Erwin Spuler, and Franz Radziwill with their images of post-war ruins. With the biblical passages, German poems from the Baroque as well as the twentieth century, and other descriptive paratexts, the author, an art historian, aimed at a wide readership with this volume. In 1948, the art critic Heinz Lüdeke criticized a photographer for having approached World War II-ruination through a romantic lens (see his "Es kommt auf die Einstellung an," *bildende kunst* 2 [1949]: 70).

experiment that would make the experience comprehensible to us. Eye-witnesses followed different impulses, seeking distance from a harrowing presence of the disaster.

This is not to say that visual artists did not occasionally deploy different pictorial idioms when they rendered the effects of a contemporary war as opposed to the iconography of ancient ruins. For example, when Bernardo Bellotto (1722–1780) painted the devastation visited on the city of Dresden during the Seven Years War (1765) – a city he had taught beholders to appreciate through numerous city views or *vedute* – he depicted the city's *Kreuzkirche* (Church of the Cross), ruined by Prussian artillery, as a heap of rubble in the midst of undamaged dwellings from which a naked wall rises into the blue sky. His frontal viewpoint and haunting vision are shockingly different from contemporary capriccios or ruins portraits (to which he and his uncle, Giovanni Antonio Canal known as Canaletto, had made trademark contributions).[51] But I would argue that the shock of this painting is precisely because it confounds the ruins code, and thus goes against our ingrained expectation of what such a scene should look like.

Representations of ancient ruins at times resonated with suggestions of causes for their ruination. The Flemish painter Maerten van Heemskerck synthesized his years of drawing ruins, torsos, and fragments in Rome in *The Rape of Helen of Troy* (1536), a synopsis of his multi-year studies of such remains in the Eternal City.[52] The scene of Helen's abduction is confined to the panel's foreground while a panoramic vision of the ancient world occupies most of the image's surface with a fantastical array of ruins in the middle ground and a splendid city at the base of a mountainous range in the background. With its roaming allusions to Troy and Rome, this painting raises the very question of how to relate the scene depicted in its foreground to the vast, largely people-less cityscapes, suspended between ruined devastation and architectural splendor.

Returning to our investigation, my point, I hope is clear: I contend that the rubble model conjures up the rhetorical force as well as the viewing frames associated with ruins. This idea, in turn, stretches the notion of ruins, these relics of the sublime. As the statements cited above by Simmel, Starobinski, and Macaulay illustrate, ruins have frequently served as boundary-markers; among other things, they are markers of both geographical and chronological thresholds. If

51 Kunsthaus Zurich, Switzerland. Some reflections on the difference between disaster ruins and other ruins in Sergio Adamo, "Constructing an Event, Contemplating Ruins, Theorizing Nature: The Lisbon Earthquake and Some Italian Reactions," *European Review* 14 (2004): 339–349.
52 Rainald Grosshans, *Maerten van Heemskerck: Die Gemälde* (Berlin: Boettcher, 1980), 116–119, ill. 20.

history is a field of knowledge, ruins and their rise to appreciation function as one period marker among others between medieval and modern times. They are said to signal the advent of historical consciousness during the Renaissance, a movement leading up to the Enlightenment and its historicist aftermath.[53] As material tokens they are held up as testimony on our long and intertwined marches toward "becoming historical" and becoming modern.[54]

In his dissertation on "Rome's Ruins," William S. Heckscher, a student of Erwin Panofsky, struggled to fit *Ruinenlust* into a neat periodization schema. He asked: what distinguished medieval invocations of Rome's ancient remains from their Renaissance counterparts?[55] To answer this question, Heckscher reversed the conventional chronological order, starting not with the phenomenon's origins but with a definition of what he called "the modern ruins thought" (*Der moderne Ruinengedanke*): "Everybody knows the word ruin as the epitome of a strange, wistfully uplifting sensation of beauty."[56] At the center of Heckscher's definition of a ruin, therefore, are not the structural features of it, but the viewer's affective reaction to it. Approaching ruins thus means to open up oneself to their semantic and structural promiscuity.[57]

Following Heckscher, we need to alter the very categories that we typically use for analysis. We cannot understand the modernity of ruins by assigning their rise to a particular period, locale, or genre. Ultimately, their modernity lies in the way they open themselves for inspection through the ruin-gazer. As architec-

---

53 Sabine Ferero-Mendoza, *Le temps des ruines: L'éveil de la conscience historique à la Renaissance* (Seyssel : Champ Vallon, 2002); Michel Makarius, *Ruines* (Paris: Flammarion, 2004).

54 A phrase borrowed from John Edward Toews, *Becoming Historical: Cultural Reformation and Public Memory in Early Nineteenth-Century Berlin* (Cambridge: Cambridge University Press, 2004).

55 Wilhelm Sebastian Heckscher [William S. Heckscher], *Die Romruinen: Die geistigen Voraussetzungen ihrer Wertung im Mittelalter und in der Renaissance* (Ph.Diss. Hamburg University, 1935) (Würzburg: Richard Mayer, 1936). This is the shorter print version of a more comprehensive dissertation. On the manuscript version, see Charlotte Schoell-Glass and Elizabeth Sears, *Verzetteln als Methode: Der humanistische Ikonologe William S. Heckscher* (Berlin: Akademie, 2008), 47–57.

56 Heckscher, *Romruinen*, 1: "Jeder kennt das Wort 'Ruine' als den Inbegriff einer ganz eigentümlichen, wehmütig erhebenden, Schönheitsempfindung."

57 Andreas Schoenle (*Architecture of Oblivion: Ruins and Historical Consciousness in Modern Russia* [DeKalb, Ill.: Northern Illinois University Press, 2011], 71) speaks of the "heterogeneity of the ruin." The term I introduce here, promiscuity, seeks to capture the interpenetration of the semantic layers at play and express the ability of ruins to forge somewhat arbitrary links.

tural critic Robert Harbison posits, they resemble "a way of seeing."[58] Attempts to contain "ruin thought" spatially, temporally, or structurally are at risk of floundering in sight of ruins' persistent ability to cross such divides. During the Renaissance, for instance, ruins stimulated "impulsive, uncontrolled, and even contradictory responses," contends Margaret McGowan, and occasional resonances between the ruins of Rome and the material destruction left in the wake of contemporary conflicts are among them.[59] If we follow Sophus A. Reinert, today's industrial and commercial ruins invoke the ancient ruin as a frame for the viewer: "To see FIAT's epic Mirafiori plant, once the pinnacle of Italian Fordism, corroding among tall weeds, or to walk the melancholy and empty halls of the former Buenos Aires branch of Harrods', is an experience not unlike Petrarch's visit to the ruins of Diocletian's baths in the midst of medieval Rome."[60] In this sense, rubble models partake of "ruin thought."

To be sure, ruins sometimes stimulate the obverse of promiscuous connecting: they instigate disconnection. In Heckscher, for instance, ruins function not only as guarantors of the rise of modernity and historicity but also as guardians of the Occident. If historical consciousness was a European achievement and if ruins played a part in its genesis, the rest of the world must lack ruins, so the reasoning goes. The counter-space Heckscher selects to prove his point, if only in passing, is Africa.[61] Since this continent lies largely outside of history, as Hegel quipped,[62] it also must have no ruins, so states Heckscher – a gesture that denies the African continent coevalness, that is, living in the same historically aware time.[63] After Horst W. Janson, another art historian and student of Panofsky, had emigrated to the US from National Socialist Germany, he, like his friend William S. Heckscher, used ruins as an emblematic divider. In an essay unpublished during his life time,

---

58 Robert Harbison, *The Built, the Unbuilt and the Unbuildable: In Pursuit of Architectural Meaning* (London: Thames and Hudson, 1991), 99. The quote in context: "Ruins are ideal: the perceiver's attitudes count so heavily that one is tempted to say ruins are a way of seeing."

59 Margaret M. McGowan, *The Vision of Rome in Late Renaissance France* (New Haven: Yale University Press, 2000), 2. See also ibid., 260–265.

60 Sophus A. Reinert, "Lessons on the Rise and Fall of Great Powers: Conquest, Commerce, and Decline in Enlightenment Italy," *American Historical Review* 115 (2010): 1423.

61 Heckscher, *Romruinen*, 4f.

62 Georg Wilhelm Friedrich Hegel, *Vorlesungen über die Philosophie der Weltgeschichte (Berlin 1822/1823). Vorlesungen*, vol. 12, ed. Karl Heinz Ilting, Karl Brehmer, and Hoo Nam Seelmann (Hamburg: Felix Meiner, 1996), 99f.

63 Johannes Fabian, *Time and the Other: How Anthropology Makes Its Object* (New York: Columbia University Press, 2002).

he issued a striking statement: "Amerika kennt keine Ruinen" – America has no ruins – translating temporal distinctions into spatial-cultural ones.[64]

Such boundary-drawing has begun to break down in recent criticism. The photographer-sociologist Camilo José Vergara vehemently claims *American Ruins* as indices of a post-industrial US society in flux.[65] For the historian Michel-Rolph Trouillot, the ruins of *Sans Souci*, a castle built after Haiti's revolution (1810–1813), occasion a meditation on the nature of historical knowledge, forever caught in a dialectics between narrative presence and narrative erasure.[66] A recent issue of *Cultural Anthropology*, edited by Ann Laura Stoler, seeks to focus our gaze from melancholic imperial ruins to debris in post-colonial situations in order "to reposition the present in the wider structures of vulnerability and refusal that imperial formations sustain."[67] Ruins have started to appear in places where they once had no home: in Russia,[68] in former Yugoslavia,[69] or in non-European contexts.[70] Global ruins photography – "ruin porn," as some critics have it[71] – has been criticized as unduly aestheticizing abandonment and urban poverty.[72] However,

---

64 Horst W. Janson, "Amerika kennt keine Ruinen" (unpublished essay). See Charlotte Schoell-Glass and Elizabeth Sears, "'Amerika kennt keine Ruinen': Horst W. Jansons Amerikabild," *Zeitschrift für Ideengeschichte* 3 (2009): 97–114; Schoell-Glass/Sears, *Verzetteln als Methode*, 71–74.

65 Camilo José Vergara, *American Ruins* (New York: Monacelli Press, 1999). See also his webpage *Invincible Cities* (http://invinciblecities.camden.rutgers.edu/intro.html).

66 Michel-Rolph Trouillot, *Silencing the Past: Power and the Production of History* (Boston: Beacon Press, 1995).

67 Ann Laura Stoler, "Imperial Debris: Reflections on Ruins and Ruination," *Cultural Anthropology* 23 (2008): 191–219, here p. 194.

68 Andreas Schoenle, *Architecture of Oblivion: Ruins and Historical Consciousness in Modern Russia* (DeKalb, Ill.: Northern Illinois University Press, 2011).

69 Andrew Herscher, *Violence Taking Place: The Architecture of the Kosovo Conflict* (Stanford: Stanford University Press, 2010).

70 See the aforementioned forum in *Cultural Anthropology* with contributions on the US, Latin America, and Africa, now published as Ann Laura Stoler, ed., *Imperial Debris: On Ruins and Ruination* (Durham: Duke University Press, 2013).

71 Thomas Morton, "Something, Something, Something, Detroit: Lazy Journalists Love Pictures of Abandoned Stuff," in *Vice* [2009] (http://www.viceland.com/int/v16n8/htdocs/something-something-something-detroit-994.php?page=1); Paul Clemens, *Punching Out: One Year in a Closing Auto Plant* (New York: Doubleday, 2011); John Patrick Leary, "Detroitism," in *Guernica*, January 15, 2011 (http://www.guernicamag.com/spotlight/2281/leary_1_15_11/). See also Ian Ference, "On 'Ruin Porn,'" in *Huffingtonpost*, January 31, 2011 (http://www.huffingtonpost.com/ian-ference/on-ruin-porn_b_816593.html); Greg Grandin, "Empire's Ruins: Detroit to the Amazon," in *Imperial Debris*, ed. Ann Laura Stoler, 115–128, here p. 116.

72 This library has become so extensive that I can only list a selection of volumes here: Harry Skrdla, *Ghostly Ruins: America's Forgotten Architecture* (Princeton: Princeton Architectural Press, 2006); Arthur Drooker and Christopher Woodward, *American Ruins* (London: Merrell,

the fact that such images transform concrete local stories into an idiom open to roaming reflections on the state of post-industrial society is not simply a form of visual exploitation. Ruins have never been exclusively about a situated past. Their appeal rests in their ability to transcend their locales and their material immanence. Ruins forge links between time and space in evocative analogies and simultaneities.[73] They are what Walter Benjamin captured as aura, namely a "presence in time and space."[74] They are the visual form that makes the coming together of space and time experiential. And this intersection is also why "ruin thought" matters in our exploration of rubble models.

With their emphasis on comprehensiveness and verisimilitude, rubble models provide an intriguing twist in a long-lasting engagement with ruins. They may in fact instill in the observer "the epitome of a strange, wistfully uplifting sense of beauty" (to quote Heckscher's definition again). As such, "rubble models" seduce the beholder's gaze to move away from the rubble, the myriad forms left by the bombs, and provide a larger image of the devastated cityscape. Rubble, after all, is material without significance; it is matter destined to be removed. By contrast, ruins invoke traditions, visual codes, and a wealth of significations. Rubble models help to transform an image of debris into an occasion to reflect and deflect. They thus perform the very move that Ann Stoler cautions us to resist, namely to open oneself to the beauty of dereliction.

This Book

This study unfolds as a series of focused readings. Its five additional chapters each revolve around a particular locale. For those who read page by page, the book's itinerary will lead them from Frankfurt to Munich, Schwetzingen (near

---

2007); Henk van Rensbergen, *Abandoned Places* (Tielt: Lannoo, 2007); id., *Abandoned Places 2* (Tielt: Lannoo, 2010); Michael Eastman, Douglas Brinkely, and William H. Grass, *Vanishing America: The End of Main Street* (Milan: Rizzoli, 2008); Brian Vanden Brink, *Ruin: Photographs of a Vanishing America* (Rockport, ME: Down East Books, 2009); Yves Marchand and Romain Meffre, *The Ruins of Detroit* (Göttingen: Gerhard Steidl, 2010); Dan Austin and Sean Doerr, *Lost Detroit: Stories behind Motor City's Majestic Ruins* (Charleston, SC: The History Press, 2010); RomanyWG, *Beauty in Decay: The Art of Urban Exploration* (Berkeley: Gingko Press, 2010).

73 See Lynn Hunt, *Measuring Time, Making History* (Budapest: Central European University Press, 2008) on the fact that "modern conceptions of time seem to require spatial representation" (4).

74 Erwin Panofsky, "Albrecht Dürer and Classical Antiquity," in *Meaning in the Visual Arts* (Chicago: University of Chicago, 1955), 236.

Mannheim), Heilbronn, and then Hiroshima. Other paths are possible, however. If you are predominantly interested in post-war culture, moving from Frankfurt to Heilbronn and Hiroshima may suit you. Or you may arrange your reading chronologically which would have you start in Munich in the sixteenth century, move on to eighteenth-century Schwetzingen, and from there to post-war Frankfurt, Heilbronn, and Hiroshima. Hinge texts – italicized – will guide you from one place and chapter to the next.

In addition, each chapter elucidates a central problematic: ideas for monuments in the wake of the unprecedented urban destruction during World War II (Chapter Two); city modeling as a medium of sovereignty (Chapter Three); the fascination with ruins that resulted in building "faux" monuments during early historicism (Chapter Four); the function of models of destruction in post-war Germany (Chapter Five); and, finally, the politics of representing and seeing disasters (Epilogue).

The chapter that follows this introduction tests the hypothesis of the *Eigen-Gewicht* (self-weight, also: dead load) of material forms of commemoration with regard to two post-war monuments: the rubble model of Frankfurt and the sculptor Benno Elkan's unrealized monument for the civilian victims of the air raids during World War II. *Eigen-Gewicht* takes its cue from *Eigen-Sinn* (waywardness, self-will), a term the historical anthropologist Alf Lüdtke coined to register the human capacity to hover between obeying and resisting.[75] By analogy, its material equivalent, *Eigen-Gewicht*, seeks to capture an object that rubs against the symbolic content and functions ascribed to it, instead accommodating a wide range of significations. As Chapter Two will show, the model of urban destruction made its first appearance as analogous to and yet different from a variety of post-war discourses much focused on rubble as a trope to characterize the moment of re-orientation after 1945.

My research of models posits that they be theorized as complex simulators. The proliferation of city models in the early 1500s was tied to a particular "production of space," to cite Henri Lefebvre, a production that needs to be approached analytically and historically. Chapter Three will investigate an epistemology that is grounded in a specific and complex form of material representation through a study of objects, their history, and the ways they were viewed. We will explore the emergence of extravagant three-dimensional city portraits as a specular technology of power and for the powerful in the context of early modern state formation with its corollaries – the conspicuous display of military, scientific, political, and

75 Alf Lüdtke, *Eigen-Sinn: Fabrikalltag, Arbeitererfahrungen und Politik vom Kaiserreich bis in den Faschismus* (Hamburg: Ergebnisse, 1993).

cultural prowess. In particular, I will focus on the sixteenth-century collection of models that showcased Bavarian cities for select viewers. Commissioned by Duke Albrecht V and constructed by Jacob Sandtner (1568–1574), a turner, these models came to hold an important place in Munich's *kunstkammer*. As Chapter Three illustrates, the technology of model-building and the surveying of urban spaces were efforts that brought together "experts" from north and south of the Alps. What is more, these urban sculptures in miniature encapsulate, if not embody, the ruler's claims to a penetrating and all-encompassing sovereign gaze.

Building models and building ruins were not antithetical to an expanding interest in the historical. Rather the reverse, they were the very grounds of historicizing; models of ruins and built ruins offered ways of experiencing the past. Chapter Four therefore explores two sides of the eighteenth-century engagement with ruins, a growing thirst for the past as well as its reliance on simulation and artifice in the production of history. The staged ruins in the landscape garden of Schwetzingen's castle (1774/1785) as well as the miniatures of Roman ruins resonated with a renewed interest in sites of historical knowledge. But the associations ruins, even built ruins, generated, emanated into the present and into the future.

The fact that ruins, even modeled ruins, occasion definition, reflection, and affective engagement made them an apt vehicle for taking stock of the debris and dereliction World War II left behind. Chapter Five will turn again to postwar Germany in a two-pronged essay surveying the construction of rubble models between 1945 and the present, as well as exploring the sculpted relief models of destruction in a particular case, part of a memorial set up in Heilbronn and opened to the public in 1963. This monument has much to tell us about the local politics of the war's representation, and the role of the past destruction in generating communities – communities founded on the sufferings that practically all citizens were thought to have shared.

Reflecting on how Germans have used models to articulate their relation to the destruction of cities from the air, my study will finally turn to a different locale to shed light on these objects and to a comparison between the German rubble models and the modeled cityscapes that are currently on display in the museum devoted to the destruction of Hiroshima, Japan, in 1945. An analysis of Alain Resnais's *Hiroshima mon amour* (1959) and the role of three-dimensional models in the film will bring to the fore the tensions between our compulsion to see disasters and the limited visual resources at our disposal to bring them into focus.

Several historical "moments" will thus shed light on our longstanding engagement with history and the human environment through models and ruins. Such an engagement has been both affective and aesthetic in nature: the sixteenth century with its antiquarianism and experiments in perspectivism; the period around 1800 with its spread of a ruins aesthetics in the context of rising historicism, revolutionary ruptures, and nascent nationalisms; and the time after 1945, which builds on these previous moments but also reflects a renewed presence of ruins that bear strong collective associations of catastrophe, tragedy, and guilt.

It is my claim, reiterated in the concluding pages ("In Conclusion"), that three-dimensional representations of ruined cities in post-war Germany gain legibility against the backdrop of these earlier layers of engagement with ruins and models. Ultimately, *Miniature Monuments* tackles a paradox: the intentional modeling of cities that have been destroyed. In the pages to come, we will explore how utterly contingent processes of crumbling and collapse – English for the Latin *ruina* – came to command such great interest that tremendous efforts were taken to render, and, most of all, recreate destruction and dereliction. When describing models of Roman ruins, early nineteenth-century writers provide us with a tentative clue as to this thematic's deep resonance: these built ruins *en miniature*, they claim unanimously, are better than the real thing.

Taken together, the essays contained in this book argue that rubble models were part of German memory culture in the post-war period. Peripheral as they may seem, they provide a compelling lens onto the commemoration of the war and the air raids after 1945.

By exploring these models' deep history, I seek to energize the dialogue between the study of history and of memory. Students of *historia* and *memoria* have, over the past two decades, engaged in an at times uneasy dialogue that has profoundly shaped both fields of studies.[76] Memory studies counts among the crucial intellectual stimuli that pressed upon practictioners of history the need to tend to the themes of visuality and spatiality. What is more, by focusing on the dynamic relations between social groups and "their" pasts, memory studies have restored a sense of moral and ethical urgency to our thinking about the past

76 Among the many contributions to this topic, I found particularly helpful: Wulf Kansteiner, "Finding Meaning in Memory: A Methodological Critique of Collective Memory Studies," *History & Theory* 41 (2002): 179–197; Ana Douglass and Thomas A. Vogler, "Introduction," in *Witness and Memory: The Discourse of Trauma* (New York: Routledge, 2003), 1–53; Jeffrey K. Olick, ed., *States of Memory: Continuities, Conflicts, and Transformations in National Retrospection* (Durham: Duke University Press, 2003); Marcus Sandl, "Historizität der Erinnerung/Reflexivität des Historischen: Die Herausforderung der Geschichtswissenschaft durch die kulturwissenschaftliche Gedächtnisforschung," in *Erinnerung, Gedächtnis, Wissen: Studien zur kulturwissenschaftlichen Gedächtnisforschung*, ed. Günter Oesterle (Göttingen: Vandenhoeck & Ruprecht, 2005), 89–119; Jeffrey K. Olick, Vered Vinitzky-Seroussi, and Daniel Levy, eds., *The Collective Memory Reader* (Oxford: Oxford University Press, 2011).

– something “documentary” history or historicism as conventionally understood has all too often failed to sustain:[77] What were and are profitable ways to make sure that “we” remember what is better not forgotten?

Miniature Monuments contributes to this ongoing dialogue by pursuing the insight that the history that matters for remembering collectively is not identical with the temporal reach of memory *per se* (which various authors have projected to be about one hundred years). The temporal expanses that matter for memory studies by far exceed the conflicts, catastrophes, and upheavals of recent generations around which memory-making, whether individual or collective, so often revolves. *Miniature Monuments* therefore foregrounds the expansive historicity and the persistent mediality of the vehicles of “our” memory-making.

Neil Gregor has suggested that the central problem of “all studies of the relationship between public representations of the past and the contents of ‘collective memory’” is that the texts (or memorials) as constructed by their authors tell us nothing about “the consumption of that text, its reception or reading.”[78] Truth be told, a study on the creation and the reception of the intriguing objects that this volume examines would be close to impossible. The paucity of documentation on model construction and how they were viewed would prevent further evaluation. But this is not to say that we are bereft of a critical apparatus to make these objects shine within the contexts where they were placed and have been viewed. In fact, the textual analogue in Gregor’s wording only goes so far. In order to model these models’ history and the history of viewing them, we need to engage their material-generic presence in modes of display and the long duration of the viewing conventions within which they make sense in order to build a case for the responses they may have occasioned in memorials and museums.

As monuments, rubble models are mobile signifiers in the double sense of the word. They are mobile in that as objects these models can be moved about but mobile also because they signify in multiple ways – ways conditioned and enabled by a history far older than the air raids of World War II. In this sense, *Miniature Monuments* brackets the persistent debate on the damages or the sufferings caused by the bombing raids, the raids’ military effects, or their ethics in order to contribute to current efforts at situating the echoes of this war within the societies that experienced it.

---

77 Dominick LaCapra, *Writing History, Writing Trauma* (Baltimore: Johns Hopkins University Press, 2001), 1.

78 Neil Gregor, *Haunted City: Nuremberg and the Nazi Past* (New Haven: Yale University Press, 2008), 20. See also Kansteiner, “Finding Meaning in Memory,” passim.

Chapter Two

Let me take you on a walk, a walk through a city, a city in the wake of destruction. Walter Benjamin used the concept of flânerie *to capture the activity of walking urban streets with their ocular attractions. A* flâneur *collects scattered impressions in what is a movement not only through space but also through time. Let us retrace the steps of urban wanderers in German cities after the Second World War.*

Ordinary ways of experiencing lived spaces were no longer possible. In cities that had seen large-scale destruction from the air, lived spaces were few and far between. Also inadequate were the ordinary ways of describing neighborhoods that had been "dehoused"(to use the euphemism of Allied military strategists). Debris piled up, paths were blocked, and leveled buildings offered new vistas where before there had been walls. Post-war flâneurs *struggled to bring such derelict and startling places into descriptive focus. How do you describe a place that is only the chimera of a city, a built environment that has been unbuilt?*

All such descriptive efforts had to confront rubble. In the legions of cities defaced by World War II, especially those cities struck from the air, rubble was everywhere. Commentators noticed heaps, piles, mountains of shattered bricks, chunks of concrete, slices of tiles, fragments of glass and wood. Rubble kept the flâneur's *gaze close to the ground, rubble got in the way. Rubble was not the stuff to keep, it was the stuff to leave behind. Rubble had precious little value, even when businesses emerged to recycle the little that could be salvaged. Yet as a descriptor, rubble allowed the* flâneur *to concatenate things and thoughts that would have belonged to categorically different registers under tranquil regimes of representation. The years after World War II became an era of not just rubble models but rubble literature, rubble photography, rubble films, and rubble music. As we will see, grappling with the reality of rubble – via word or via image – created radically different results and, in the case of memorials and models, ultimately revealed the fundamental problematic of visual representation. The insistence on the descriptor "rubble" kept debates open; the term ruin was often reserved for a specular solution to the prevalent disorder and chaos.*

Frankfurt am Main, the city we will explore now, is one of many German cities scarred beyond recognition by aerial attacks. In each place the destruction and its aftermath took a different path; a city's geographic location, its topography, the primary building materials, even the dates of the bombings and similar such factors made every case particular. What suggests Frankfurt as paradigm for Germany is less the specifics of its destruction than its rapid re-development after 1945. Here, post-war discussions about usable pasts, presents, and futures offer an early window on reactions and conflicts relevant for other German communities.

In order to orient ourselves in this city of rubble, we will crisscross Frankfurt's center several times. To get a better view amidst the rubble – both actual and metaphoric – we will use different guides. We will tag along with an artist walking through the old city, and we will re-encounter the same artist engaged in a monument to commemorate the many lives lost in attacks from the air. We will also cover the same ground by using a miniature version of the destroyed city center as a lens – a relief model produced to offer guidance and reflection, a relief model that raises its own questions about what is usable in the past, present, and future. 'How to gain distance and *keep a record of these memorable sights?' this object seems to ask.*

In the midst of the rubble emerged the desire to shape a memento of these arresting sights – a view unprecedented in terms of sheer material destruction and the various losses figured through it. Recourse to forms of memorialization familiar from previous moments of trial – public monuments, models, descriptions of walks through a city, and rebuilding – was certainly one possible response. After all, the entirely new beginning that some critics had hoped for – in everything from social life to architecture, politics to languages – never materialized after 1945. At the same time, eclecticism remained vulnerable to critique when, during the rubble years, the wounds of the recent past went deep and were tied, at least for some critics, into a reflection on Frankfurters' own responsibility in having caused the city's demise. Past aesthetic forms were suspect because they were felt to be tainted together with the past. As a result, rubble and loss could not easily be turned into a monument to Frankfurt's destruction, even as the actual process of clearing up progressed quickly. The two monuments we will bring into dialogue in the pages to come, a planned monument for the civilians lost to the air raids and the rubble model of downtown Frankfurt, bear witness to the post-war desire to mourn and move on as well as to the simultaneous hesitation to do so. They are testimony to the difficulties of erecting mementos of destruction and loss in the wake of war and defeat.

Rubble City, Frankfurt

> Das Kennzeichen unserer Zeit ist die Ruine. Sie umgibt unser Leben. Sie umsäumt die Straßen unserer Städte. Sie ist unse Wirklichkeit. In ihren ausgebrannten Fassaden blüht nicht die blaue Blume der Romantik, sondern der dämonische Geist der Zerstörung, des Verfalls und der Apokalypse. Sie ist das äußere Wahrzeichen der inneren Unsicherheit des Menschen unserer Zeit. Die Ruine lebt in uns wie wir in ihr. Sie ist unsere neue Wirklichkeit, die gestaltet werden will.[1]
> (The sign of our times is the ruins. They surround our lives. They line the streets of our cities. They are our reality. In their burned-out façades there blooms not the blue flower of Romanticism but the daemonic spirit of destruction, decay, and the apocalypse. They are the outer symbol of man's inner insecurity in our age. The ruins live in us as we live in them. They are our new reality which is asking to be reshaped.)

Five years after the end of the Second World War, a former resident of Frankfurt am Main, Benno Elkan, visited the city, recording his impressions in an article published in the local press.[2] The author, an artist and Jewish émigré, approached the city with considerable trepidation. Yet once he reached the *Römerberg*, the city's historic center, apprehensiveness gave way to shock. "On the Hills of Sorrow" (*Auf den Hügeln des Jammers*) captures a loss of orientation in what the author describes as a derelict wasteland.[3]

In Elkan's description, disconnected sounds, material objects, and vistas surface as distant echoes of a lost urbanity. These evocations barely sediment into the aesthetic form of "ruins," a word that appears only once in his short text. More common is the messier term, "chunks" (*Brocken*), with its associations of chaos and dereliction.[4] The city's center is presented as a space neither urban nor rural, a "desolate heap" overgrown with plants and a space marked above

---

1 Hans-Werner Richter, "Literatur im Interregnum," *Der Ruf* 1 (1947): 10.

2 Benno Elkan, "Auf den Hügeln des Jammers," *Frankfurter Neue Presse*, October 7, 1950; Institut für Stadtgeschichte, Frankfurt am Main, Kulturamt 949, 63. On Elkan, see Fritz Hofmann and Peter Schmieder, *Benno Elkan: Ein jüdischer Künstler aus Dortmund* (Essen: Klartext Verlag, 1997).

3 In a diary entry of 1946, the writer Max Frisch compares Frankfurt's remains with those of Munich: "Wenn man in Frankfurt steht, zumal in der alten Innenstadt, und wenn man an München zurückdenkt: München kann man sich vorstellen, Frankfurt nicht mehr." See id., *Tagebuch 1946–1949* (Frankfurt am Main: Suhrkamp, 1960), 37.

4 The tension between "rubble" and "ruin" surfaces frequently in contemporary descriptions. See, for instance, Ernst Beutler's "An Goethes hundertundzwölftem Todestage, dem 22. März 1944, starb auch das Haus seiner Kindheit, starb die Stadt seiner Jugend" (1944/45), in *Goethe im Urteil seiner Kritiker: Dokumente einer Wirkungsgeschichte Goethes in Deutschland*, vol. 4, ed. Karl Robert Mandelkow (Munich: Beck, 1984), 258–260.

all by absences. "Emptiness" (*Leere*) and "nothingness" (*Nichts*) reign supreme. Elkan's scattered recollections of a walk through the bombed-out center of Frankfurt do not speak of the sounds of construction.[5] Barely a human soul populates his narrative. Rather, the few signs of life amidst the devastation – the ads, the cars racing through, and the sounds of jazz – disrupt the author's elegiac mourning for a city declared dead.

In death, the *Altstadt* or old city assumes a heightened presence.[6] Anthropomorphic images provide a vibrant index of past urban life. The cathedral that once anchored a sea of old houses now towers above a scene of destruction, a beacon of solitude. But these reflections of a former life cannot cohere. They cannot create a sense of completion. Elkan stabs at many ideas, many themes. Overcome by the sheer amount of rubble, the author explicitly relinquishes questions of guilt and responsibility. Somewhat uneasily, the description oscillates between stylistic, aesthetic, and moral registers; ultimately, Elkan adds his own verbal debris to a Frankfurt in rubble.

By 1950, the metaphors and rhetoric of Elkan's uneasy meditation on an urban wasteland fit into a genre of writings. Starting even before the war had ended, urban rubble began to surface in letters, travelogues, diaries, essays, and poems. From the start, the rubble interrupted our conventional modes of seeing and challenged our conventional modes of documenting.[7] "There was Frankfurt, or was it?" writes Walter H. Rothschild, a naturalized US officer and former Frankfurter. In a letter dated April 3, 1945, written days after American troops

5 By decision of the council, the city government prohibited reconstruction in the old city (*Innenstadt*) from 1945 to 1949, a decision renewed for another three years. Rebuilding only began in 1952. See Thomas Bauer, *'Seid einig für unsere Stadt': Walter Kolb – Frankfurter Oberbürgermeister 1946 – 1956* (Frankfurt am Main: Waldemar Kramer, 1996), 87.

6 See, for an introduction and quotations from similar reports, Hermann Glaser, "So viel Anfang war nie," in *So viel Anfang war nie: Deutsche Städte 1945–1949*, ed. H. Glaser, Lutz von Pufendorf, and Michael Schöneich (Berlin: Siedler, 1989), 8–23. Cf. Carl Zuckmayer, *Deutschlandbericht für das Kriegsministerium der Vereinigten Staaten von Amerika*, ed. Gunther Nickel, Johanna Schrön, and Hans Wagener (Frankfurt am Main: Fischer, 2007); Hannah Arendt, "The Aftermath of Nazi Rule: Report from Germany," *Commentary* 10 (1950): 342–352. This genre is distinct from eyewitness reports, such as Fried Lübbecke's (see below), on the destruction of his hometown, Frankfurt.

7 For other examples concerning Frankfurt see Marie Luise Kaschnitz, "Rückkehr nach Frankfurt," in *Gesammelte Werke*, ed. Christian Büttrich and Norbert Miller, vol. 5 (Frankfurt am Main: Insel, 1985), 142–153 (first published in *Die Wandlung* 1, 1945/1946). On the popularity of poems in post-war Germany in general and Marie Luise Kaschnitz's in particular, see Gustav Zürcher, "'Vom elenden, herrlichen Leben': Die Nachkriegsgedichte von Marie Luise Kaschnitz," in *Marie Luise Kaschnitz*, ed. Uwe Schweikert (Frankfurt am Main: Suhrkamp, 1984), 193–208.

had gained control of the city, he summarized what he saw as "[a]n absolutely erschuetternde [harrowing] sight." His sudden switch into one word of German in a letter composed in English appears to register his shock. Another letter of July 29, 1945, speaks of the "creeping uncertainty [of] what you will see [when going to Frankfurt], and the fear of being hurt very much": "If I only had words to describe it to you."[8] For Theodor W. Adorno, the city's *Altstadt* was a "desolate dream where everything went topsy-turvy" (*wüster Traum, in dem alles durcheinander geriet*).[9] The Swiss writer Max Frisch captured Frankfurt in May of 1946 as a place where even the ruins "lie submerged in their own rubble."[10] The sheer amount of rubble covering the streets meant that these visitors no longer walked on street level, but on a slightly elevated, broken plane. Frisch continues: "It is all as one knows it from pictures; but here now it is, and at times one is astonished to experience no further awakening."[11] By 1946, in other words, the images of cities in rubble were familiar, so much so in fact that traveling to see authentic sights of urban destruction failed to catapult the observer to a loftier vantage point.

Yet Elkan's description of a walk through what once had been the core of Frankfurt also has an unlikely material counterpart in a model of the city's ruined center, undated but manufactured in the immediate wake of war for a 1946–1947 exhibition in Wiesbaden, the capital of the newly re-constituted state of Hesse. This was the first post-World War II rubble model made in Germany, made in a period of scarce resources when the city, especially its historic center, lay derelict (fig. 1).[12] The city's ruinous conditions are precisely what this object purports to represent, in dramatic sculpted relief. The whole model, some two by two meters, consists of wood, cardboard, and sand. The ruined buildings and façades

8 Sabine Hock, "Frankfurt am Main zur Stunde Null 1945: Zwei Briefe von Walter H. Rothschild," *Archiv für Frankfurts Geschichte und Kunst* 63 (1997): 535–557, here pp. 540 and 543.

9 Theodor W. Adorno, *Briefe an die Eltern 1939–1951* (Frankfurt am Main: Suhrkamp, 2003), 530 (letter of November 12, 1949).

10 Max Frisch, *Sketchbook 1946–1949*, trans. Geoffrey Skelton (New York: A Helen and Kurt Wolff Book, 1977), 21; id., *Tagebuch*, 32: [die Ruinen] "versinken in ihrem eigenen Schutt."

11 Frisch, *Sketchbook*, 21; id., *Tagebuch*, 33: "Es ist alles, wie man es von Bildern kennt; aber es ist, und manchmal ist man erstaunt, daß es ein weiteres Erwachen nicht gibt."

12 Frankfurt am Main, Historisches Museum, Plastische Skizze von der durch Kriegseinwirkung 1939–1945 zerstörten Altstadt von Frankfurt am Main (Three-dimensional sketch of the destroyed Old City of Frankfurt). It is known as the "Rubble Model," Frankfurt, 201 × 186 × 40 cm (made of wood, cardboard, and sand). The model is not dated. See *FFM 1200: Traditionen und Perspektiven einer Stadt*, ed. Lothar Gall (Sigmaringen: Thorbecke, 1994), 340: "Das 'Trümmer-Modell' war vermutlich eine Auftragsarbeit von Befürwortern einer radikalen Neugestaltung." Similarly *Das Frankfurter Altstadtmodell der Brüder Treuner*, ed. Jan Gerchow and Petra Spona (Frankfurt am Main: Henrich Editionen, 2011), 8f.

have been crudely painted to heighten their dramatic effect. The reddish coloring reflects one of the local building materials, red sandstone. But in its uneven flourishes, the color also evokes the afterglow of the firestorm that ravished the center after the fateful bombings of March 1944. The debris on the ground is rendered in high realism. The city center or *Römerberg* district appears almost completely leveled. Only the façades of several buildings – most of them structures of historic significance like the cathedral (*Kaiserdom*), St. Paul's Church (*Paulskirche*), *Old Nicolai Church*, and city hall (*Römer*) – stand above the squalor below. The streets and squares that we know must have formerly been there are covered with rubble; passage seems impossible.

If today this three-dimensional model of Frankfurt bears the caption "rubble model," this name derives not from the time of its making; it probably stems from the time when the model was first exhibited in Frankfurt's Museum of History (*Historisches Museum*), sometime in the late 1970s or early 1980s. The edge of the object itself merely bears the modest inscription "Plastic Sketch." The term is apt in that the topographic situation of the city's center with its hills is barely captured. What is more, comparisons with the ample photographic record of the time show that the relief model overstates, if not dramatizes, the state of destruction. Yet "rubble model" is an apt descriptor in that it analogizes the model with "rubble literature" and "rubble film." Such terms were somewhat defiant assertions. They seemed to assert that even in the midst of utter dereliction and starvation, culture still existed, and a culture that in retrospect recommended itself through an intense urgency. When Heinrich Böll embraced the term in his 1952 essay "Commitment to Rubble Literature," post-war German literature had already transitioned into a new phase, yet the writer wanted to retain the particular pure and stark mode of seeing he associated with "rubble literature."[13] In the case of the model, an image retained destruction's unsettling beauty for future generations to behold.

Let us explore the relationship between two objects designed to commemorate urban destruction in the wake of defeat. One is the relief model of Frankfurt's center at the end of the war, and the other is a design for a monument to the victims of the air raids, a design executed by the very same Benno Elkan who sought to mourn the lost Frankfurt in his 1950 newspaper article. Different as these objects are in rendering ruination – with the one focused on human loss whereas the model, at least on the surface of it, is devoid of representations of human life altogether. The monument was never realized, neither in Frank-

13 Heinrich Böll, "Bekenntnis zur Trümmerliteratur," in *Essayistische Schriften und Reden*, vol. 1, ed. Bernd Balzer (Cologne: Kiepenheuer & Witsch, 1979), 31–35.

Fig. 1: Robert and Hermann Treuner, Model of the destroyed center of Frankfurt (Römerberg), "Plastische Skizze von der durch Kriegseinwirkung 1939-1945 zerstörten Altstadt von Frankfurt am Main," ca. 1946, Historisches Museum Frankfurt am Main, X.2009.2961a-b (Photo: Horst Ziegenbusz)

furt nor elsewhere – only photographs of a *maquette* or model exist[14] – and the "rubble model" was exhibited in public only for a short period, if at all, at least until several decades later when this object entered the collection of the city's historical museum. What do these stunted efforts tell us about commemorating the air raids in the decade after 1945? Why was there such caution, if not anxiety, around monuments of the air raids?

14 Hofmann/Schmieder (*Benno Elkan*, 79) state that the *maquette* is lost and can no longer be located.

The Memory of Material Loss

Between June 4, 1940, and March 24, 1945, Frankfurt experienced 33 air raids.[15] In late 1943, these attacks grew more devastating. The attack of October 4 alone cost approximately 600 human lives.[16] By the end of the war, roughly 23,000 Frankfurters had died as a result of military actions.[17] Of them, 5,647 were civilian casualties of the air raids; the others were soldiers and military personnel, most of whom died in combat.[18] The horrific effect wrought by bombs dropped over densely built and populated areas makes it impossible to give an exact account of the human loss.

Of Frankfurt's 553,000 inhabitants in 1939, 269,000 still lived in the city after the end of hostilities – numbers that swelled rapidly in the ensuing months when former inhabitants and refugees flocked to the city.[19] Prior to the war, Frankfurt had approximately 177,600 apartments. Only 44,000 apartments were classified after the war as "without damage." Overall, approximately 83,000 apartments were uninhabitable and of the remaining 50,000 many were heavily damaged. As a result of the air raids, the city lay buried under more than 10 million cubic meters of rubble (other accounts estimate as high as 13 million cubic meters).[20] Inevitably, the levels of destruction varied from neighborhood to neighborhood, and street to street.[21] Yet nowhere did the destruction become as visible as in the

15 Hans-Reiner Müller-Raemisch, *Frankfurt am Main: Stadtentwicklung und Planungsgeschichte seit 1945* (Frankfurt am Main: Campus, 1996), 21; see also Armin Schmid, *Frankfurt im Feuersturm: Die Geschichte der Stadt im Zweiten Weltkrieg* (Frankfurt am Main: Frankfurter Bücher, 1965); second edition (Frankfurt am Main: Societätsverlag, 1984).

16 Bauer, '*Seid einig*,' 31.

17 Jutta Heibel, *Vom Hungertuch zum Wohlstandsspeck: Die Ernährungslage in Frankfurt am Main 1939–1955* (Frankfurt am Main: Waldemar Krause, 2002), 107. Cf. Werner Bendix, *Die Hauptstadt des deutschen Wirtschaftswunders: Frankfurt am Main 1945–1956* (Frankfurt am Main: Waldemar Kramer, 2002), 26.

18 Bauer, '*Seid einig*,' 31. Cf. Bendix, *Die Hauptstadt*, 26; Müller-Raemisch, *Frankfurt am Main*, 21.

19 Heibel, *Vom Hungertuch zum Wohlstandsspeck*, 106; Bauer, '*Seid einig*,' 31; Müller-Raemisch, *Frankfurt am Main*, 21.

20 Bauer, '*Seid einig*,' 31. For comparative data, see Jeffry M. Diefendorf, *In the Wake of War: The Reconstruction of German Cities after World War II* (New York: Oxford University Press, 1993), 15 (for Frankfurt, Diefendorf quotes the figure of 11,700,000 cubic meters with Berlin topping the list of other German cities, 55,000,000; this translates to a per capita amount of 21.1 cubic meters for the city).

21 Heibel, *Vom Hungertuch zum Wohlstandsspeck*, 108; Bauer, '*Seid einig*,' 31; Bendix, *Die Hauptstadt*, 7–8; Müller-Raemisch, *Frankfurt am Main*, 21. With a rate of destruction of one third, Frankfurt had received average losses. Rates in Cologne or Hamburg were significantly higher.

historic center, the *Altstadt*. This area, which would soon be depicted in the country's first rubble model, was known for its narrow streets and timber-frame structures. These houses were easy prey to the fires that engulfed the city in the wake of the bombs, and rubble was what remained of them. Laconically, a historian of Frankfurt notes: "The Second World War ended with the destruction of Frankfurt. The city of today has very little to do with the old Frankfurt."[22]

For Frankfurt, "total war" had resulted in unprecedented destruction. Starting even before the war ended, and continuing for years after, these devastations were assiduously measured, counted, published, and archived by state bureaucrats. But the country's documentation and discussion of destruction took many forms. After 1945, many Germans came to embrace the notion of "zero hour" (*Stunde Null*), as a means to describe Germany's defeat and to mark the moment, at war's end, of beginning anew. The popular formula has not fared well in historiography about post-war Germany, however.[23] Against the term's suggestion of a complete break, historians of post-war Germany have insisted on a plethora of continuities. National Socialist Germany, in power since 1933, these scholars contend, had far more to do with the post-1945 Germany than this trope has us imagine. Forms of pre-1945 political life did not vanish as the bombs fell; the nation was not reduced to rubble with the built infrastructure of its cities. In the midst of ruination, bureaucracies persisted, laws from the National Socialist period remained in effect, and mentalities were slow to change.[24]

More recently, however, historians of post-war Germany have insisted that these early years after the war were not only a time of hidden continuities but

---

See also a reprint of the color map of 1947 in Bendix, *Die Hauptstadt*, 30. Of the inhabitable dwellings, US headquarters demanded 8,000 for their own housing as well as for staff. According to a different calculation, of 45,000 buildings 36,000 had been destroyed or damaged. With regard to 12,000 of these, the buildings were classified as more than 70% destroyed (Hans Dauer and Karl Maury, *Frankfurt baut in die Zukunft* [Frankfurt am Main: Kramer, 1953], 20.)

22 Erich Helmendorfer, *Frankfurt – Metropole am Main: Geschichte und Zukunft* (Düsseldorf: Econ, 1982), 278.

23 Frank Biess, "Histories of the Aftermath," in *Histories of the Aftermath: The Legacies of the Second World War in Europe*, ed. Frank Biess and Robert G. Moeller (New York: Berghahn, 2010), 1–10 (with bibliography). From a literary perspective, see Stephen Brockmann, *German Literary Culture at the Zero Hour* (Rochester, NY: Camden, 2004). See esp. pp. 241f. on the history of the term.

24 Rebecca Boehling, "*Stunde Null* at the Ground Level: 1945 as a Social and Political *Ausgangspunkt* in Three Cities in the U.S. Zone of Occupation," in *Stunde Null: The End and the Beginning Fifty Years Ago*, ed. Geoffrey J. Giles (Washington, DC: German Historical Institute, 1997), 105–128, on Frankfurt see pp. 107–113; Jeffrey K. Olick, *In the House of the Hangman: The Agonies of German Defeat, 1943–1949* (Chicago: University of Chicago Press, 2005), 135 and passim.

also a time of possibilities.[25] The notion of the "zero hour" did not arise immediately with Germany's defeat; it rose to prominence at a time when German society turned away from the war, to quote Konrad Jarausch, and when the future re-asserted itself.[26] In recent studies, the repressive hypothesis developed in the 1960s about post-war Germans' inability to confront their Nazi past has been replaced by a contradictory image of discontinuities and continuities.[27] In fact, the debates among today's historians of post-war Germany resonate powerfully with discussions in Germany in the years after 1945.[28] The term "restoration," used by historians to characterize post-war Germany's return to the country's established political, ethical, and social traditions,[29] was already being deployed critically at the time.[30] By contrast, and more recently, Jeffrey Herf has sought to broaden our awareness of the messiness of post-war reality; not content with the singular usage of our terminology, he emphasizes the "multiple, pluralistic, and enduring nature of the postwar restorations of German political traditions."[31] Similarly,

---

25 Aleida Assmann, "1945 – Der blinde Fleck der deutschen Erinnerungsgeschichte," in *Geschichtsvergessenheit – Geschichtsversessenheit: Vom Umgang mit deutschen Vergangenheiten*, ed. Aleida Assmann and Ute Frevert (Stuttgart: Deutsche Verlags-Anstalt, 1999), 97–138. See also Malte Thießen, *Eingebrannt ins Gedächtnis: Hamburgs Gedenken an Luftkrieg und Kriegsende 1943 bis 2005* (Hamburg: Dölling und Galitz, 2007), 366.

26 Konrad Jarausch, *Die Umkehr: Deutsche Wandlungen 1945–1995* (Munich: DVA, 2004).

27 The threat or promise of forgetting was already part of the post-1945 discussion, for instance in Marie Luise Kaschnitz's play "Danse Macabre" (*Totentanz*), written in 1944 after Frankfurt's demise but set 10–15 years after the war. See Marie Luise Kaschnitz, *Totentanz und Gedichte zur Zeit* (Hamburg: Claassen & Goverts, 1947). See also Bradford Vivian, *Public Forgetting: The Rhetoric and Politics of Beginning Again* (University Park, PA: Pennsylvania State University Press, 2010).

28 Attempts to survey the contradictory responses to the Nazi past in West Germany in the years after 1945 in Jeffrey K. Olick, *In the House of the Hangman*; Kurt Finker, *Der Dämon kam über uns: Faschismus und Antifaschismus im Geschichtsbild und in der Geschichtsschreibung Westdeutschlands (1945–1955)*, ed. Friedrich-Martin Balzer (Bonn: Pahl-Rugenstein Nachfolger, 2008).

29 Lothar Kettenacker, *Germany since 1945* (Oxford: Oxford University Press, 1997), 161.

30 See, for instance, Alfred Weber, "Haben Wir Deutsche seit 1945 Versagt?" [1949] in *Politik im Nachkriegsdeutschland*. Alfred-Weber-Gesamtausgabe, vol. 9, ed. Eberhard Demm (Marburg: Metropolis, 2001), 91–107.

31 Jeffrey Herf, "Multiple Restorations: German Political Traditions and the Interpretation of Nazism, 1945–1946," *Central European History* 26 (1993): 21–55, here p. 54. A shorter version has been published as Jeffrey Herf, "Divided Memory, Multiple Restorations: West German Political Reflections on the Nazi Past, 1945–1953," in *Revisiting Zero Hour 1945: The Emergence of Postwar German Culture*, ed. Stephen Brockmann and Frank Trommler (Washington, DC: American Institute for Contemporary German Studies, 1996), 89–102. See also Lutz Niethammer, "Privat-Wirtschaft: Erinnerungsfragmente einer anderen Umerziehung," in *'Hinterher merkt man, daß es richtig war, daß es schiefgegangen ist': Nachkriegserfahrungen im Ruhrgebiet*, ed. Lutz Niet-

Christoph Klessmann has argued for a new cultural history of the post-World War II moment to adequately capture the web of continuities and discontinuities during the years before the foundation of the two Germanies in 1949. While issuing the caveat that we cannot take the rhetoric of renewal and departures from these years at face value, Klessmann also insists that the situation is too complex to be rendered by a simple alternative – a rhetoric of either restoration or renovation and change that remains steeped in post-war controversies.[32] Controversies not only arose from the rubble in post-war Germany; they turned the same rubble into something of a looking-glass. And the urban landscape and urban planning became venues of discussion about the unparalleled challenges post-war Germans faced.[33]

At first sight, the "rubble model" is a simple object. Yet its seemingly straightforward material enables us to approach post-war discourses about rubble and rebuilding, discourses that were never about material remains alone. The multiple levels of all such discourses – emotional and intellectual, physical and psychological, all at the same time – are made evident by several ambitious essays published for ordinary German readers in 1946.[34] In "Before the Ruins of

hammer (Berlin/Bonn: J. H. W. Dietz Nachf., 1983): 17–105; id., "War die bürgerliche Gesellschaft in Deutschland 1945 am Ende oder am Anfang?" [1990] in id., *Deutschland Danach: Postfaschistische Gesellschaft und Nationales Gedächtnis*, ed. Ulrich Herbert et al. (Bonn: J. H. W. Dietz, 1999), 18–35; Geoffry G. Giles, ed., *Stunde Null: The End and the Beginning Fifty Years Ago* (Washington, DC: German Historical Institute, 1997); Uta Gerhardt, *Soziologie der Stunde Null: Zur Gesellschaftskonzeption des amerikanischen Besatzungsregimes in Deutschland 1944–1945/1946* (Frankfurt am Main: Suhrkamp, 2005).

32 Christoph Klessmann, "'Das Haus wurde gebaut aus den Steinen, die vorhanden waren': Zur kulturgeschichtlichen Kontinuitätsdiskussion nach 1945," *Tel Aviver Jahrbuch für deutsche Geschichte* 19 (1990): 159–177.

33 See Werner Durth and Niels Gutschow, *Träume in Trümmern: Planungen zum Wiederaufbau zerstörter Städte im Westen Deutschlands 1940–1950*, vol. 2: *Städte* (Braunschweig: Friedrich Vieweg & Sohn, 1988), 147f. The fact that 1945 did not constitute a turning point in Germany or in other European countries is established in the following anthology: Jeffry M. Diefendorf, ed., *Rebuilding Europe's Bombed Cities* (Basingstoke: Macmillan Press, 1990). See the editor's introduction, "Introduction: New Perspectives on a Rebuilt Europe" (1–15) as well as the contributions by Tony Mason and Nick Tiratsoo ("People, Politics and Planning: The Reconstruction of Coventry's City Centre, 1940–53," 94–113), Niels Gutschow ("Hamburg: The 'Catastrophe' of July 1943," 114–130), and Friedhelm Fischer ("German Reconstruction as an International Activity," 131–144). Continuity also characterized the lives of individual 'experts' in architecture and urbanism before and after 1945, see Sylvia Necker, *Konstanty Gutschow 1902–1978: Modernes Denken und volksgemeinschaftliche Utopie eines Architekten* (Hamburg: Dölling & Galitz, 2012).

34 In addition to the ones mentioned below, see also Friedrich Meinecke, *Die deutsche Katastrophe: Betrachtungen und Erinnerungen* (Wiesbaden: Brockhaus, 1946) – an essay so focused on

Germany: A Call to Historical Self-Reflection" (*Vor den Ruinen Deutschlands: Ein Aufruf zur geschichtlichen Selbstbesinnung*), Franz A. Kramer uses the actual devastations as a rhetorical backdrop for activating Germans to recognize their own responsibility in bringing about the country's ruin – a recognition, he hoped, that would generate the intellectual forces needed for reconstruction.[35] For Wilhelm Hoffmann, author of "After the Catastrophe" (*Nach der Katastrophe*), the material destruction is symptomatic, namely an outer manifestation of a German culture tainted to the core.[36] In Karl Jaspers' "The Question of Guilt" (*Die Schuldfrage*), the material conditions surface on the margins of his explication of different types of guilt, as this philosopher rejects arguments that equated the sufferings Germans inflicted on others with the sufferings Germans experienced through the air raids and as a result of the war.[37]

In these pleas, the invocation of debris was designed to move and mobilize readers – something that extended also to publications on Germany from abroad. For Victor Gollancz, the British philanthropist, the horrid living conditions in the defeated Germany would ultimately result in moral destitution.[38] Hannah Arendt re-interprets the term *Schadenfreude* (literally, damage-joy) to capture the German post-war mentality of forming dogged attachments to their own powerlessness – a German word she renders as "malicious joy in ruination."[39]

Yet the notion of a rupture in the defeated Germany crystallized above all around the destroyed cities and their centers. The urban wastelands offered themselves as ciphers, spawning descriptions, musings, and reflections in photographic, literary, and modeled forms. Material loss figured as a signifier for an all-encompassing sense of disorientation. Rubble appeared as a sign of a crisis, a crisis of representation. "Surrender and occupation cut loose the familiar

---

saving German culture (*Geist*) in the "catastrophe" that material conditions remain outside its purview. An overview of post-war German discourses about the legacy of the past in Olick, *In the House of the Hangman*, 139–233.

35 Franz A. Kramer, *Vor den Ruinen Deutschlands: Ein Aufruf zur geschichtlichen Selbstbesinnung* (Berlin: Wedding-Verlag, [1945]).

36 Wilhelm Hoffmann, *Nach der Katastrophe* [1946] (Stuttgart: Lithos-Verlag, 2001), see esp. 48–51 and passim. The air raids' impact on the psyche in National Socialist Germany occasion extensive reflection in this context (19–27).

37 Karl Jaspers, *Die Schuldfrage* (Heidelberg: Lambert Schneider, 1946); id., *The Question of Guilt*, trans. E. B. Ashton (New York: Dial Press, 1947). The city of Frankfurt awarded Jaspers the Goethe Prize in 1947. According to Hoffmann (*Nach der Katastrophe*, 48), a discussion of the Allied war from the air is premature in light of a lack of a fuller understanding and would detract from Germany's need to reflect on its own state.

38 Victor Gollancz, *In Darkest Germany* (London: Victor Gollancz, 1947).

39 Arendt, "Aftermath," 343.

tropes that anchored representation; 'meaning' abruptly flew in new directions," writes Abé M. Nornes with regard to the defeated Japan in a comment that could also describe its defeated war ally, Germany.[40] Such descriptions singled out a place's historic cores as the symbolic center of that community, and, at least in some renderings, a space ready for re-inscription. The urbanisms that emerged in this context became a focal point and a measuring stick for where the city, the region, the country, and even the world were headed. In post-war Frankfurt as elsewhere in Germany and Europe, the urban past and its possible futures became a severely contested territory after destruction. "The experience of the aerial warfare and of the Third Reich created an invincible faith in a better future, as if a look back into history would allow only a look into an unfathomable pit," writes Niels Gutschow.[41]

The anticipation of a better, hygienic, and beautiful future for Germany's cities had already been a component of Nazi propaganda toward the end of the war, as more and more cities fell into ruin.[42] But after the war the theme of construction rose to prominence with renewed vigor. While debates, tensions, and conflicts over a city's future became a feature of many German communities ravaged by the aerial war, in Frankfurt such contestations had a particular urgency. Like in other major German cities, local National Socialist planning authorities had left the city with urban designs that guided post-1945 construction efforts, though these visions for the future were more modest than elsewhere. After all, Frankfurt, a city with democratic and Jewish associations, had occupied only a peripheral place in the National Socialist state or in Nazi visions for future urban grandeur. Still, in Frankfurt as elsewhere there was, overall, considerable continuity in both personnel and ideas.[43]

What is particular about Frankfurt is that few German cities experienced as rapid a post-war expansion. Within eleven years of the war's end, Frankfurt, after having been brought to the brink of its existence, surpassed the level of its

40 Abé Mark Nornes, *Japanese Documentary Film: The Meiji Era through Hiroshima* (Minneapolis: University of Minnesota Press, 2003), 183.

41 Niels Gutschow, "Hamburg: The 'Catastrophe' of July 1943," in *Rebuilding Europe's Bombed Cities*, ed. Jeffry Diefendorf (Basingstoke: Macmillan, 1990), 126.

42 Joseph Goebbels, *Goebbels-Reden*, vol. 2: *1939–1945*, ed. Helmut Heiber (Düsseldorf: Droste, 1972), 297, 299, 338f, 453.

43 Almut Gehebe-Gernhardt, *Architektur der 50er Jahre in Frankfurt am Main – am Beispiel der Architektengemeinschaft Alois Giefer und Hermann Mäckler* (Frankfurt am Main: Waldemar Kramer, 2011), 43–57. On these traditions in general, see Werner Durth and Niels Gutschow, *Architektur und Städtebau der fünfziger Jahre* (Bonn: Deutsches Nationalkomitee für Denkmalschutz, 1990), 11.

pre-war population and economic output.[44] Drawing on a rich history as a center of German political life,[45] its central geographic location, its vital role in the country's industrial production and banking, as well as its cultural cachet, Frankfurt vied to become the provisional capital of a new Germany, a campaign launched shortly after the end of the war. In June 1946, the city became the administrative center for the *Bizone*, the combined US and British occupation zones, which resulted in the rapid construction of new office and apartment quarters. In 1947, the renowned modernist architect Walter Gropius authored a confidential report for Lucius D. Clay, the US Military Governor in Germany, on why Frankfurt should be the capital city of a West German state.[46] When two 1949 elections saw Frankfurt lose to its contender, Bonn, as the capital of the Federal Republic, the result was due, among other reasons, to the perception that the city made so much sense as a capital that its choice would have rubbed against West Germany's claim to be only a provisional state and would have eclipsed Berlin as the future capital of a united Germany.[47] Yet, despite this setback, Frankfurt could still lay claim to be the "capital of the economic miracle."[48]

Visions for this miraculous new city drew on images of the past, but it was a past that had to be overcome, incorporated, reinstated, or reinvented. In Old-Frankfurt, the past had been a bricolage. The city's century-long history was evident in the aggregation of landmark buildings, buildings of different historical styles, and the fabric of individual houses that had been resized, refit, and upgraded without completely excising what had been there before. It was this temporal layering that could not be mimicked after 1945. The past had literally been flattened. City planning thus became a forum for social, cultural, political, and historical debate.

Architecture has always been an idiom replete with symbolisms. But amidst the sheer vastness of destruction, urban planning and building risked collapsing under the weight of its functions and significations. While construction started to rapidly transform many neighborhoods, both business and residential, the revival was stalled in the city's old center and the past constituted an open wound

44 Bendix, *Die Hauptstadt des deutschen Wirtschaftswunders.*
45 In June of 1947, Walter Kolb, Frankfurt's mayor, explicitly referred to the city as (the former) imperial city in the context of a campaign to make the city capital of the Federal Republic.
46 Jeffry M. Diefendorf, "America and the Rebuilding of Germany," in *American Policy and the Reconstruction of West Germany, 1945–1955*, ed. Jeffry M. Diefendorf, Axel Frohn, and Hermann-Josef Rupieper (Cambridge: Cambridge University Press, 1993), 331–351, here p. 337.
47 Gehebe-Gernhardt, *Architektur der 50er Jahre*, 66f.
48 Müller-Raemisch, *Frankfurt am Main*, 28f.

at a time when the model of destroyed Frankfurt was made and Elkan wandered "on the hills of sorrow." The city government declared the *Altstadt* a zone where private owners were barred from building until the city issued a master plan. Only in 1952, after the most egregious urban needs in other neighborhoods had been addressed, the center started to catch up with the rest of the city. The questions about its shape, however, have never vanished, even as block by block a new *Altstadt* emerged from the rubble. Frankfurt thus is a paradigmatic case study for the complex, often tortured, relationship of German communities to their lost urban pasts.

Viewed thus, the Frankfurt model functions metonymically, its own rubble gestures toward a variety of post-war discourses and realities, referencing various temporal layers. In all its emotive qualities, this model, now in the city's history museum, shows a haunting vision of ruined Frankfurt rather than the grim reality of a city in rubble. The presentation borders on the theatrical (fig. 2). This modeled vista reorders the rubble and debris of which the post-war urban wanderer speaks into the well-focused idiom of ruins. Not unlike Marie Luise Kaschnitz, who in the first poem of her 1946 cycle of elegies about the destroyed city, "Return to Frankfurt" (*Rückkehr nach Frankfurt*), crafted an anthropomorphized city for an existentialist oracle in poetic form, the model is a work of translation, a translation that turns destruction into a recognizable language.[49] For one, the model could be read as equivalent to the myth of a rupture: the worse the state of destruction, the more powerful the city's ensuing rebirth (and this is what the caption states in the museum where the model is exhibited today). Yet while this object fits into the "zero hour" narrative, the object also exceeds this discourse about new beginnings by conjuring up a haunting image of the past together with both the present and a future as yet unbuilt at the time of the model's creation.

Modeling the Past, Present, and Future

The modeled scene of urban devastation powerfully evokes a rich historical past, interweaving local with national history through an image of the ruined center of Frankfurt.[50] Dwarfing other buildings, St. Bartholomew, the *Kaiserdom*,

49 Kaschnitz, "Rückkehr," 142.

50 In his report of July 1946, Mayor Kurt Blaum had a strikingly similar vision for the post-war Frankfurt that wedded its economic centrality to the city's rich historical traditions, see Gehebe-Gernhardt, *Architektur der 50er Jahre*, 34.

was the church[51] where the electors of the Holy Roman Empire gathered to cast their vote on the future German king, a ceremony first documented for the city in 1147, regulated in 1356, and last carried out in 1792. After 1562, the coronations also took place in the cathedral.[52] The newly elected rulers were honored with a festive celebration in city hall, the so-called *Römer*, to the cathedral's west and on the main square – a landmark façade recognizable even in its ruined state. On October 8, 1866, its emperors' hall (*Kaisersaal*) provided the setting for the city's incorporation into Prussia – an act that ended Frankfurt's centuries of political independence as a free imperial city and its status as the capital of the German Confederation (*Deutscher Bund*) in the period after 1815.[53] Towards the northern edge of the relief, the *maquette* of the classicist *Paulskirche*'s empty shell with its striking oval nave calls forth memories of the first German parliament. In 1848, parliamentarians gathered there after Frankfurt's city hall had proved too small for their great number.

Viewed through the lens of modeled destruction, these buildings reference historical layers for those in the know. As a ruined church, the *Kaiserdom*, for instance, takes on a medieval aura, reminiscent of the haunting ruins of cathedrals and abbeys in nineteenth-century paintings from a Romantic era when medievalism first emerged as a rallying point against the rationalism of the late Enlightenment or France's cultural hegemony over Germany. Yet before its devastation during the 1944 air raids, the church, especially the tower, had been damaged by fire in 1867; its tower was finally completed in 1880, on the basis of a medieval plan; and the historicist reconstruction of Johannes Janssen showed patched-together altars and interior decorations in an eclectic Gothic style with national overtones. In modeled ruination, the past of particular buildings emerges as more homogeneous and the city as a place imbued with "beauty," to use a word from Elkan's description of bombed-out Frankfurt.[54]

---

51 Formally speaking, the church was not a bishop's see. The honorific title "cathedral" (*Dom*) became common in the early modern period.

52 Matthias Theodor Kloft, *Kaiserdom St. Bartholomäus Frankfurt am Main*, 2nd ed. (Regensburg: Schnell & Steiner, 1999); Wolfgang Klötzer, "Zur Geschichte der Frankfurter Wahlkapelle," in *Keine liebere Stadt als Frankfurt: Kleine Schriften zur Frankfurter Kulturgeschichte*, vol. 2 (Frankfurt am Main: Waldemar Kramer, 2000), 397–408; Gehebe-Gernhardt, *Architektur der 50er Jahre*, 176–182 (on the cathedral's post-war reconstruction).

53 Wolf-Arno Kropat, *Frankfurt zwischen Provinizialismus und Nationalismus: Die Eingliederung der "Freien Stadt" in den preußischen Staat* (Frankfurt am Main: Waldemar Kramer, 1971), 23.

54 Diefendorf (*In the Wake of War*, 4) quotes George Kennan on a visit to Berlin 15 years after the war: "And what ruins! In their original state they had seemed slightly imitative and pretentious. Now they suddenly had a grandeur I had never seen even in Rome ... There was a stillness, a

Starting in the early twentieth century, the pace of urban change accelerated considerably, something also visible in the model of the city in ruins. Fin-de-siècle urban renovations facilitated circulation within the city by cutting thoroughfares into the historically textured center, a renewal propagated as a "rational" median course between zealous traditionalism on the one hand and reckless modernizing on the other.[55] During the Weimar Republic, under the aegis of the internationally renowned city planner Ernst May, the focus of development shifted to satellite suburbs with their promise of social reform and "The New Frankfurt" (*Das Neue Frankfurt*) – the title of a journal published during the golden years of "new building" (*Neues Bauen*), 1926–1932.[56] With the exception of urban projects billed as sanitation, the old city with its dark streets and increasingly impoverished inhabitants lay largely neglected, its relation to the bustling new Frankfurt unresolved.[57]

At this juncture, in 1922, the art historian and preservationist Fried Lübbecke (1883–1965)[58] founded the "Association of Active Friends of the Old City" (*Bund tätiger Altstadtfreunde*) in order to foster a climate of appreciation for the historic Frankfurt, improve the "living conditions in this part of town," and prevent any further loss of the city's historically grown fabric.[59] The *Bund* spawned alliances

---

beauty, a sense of infinite, elegiac sadness and timelessness such as I have never experienced" (George F. Kennan, *Sketches from a Life* [New York: Pantheon Books, 1989], 194).

55 Jörg R. Köhler, *Städtebau und Stadtpolitik im Wilhelminischen Frankfurt* (Frankfurt am Main: Waldemar Kramer, 1995).

56 Diefendorf, *In the Wake of War*, 76–78; Susan Rose Henderson, *The Work of Ernst May, 1919–1930* (Ph.D. diss., Columbia University, 1990), vol. 2, 302f and passim; Justus Buekschmitt, *Ernst May* (Stuttgart: Verlagsanstalt Alexander Koch, 1963).

57 A model of an urban block in the old city with a moveable inner core of buildings was meant to demonstrate the beneficial effects of urban sanitation for visitors of the German Construction and Settlement Exhibition (*Deutsche Bau- und Siedlungsausstellung*) in Frankfurt in 1938. See photograph in Johannes Cramer and Niels Gutschow, *Bauausstellungen: Eine Architekturgeschichte des 20. Jahrhunderts* (Stuttgart: W. Kohlhammer, 1984), 35.

58 Fried Lübbecke, *Die gotische Kölner Plastik* (Strassburg: Heitz, 1910); *Die Plastik des deutschen Mittelalters* (Munich: Piper, 1922).

59 "Frankfurter Angelegenheit," *Frankfurter Zeitung*, April 14, 1922, 2 (Morgenausgabe) (report on the founding of the association): "Geplant ist nicht nur Schutz der Altstadt und ihrer Schönheiten, sondern auch die Hebung der Wohnverhältnisse in diesem Stadtteil." See also Andreas Hansert, *Georg Hartmann (1870–1954): Biografie eines Frankfurter Schriftgießers, Bibliophilen und Kunstmäzens* (Vienna: Böhlau, 2009), 99f, 249–251. See also Fried Lübbecke, "Fried Lübbecke über sich selbst," in *Die Frankfurter Altstadt: Eine Erinnerung*, ed. Wolfgang Klötzer (Frankfurt am Main: Waldemar Kramer, 1983), 427–431. This volume also contains a selection of his writings on Frankfurt between 1922 and 1965.

across the political spectrum and artistic ideologies – a vibrancy evident in the association's 1925 *Festschrift*, edited by Benno Elkan, an illustrated book created on the occasion of the old city's repainting, with a burlesque experimentation that wedded carnival tradition to the aesthetic avant-garde. In one of the contributions, Siegfried Kracauer of the *Frankfurter Zeitung* utters in jest: "The old city does not exist; it is but a great ideology of the Association of Active Friends of the Old City."[60] The confrontation between proponents of a "New Frankfurt" and an "Old Frankfurt" – the programmatic title of a series of photography albums issued by the *Bund* – would re-surface after 1944, as we will see, when the task to rebuild Frankfurt pitted modern urbanists against preservationists.[61]

Moved by fears of modern-day "destruction," be it through sheer neglect, new building projects, or the destructive needs of the modern city, especially its traffic – the association launched initiatives to archive the historic city for future reference.[62] It was thus in the heady political, social, and urbanistic climate of the Weimar Republic that a penchant for the relief modeling of Old Frankfurt was born, namely as a small-scale bulwark against the destructive forces of change. For proponents of the historical *Altstadt*, models promised a record of ancient structures scheduled for demolition. Since the early 1900s, museum officials, local historians, and the *Bund* commissioned replicas of houses or small urban sections – models that paved the way for the idea of a comprehensive relief sculpture of *Alt-Frankfurt*.

---

60 Siegfried Kracauer, "Die Nichtexistenz der Altstadt: Eine philosophische Deduktion," in *Römer-Maske: Eine Festschrift Phantastischer Satire und satirischer Phantasie* (Frankfurt am Main: Hauser, 1925), 48: "Die Altstadt existiert nicht, sie ist vielmehr eine große Ideologie des Bundes tätiger Altstadtfreunde." The paint applied to the old city was equaled to the old city masking itself for carnival.

61 For an introduction to post-war reconstruction on the backdrop of building in Weimar and Nazi Germany, see Diefendorf, *In the Wake of War*. With regard to Frankfurt and the controversial plans to involve Walter Gropius, see p. 184. See also Friedhelm Fischer, "German Reconstruction as an International Activity," in *Rebuilding Europe's Bombed Cities*, 131–154, here pp. 140–142. On the history of architecture, see Jörg Paczkowski, *Der Wiederaufbau der Stadt Würzburg nach 1945*, 2nd ed. (Würzburg: Ferdinand Schöningh, 1995) .

62 Paul Wolff and Fried Lübbecke, *Alt-Frankfurt*, vol. 3 (Frankfurt: Englert & Schlosser, 1926), 9. Cf. Georg Hartmann and Fried Lübbecke, *Alt-Frankfurt: Ein Vermächtnis* (Frankfurt am Main: Der Goldene Brunnen, [1950]), a re-edition of 252 full-page black and white photographs of the old city with 18 shots of ruined Frankfurt in the aftermath of war. The preface states that "this book contains pictures from Frankfurt's old city that to the largest part were taken in dark prescience of the horrible end" (*Dieses Buch enthält Bilder aus der Frankfurter Altstadt, die zum größten Teil während des Krieges in dunkler Vorahnung des furchtbaren Endes aufgenommen wurden*) (unnumbered page).

In 1926, the brothers Robert and Hermann Treuner seized the moment and started to model old Frankfurt *in toto* – the year 1927 serving as the date of reference. Their project lasted into the post-war years, and remained unfinished when the last of the two brothers died in 1962. Building by building, street by street, the two model-makers meticulously researched cadastre records, produced on site-drawings, made measurements, and carved wooden blocks – with the imposing scale of 1:200 – painted to increase their realist appeal. Public and private support for what was largely a labor of love was intermittent and progress slow.

When the old city fell into rubble during the devastating air-raids of March 18 and March 22 of 1944, its miniature replica – as much as had been finished by the time – survived in a bunker, evidence that it was highly treasured as an object. This model thereby became a document of and a monument to an urban space damaged beyond repair.[63] "The old city is still alive," as the title to a 1946 newspaper article has it, only to add the subtitle "in the models of the brothers Treuner."[64] The Treuners' "precious model" was even mentioned in a charter issued at the occasion of the inauguration of post-war construction work on the old downtown on May 15, 1952, although the new *Altstadt* that came to replace what had been lost referenced the information contained in the model only occasionally.[65] After the war, the brothers continued their work on sculpting the city of old in miniature, drawing on their and others' records of what had been destroyed. When the planners of the first state-wide exhibit in post-war Hesse decided to include a model of the destroyed Frankfurt, they turned to the Treuners to have them model the downtown of the state's premier city in 1946.[66] The exhibition (*Landesausstellung Hessische Wirtschaft*), one of the first of its kind in post-war Germany (October 1946–July 1947), was intended to showcase the return to peacetime economy, the state's future economic potential, and the German people's will to peaceful existence in the concert of nations.[67]

---

63 Fried Lübbecke, *Treuner's Alt-Frankfurt: Das Altstadtmodell im Historischen Museum* (Frankfurt am Main: Waldemar Kramer, 1960); Gerchow/Spona, *Das Frankfurter Altstadtmodell.*

64 "Die Altstadt lebt noch – In den Modellen der Gebrüder Treuner," *Frankfurter Neue Presse*, December 23, 1946, 5.

65 Dauer/Maury, *Frankfurt baut in die Zukunft*, appendix.

66 "Die Altstadt lebt noch," *Frankfurter Neue Presse*, 5. I thank Dorothee Linnemann from Frankfurt's Historical Museum for having shared this finding with me.

67 Hessisches Hauptstaatsarchiv Wiesbaden, Eröffnung der Landesausstellung am 16.10.1946, Abt. 1126, Nr. 32c and 34a; ibid., Hessische Exportschau 1946/47, Abt. 3008/1 Nr. 2035 (photograph); ibid., WK Nr. 103v, 123 v, 129v, 133v, 140v, and 143v. The scant available documentation on the show I have so far been able to unearth does not contain information on how and in what context the rubble model was on display. If it was, the rhetoric of the display would be

Fig. 2: Robert and Hermann Treuner, Model of the destroyed center of Frankfurt (Römerberg), "Plastische Skizze," ca. 1946, detail, Historisches Museum Frankfurt am Main (Photo: Author)

As becomes evident if one compares their rubble model with photographs of the destroyed city, the modelmakers did not render a number of remnants of houses that were still standing. What this "plastic sketch" lacked in verisimilitude – a quality often mentioned with regard to the Treuners' rendering of Old Frankfurt – it made up in authenticity: The makers used actual debris for their model, thus turning the object into a monument of sorts. It offers not only a haunting image of the rubbled city but also serves as a monument made in part of its own rubble.[68]

---

comparable to other exhibits after 1945 discussed in Chapter Five that, as a rule, used the rubble to look back in order to then have viewers look into the future. With thanks to Dr. Volker Eichler and Peter Haberkorn from the Hauptstaatsarchiv Wiesbaden for their help. Another city in Hesse, Kassel, organized an exhibit on reconstruction as early as May 1946 ("Kassel baut auf!"), Landesamt für Denkmalpflege Hessen, ed., *Baudenkmale in Hessen: Stadt Kassel I* (Braunschweig: Friedrich Vieweg & Sohn, 1984), 23. See also Wolf-Arno Kropat, *Hessen in der Stunde Null 1945–1947: Politik, Wirtschaft und Bildungswesen in Dokumenten* (Wiesbaden: Selbstverlag der Historischen Kommission für Nassau, 1979); id., ed., *Aufbruch zur Demokratie: Alltag und politischer Neubeginn in Hessen nach 1945.* Exhibition Catalogue (Wiesbaden: Hessisches Hauptstaatsarchiv, 1996).

68 "Die Altstadt lebt noch," *Frankfurter Neue Presse*: "Bei den weiten Trümmerflächen der heutigen Altstadt [im Modell] wurde zerschlagenes Originalmaterial mitverwandt."

Yet the model of destroyed Frankfurt was not only oriented toward the old but also toward the new Frankfurt, offering a blueprint for the future city and new *Altstadt*. The model of the ruined city conjures up a map of open spaces that city planners were called upon to fill. During post-war reconstruction, city planners then sculpted an urban space in which repaired or rebuilt individual edifices, deemed historically significant, shone within a newly constituted urban fabric. The density of old gave way to an urbanism of open spaces, car-accessible streets, and what was advertised as spacious living quarters. In many instances, parts of buildings that had survived the air raids were taken down to make place for the new.[69] Post-war Frankfurt became a decidedly modern city whose historical depth was nonetheless readily apparent. The new neighborhoods that arose in lieu of the old center provided a frame for the reconstructed landmark buildings. It became an open-air museum for the post-war *flâneur* or the growing number of people who moved through the city by car. As a result, the city's attractions became more insular than before the war as historical buildings were "released from the deadly clutch of trivial building blocks," in the words of Walter Kolb, the city's mayor from 1946 to 1956.[70] Post-war Frankfurt was configured as an urban stage upon which the city's past could be appreciated, a historical spectacle condensed into architectural highlights, something the "rubble model" foreshadows and reflects. With its hyperbolic statement on the state of the city's destruction, the model seems to have been accorded the task of invigorating such visions of a new beginning via a haunting image of the present and the past – a past that due to the use of debris from the destroyed city was materially present in this miniature monument.

69 Gehebe-Gernhardt, *Architektur der 50er Jahre*, 293, 296.

70 Quoted after Bauer, '*Seid einig*,' 95f: "Wirkliche Baudenkmäler von Rang sind im Gegenteil zum Mittelpunkt einer neuen Gestaltung gemacht worden und aus der tödlichen Umklammerung belangloser Baublocks bewusst befreit worden." This comment echoes a comment by Johann Wolfgang Goethe who, when passing through Frankfurt in 1787, first saw the recently erected *Paulskirche* and remarked that its modern form and its densely built urban context were at odds with one another: "Die neue lutherische Hauptkirche gibt leider viel zu denken ... da kein Platz in der Stadt weder wirklich noch denkbar ist, auf dem sie eigentlich stehen könnte und sollte, so hat man wohl den schwersten Fehler begangen, daß man zu einem Platz eine solche Form wählte. Sie stickt, da man ringsherum wohl schwerlich viel wird abbrechen lassen, zwischen Gebäuden, die ihrer Natur und Kostbarkeit wegen unbeweglich sind." (Quoted after Dieter Bartetzko, *Denkmal für den Aufbau Deutschlands: Die Paulskirche in Frankfurt am Main* [Königstein im Taunus: Karl Robert Langewiesche Nachfolger, 1998], 3). Stadtrat Wolf explicated the concept thus, historical buildings "as pillars" of their architectural context (*Bauwerke als Pfeiler der Gesamtbebauung*). See Dauer/Maury, *Frankfurt baut in die Zukunft*, 10.

To be sure, in actual post-war Frankfurt, the architectural past raised its head from the rubble selectively. The many projects that aimed to fill in the open spaces left by destruction catalyzed various relationships to the past, from attempts at reconstructing, to moderate nods to that same past, to an architecture that, more or less radically, departed from past solutions. Not surprisingly, buildings that carried connotations of a "good" Germany received preferential treatment after 1945. In light of the impending one-hundred year anniversary of the 1848-revolution when political representatives had gathered in St. Paul's, the city government decided to rebuild the church as early as April of 1946 (the *Paulskirche* marks the northwestern end of Frankfurt's rubble model). Other than making the streets passable and repairing streets, St. Paul's was the city's first major construction project, and arguably one of the first major renovation projects anywhere in the country. As such, it offered an opportunity to promote Frankfurt's preeminence in the emerging political order of occupied Germany.[71] The demise of the nation within the defeated Germany allowed local governments to lay claim to political authority and national prestige in a degree unprecedented since the unification of Germany in 1871 (fig. 3).

The 1949-bicentenary of Johann Wolfgang von Goethe's birth – the most famous Frankfurter – ushered in another construction project, the plan to rebuild the writer's parental home (not rendered on the relief model), owned since 1863 by the *Freie Deutsche Hochstift,* a Frankfurt-based national civic association (founded in 1859). In post-war Germany as well as internationally, Goethe figured as a potent projection screen – an emblem for the national character as well as for a cosmopolitan Germany.[72] Though the city government needed to approve

---

71 Mayor Kurt Blaum explicitly mentioned that the church could be used as an assembly hall for the new German parliament (Bauer, '*Seid einig,*' 40). Already before 1848, the amphitheatrical seating order in the church's interior held connotations of democracy, see Bartetzko, *Denkmal*, 21, and Müller-Raemisch, *Frankfurt am Main*, 41–43.

72 G. P. Gooch et al., *The German Mind and Outlook* (London: Chapman, 1946), 70–91, 215–218. The authors herald Goethe as cure for the "diseased" (215) German mind that this collection of essays diagnoses. In a chapter devoted to this writer's thinking and in the concluding section he comes across as a praxis-oriented philosopher of freedom. See also Meinecke, *Die deutsche Katastrophe*, 21, 157, 168, 174–176 with its suggestion to launch Goethe circles in all German towns in order to celebrate the achievements of the German mind (*Goethegemeinden*). On the German discussion, see Karl Robert Mandelkow, ed., *Goethe im Urteil seiner Kritiker*, iv, 258–307. On the invocation of Goethe among post-war Germans, see Hermann Glaser, *Kleine Kulturgeschichte der Bundesrepublik Deutschland 1945–1989*, 2nd ed. (Bonn: Bundeszentrale für politische Bildung, 1991), 137–139; Olick, *In the House of the Hangman*, 152–154, 165. Cf. Kaschnitz, "Rückkehr," 149–151 (a 1946 poem that moves from the ruined *Goethehaus* and a sign that states "property of the nation" – *Besitz der Nation* – to the immovable intellect of Goethe). See Bettina Meier, *Goethe in*

the plan for this new *Goethehaus*, an association – the *Hochstift* – was in charge of the task in this case.

The rebuilding of these two monuments, while initiated locally, was billed as a national or international imperative, a strategy, among other things, devised to generate financial support and other forms of aid.[73] But the rhetoric of the Frankfurt government and the *Hochstift* was also directed at critics of large-scale public projects in a time of severe material shortages.[74]

These two showcase buildings, the *Goethehaus* and the *Paulskirche*, pioneered different solutions to the task of architectural renewal from urban destruction.[75] Little of the *Goethehaus*'s architectural substance remained in 1945, whereas the hollowed out *Paulskirche* provided a matrix for renovation. In the latter case, a competition was held to determine the building's future design. The architects who were finally entrusted with the project (Rudolf Schwarz, Johannes Krahn, Gottlob Schaupp, and Eugen Blanck) took inspiration from the church's ruinous hulk. In the rebuilt building, they sought to preserve its surviving structural shell, with its associations of, as they saw it, Rome's Pantheon and ancient ruins, in the rebuilt edifice. The building's structural organization also mimicked the ongoing reconstitution of German democracy: the architects introduced a symbolism of conversion from the dark, low vestibule on the ground floor, a newly added feature, to the spacious, light-flooded main hall with its many seats placed on the same level: a haven for the polity. They created, in the guise of architecture, a symbolic purification of sorts.[76] In a letter, Schwarz, one of the most eminent architects in post-war Germany, spoke of a "giant circle of naked stones that had ceased to glow" (*riesiges Rund aus nackten ausgeglühten Steinen*), suggesting that the experience of the firestorm was preserved in the church's reconstruction. But he also offered "Roman grandeur" as a description of the

---

Trümmern: Zur Rezeption eines Klassikers in der Nachkriegszeit (Wiesbaden: Deutscher Universitätsverlag, 1989).

73 Bartetzko, *Denkmal*, 48f.

74 Bauer, '*Seid einig*,' 41.

75 The juxtaposition of the two buildings in the context of debates about reconstruction in Frankfurt, with their different ownerships and histories, runs like a leitmotif through the historiography – a direct continuation of the post-war controversy. Hansert points out how in recent years the pro-reconstruction faction has won, though in the years after the war they saw themselves as having lost the debate (see his *Georg Hartmann*, 309).

76 In a competition held by the city in late 1946, the first prize went to Gottlob Schaupp. His design abandoned the galleries and created one integrated interior space reminiscent of the ruinous hulk. Otto Bartning, an architectural critic and consultant for this project, remarked in 1948: "ein Beispiel ..., wie eine wertvolle Ruine nicht zu rekonstruieren, sondern aufzubauen ist" (Müller-Raemisch, *Frankfurt am Main*, 43). See Durth/Gutschow, *Träume*, 88.

rebuilt hall, and even claimed that the new *Paulskirche*, completed in 1948, was "more magnificent than the earlier building."[77] For the so-called traditionalists, however, Fried Lübbecke among them, the plainness of the *Paulskirche*'s renovated interior constituted a loss of historical substance.[78] The rebuilding of the *Paulskirche* is therefore a good example of the multiple functions and meanings that building and rebuilding held in post-war Germany.

The *Hochstift*'s director, Ernst Beutler, was well prepared for the eventuality of the *Goethehaus*'s loss. In light of its historical significance, the association decided to erect the building as an approximation of the original. Comprehensive documentation, collected during the war, made it possible to plan a replica of what had been lost to the bombs. While opponents lampooned the project as window dressing, proponents in fact understood that a reconstruction would never equal the original.[79] Even though a majority of the city's officials backed the plan, the recreation of the *Goethehaus* was a sore point for architects and city planners committed to modernist architecture and societal reform. Yet the *Goethehaus*-replica was not an exemplar for the reconstruction of the city as a whole. If anything, it was a *pars pro toto;* the fact that the building had been carefully re-erected offered a rationale to level partially destroyed remnants of the old

---

77 Bartetzko, *Denkmal für den Aufbau Deutschlands*, 40. See also the quotation from a letter by Rudolf Schwarz cited in Gehebe-Gernhardt, *Architektur der 50er Jahre*, 63. Recently, Schwarz has attracted much critical attention; his writings and oeuvre allow critics to explore alternate paths within the history of modern architecture – narratives usually centered on the *Bauhaus* and its reception. See, for instance, *Rudolf Schwarz (1897–1961): Werk, Theorie, Rezeption*, ed. Conrad Lienhardt (Regensburg: Schnell & Steiner, 1997); Dorothee Sorge, *Baukunst als Formung des eigenen Schicksals: Das Architekturverständnis von Rudolf Schwarz* (Cologne: Abteilung Architekturgeschichte der Universität Köln, 2008); Thomas H. Beeby, "Rudolf Schwarz and Mies van der Rohe: The Form of the Spirit," in *Constructing the Ineffable: Contemporary Sacred Architecture*, ed. Karla Cavarra Britton (New Haven: Yale School of Architecture, 2010), 82–95; and Gehebe-Gernhardt, *Architektur der 50er Jahre*, 99–128, 134–138.

78 On Lübbecke's critique of the new *Paulskirche*, see Gehebe-Gernhardt, *Architektur der 50er Jahre*, 64f.

79 See Beutler, "An Goethes hundertzwölften Todestage," 258–260. Cf. Hansert, *Georg Hartmann*, 251–253, 257f. One critic speaks of the *Goethehaus* as if it were a model. See also Gehebe-Gernhardt, *Architektur der 50er Jahre*, 67–71, 290; Durth/Gutschow, *Träume*, 34. On the history of the *Freie Deutsche Hochstift* and particularly the reconstruction of the *Goethehaus*, see Joachim Senge, *Goethe-Enthusiasmus und Bürgersinn: Das Freie Deutsche Hochstift – Goethemuseum, 1859–1960* (Göttingen: Wallstein, 2009), 498–544; Hansert, *Georg Hartmann*, 296–309; Meier, *Goethe*, 16–85; Diefendorf, *In the Wake of War*, 71f; Wilhelm Nerdinger, *Architektur der Wunderkinder: Aufbruch und Verdrängung in Bayern 1945–1960* (Salzburg: Anton Pustet, 2005), 248.

Frankfurt elsewhere.[80] Mayor Kolb in fact re-assured critics that the *Goethehaus* would not serve as a model for Frankfurt's post-war construction.

Kolb took pains to emphasize "a synthesis between the old and the new" in Frankfurt's re-constitution. But such a formula, eager to please all constituencies, simplified a far more complex situation, and covered over confrontations about particular buildings.[81] The formula captures well, however, what the ample historiography on post-war Frankfurt – with its juxtaposition of the *Goethehaus* and the *Paulskirche* as paradigmatic counter-examples – glosses over, namely the many ways in which gestures toward the lost historical core shaped the post-war city. The presence of the past is clear, even if we concede, as does the literature, that the modernist faction with their far-reaching visions of a new society and urbanism most certainly carried the day in the wake of the war. A most attentive observant of post-war Germany, the British writer Stephen Spender, says as much when in 1955 he singles out Frankfurt for having been "more enterprising than most other German towns," and continues: "It has not gone in for the banal restoration of a recent past; nor, like Düsseldorf, does it rely on 'planning' broad streets. The new buildings on the Altemarkt are built in a style that acknowledges the manners of those traditional ones which survived well enough to be restored."[82]

Frankfurt's print media with their trans-regional circulation propelled the discussions about the city's future beyond its confines. At a time when paper was scarce, journals such as the *Frankfurter Hefte* (1946–1984), edited by Eugen Kogon, the widely respected author of *The SS State* (1946), and Walter Dirks, quickly emerged as one of the leading intellectual venues in occupied Germany, alongside *Die Wandlung* (Heidelberg, 1946–1949), *Baukunst und Werkform* (Nuremberg, 1947ff), and the Frankfurt-based journal of urbanism, *Die neue Stadt* (1947–53), whose second issue was devoted to the city's reconstruction.[83] Among other focal points, these publications became a forum to discuss urban renewal

80 Christian Welzbacher, "Der Wiederaufbau des Frankfurter Goethehauses: Altstadtsanierung – Schöpferische Rekonstruktion – Kulturpessimismus – Symbolpolitik," *Die Alte Stadt* 33 (2006): 325; Marianne Rodenstein, "Goethehaus, Frankfurt am Main," in *Geschichte der Rekonstruktion: Konstruktion der Geschichte*, ed. Winfried Nerdinger (Munich: Prestel, 2010), 434–436.

81 For the intricacies of the discussion around the *Goethehaus*, see Welzbacher, "Der Wiederaufbau," 317–330; Senge, *Goethe-Enthusiasmus und Bürgersinn*, 498–544.

82 Stephen Spender, *Journals 1939–1983*, ed. John Goldsmith (London: Faber and Faber, 1985), 167.

83 Michael S. Falser, *Zwischen Identität und Authenzität: Zur politischen Geschichte der Denkmalpflege in Deutschland* (Dresden: Thelem, 2008): 71–97. See also Klessmann, "Zur kulturgeschichtlichen Kontinuitätsdiskussion," 167–169. The journals continue discussions that were in-

and construction where diverse voices could be heard, billed by the editors of the *Frankfurter Neue Hefte* as an "important subject matter."[84] This debate addressed local issues as exemplars of post-war developments across the country: "That [this forum] pertains to Frankfurt am Main shall not mean a limitation; our wish is to address all those who plan the reconstruction of old cities."[85]

Otto Bartning, one of the co-founders of the *Bauhaus*, opened the debate 1946 with his "Heretical Thoughts near Heaps of Rubble."[86] Like many other experts, urbanists, and architects, he advocated a radical departure from the old, provocatively linking the language of the bombs with modernist aesthetics; he argued for an embrace of ruins instead of "half-truths," and criticized those traditionalists who would erect a "death-mask" to cover over the traces of destruction. Characteristically, like other contributors to the debate, Bartning widened the scope of the discussion from architecture proper to questions of morality, responsibility, and guilt.

The writing of these urbanists and architects, in fact, became a crucial means by which Germans – or at least the intellectual elite – began to discuss their role in war's destruction. As a result, the buildings of Frankfurt and other cities, of crucial concern to these writers, became not just physically and emotionally important, but also intellectually and symbolically central, to a much wider swath of the country. In a programmatic article, "Courage to Say Good-Bye" (*Mut zum Abschied*), Walter Dirks, a writer, publicist, and proponent of Christian Socialism, declared in 1947: "The house on the *Hirschgraben* [i.e., the *Goethehaus*] was not destroyed by a fire caused by an iron or lightning or arson. It was not destroyed accidentally, or to be more exact in a chain of causes that had no relation to the particular nature of this house and would thus be external to it ... Had the nation of poets and philosophers not betrayed the spirit of Goethe, the spirit of moder-

augurated by a series of publications on behalf of the urban authorities as early as November 1945. See Gehebe-Gernhardt, *Architektur der 50er Jahre*, 36f.

84 Alfons Leitl, "Erwägungen und Tatsachen zum deutschen Städte-Aufbau," *Frankfurter Neue Hefte*, vol. 1 (1946): 60–67, here p. 67 (Nachwort der Schriftleitung): "Wir werden die Diskussion über diesen wichtigen Gegenstand fortsetzen und praktische Lösungen, die schon in Angriff genommen oder geplant sind, aufzeigen." See also Josef Dünninger, "Auf der Suche nach dem Lebensgesetz einer zerstörten Stadt: Brief aus Würzburg," ibid., 49–53; Ursula Hofmann, "Wunsch an die Städteplaner," ibid., 593–600.

85 Ursula Hofmann, "Wunsch an die Städteplaner," *Frankfurter Neue Hefte*, vol. 1 (1946), 593: "Daß die Erinnerung Frankfurt am Main gilt, soll keine Beschränkung bedeuten; unser Wunsch geht an alle Planer des Neubaues alter Städte."

86 Otto Bartning, "Ketzerische Gedanken am Rande der Trümmerhaufen," *Frankfurter Neue Hefte* 1 (1946): 70f.

Fig. 3: Mayor Walter Kolb inaugurating a campaign to clear Frankfurt's rubble in front of city hall on October 17, 1946, Institut für Stadtgeschichte Frankfurt am Main, S7Z 1946/44 (Photo: Fred Kochmann)

ation and humanity, then it would not have undertaken this war and would not have provoked the house's destruction."[87] The destruction of the prewar city thus acquired a profound significance for Dirks that any architectural resuscitation of the old could only undo. To reconstruct, he contends, would be to breed new disaster. It was politically mandatory, this manifesto claims, to recognize loss's permanence. Walter Gropius, the Weimar architect who emigrated to the US and taught at Harvard University, expressed similar concerns to the US authorities, recommending urban construction in form of small residential nuclei as a form of political reform: "there is a political corpse buried in Germany's rubble and it is the job of the reconstruction planners to insure that it isn't revived."[88] These controversies over construction vs. reconstruction, as well as the city's prominent projects, ensured that the rebuilding of Frankfurt became a much-debated example for the interested public across Germany. In the late 1940s and early 1950s, experts looked to Frankfurt as a paragon of urban renewal, even as the city and its constituencies debated what that renewal should look like.

The slowly reconstituted cityscape never put to rest the specter of individual or collective responsibility and guilt. Indeed, perhaps it is hard, if not impossible, for buildings (or models for that matter) to answer questions of morality. But it is clear, as we have seen, that these questions were a powerful subtext to the debates about the city's reconstruction, and thus to the emerging new buildings.[89] As the city began to rebuild and build, some Frankfurters continued to ask: Who caused the devastation? Were the bombings justified? And how should we remember the devastation?

---

87 Walter Dirks, "Mut zum Abschied," quoted after Müller-Raemisch, *Frankfurt am Main*, 44. (Frankfurter Hefte 8, 1947): "Das Haus am Hirschgraben ist nicht durch einen Bügeleisenbrand oder einen Blitzschlag oder durch Brandstiftung zerstört worden. Es ist nicht 'zufällig' zerstört worden, genauer gesagt in einer Kausalkette, die keine Beziehung zu dem eigentümlichen Wesen dieses Hauses hätten und also ihm gegenüber äußerlich wäre ... Wäre das Volk der Dichter und Denker (und mit ihm Europa) nicht vom Geiste Goethes abgefallen, vom Geist des Maßes und der Menschlichkeit, so hätte es diesen Krieg nicht unternommen und die Zerstörung des Hauses nicht provoziert." Dirks withdrew his membership of the *Freie Deutsche Hochstift*, the association in charge of reconstruction, in a letter addressed to Ernst Beutler of April 24, 1947. He expressed his opposition in a letter to Mayor Walter Kolb of April 18, 1947 (see Senge, *Goethe-Enthusiasmus*, 515f). Dirks echoes comments the poet Reinhold Schneider had made in a 1945 article: "Goetheverehrung oder Goethekult? Eine Frage," *Freiburger Nachrichten*, December 14, 1945, 3; see also Schneider's "Fausts Rettung" (1946), in *Goethe im Urteil seiner Kritiker*, 266–273, esp. p. 272. On Dirks, see Hansert, *Georg Hartmann*, 300–302.

88 Diefendorf, "America and the Rebuilding of Germany," 335. As Diefendorf shows, the US dedicated few resources to the reconstruction of German cities.

89 See Hansert, *Georg Hartmann*, 269f.

Monumental Efforts

These haunting questions became prominent in the wake of Elkan's visit to Frankfurt. Fried Lübbecke – who, we will remember, founded the "Association of Friends of the Old City" in the 1920s and opposed the new *Paulskirche* – proposed that Frankfurt secure Elkan's planned monument for the victims of the air raids.[90] In a 1953-letter to a local politician, Lübbecke wrote: "It would be *the* monument of our destroyed old city; between its new buildings, it should remind, deter, console future generations of the lunacy of world war." To bolster his argument, he attached a copy of Elkan's "On the Hills of Sorrow."[91] In a way, what Lübbecke proffered in this instance was not so far removed from what many forward-looking forces envisioned, namely a post-war return to Frankfurt's 1920s traditions. However, Lübbecke was not only one of the most vocal critics of the new Frankfurt that emerged after 1945.[92] Urbanists' search for a continuation, if not triumph, of the "new building" in a Europe whose many cities lay devastated also was fundamentally different from wanting to revive the defunct artistic traditions of that same era under the aegis of the Cold War. If the émigré Elkan had hoped to renew his bond with Frankfurt and Germany, his hopes, like those of many others, were thwarted.[93] In the aftermath of his 1950-declaration of love to the city – the short article with which this chapter set out – a controversy arose in Frankfurt over if and how to commemorate the bombings and their casualties. Elkan was at the center.

As early as October 1946, the city government resolved to do after 1945 what had been done in the aftermath of previous wars, honor the fallen members of

---

90 Institut für Stadtgeschichte, Frankfurt am Main, Kulturamt, 949, 63 (April 14, 1953). The mayor's office asked for an opinion by the magistrate in charge of "science, art, and people's education," Vom Rath, who stated unequivocally and without giving a reason that the proposal should be rejected and opinions by two experts should be obtained (in this order). The idea might not have been welcome because of the initiator and his past affiliation with the city government. Lübbecke was entrusted with the preparation of the *Paulskirche*-anniversary, until he resigned in 1947 during a controversy over the prize-winning design of the architects of the *Paulskirche* (Bauer, '*Seid einig*,' 39–46).

91 Institut für Stadtgeschichte, Frankfurt am Main, Kulturamt, 949, 63, Letter of April 16, 1953 (Lübbecke to Vom Rath): "Es wäre das Denk-Mal unserer zerstörten Altstadt und sollte zwischen ihren neuen Bauten noch späte Geschlechter an den Wahnsinn des Weltkrieges mahnen, abschrecken und tröstend erinnern."

92 In an article of August 1948, Lübbecke compared May with Mussolini. See Gehebe-Gernhardt, *Architektur der 50er Jahre*, 76 and 79.

93 Olivier Guez, *L'impossible retour: Une histoire des juifs d'Allemage depuis 1945* (Paris: Flammarion, 2007). On Elkan see Menzel-Severing, "Benno Elkan," 93.

the community. The novel experience, however, of comprehensive war from the air called for a new type of monument, a monument to the victims of the air raids. It was decided to use a location that offered space for rallies. The first plan was to use the city's Bismarck monument, damaged by the war: a sarcophagus at the base of the existing monument, to be filled with the remains of the first un-identified victim recovered from the debris. But the head of the city's construction department, along with a bevy of architects and artists, rejected the design for reasons of due process and artistic merit; it was the first of many designs for an air raid monument that would not be realized.[94]

Elkan's monument design originated with his personal experience of the aerial war during the Blitz of 1941/42, when German bombs severely damaged his London home. His plan seemed at first a fortuitous coincidence. The city was committed to erecting a monument to the victims of the air raids, and Elkan was an artist connected to Frankfurt, devoid of Nazi allegiance, and was working on just such a design. But coincidence quickly became mired in controversy. With its focus on the person of the artist, the monument's style, and the question of a monument's manifold meanings, the debate over Elkan's design demonstrates the painful stakes of the material representation of the air raids for a German public.

In Elkan's words, his was a monument to the "unknown citizen," focused entirely on the existential human tragedy caused by an air raid (fig. 4).[95] He proposed a sculpted mass of contorted, naked figures scattered in a variety of poses over a wide rectangular, ruinous space. His proposed sculpture sought to capture men, women, and children at the mercy of forces beyond their control, about to become or already having become victims of a violence whose agents remain invisible, a violence that befell them from above. Elkan thus responded to the monumental horrors of the air raids with a monumental design (quite different from the Treuners' miniature monument). This penchant for size was also reflected in the classical language of bodily suffering he deployed in the sculpture's *maquette*, a language simultaneously referencing Christian iconography, Renaissance sculpture, the oeuvre of Auguste Rodin (whom Elkan had met in Paris in 1905), and the neoclassic style of the interwar period with its connota-

94 Institut für Stadtgeschichte, Frankfurt am Main, S3/K2122, Mahnmal der Opfer des Bombenkriegs: Letter, Berufsverband Bildender Künstler, October 14,1946; letter Hebebrand's to mayor Kolb, October 16, 1946; letter, AG Frankfurter Architekten, October 16, 1946; Hans Bütow, "Mut zu Denkmälern," *Frankfurter Rundschau*, August 22, 1953.
95 Letter of April 16, 1953, by F. Lübbecke to Vom Rath, referring to correspondence with the artist. See Institut für Stadtgeschichte, Frankfurt am Main, Kulturamt, 949, 63.

tions of internationalism.[96] Whereas Elkan's art defies easy categorization, his design for the sculpture bears some resemblance to Pablo Picasso's painting *Guernica* (1937), then and now the most famous artwork depicting an air raid.[97] Like *Guernica*, Elkan's planned monument to the "unknown citizen" focused on the sufferings on the ground while eschewing a depiction of the aggressors. (In the case of the Basque city, the aggressor was the German Legion Condor that, with some support from others, had carried out the attack at the behest of the Spanish Falangistas, a trial run for a military strategy from the air devised by the German Air Force that would later bring destruction to other European and ultimately to German cities.)

Fig. 4: Benno Elkan, "Mahnmal für die wehrlosen Opfer des Bombenkriegs," maquette as published in the Frankfurter Neue Presse, July 13, 1954 (Photo: Author)

Perhaps inevitably, the grand gestures and dimensions of Elkan's monument plan raised objections among experts and citizens alike. Representatives of the *Deutscher Werkbund* (German Work Federation) – an association of architects and artists that traced itself back to the beginning of the century and established itself as a guardian of modernist traditions in post-war Germany – declared his design a tribute to an aesthetic that had vanished with the old cities, one that should not be resuscitated in the post-war world.[98] Even before the artist presented his project (at the city's behest) in Frankfurt in July of 1954, a heated dis-

96 Hofmann/Schmieder, *Benno Elkan*, 79 (with illustration). The *maquette* rendered is dated 1959. A photograph of this *maquette* is part of an article published in the *Frankfurter Allgemeine Zeitung* July 8, 1954, 23 ("Diskussion um ein Mahnmal").

97 Cf. Hofmann/Schmieder, *Benno Elkan*, 78.

98 On the *Deutscher Werkbund*, its history and role in post-war Germany, see Diefendorf, *In the Wake of War*, xv, 45–47, 54–66, and Gehebe-Gernhardt, *Architektur der 50er Jahre*, 101–120.

cussion flared up in the local press, involving letters to the editor both critical and supportive. In this context, photographs of the monument's *maquette* circulated. One opinion warned of the "traumatic injuries" that the sight of the monument would inflict upon children. Others said the monument lacked precisely what it needed most, a realistic depiction of an aerial attack. To them Elkan's design failed to depict the horrors of the bombings, a suffering – some insisted – that exceeded what his, or any, art could possibly capture. Still others questioned the wisdom of portraying the war for civilians in the first place; as long as people were suffering from war-induced devastation and destitution, so the argument ran, the finances necessary for the monument's realization would better be spent on social housing and welfare. One critic went as far as to suggest that every rebuilt house gave better testimony to the horrors that had happened than a monument, whose dimensions and rhetoric would rightly call forth critical responses.[99] According to some art experts, for example, the appropriate goals for a monument were *Vergeistigung*, or "spiritualization," and not the representation of suffering; peace and not confrontation; consolation and not disturbance. On all these fronts, they stated, Elkan's design failed to deliver. From the outset, the discussion among officials, experts, and citizens had a categorical bent that undermined the prospect of realizing Elkan's somewhat eclectic monument.

By the early 1950s, abstract and figurative art, cast as diametrical opposites, carried political overtones. Elkan's recourse to neoclassicism was bound to call forth critical responses among proponents of modernism who saw any kind of "realism" as a nod to a problematic aesthetic or political past, or, worse, an instantiation of the socialist realism said to reign supreme east of the Iron Curtain. Less than two decades earlier, commentators had expressed comparable concerns regarding Picasso's *Guernica*, doubting whether the painting offered consolation.[100] By the 1950s, the renown of Picasso's by then canonical piece invalidated that argument. Two of Elkan's critics even cited Picasso and the German painter Otto Dix as experts of capturing war atrocities in art, and

99 According to Lübbecke, the artist imagined an installation in a grotto or a church. See Institut für Stadtgeschichte, Frankfurt am Main, Kulturamt, 949, 63, letter of April 16, 1953. In a talk about the project, Elkan stated the dimensions as 10–11 meters in length as well as height and width of 3–4 meters, made of shell limestone or granite, see *Frankfurter Neue Presse*, July 14, 1954.

100 Carlo Ginzburg, "The Sword and the Lightbulb: A Reading of *Guernica*," in *Disturbing Remains: Memory, History, and Crisis in the Twentieth Century*, ed. Michael S. Roth and Charles G. Salas (Los Angeles: The Getty Research Institute, 2001), 111–177. Ginzburg's enlightening essay falls short of offering a reading of Guernica, as the title says. But he resuscitates an important nexus of debates on the relationship between pictorial language, composition, and subject matter that is of relevance here.

compared Elkan unfavorably to them.[101] The most troubling criticism, however, was that Elkan's design offered nothing but convoluted bodies *en masse*, and as a result that it failed as a political monument. As one critic put it: "One may think that the sight of horror could prevent people from committing atrocities: This [notion] is contradicted by the facts of history."[102] Elkan's monument refused to bestow meaning on the events, they stated, thus evacuating the realm of interpretation and leaving these questions to the viewer.[103] A work of art could be interpreted in various and unpredictable ways, they surmised, even as an exculpation of German civilians – an interpretation that was anathema to these critics.[104]

How would viewers respond to a public monument of this type? some asked. Could such a monument centered on German civilian victims be appropriated as an indictment of the occupying forces? How could a monument instill in viewers a meditation on their own role in bringing disaster to the city and to Germany? With remarkable sophistication – and an equal measure of blindness to the limits of what monuments can achieve – this debate homed in on the politics of representation. As the city of Frankfurt sought to commemorate its victims, and as it tried to build a monument under the aegis of defeat, the "openness" of the work of art to myriad "interpretive possibilities" – even in an explicitly referential sculpture like Elkan's – surfaced less as a promise of "infinite potential" than as a politically problematic vagueness.[105]

Not surprisingly, the controversy became inseparable from the artist's persona and the monument's major proponent, Fried Lübbecke, the spokesper-

101 Holtzinger, Mettel, June 9, 1953, Institut für Stadtgeschichte, Frankfurt am Main, Kulturamt, 949, 63.

102 Ibid., "Es mag einer denken, der Anblick des Grauens könne die Menschen vor grausigem Tun bewahren: Dem widersprechen die historischen Tatsachen."

103 Ibid., "Sicher ist es eine Anklage, aber die meisten werden es nur als Anklage gegen Deutschlands Gegner im Krieg empfinden, nicht als Anklage gegen sich selbst, worauf es doch ankäme bei so viel eigener Schuld. Damit würde ein solches Denkmal aber nicht nur missverstanden, sondern geradezu zur geistigen Gefahr. Es käme darauf an, die Menschen zum Nachdenken darüber zu bringen, dass sie mit ihrere alten Stadt ein Lebenselement verloren haben und warum sie es verloren haben."

104 An "accusation against the destructive spirit of war" (Anklage gegen den Ungeist des Krieges) was issued in the introduction to a book on Frankfurt's lost city center – a book itself conceived as a monument – without accusing the Allies directly. See Georg Hartmann and Fried Lübbecke, *Alt-Frankfurt: Ein Vermächtnis*, ed. Georg Hartmann (Frankfurt am Main: Der Goldene Brunnen [1950]). See also Meier, *Goethe*, 41, 66, 196f.

105 Umberto Eco, *The Open Work*, trans. Anna Cancogni (Cambridge, Mass.: Harvard University Press, 1989): 84, 91 (originally published in1962). Eco's essays were much inspired by avant-garde works of art from the 1950s and early 60s.

son of the old city who had personal ties to the sculptor dating back to the time before 1914.[106] To be sure, Elkan had expert credentials as a designer of monuments. In the German city of Dortmund, his birthplace, he had created tombstones and funerary sculptures before World War I.[107] Shortly after the war's end, the city of Frankfurt where the artist had relocated commissioned him to create a monument to commemorate the fallen soldiers – a design whose enormous projected dimensions made its realization impossible. Instead, the city acquired *Heldenklage* (Lament for Heroes) of 1913–1914, a naked female mourning figure that was widely admired but also attacked for its lack of heroism.[108] Not surprisingly, after the National Socialists came to power, they immediately dismantled the memorial with its relentless focus on mourning. But then in 1946, in the year when the Treuners sculpted a "plastic sketch" in rubble and just a few years before the debates over the artist's air raid proposal would begin, a Frankfurt government eager to break their ties with the past decided to reinstall the statue.[109] The resonance between two post-war moments with their urgent searches for an appropriate way to commemorate human loss did not escape notice in 1954 when one critic praised Elkan's World War I monument over his planned monument for the victims of the air raids.[110]

From the outset, the artist's Jewishness was a powerful subtext to the debates about the project's artistic merits. His faith empowered the project's main proponent, Lübbecke, and his fellow supporters: a German-Jewish artist who had been forced into emigration, Lübbecke reasoned, was above suspicion; pursuing a commission from him would not only foster reconciliation but also immunize a potential monument against suspicions of nationalism.[111] At the same time, when Lübbecke initially approached the city he did not fail to mention that Elkan had served as a soldier in World War I, characterizing "the grand master," as he described him, as a true German despite his having acquired British citizenship

106 See his pre-World War I article on the artist, Fried Lübbecke, "Benno Elkan – Alsbach i.H.," *Deutsche Kunst und Dekoration* 30 (1912): 21–28.
107 Hofmann/Schmieder, *Elkan*, 27–42.
108 Menzel-Sievering, "Benno Elkan," 84–87, 92.
109 <http://www.ffmhist.de/ffm33-45/portal01/portal01.php?ziel=t_hm_elkan>.
110 Doris Schmidt, "Diskussion um ein Mahnmal," *Frankfurter Allgemeine Zeitung*, July 8, 1954.
111 Institut für Stadtgeschichte, Frankfurt am Main, Kulturamt, 949, 63, letter, April 16, 1953 (Lübbecke to Vom Rath): "Niemand wird uns nationalistischer Propaganda zeihen können. Ein aus seiner Heimat vertriebener Jude, für die er selbst vier Jahre als Soldat im Felde stand." He gives this work of art as a gift (!) to his "immer noch über alles geliebten Stadt ... und vergisst die 35000 Juden, die aus ihr in Tod und Verbannung sich schleppten." See also other letters by Lübbecke in the same file.

and a following among the British political elite.[112] Furthermore, the artist's 1950-piece in the *Frankfurter Neue Presse*, "On the Hills of Sorrow," about his visit to Frankfurt's derelict *Altstadt* carefully avoided a moral reckoning with National Socialist Germany and the Nazi past, though this stance remained unsaid. Elkan may even have felt indebted to a city that had re-erected his World War I monument.

Conversely, opponents of the artist were vulnerable to the charge of anti-Semitism, a rhetorical weapon wielded freely by the pro-monument faction in a city whose Jewish community quickly re-constituted itself after 1945 (though the same community does not seem to have participated in the debate).[113] These accusations became even more entrenched when the artist's health deteriorated and rumors circulated that his frailty had been caused by the acerbic tone of the debate.[114] The somewhat enigmatic but slashing formula of the monument's "counter-natural form," offered by the *Werkbund*, surfaced as an explanation for his condition; Lübbecke even detected the legacy of "Hitler's poison" in the comment.[115]

To complicate things further, discussions over the monument's aesthetic merit and political message were enmeshed with procedural questions. Had the artist sought his own advantage by offering the monument to the city?[116] With a commission of such prominence, wasn't a public competition necessary, all the more so since the projected costs for the realization of Elkan's monument would

112 Institut für Stadtgeschichte, Frankfurt am Main, Kulturamt 949, 63, Lübbecke to Vom Rath, April 16, 1953, and May 6, 1953.

113 Godo Remszhardt, "Glück und Unglück, oder: Das Mahnmal," *Frankfurter Rundschau*, July 8, 1954. Cf. Beate Kemfert, *Hermann Goepfert (1926–1982): Nachkriegskunst in Frankfurt am Main* (Frankfurt am Main: Waldemar Kramer, 1999); Alon Tauber, *Zwischen Kontinuität und Neuanfang: Die Entstehung der jüdischen Nachkriegsgemeinde in Frankfurt am Main 1945–1949* (Wiesbaden: Kommission für die Geschichte der Juden in Hessen, 2008).

114 Institut für Stadtgeschichte, Frankfurt am Main, Kulturamt, 949, 63, letter of August 14, 1954 (Lübbecke to Hans Maria Wingler). A comparison between the photograph published in the Frankfurt press of Elkan's *maquette* for the monument and the state of the project in 1959 shows that Elkan continued to rework the design and may in fact have responded to some of the criticism that had surfaced in the debate, especially with regard to one female nude whom some critics had singled out as un-realistic and all too beautiful for the victim of an air raid.

115 Institut für Stadtgeschichte, Frankfurt am Main, Kulturamt, 949, 63, letter of August 16, 1954 (Lübbecke to Vom Rath).

116 This question was a leitmotif of the discussion. Lübbecke who said he and Elkan had been friends for forty years, oscillated between acting as a mediator and an initiator. See Institut für Stadtgeschichte, Frankfurt am Main, Kulturamt, 949, 63, letter, May 6, 1953 (Lübbecke to Vom Rath). Elkan contradicted these rumors in the press (*Neue Presse*, April 30, 1953).

have exceeded those of previous artwork commissioned by the city? Shouldn't the city request proposals from local artists and not just an "outsider"? Neither the artist's public presentation in Frankfurt nor a delegation to the artist's studio in London did much to disentangle the controversial positions that had clustered around the project.[117] Around this time, Elkan became convinced that public opinion had turned against him in Frankfurt and approached another city, Dortmund, with the same monument proposal; there, preference was given to a monument that pictured an act of resistance in the city.[118] Interestingly enough, Lübbecke had initially made the sculpture sound as if it were a work of art created by a one-time resident of Frankfurt for the city in response to Elkan's 1950-visit. But the monument, if realized, would have transcended its own locality and connected Frankfurt with other cities across Europe, populations of former Axis and Allied powers alike devastated by the indiscriminate fury of the bombs. It would not so much have been a local monument but a monument on the air raids *tout court*.

Commemorating the air raids remained a complicated affair in the shadow of the rubble despite the fact that the rubble itself became increasingly rare, even in the city's old downtown. Frankfurt's 1946-plan to commemorate the loss and suffering of its citizens as a result of the air war continued to reverberate through city politics for many years. After the media flurry, in 1954, the city government reviewed Elkan's design one last time. When it was rejected, the city then announced a public competition; but none of the entries was realized. Over the years, several locations were discussed as a site for the monument, the former library's portico and the Carmelite Monastery among them. Another proposal, a simple field of rubble, could no longer be turned into a monument since no such plot existed by the late 1950s; the rebuilding of the city continued at such a furious pace that most of the *Altstadt*'s debris had been carted away and the land rebuilt. In the process, it seems, the city shied away from creating an artful equivalent of the rubble that had so recently been omnipresent: only authentic rubble could pass as ruins worthy to gaze at.

Despite an early commitment to commemorate the air raids on Frankfurt and their victims, despite Lübbecke's initiative, and despite a public competition,

---

117 Institut für Stadtgeschichte, Frankfurt am Main, Kulturamt, 949, 63, invitation by the city to Elkan for July 13, 1954.

118 The magistracy rejected the proposal on April 27, 1953, before the expert opinion was available. The parliament (*Stadtverordneten-Versammlung*) recommended that the proposal be again considered (June 22, 1954). Further expert opinions were obtained by the *Berufsverband Bildender Künstler*, Frankfurt (Hanke and Becker, July 12, 1954).

Frankfurt never erected a central monument for the victims of the air raids.[119] Instead, a nexus of plaques,[120] public artworks, and the like came into existence to remind Frankfurters or tourists of what was there before the pandemonium that put an end to the city of old. Today's *flâneur* who seeks to follow Benno Elkan's steps will find a rich memory-scape with a multitude of references to the city's demise and reconstitution, reminders created in a variety of styles, forms, and media, put up over several decades. St. Catherine's Church (*Katharinenkirche*), for instance, features modern glass windows depicting the date and hour of the most devastating air raid.[121] With the recreation of certain landmark structures during the 1950s, architects integrated original elements, like the carved wooden reliefs from the Middle Ages that adorn houses near city hall – clearly modern houses but built in an architectural idiom of a moderate modernism.[122] As one enters the city's main square from the north, a mosaic of a Phoenix rising from the ruins of a city, marked by crosses, blankets a building's façade just in front of you, invoking the human losses on which the new Frankfurt rests: reconstruction as rebirth. Because of its high visibility, Stefan Timpe has called this mosaic "*the* central monument in Frankfurt for the commemoration of wartime destruction and reconstruction."[123] His assertion makes sense, and yet the piece has never officially been accorded this status. Frankfurt, it seems, continued to search for ways to commemorate its devastation, but has never been able to decide on the adequate form. When in 1978 the city finally settled for a modest bronze plaque let into the ground, verbal information rather than visual daring carried the day. Designed by the sculptor Willy Schmidt, the small relief shows the cathedral

119 That plans for a monument were not realized is also true of other cities such as Magdeburg where in February of 1949 the city committed to erecting two monuments, one dedicated to the memory of the victims of fascism and one to the memory of the victims of air war, see Jörg Arnold, "'Nagasaki' in der DDR: Magdeburg und das Gedenken an den 16. Januar 1945," in *Luftkrieg: Erinnerungen in Deutschland und Europa*, ed. J. Arnold, Dietmar Süß, and Malte Thießen (Göttingen: Wallstein, 2009), 246.

120 In Frankfurt and in other German cities, many buildings built during post-war renovation programs are adorned with metal plaques with the date of their completion. In rare cases of particularly well-known houses, new buildings in Frankfurt's *Altstadt* bear relief images of the facades of their predecessor buildings. See Dauer/Maury, *Frankfurt baut in die Zukunft*, 56 (*Fürsteneck, Mehlwaage, Goldene Waage*).

121 Designed by Charles Crodel (1954).

122 Stefan Timpe, "Denkmalgestaltung als Prozess: Zur jüngsten Restaurierung der Fassaden des Frankfurter Römers," *Denkmalpflege und Kulturgeschichte* 1 (2005): 2–8, here p. 4. Designed by Otto Apel, Rudolf Letocha, William Rohrer, and Martin Herdt together with the city's construction department, 1951–1953.

123 The mosaic is by Wilhelm Geißler. Timpe, "Denkmalgestaltung," 5.

tower engulfed in flames while the text spells out the destruction matter-of-factly: "At the end of war 17 million cubic meters rubble covered the city that mourned over 14,701 fallen soldiers and 5,559 victims of the bombs."[124]

Today, the so-called rubble model of Frankfurt, a monument to the city's darkest hour, built shortly after the city's destruction, is on display in one of the buildings of the historical museum. There, the aforementioned model by the brothers Treuner of *Alt-Frankfurt* sits in dialogue with the rubble model. They are within sight of each other. Whether intentional or not, the display for these models in tandem is now a well-established strategy: pairing images of before and after has become the dominant iconography of destruction (and rebuilding) that arose in post-war Frankfurt as well as other German cities.

Fig. 5: [Paulskirche before and after the attacks of March 1944] Georg Hartmann and Fried Lübbecke, Alt-Frankfurt: Ein Vermächtnis, Frankfurt am Main: Der Goldene Brunnen, [1950]), 268f (Photo: Author)

124 Bauer, '*Seid einig*,' 36f. The full text: "1939 Zur Erinnerung 1945. Zwischen dem 4. Juni 1940 und dem 24. März 1945 wurde Frankfurt von 33 Luftangriffen, zahllosen Störflügen und Tieffliegerangriffen heimgesucht. Tausende Tonnen Spreng- und Brandbomben zerstörten oder beschädigten vier Fünftel aller Bauten. Am 22. März 1944 löschte ein Grossangriff den Alstadtkern völlig aus. Bei Kriegsende bedeckten 17 Mio. CBM Trümmer die Stadt, die um 14701 Gefallene und 5559 Bombenopfer trauerte." This was part of a series of plaques commemorating other historical events, like the Nazi book-burning. Photograph in Klötzer, *Die Frankfurter Altstadt*, 432.

In Frankfurt, for instance, postcard vendors across the city have for a long time sold aerial views of the *Römerberg* district, at unspecified dates after the war, some of them showing photographic vistas of scenes of urban devastation and some of them juxtaposing a view of the ruined cityscape with the rebuilt Frankfurt. Whether the comparative mode is made visually explicit, as with the latter case of paired images, or implicit as in the former case (since an image of the destroyed city invokes the city "as is" which the buyer can see with his own eyes), these postcards encourage the beholder to gauge the distance that separates Frankfurt's past from the present. The urban devastation of World War II is thus seen to constitute the ground zero of the community. One wonders what buyers of such cards write when sending them to friends and loved ones. The popular appeal of such images may lie, among other things, in their ironic anti-tourism that, as James Buzard remarks, is the mark of the true tourist. But the rhetoric of visual counterpoints emerged in the years after 1945 from a particular aesthetic and emotional nexus.[125]

Within this comparative mode of seeing, mourning over what was lost informs Fried Lübbecke's *Alt Frankfurt: A Legacy* (fig. 5); Sebald sees a city's pride in a quick return to civic normalcy in the postcard entitled "Frankfurt: Yesterday and Today," included in *On the Natural History of Destruction.*[126] These are just two of a phalanx of essays, history books, photography books, museum exhibitions, and the like that echo similar counterpoints, post-war creations that differ in their emphases, but all emerge from that same complex of aesthetics, reflections, and emotions – the desire to document the "rebirth" of a people, and their city, through the built environment. Arendt famously remarked in 1950 about how Germans, "amid the ruins, ... mail each other picture postcards still showing the cathedrals and market places, the public buildings and bridges that no longer exist."[127] There may be other ways to interpret this practice, however, than Arendt does, namely as a sign for Germans' callousness or a dogged refusal to move on. What developed in other words was a *comparative specularity*. This mode of engagement utilizes images of the built or unbuilt environment to suggest the spectacular shift of history, to goad a collective awareness, and to inject a sense

125 James Buzard, *The Beaten Track: European Tourism, Literature, and the Ways to Culture, 1800–1918* (Oxford: Oxford University Press, 1993).

126 W. G. Sebald included one such postcard in *Air War and Literature*, "Frankfurt: yesterday and today" (*Frankfurt gestern und heute*). See W. G. Sebald, *Luftkrieg und Literatur: Mit einem Essay zu Alfred Andersch* (Munich: Hanser, 1999), 15; id., *On the Natural History of Destruction: With Essays on Alfred Andersch, Jean Améry and Peter Weiss*, trans. Anthea Bell (London: Hamish Hamilton, 2003), 8.

127 Arendt, "Aftermath," 342.

of frailty into the everyday.[128] It became a poignant mode to tear open the architectural surface with suggestions of an urban fabric's deeper history.[129]

In yet another example of the ways that the echoes of the past destruction never seem to end, Frankfurt's museum of history was taken down in 2011. Located in the center of the *Altstadt*, the main building of the city's museum of history, built in 1972, was arguably the most contested structure of post-war Frankfurt. Both its material – unadorned concrete – and its architectural form, with its stress on horizontality and formal antagonism, signaled a rupture with the urbanism that had shaped the reconstitution of the city center during the previous two decades. This building, now demolished, announced its modernity unabashedly. What irked the building's critics in particular was that in turning away from the architecture of the past, even the moderated modernism of 1950s designs, the museum also seemed to condemn this same past. In fact, the museum's now defunct central exhibit on the city's history matched the building's architectural antagonism, interpreting Frankfurt's past as a series of class conflicts. This antagonizing institution has, for almost four decades, served as a repository for the city's history and the artifacts saved from the destruction of World War II. Its uneasy place in the city's center reflects the difficulty of finding a form – be it the written word, or a miniature model, or a whole museum – adequate to the task of preserving the intangibility of the past.

When the current plans for the city's new museum of history come to fruition, comparative specularity will finally find a triumphant architectural expression. And, once again, city models will compensate for – or invite comparison to – what Frankfurt has become. The new building is scheduled to be inaugurated in 2017. Not surprisingly, the historical buildings now part of the museum will be kept intact (where the models of *Alt-Frankfurt* as well as the rubble model are currently on display). The plans for the new building suggest the remarkable continued relevance of miniature depictions of history. From a square in the midst of the planned museum complex that can be reached by walking up an open flight of stairs, *flâneurs* will be able to gaze through an ocular window in the ground – what a journalist has described as a "fountain of history" – into the lower level.

---

128 Needless to say, the verbal and visual rhetoric of old vs. new also emerged for other cities such as Dresden, see Matthias Meinhardt, "Der Mythos vom 'Alten Dresden' als Bauplan: Entwicklung, Ursachen und Folgen einer retrospektiv-eklektizistischen Stadtvorstellung," in *Städte aus Trümmern: Katastrophenbewältigung zwischen Antike und Moderne*, ed. Andreas Ranft and Stephan Selzer (Göttingen: Vandenhoeck & Ruprecht, 2004), 172–200, here p. 176.
129 In *The Future of Nostalgia* (New York: Basic Books, 2001), Svetlana Boym imaginatively explores "the repetition of the unrepeatable, the materialization of the immaterial" in human experiences of the cityscapes through the lens of nostalgia.

The exhibit we will behold – as if we happened upon an archeological dig or a window onto the past – is a model of Frankfurt, as modeled by the Treuners.[130] We can't help but wonder whether the rubble model with its image of the city's destruction will be visible as part of this modeled trajectory of the city, or whether it will be excluded because of its exaggerated depiction? In other words, will modeled destruction also be erased from view?

Just as the rubble city of 1945 forced a fundamental debate over Frankfurt's future, the mundane built environment that emerged after the war in the city's center – and that citizens and critics have been debating for more than a half century – seems to ask just as many questions of architectural semantics and historical substance. Even as the post-war architecture boom indexed what was erased by the bombs, this new old city never has been able to rid itself of the haunting chimera that lay at its origin.

Post-war Frankfurt inevitably has called forth comparisons to the old. It is this inescapability of the past, I believe, that many advocates of modernist renewal seem to have disregarded too readily in the wake of war. But the past, it seems, is bound to return – the only question is what particular form it will take. It is therefore not surprising to observe that, during the last two decades, visions of the medieval urban past have returned with a vengeance to the *Altstadt*, and a penchant for erecting quasi-medieval houses has been its visual manifestation.[131] The layered past that has emerged since 1945 and the 1980s with every generation of city planners leaving built traces in order to fill the center's voids has been and continues to be partially erased in order to make room for recreations of the past somewhat unmoored from the place's history and with a somewhat uniform look. Another round of destructions, though of an entirely different kind, has been, and will be, the result.

At any rate, in the twenty-first century, unlike immediately after 1945, *Alt-Frankfurt* and its proponents evidently carry the day. The case of the city's history museum as well as the recent and ongoing reconstitution of the *Altstadt* gestures towards a departure from comparative specularity and towards the

---

130 The architects of the new museum building are Lederer Ragnarsdóttir Oei, Stuttgart. See Matthias Alexander, "Neubau am Römerberg: Haus mit Doppeldach für Historisches Museum," *Frankfurter Allgemeine Zeitung*, January 30, 2008. <www.faz.net/s/RubFAE83B7DDEFD4F2882ED5B3C15AC43E2/Doc~E1B0DCE9BC8504AC8947E2A32D70BED12~ATpl~Ecommon~Scontent.html>; id., "Kommentar: Selbstbewusst und einfühlsam," ibid., January 30, 2008 <www.faz.net/s/Rub3DFC0DABC5664C30AC70700DD10A965D/Doc~E75B57DB8B52A4A81BAA42B5CFE28A349~ATpl~Ecommon~Scontent.html >.

131 Marianne Rodenstein, "Römer und Römerberg," in *Geschichte der Rekonstruktion: Konstruktion der Geschichte*, ed. Winfried Nerdinger (Munich: Prestel, 2010), 314f.

gradual emergence of yet another visual regime, almost seventy years after the end of World War II: Complex layers of avowedly modern construction efforts erected by generations after 1952 slowly vanish from view in the city's historic core. These destructions express a search for the pre-1944 Frankfurt, a past untainted by National Socialism and the devastations of World War II; in fact, similar attempts to erase the omnipresent architecture of post-war decades are manifest across Germany.[132] The historicizing structures that have already gone up or are planned in lieu of these edifices (or the voids left by war-time destruction) reference the pre-1944 era in their design, layout, and cadastral plan. They work well as backdrops to the portraits travelers to the city take in front of these built suggestions of old Frankfurt. But compared to the buildings whose memory they seek to perpetuate their clean and symmetrical façades appear lifeless. It is as if they followed the cues of timber-frame houses *en miniature* that are for sale in tourist shops around the *Römerberg*. In other words, it is as if in the latest manifestation of the city's search for a livable built past today's urbanism followed the cues of miniature models.[133] In short, the models with their promise to repair what was lost to the bombs seem to take precedence over the notion of an irredeemable past that, at least among experts, reigned supreme for many years after 1945.

Comparative specularity, as it emerged after the end of World War II, is unlikely to vanish, however. In a way, it is more widely available than ever. Since 2011, one can once again take a walk through the lanes, streets, and squares of Old Frankfurt – in 3D. The armchair *flâneur* is invited to explore "a world that nobody has seen since 1944," as Jörg Ott, the model's creator, bills his widely acclaimed project. 100 streets and one square kilometer of the old city are already walkable in a virtual mode; expansions are in the planning. 1,700 buildings have thus been re-erected in the pristine condition the medium bestows on the built environment – everything illuminated by a midday sun that never changes. Yet this new type of model would have been unthinkable without the old. The Treuners' material monument delivered not only much of the information contained in this computer-generated *Alt-Frankfurt* (whose expanse is wider than the Treuners') but also its initial inspiration.[134] And even more than its predecessor, the

132 See, for instance, Meinhardt, "Der Mythos vom 'Alten Dresden,'" 188.
133 Interestingly enough, Gehebe-Gernhardt (*Architektur der 50er Jahre*, 31, 313) speaks of model-like interpretation of the past ("modellartige Interpretation der Vergangenheit"). See her discussion of recent changes regarding architecture from the 1950s, ibid., 29–32, 310–314.
134 <http://www.virtuelle-altstadt.de/das-altstadtmodell.html>. The webpage contains a tab "Veröffentlichungen" or publications that documents the various newspaper and other publications on the model. They show how this 3D model has begun to shape the debate over Frank-

virtual old city has begun to shape the discussions and contestations over the right urbanism for the present. To many observers, *Alt-Frankfurt* in 3D has persuasive force: What exists in computer-generated form ought to be erected in the actual city. The earliest models of old Frankfurt were meant to compensate for the loss of historical fabric in the modernizing city. It would seem that the modeled past has now returned to triumph over the present.

* * *

Post-war Frankfurt, like much of the world in the wake of world war, was moved to reflect extensively on what had just happened. Visual depictions of destruction – whether model or monument – were, needless to say, just one of a host of efforts to remember and comprehend. In fact, in the first decade after the war, words, a torrent of spoken, sung, and written language seem to have become the preeminent means of providing consolation and orientation. To name just a few of these voices, the orator's spoken words (Mayor Walter Kolb), the poet's oracular utterances (Marie Luise Kaschnitz), the disembodied voice of the radio (Hans Mayer and Theodor W. Adorno on Radio Frankfurt),[135] or the singer's performance (Dietrich Fischer-Dieskau performing Franz Schubert's song-cycle *Die Winterreise* [Winter Journey], a story of alienation, first on Berlin radio, RIAS, in 1948, in a strikingly word-centered declamatory voice).[136]

By comparison to the utopian, infinitely flexible promise of words, of spoken words especially, material acts of signification about the war's losses were less flexible. By definition, monumental sculptures are definitive in their materiality and, as a result, less mobile as signifiers. In the context of the debate over Elkan's monument to the "unknown citizen" and victim of the bombings, for instance, the verbal notion that the air raids defied visual representation strongly asserted itself. What is more, under conditions of scarcity, questions about monuments' necessity weighed on their realization. In their need to concretize, they became

furt's cityscape in the old center. See also the interview with Jörg Ott, the model's creator, on his indebtedness to the Treuner model (Presse- und Informationsamt der Stadt Frankfurt, www.frankfurt.de, published May 10, 2011).

135 Rolf Messerschmidt, "' ... in freier, gleicher, offener und furchtloser Weise dem ganzen Volk dienen': Zur Entstehung und Rolle des Hessischen Rundfunks in den ersten Nachkriegsjahren," in *Hr – 50 Jahre Rundfunk für Hessen*, ed. Heiner Boehnke et al. (Frankfurt am Main: Insel, 1995), 19–28.

136 With regard to radio broadcasting in post-war Germany, see Peter Marchal, *Kultur- und Programmgeschichte des öffentlich-rechtlichen Hörfunks in der Bundesrepublik Deutschland: Ein Handbuch*, vol. 1: *Grundlegung und Vorgeschichte* (Munich: kopaed, 2004), 273–385.

suspect above all to relinquish the range of future possibilities post-war interpreters accorded this moment.[137]

In the shadow of declarations, discourses, and debates – in other words in the shadow of the endless malleability of words – material modes of commemoration have nevertheless asserted themselves, rubble models among them. Built in the aftermath of war, these objects held, as I will show, the promise to elevate Germans from the minutiae of their individual lives and from sights, if not experiences, of moral, social, and economic destitution, to a vantage point that was elevated and about communities.[138]

In German cities where such models were commissioned in the decades after 1945, these images of constructed destruction did not face the scrutiny borne by public monuments.[139] Still, the Frankfurt "plastic sketch" was exhibited only for a short time, before it was "discovered," sometime in the late 1970s or early 1980s, in the attic of the Hessian Ministry of Construction in Wiesbaden from where it was transferred to Frankfurt's Historical Museum. There, it has been prominently displayed ever since. (And that display, incidentally, helped stimulate the creation of other such models in Würzburg and other places in the years after 1980.) The fact that the model was made so soon after Frankfurt's destruction, and its sense of theatric hyperbole, may help explain why there are few traces of its exhibition until its rediscovery. Though it was produced at considerable expense during a time of severe economic uncertainty, the finished product may have simply been seen as too inflammatory. A comparison with the ample photographic record reveals the model's constructedness, challenging the medium's association with verisimilitude. Looking at photographs taken by Albert Riethausen (b. 1920), for example, side by side with the rubble model, we see that many buildings were not damaged as severely as the model implies. The informed viewer, as a result, could not help but notice the model's potential to be used ideologically, be it as

137 The primacy of the written word in the construction of urban memory culture is emphasized by Thießen in his excellent *Eingebrannt ins Gedächtnis*, 18. This is not a general characteristic of memory culture but the product of specific constellations of media and the place of texts within them.

138 For the complex mental and emotional map of a particular city, Berlin, see Jennifer Evans, *Life among the Ruins: Cityscape and Sexuality in Cold War Berlin* (New York: Palgrave Macmillan, 2011).

139 In his study of the first decade of post-war German art, John-Paul Stonard makes a similar argument for post-war ruin photography. Citing a 1948-critique of a contemporary ruin photograph as in a picturesque mode, he states: "precisely because photography stopped short of full artistic status, it was an appropriate mode for the ruins" (*Fault Lines: Art in Germany 1945–1955* [London: Ridinghouse, 2007], 56).

an argument in favor of the emerging post-war urbanisms or in a debate about the justice or injustice of the bombings.

Among the many forms of preserving memories of the air war and its deadly effects, rubble models have played a striking, though under-appreciated, role. Here, in order to shed initial light on this genre of objects as a whole, we have explored one particular model as a way to understand the larger discourses of destruction and reconstruction. This strategy, however, only begins to assess the models' unassailable impact as objects. I will therefore return to analyze objects like the Frankfurt rubble model from a different angle.

Models of destruction take a pregnant historical moment and offer the comfort of scaled representations. Precision implies truth, and a miniature view – even if representing the aftermath of a horrific event – makes the world feel comprehensible. It is no surprise, then, that, due to their verisimilitude, models of destruction have usually escaped the controversies that almost inevitably surround artistic manifestations of a catastrophe. In scale, make, and presentation, rubble models reference a tradition of constructing cityscapes in relief and with geometrical exactitude in existence since the Renaissance. At the same time, they disrupt this viewing tradition by rendering panoramas in ruination. Their rhetoric as visual objects simultaneously relies on conspicuous absences, on the things that they don't reveal. They necessitate, for example, the absence of people, whose problematic presence is at the heart of artistic representations like Picasso's *Guernica* and Elkan's *maquette*. They are a material synecdoche – miniatures whose relation to pain and loss is oblique (though with the debris from the destroyed city that literally grounds the Frankfurt model this nexus is made explicit). What is more, they obfuscate the specifics of individual guilt or collective entanglements behind an all-encompassing cipher of disaster. In that sense, they may be said to be escapist at the same time as they insist on their status as truth.

Put differently, when we confront these built evocations of destruction, in their utter strangeness they call upon us to bring our own associations. The appeal of these objects thus lies in their readiness for inscription. Monument-like they are indeed in that the models of a ruined cityscape invite us in: they invite us as viewers to contribute our own affective responses, our own narrations of their people-less story, our own meaning-giving.

In that sense, the dialogues I have forged in the preceding pages were an effect of the Frankfurt model itself with its ability (like all rubble models) to accommodate far-reaching associations of times and spaces past, present, and future. We can now build on a formula coined at the outset of this book: this chapter has demonstrated how a model's miniature monumentality is a spatial form thick with temporal layers, a frozen moment of history that exists both within time and outside of it.

Chapter Three

The notion that space is not a given but socially constructed – an approach inspired by and associated with the French theorist Henri Lefebvre – has gained broad acceptance in the humanities, the social sciences, and architectural theory. This recent shift of perspective may enable us to acknowledge the ways that sculpted reliefs of cities don't just mirror the existing conditions of a place, but actually shape humans' spatial experience in history. Viewed thus, models are always social spaces, even though they frequently are devoid of humans

The visual exploration of crafted three-dimensional spaces – by which I mean the spaces we can roam with our eyes but not with our bodies – has the potential to transform one's relation to the world. The makers of models produce parts of an actual, represented, or imagined world in miniature – a machine, a building, a city. They do so in order to activate and mobilize viewers: such models entertain, they instruct, and they can be put to myriad uses. The more or less systematic translation of ordinary conditions into a material object alerts the viewer to possibilities that may otherwise remain unrecognized, as we will see.

This way of looking has become so natural for many, especially in the so-called West, that it is useful to remind us of a prior regime of representation – one that I characterize, somewhat ineptly, as medieval – where relations between objects in different sizes were not geometrically conceived. Medieval manuscript illumination, Gothic ivories, reliquaries, painted glass windows, and architecture could substitute for one another, without scalar mediations regulating their relations.

With city models as well as many other models, the relation between the world 'as is' and the world 'as if' rests on the controlled transposition of data (altitudes, proportions, distances, heights, etc.). Without accuracy in rendering the world we inhabit, a modeled object cannot accomplish its task of attracting the viewer into recognizing differently what they already know or wish to know. If the transposition is all too evident as such or, worse, overtly reductive, the model ceases to function as a valuable vehicle, calling attention to its own making rather than to what it references – as may be the case with the Frankfurt rubble model. (There are, of course, models of things one can only intuit, not know – models of the long-destroyed Temple in Jerusalem, for instance – that reference not so much a visual reality but a text or an idea.) At any rate, such transpositions are necessarily selective, though there is, as a rule, a system to the selection process. They simplify the actual environ, and simplification is precisely the point. City models can therefore be understood as sculpted objects whose urban point of reference is recognizable – an object analogous to a visual experiment.

Yet what does it mean to inspect a modeled city, whether it depicts a destroyed city as in the case of the Frankfurt rubble model or a built and inhabitable one as in many museums? Even in an age that has fulfilled humans' dream to fly, air travelers can hardly escape the sense of mastery when seeing the surface of the earth turn into a miniature toy-land spread out beneath them after take-off. The thesis advanced in this chapter is that models, city models in particular, are agents. They not only mobilize the viewe, but also turn the viewer into an agent. Positioning one's body and mind in relation to a modeled space means to assume a privileged position, one that offers both oversight and insight.

In the history of Europe, the modeling of urban spaces originated, as a practice and a skill, in the Renaissance. The elevated viewpoint offered by the early models, as we will see, was largely reserved for rulers and their entourage. Sovereignty, the Renaissance idea of rulership, derives from the medieval coinage of the Latin term 'superanus,' an adjective derivative of the preposition super: "the one positioned above." The word sovereign therefore implies a comparison; the sovereign's social standing above others or his high position in space. In Jean Bodin's understanding the ideal sovereign becomes associated even with the superlative mode ("the ruler is highest") and claims to a position of absolute, unmitigated power. Models were one of the spatial forms to give profile to this notion of rulership. Rulers' mastery over space brought with it the potential of a heightened emotional state for the viewer-subject as well as the potential for re-imagining the environs in an experimental fashion. We might call this scopic stance the sovereign's or the sovereign gaze. This nexus was forged at a moment when ruling, at least as educators prescribed it, demanded the exercise of the ruler's intellect and a ruler's learning expanded beyond textual canons to include the material world and training in imaginibus. During the Renaissance, the rise of central perspective, geometry, artillery, military science, the planned city, and other similar phenomena offered incentives to re-envision the social environment on a grand scale but, at least initially, in miniature form. In their original contexts – as an aid to rulership, military planning, and as an asset to princely collections – the first models, not least because of their startling novelty, left considerable traces of their conception. Yet the sense of corporeal-sensual mastery over the (material) world is so deeply ingrained in this genre of objects that even when city models were beheld by non-elite viewers and even when model-making became something of a profession, this appeal to command over a modeled space spread out below counts among these objects' primary effects. The city model interpellates the subject, allowing the viewer to experience himself (or herself) as sovereign.

Cities as Models in Munich

In 1529, Pope Clement VII, bent on regaining Medici control over Florence, prepared to lay siege to the city. To plan the campaign, he ordered that a new map of the city, its defenses, and its environs be drawn up "secretly" (*segretamente*).[1] When the sculptor Niccolo del Tribolo[2] joined the clock- and instrument-maker Lorenzo di Benvenuto della Volpaia in executing the task, he suggested creating a plan in relief rather than a two-dimensional map. Giorgio Vasari, who tells the story in his *vita* of Tribolo, adds that a three-dimensional representation provided "better consideration of the height of the mountains, the depth of the low-lying parts, and all other particulars" (*a ciò meglio si potesse considerar l'altezza de' monti, la bassezza de' piani e gl'altri particolari*).[3] In early modern warfare, relief models were cherished as something of a miracle weapon. Military science was a growth industry during this war-prone era, and its practitioners saw vast applications for scale models.[4]

---

1 Giorgio Vasari, *Le vite de' più eccellenti pittori scultori e architettori*, vol. 5 (Novara: Istituto Geografico de Agostini, 1967), 449; Giorgio Vasari, *Lives of the Painters, Sculptors and Architects*, trans. Gaston du C. de Vere (London: Random House, 1996), vol. 2, 227f, here p. 227. On this model see Filippo Camerota,"Tribolo e Benvenuto della Volpaia: Il modello ligneo per l'assedio di Firenze," in *Niccolò detto Il Tribolo tra arte, architettura e paesaggio*, ed. Elisabetta Pieri and Luigi Zangheri (Poggio a Caiano: Comune di Poggio a Caiano, 2000), 87–104. An earlier version of this chapter was published as Helmut Puff, "The City as Model: Three-Dimensional Representations of Urban Space in Early Modern Europe," in *Topographies of the Early Modern City*, ed. Arthur Groos, Hans-Jochen Schiewer, and Markus Stock (Göttingen: Vandenhoeck & Ruprecht, 2008): 193–217. I first presented this chapter as a talk at Cornell University and at the Eisenberg Institute for Historical Studies at the University of Michigan, Ann Arbor. I want to thank both audiences for the feedback I received, especially Will Glover for his excellent comments.

2 Vasari, *Le vite*, 419, calls him a "pittore." In his "History of Florence" (ix.28), Benedetto Varchi calls the same artist a "scultore": Benedetto Varchi, *Storia fiorentina* (Florence: Salani, 1963), 549.

3 Vasari, *Le vite*, 449; Vasari, *Lives*, 227.

4 In 1521, the Grand Master of the Knights Hospitallers, Philippe de Villiers de l'Isle Adam, had a model of the city and fortress of Rhodes made to prepare for an imminent attack by the troops of Sultan Suleiman II. Unlike in Florence, the "miracle" did not happen. After an extended siege, the Ottoman Empire emerged victorious. See Isabelle Warmoes, *Musée des Plans-Relief: Historic Models of Fortified Towns* (Paris: Patrimoine, 1999), 7; Albert Gabriel, *La cité de Rhodes* (Paris: E. de Boccard, 1921), 116. The scale model of Rhodes probably served as a planning device in upgrading the port's fortifications and bastions before the attack. See Ernle Bradford, *The Shield and the Sword: The Knights of St. John* (London: Hodder and Stoughton, 1972), 110; Helen Nicholson, *The Knights Hospitaller* (Woodbridge: Boydell Press, 2001), 59–67. Pope Leo X, Clement's uncle, received the model of Rhodes as a gift. According to Benedetto Varchi, Clement came to own the model. He does not mention it as his commission "un modello di legname, il quale ebbe

The elaborate preparations paid off. By 1530, when troops entered the city after a ten-month siege, Florence once again came under Medici rule, setting the stage for a transformation of this eminent city republic into a duchy. Although the relief model of Florence might have played only a minor, if any, role in the Medici's victory, the outcome seems to vindicate the artists' tremendous efforts to produce what Vasari called a "truly rare and marvellous" object (*cosa nel vero rara e maravigliosa*).[5]

Approaching the historical semantics of the city model is an intriguing challenge. Three-dimensional renderings of urban spaces have rarely been subjected to scholarly examination. The visual workings of models have typically been taken for granted, and authors tend to approach them as easily legible wonders of verisimilitude. David Buisseret, one of the few scholars to give these objects more thorough consideration, aptly describes them as "the least abstract of all representational types."[6] This chapter attempts to pressure our conventional understanding of city models as straightforward vehicles of the authentic; as soon as we look further, we see that the contexts for which these models were made point to levels of signification far beyond a mere rendering of the environment with exactitude.

As three-dimensional city models became a legitimate genre, surveying was a new science with immediate political implications. Models were instruments that could serve as planning devices or, as Clement demonstrated, as tools in the context of military campaigns. Yet the knowledge contained within these small-scale representations often demanded secrecy. While excelling in artistry, models thus emerged within the frame of early modern rulership. I will discuss two main examples: Vasari's account of the Florence model, mentioned above, and the sixteenth-century collection of modeled cities manufactured for the dukes of Bavaria. From these contexts, we can wrestle with the ways in which these marvelous objects might have been appreciated. From this sense of a genre's origins and its reception, my hope is that we can get a sense of how city models, in the sixteenth century and in our own era, are a potent means of shaping our perception of the world.

---

opoi papa Clemente e lo tenne in camera sua tutto il tempo che egli vivette" (Benedetto Varchi, *Storia fiorentina*, 549). Vasari's account does not acknowledge potential sources of inspiration, as if the artists' *ingenio* were solely responsible for its creation.

5 Vasari, *Le vite*, 450; Vasari, *Lives*, 228.

6 David Buisseret, *Modeling Cities in Early Modern Europe*, in *Envisioning the City*, ed. David Buisseret (Chicago: University of Chicago Press, 1998), 125–143, here p. 141.

A Rare and Marvellous Object

These three-dimensional renderings of urban space relied on and corresponded to existing forms of representation. They needed to utilize such forms to ensure that the viewer understood what they were seeing. Today we take for granted miniature creations done to scale; they make inherent sense to us because, through sheer repetition, we are able to understand that this is a reduced depiction of an actual physical space. But without that familiarity – without the globe in every primary school classroom, without the maps in our parents' car, or without architectural models – imagine how bizarre a miniature model of a city might seem. The first generations of model makers thus had to create a sense of familiarity through related creations.

To begin with, architectural models of buildings, also known in antiquity, had been in use since at least the fourteenth century. More widely dispersed were paintings or sculptures of donor figures and patron saints, a form of representation that proliferated toward the end of the Middle Ages. The men (and occasionally women) depicted often hold in their hands miniature buildings or places with which they were identified – thus linking embodied sainthood with individual buildings or entire towns.[7]

Renderings of cities in high relief also emerged in a close nexus with two-dimensional modes of topographical representation.[8] Images of cities had already become a focal point of interest by 1493 as exemplified by the so-called *Nuremberg Chronicle*, a comprehensive world history accompanied by lavish imagery.[9] This extraordinary printing venture featured an unprecedented number of woodcuts of urban skylines. Some were meticulously rendered actual portraits – one particularly remarkable example is the commanding view of Nuremberg with its church steeples and the imperial castle – while others were used to lend visual form to a number of cities.[10] Models, by contrast, whether painted or actual,

7 Elizabeth Lipsmeyer, *The Donor and His Church Model in Medieval Art from Early Christian Times to the Late Romanesque Period* (Ph.D., Rutgers University, 1981).

8 See Carry van Lakerveld, *Opkomst en Bloei van het Noordnederlandse Stadsgezicht in de 17de Eeuw: The Dutch Cityscape in the 17th Century and Its Sources* (Amsterdam: Amsterdams Historisch Museum, 1977); *Città d'Europa. Iconografia e vedutismo dal XV al XVIII secolo*, ed. Cesare de Seta (Naples: Electa, 1996).

9 Hartmut Kugler, *Die Vorstellung der Stadt in der deutschen Literatur des Mittelalters* (Munich: Artemis, 1986).

10 Hartmann Schedel, *Weltchronik: Kolorierte Gesamtausgabe von 1493*, ed. Stephan Füssel (Cologne: Taschen, 2001).

required the beholder to train his or her gaze: small-scale replicas had to be set in relation to *realia*.

Despite these precursors, miniature models of cities and their environments were still something of a novelty in the sixteenth century. Vasari lavishes praise on the relief created by Della Volpaia and Tribolo, as mentioned above, calling it a "truly rare and marvellous" object (*cosa nel vero rara e maravigliosa*).[11] *Rara* and *maravigliosa* held manifold meanings in his *Vite*. In this particular context, the phrase posits the model as a rarity in comparison to other objects, and seeks to express the tremendous effect it had – as a thing of *marvel* – on the viewer.[12] But the phrase also hints at novelty, as it links the sculpted urban terrain to the category of the curious and the wondrous.[13]

The model itself has not survived the intervening half-millennium. But just as intriguing is that Vasari deemed it worthy of extensive description, since descriptions of such models are themselves rare. Vasari's account even has a parallel in Benedetto Varchi's *Storia fiorentina* (History of Florence), written in 1547/48. This vast historical project revolves around the decade of change between the Medici's ousting and their rise as dukes of Tuscany, and includes a short passage on the same relief model.[14]

Both accounts reveal some of the "secrets" that went into the model's construction. Vasari and Varchi stress, for instance, the elaborate measurements necessary to produce Florence *en miniature*, a project that took considerable time – six months according to Varchi.[15] Vasari reveals that the artists were staying out "all night to measure the roads and to mark the number of *braccia* between one place and another, and also to measure the height of the summits of the belfries and towers, drawing intersecting lines in every direction by means of the

11 Whether Vasari had himself seen the object is not clear from the description.

12 A similar description appears in the context of Lorenzo Ghiberti's Vita: "la più rara e maravigliosa cosa che si possa veder" – an expression referring to bronze ornamentation made for a Florentine church. The project was finished by Ghiberti's grandson, Bonacorso, and it is his work that is praised in this context. See Giorgio Vasari, "Lorenzo Ghiberti," in *Le vite*, vol. 3 (testo), ed. Rosanna Bettarini (Florence: Sansoni, 1971), 101.

13 Lorraine Daston and Katharine Park, *Wonders and the Order of Nature 1150–1750* (New York: Zone, 1998) – in particular their discussion of "Marvellous Particulars," pp. 135–172. On the nexus of the rare and the curious, see also Lorraine Daston, "Neugierde als Empfindung und Epistemologie in der frühmodernen Wissenschaft," in *Macrocosmos in Microcosmo: Die Welt in der Stube: Zur Geschichte de Sammelns 1450 bis 1800*, ed. Andreas Grote (Opladen: Leske & Budrich, 1994), 35–59, here p. 43; Lina Bolzoni, "Das Sammeln und die ars memoriae," ibid., 129–168, here p. 142.

14 The one account doesn't seem to rely on the other. Because of its length, I will treat Vasari's primarily and draw Varchi in only as a comparison.

15 Varchi, *Storia fiorentina*, 549.

compass, and going beyond the walls to compare the height of the hills with that of the cupola [of Florence's cathedral], which they had marked as their center" (*tutta la notte a misurar le strade e segnar le misure delle braccia da luogo a luogo e misurar anche l'altezza e le cime de' campanili e delle torri, intersegnando con la bussola per tutti i versi et andando di fuori a riscontrar con i monti la cupola, la quale avevano segnato per centro*).[16] Varchi concurs that the two artists worked at night, thus avoiding the hustle and bustle of Florentine city life.[17]

Both writers also provide information on the materials used in transferring the newly collected topographical data into a relief model. "[F]or the sake of lightness" (*perché fusse più leggiera*), Vasari explains, the two artist-artisans executed the model in cork.[18] By contrast, Varchi says it was made of "wood" (*legname*).[19] In any case, the model's supposedly light weight made it easier to transport. If we follow Vasari, it consisted of several pieces and thus was smuggled out of the threatened city "in some bales of wool" (*in alcune balle di lana*).[20] Apparently, the economically active city could not be sealed off. Even in times of conflict, Florence depended on the mobility of people, goods, and knowledge. Ultimately, this permeability left the city vulnerable, contributing to its military demise.

The model's scale can be inferred from information we possess. According to Vasari, Pope Clement had asked for a model that captured the city with one mile of plateau around the city. One Florentine mile equals 1654 m; the model's dimensions are given as four *braccia* (approximately 225 cm).[21] If we extrapolate from these measurements, we get a scale of roughly 1:1470. This is not unlikely in light of the model's function as a planning device for a military campaign. While

---

16 Vasari, *Le vite*, 450; Vasari, *Lives*, 227: "all night to measure the roads and to mark the number of *braccia* between one place and another, and also to measure the height of the summits of the belfries and towers, drawing intersecting lines in every direction by means of the compass, and going beyond the walls to compare the height of the hills with that of the cupola [of Florence's cathedral], which they had marked as their center."

17 Cf. Varchi, *Storia fiorentina*, 549, on this point: "non lavorando se non la notte, per non essere, secondo l'uso del popolo di Firenze, impediti dalla gente." On this question of surveying as something possible at night and other measurements that had to be collected during the day, see Camerota, "Tribolo e Benvenuto della Volpaia," 88f. Camerota also discusses the possibility that the artists could draw on data Antonio da Sangallo collected for the improvement of Medici Florence's fortifications only a couple of years before Tribolo's and Della Volpaia's model (89–92).

18 Vasari, *Le vite*, 450; id., *Lives*, 227.

19 Varchi, *Storia fiorentina*, 549.

20 Vasari, *Lives*, 450; id., *Le vite*, 227.

21 Ronald Edward Zupko, *Italian Weights and Measures: From the Middle Ages to the Nineteenth Century* (Philadelphia: American Philosophical Society, 1981).

most early models of cities adopted a much smaller scale, models representing cities or fortresses *and* their surroundings commonly used a larger scale. With this scale, it might just about have been possible to see "the squares and streets within" (*dentro le piazze e le strade*), as Clement had wished.[22]

Vasari locates the value of this "rare and marvelous" model in its utility and, one might add, the evidence it provides of the artist's protean ability – his *ingenio* – to be useful, especially to the house of Medici. Throughout the military campaign, Clement VII apparently kept the model in his private chambers, where he was able to follow the army's every move even while 230 kilometres from the theatre of war. The model served as a scopic device – an instrument that allowed the pope and commander to watch the progress of military activities from afar. It thus helped to translate information from one register to another. Messages in the form of "letters and despatches" (*lettere e gl'avisi*) about the campaign's progress could be converted into the sense of sight, as if this instrument annihilated the distance between Rome and Florence.[23]

The differences between Vasari's and Varchi's descriptions are revealing, not least because they provide us with traces of the different contexts in which such models were created and understood. Vasari's narrative centers on the ingenious artists behind the model. In their indefatigable ability to mimetically model urban topography, Della Volpaia and Tribolo become indispensible to the ruler – a story emphasized by the notion of the secrecy of their activity. Varchi's short account takes an entirely different rhetorical thrust. This writer launches into an excursus on Florence's historical topography, comparing the Florence of 1547 with Florence before the siege. He claims to model his own description of the city on the model in question (which makes it probable that he saw the model first-hand). Under Varchi's pen, the model became a historian's tool, providing

22 Vasari, *Le vite*, 449; id., *Lives*, 227. Based on the assumption that "l'area interessata poteva essere circoscritta da un quadrato di circa sei chilometri per lato," Camerota arrives at a different hypothesis about the model's scale, either 1:2500 or 1:5000. The sixteenth-century models of similar size from Nuremberg and Augsburg Camerota adduces to discuss the size are not comparable, however, since these objects do not show the city in its geographic context.

23 Vasari, *Le vite*, 450; id., *Lives*, 228. Varchi, *Storia fiorentina*, 549 only mentions that Clement kept the model in his chamber all his life ("lo tenne in camera sua tutto ul tempo che egli vivette"). On the history of these models and their multiple functions, see Antonio Manno, "Rilievi scultorei e plastici di fortezze: Annotazioni e proposte per una storia delle idee di città e della guerra nel patriziato veneziano" (49–64) and Marino Vigano, "La fortezza in casa: Modelli di piazzeforti tra guerra e conoscenza del territorio (XVI–XIX secolo)," in *Europa Miniature: Die kulturelle Bedeutung des Reliefs, 16.–21. Jahrhundert*, ed. Andreas Bürgi (Zürich: Verlag Neue Zürcher Zeitung, 2007), 79–90.

him with a window onto Florence's past as well as a model for his own writing of history. In its ability to conjure up the changing city in its entirety, this "rare and marvelous" object became – not unlike the post-World War II rubble models four centuries later – an emblem for visual accessibility, comprehensiveness, and truthful representation.[24]

Visual Technologies of Urban Space

Cities posed tremendous challenges to the *kunst der perpsectiff* or "art of perspective," to quote the Nuremberg writer Hans Sachs[25] – challenges that seem to have attracted increasing numbers of artisans, artists, and printers in the sixteenth century. Portraitists of cities had to depict vast numbers of buildings, and their attendant layout, and forge them into a unified image.

In 1500, Jacopo de' Barbari created a masterful print that purported to show a geometrically exact view of Venice from an imagined viewpoint, with an unprecedented wealth of urban detail. In reality, this masterpiece of monumental size provides a plenitude of viewpoints integrated into one image of a city, seen from high above and spread out before the viewer. It solves the problem of providing access to this sea of islands, canals, and buildings by suggesting, among other things, that a bird would see the curvature of the globe. *A volo d'uccello* (as its mode of representation is described on this print) means "in bird's flight," a description that captures the image's sense of movement through space.[26] Yet mathematically calculated representations of cities contained significations that went beyond mere geometrical accuracy and urban naturalism. Barbaro's Venice gestures toward various symbolic layers of meaning, invoking benevolent deities, for instance. It is in this context of visual experiments in perspectival seeing that city views of any kind, including the nascent genre of urban scale models, gained legibility. Such ways of seeing have since been standardized, but in the sixteenth century were still being formed.

Vedute of individual cities were predicated on the conjunction of applied mathematical knowledge and artisanal expertise. Rendering urban spaces

---

24 Varchi, *Storia fiorentina*, 549.

25 Quoted after *Frühneuhochdeutsches Wörterbuch*, ed. Ulrich Goebel and Oskar Reichmann, vol. 3 (Berlin: de Gruyter, 1998), col. 1536 (Hans Sachs, 1565, 23, 278).

26 See Giandomenico Romanelli, Susanna Biadene, and Camillo Tonini, eds., *'A volo d'uccello' : Jacopo de' Barbari e le rappresentazioni di città nell'Europa del Rinascimento* (Venice: Arsenale, 1999).

required cooperation across crafts and disciplines; when successful, divisions between *artes liberales* and *artes mechanicae* disappeared. In this rarefied milieu, projects of mapping the urban world by means of a scrutinizing gaze were pursued systematically. In 1502, only two years after Jacopo de' Barbari's view of Venice, Leonardo da Vinci rendered the Italian city of Imola ichnographically – a form of mapping by which a plan of the city's plots of land was combined with horizontal sections of every building. His is not a bird's eye view of an area in which certain places were condensed into a summary view, as was the case with Barbari's Venice; his is a view that innovatively renders all elevations on the same orthogonal scale as traces on a flat surface.[27]

Albrecht Dürer was in fact something of a patron saint for these visual-artisanal innovations. In the decades after his death, interest in recording the urban landscape both visually and spatially was traced back to his vast oeuvre, which included watercolors of cities as well as views of parts of cities or *vedute*;[28] his interest in measuring the human body to serve his art, which lent itself to the expansion of the interface between geometry and the arts; and his treatise on fortifications, which testifies to the new ways that knowledge about the material world and its representation were valued. Dürer thus pioneered new roles for the artisan-scholar. He epitomized the fusion of ingenious artisanal expertise with the claims to learning through images. Not surprisingly, Georg Braun, editor of the first comprehensive atlas of city views, invoked Dürer's guiding spirit in the preface to the work's third volume, published in 1582.[29]

The growing interest in various city views during the fifteenth and early sixteenth centuries coincided with the first creation (since antiquity) of three-dimensional models of cities. Sixteenth-century Nuremberg as well as Augsburg seem to have pioneered three-dimensional representations of urban space north of the Alps: Both cities were centers of printing whose output included capital-inten-

---

27 Peter Bosselmann, *The Representation of Places: Reality and Realism in City Design* (Berkeley: University of California, 1998).

28 I am using city views, *vedute*, and portraits in contradistinction to cityscape: "'a painting, drawing or print of a prospect of a city or a part of a city, such as can be taken in at a glance from one point of view.' The latter restriction is important, because it excludes most of the profiles, panoramas, bird's-eye views and the like. Such views were generally composed of a number of separately observed parts which, although they were combined to form one picture, cannot be taken in at a glance" (*The Dutch Cityscape*, 10).

29 Georg Braun and Frans Hogenberg, *Beschreibung und Contrafactur der vornembster Stät der Welt*, ed. Max Schefold (Plochingen: Müller & Schindler, 1965–1970), vol. 3, (*)r. See also Georg Braun and Frans Hogenberg, *Civitates orbis terrarum: 'The Towns of the World,' 1572–1618*, ed. R. A. Skelton (Cleveland: World Pub. Co., 1966).

sive ventures alongside more conventional fare. Their famous instrument-makers supplied surveyors with tools to measure buildings and spaces. These cities – which lacked the traditional intellectual frame provided by a university – also engendered social milieus in which humanist scholars and artisans mingled and exchanged ideas. Finally, the strategic position of both cities as mercantile centers with close ties to the north of Italy enabled urban elites to follow the pulse of technological and artistic innovation south of the Alps.[30] The aforementioned Jacopo de' Barbari, for instance, collaborated with the German merchant Anton Kolb, a merchant from Nuremberg who was resident in Venice. Barbari was a friend of a fellow Renaissance artist from Nuremberg, Albrecht Dürer, and died a court artist in northern Europe.

Under the aegis of urban topography as a new expertise, many forms of representation flourished. Yet models executed in scale were distinct from two-dimensional urban representations. Cities in relief had a pronounced edge over their two-dimensional rivals and relatives: they solved a problem that haunted city views and maps – how to render elevation. As Vasari indicates, mapmakers of the sixteenth century were unable to render the natural terrain with any degree of exactitude (which is not to say that all city models made use of an exact rendering of elevation). Conversely, models were sensorily accessible from various angles, offering themselves as syntheses of various urban views. They were able to blend the most successful attributes of recent two-dimensional innovations, since three-dimensional portraits could harness both the considerable advantages of a bird's eye perspective as well as the comprehensive information that came with the orthogonal scale. Their intrinsic multiperspectivism amounted to a revolutionary change in representing city spaces. What is more, unlike maps and

---

30 Andrew John Martin, "Stadtmodelle," in *Das Bild der Stadt in der Neuzeit: 1400–1800*, ed. Wolfgang Behringer and Bernd Roeck (Munich: Beck, 1999), 66–72; Angela Marino, "Modelli e storia urbana: Da immagine simbolica a strumento di progetto," in *Europa Miniature: Die kulturelle Bedeutung des Reliefs, 16.–21. Jahrhundert*, ed. Andreas Bürgi (Zürich: Verlag Neue Zürcher Zeitung, 2007), 65–77. For the larger context, see Eva-Maria Seng, *Stadt – Idee und Planung: Neue Ansätze im Städtebau des 16. und 17. Jahrhunderts* (Munich: Deutscher Kunstverlag, 2003). The three models of Nuremberg manufactured in sequence seem to have been made in response to the council's 1538 decision to update the city's fortifications: Hans Sebald Beheim, Nuremberg (1540); Hans Payr, Nuremberg (1541); Georg Pencz and Sebald Peck, Nuremberg (1543). Hans Rogel portrayed Augsburg in relief (1560–1563). On the cultural milieu, for Nuremberg, see David Hotchkiss Price, *Albrecht Dürer's Renaissance: Humanism, Reformation, and the Art of Faith* (Ann Arbor: University of Michigan Press, 2003); *Nürnberg 1300–1550: Kunst der Gotik und Renaissance*, ed. Gerhard Bott (Munich: Prestel, 1986); on Augsburg, *Geschichte der Stadt Augsburg: 2000 Jahre von der Römerzeit bis zur Gegenwart*, ed. Gunther Gottlieb (Stuttgart: Konrad Theiss, 1984).

views of cities, which were usually printed and therefore available in multiple copies, models were one of a kind, a fact that appealed to city councilors, aristocratic collectors, and members of the power elite.

Modeling Bavaria

A pioneering text of 1565, Samuel Quiccheberg's (1529–1567; also Quicchelberg) *Inscriptiones vel tituli theatri amplissimi*, further cements the idea that city models were a crucial visual technology for Renaissance rulers. Models, here called *exempla ex arte fabrili* (literally, "specimens from the carpenter's trade"), form an intriguing part of the author's argument. Composed for Duke Albrecht V of Bavaria (r. 1550–1579), a stalwart Catholic and a patron of the arts, this treatise is one of the incunabula of modern museum studies.[31] In little more than 60 pages, Quiccheberg – the duke's "Flemish advisor on matters artistic"[32] – offered an all-encompassing blueprint for assembling a *kunstkammer*, or cabinet of curiosities. The term, a sixteenth-century coinage, describes more or less systematic collections that combined objects found in nature with objects created by humans. Included in the catalogue's first "class" – a collection that makes a collector's identity manifest – are "artisans' models of edifices, for instance, of houses, castles, temples, *cities*, castra, and fortifications made of little wooden slats, paper, and feathers, sometimes ornamented with colors" ([*a*]*edificiorum exempla ex arte fabrili: ut domorum, arcium, templorum, urbium, castrorum, munitiornum, ex asserculis, chartis, pinnulisque combinata: ac coloribus forte ornate*).[33] City models thus are grouped with genealogies, portraits, maps, *vedute*, representations of events or processions, and stuffed animals.

The ducal collection was still in its beginnings in 1565, the year when the *Inscriptiones* appeared in print and the year when decrees by Duke Albrecht and his wife Anna declared "nineteen valuables as being inalienable heirlooms of the

31 *Der Anfang der Museumslehre in Deutschland: Das Traktat 'Inscriptiones vel Tituli Theatri Amplissimi' von Samuel Quiccheberg*, ed. Harriet Roth (Berlin: Akademie, 2000.) (I will quote this volume under Quiccheberg's name when citations refer to the edited text and under Roth if it concerns the editor's extensive commentary on this text.) See also Seng, *Stadt*, 28–32.

32 Lorenz Seelig, "The Munich *Kunstkammer*, 1565–1807," in *The Origins of Museums: The Cabinet of Curiosities in Sixteenth- and Seventeenth-Century Europe*, ed. Oliver Impey and Arthur MacGregor (Oxford: Clarendon, 1985), 76–89, here p. 76.

33 *Der Anfang der Museumslehre*, 44. Italics added.

princely household, to be handed down to the successive rulers forever."[34] As far as we know, their inventory did not yet feature three-dimensional renderings of cities or fortresses. Quiccheberg's text might have offered a stimulus to fill this "gap" in the collection. After all, the *Inscriptiones* was a two-pronged publication: it constituted a theoretical treatise on the *kunstkammer* as a mirror of the ordered world, but also served as a practical manual on what to collect and how to build a collection. Just a few years after *Inscriptiones* was published, the first such model entered the Bavarian collection.[35] By the end of the decade, the wood turner and model-maker Jacob Sandtner started to work on a series of models portraying Bavarian cities for the duke.

Not accidentally, the cities represented in scale were centers of ducal administration, the so-called *Residenzstädte* or seats of government within the duchy: Munich (1570) (fig. 10),[36] Landshut (1571) (fig. 8),[37] Ingolstadt (1572),[38] and Burghausen (1574) (fig. 9).[39] The model of Straubing, hometown of Jacob Sandtner, is distinguished from the other models by its different scale and earlier date of completion, 1568 (fig. 6).[40] Some speculate that it might have been the Straubing model that inspired the duke's decision to commission renderings of other

---

34 Seelig, "The Munich *Kunstkammer*," 76.

35 Sandtner's models count among the oldest objects in the Munich *kunstkammer*'s inventory. For Renaissance understandings of museums, see Paula Findlen, "The Museum: Its Classical Etymology and Renaissance Genealogy," in *Museum Studies: An Anthology of Contexts*, ed. Bettina Messias Carbonell (Oxford: Blackwell, 2004), 23–50.

36 199 × 189 cm, scale ca. 1:616 to 1:750. Limewood, partly polychrome (Bavarian National Museum, Inv. No. Mod 1).

37 193 × 155 cm, scale ca. 1:750. Limewood, partly polychrome (Bavarian National Museum, Munich, Inv. No. Mod 2).

38 160 × 160 cm, scale ca. 1:685. Limewood, partly polychrome (Bavarian National Museum, Munich, Inv. No. Mod 3).

39 221 × 108 cm, scale ca. 1:662. Limewood, partly polychrome (Bavarian National Museum, Munich, Inv. No. Mod 4).

40 81 × 64 cm. On Sandtner's life, see Alexander Freiherr von Reitzenstein, *Die alte bairische Stadt in den Modellen des Drechslermeisters Jakob Sandtner, gefertigt in den Jahren 1568–1574 im Auftrag Herzog Albrechts V. von Bayern* (Munich: Callway, 1967), 6f. More than in subsequent generation of modelmakers, Sandtner became an artist-artisan with name recognition. Johann Baptist Seitz built a model of nineteenth-century Munich (1841–1863), explicitly referring to Sandtner's example (Franz Schiermeier, *"Relief der Haupt- und Residenzstadt München": Das Stadtmodell von Johann Baptist Seitz 1841–1863*, ed. Renate Eikelmann [Munich: Bayerisches Nationalmuseum, 2000]). See also Josef Dinges from Landsberg, who referred to a copy he made of Sandtner's model of Burghausen when offering his services to the German Archaeological Institute in 1933 (Deutsches Archäologisches Intitut, Rom, "Allg. Korr.-Dinges.")

Fig. 6: Jacob Sandtner, Model of Straubing, © Bavarian National Museum, Munich

places in a similar fashion. Be that as it may, the models' material presence at court symbolically brought these administrative strongholds into the center of the newly strengthened Bavarian state, the city of Munich. Together, the models, now at the Bavarian National Museum, constitute one of the oldest, if not the earliest, existing collections of such *maquettes*.

These models differ in kind from the one commissioned by Clement VII for the siege of Florence. Full-scale representations manufactured for military functions usually represented a settlement together with its surrounding terrain, as did the model of Florence created by Tribolo and Della Volpaia whose work was admired by Vasari, making such an object useful for planning attacks or updating defense systems. In Zurich, for instance, Hans Ulrich Bachofen and Hans Conrad Gyger created a wooden model of the city and its environs around 1625 that served as a planning device for erecting new fortifications (built after 1642) (fig. 7). While the dense texture of the built urban environment is rendered in red paint only, without any elevation (much like in a city map of today), the tall buildings – churches, towers, major buildings as well as buildings outside the city walls – were executed in three dimensions. Thus, military

Fig. 7: Hans Ulrich Bachofen, Relief Model of Zurich, 1627, Swiss National Museum, Zurich

planners were able to calculate the effects of artillery fire from the city's hilly surroundings.[41]

By comparison, the models of Bavarian cities did not, at least as far as we know, function as a vehicle for military knowledge. The models of Straubing, Munich, Landshut, Ingolstadt, and Burghausen show the cities and their fortifications only, without the urban hinterlands critical to military planning. The models were carved out of limewood, a pliable material commonly used for Gothic sculpture in Germany. Individual houses and buildings retained the quality of the wood, thus blending the sea of roofs and gables into a whole; unbuilt areas were painted with a striking green color and supplied with generic miniature trees. Importantly, these miniature *Residenzstädte* all share the same principles of production and design, which yields a uniform look – a look that transforms the objects into a collection of cities meant to be viewed as an ensemble.

41 Zurich, Swiss National Museum, 1:3000 (1627); Inv. 62.5625. See Otto Sigg, "Das 17. Jahrhundert," in *Geschichte des Kantons Zürich* (Zurich: Werd-Verlag, 1996), 320f, 351f.

Fig. 8: Jacob Sandtner, Model of Landshut, detail, © Bavarian National Museum, Munich (Photo: Marianne Stockmann)

Fig. 9: Jacob Sandtner, Model of Burghausen, detail, © Bavarian National Museum, Munich

With all their naturalist exuberance, these models still deviated from the actual urban space. Some distortions and omissions are obvious: Sandtner's Munich has few chimneys, for instance. More important than the particular omissions, however, is their overall effect: to create a sense of unity in cities that did not look very similar to each other. Habitations are further unified in their look since the three-dimensional map does not render one of Munich's most distinctive features – painted house façades. More importantly, the width of streets is exaggerated, as is the height of signature buildings such as churches, towers, and castles. These changes are apt to heighten the viewer's impression of the urban scene's grandeur. Distortions and omissions also connect these full-bodied representations with representations on paper, where similar such distortions were introduced in order to assist graphic clarity.[42] The "Cities of the World" (*Civitates orbis terrarum* or *Beschreibung vnd Contrafactur der vornembster Stät der Welt*) says as much, when Georg Braun, the editor, explains that such visual adjustments allow "that the reader can look into all streets as well as look at buildings and open squares" (*daß der Leser in alle Gassen vnd Strasen sehen / auch alle gebäw vnd ledige platzen anschawen kan*).[43]

In our age of global positioning systems it is hard to imagine the tremendous efforts necessary to construct models that were accurate, or at least seemed to be. Their production required intensive measurements in situ, as the geodetic data were collected from scratch. If Sandtner was not alone in creating the database necessary for his models, no trace of such collaborations remains.[44] The extensive data gathering that must have preceded the models' production is reminiscent of Vasari's and Varchi's accounts of how the Florence model was made. We can imagine Sandtner, and perhaps an apprentice or two, dragging equipment through the streets, triangulating his coordinates in order to measure the heights of certain buildings, the length of each avenue, or the altitude of the elevations in the natural environment.

In Sandtner's case, years lay between the dates of completion for the different models, proudly noted on the objects themselves. Significantly, Sandtner seemed to have had a ducal permit to enter into every building in order to com-

---

42 Max Schefold, "Einleitung," in *Beschreibung*, vol. 1 (Kommentarband) (Plochingen: Müller & Schindler, 1965), 10: "Die klare Gliederung und leichte Überschaubarkeit des Stadtganzen erforderte die Überbetonung der Straßen und Plätze – im Falle von Venedig (I, 44) die der Kanäle – doch geschah dies auf Kosten der Häusergruppen, die dadurch allzu sehr eingeengt wurden; so war der Wunsch, jedem Gebäude, jedem Bürgerhaus gerecht zu werden, kaum zu erfüllen."

43 Braun, "Vorwort," in *Beschreibung*, vol. 3 (1581), reprint (Stuttgart: Müller & Schindler, 1968), (*)r.

44 Reitzenstein, *Die alte bairische Stadt*, 12.

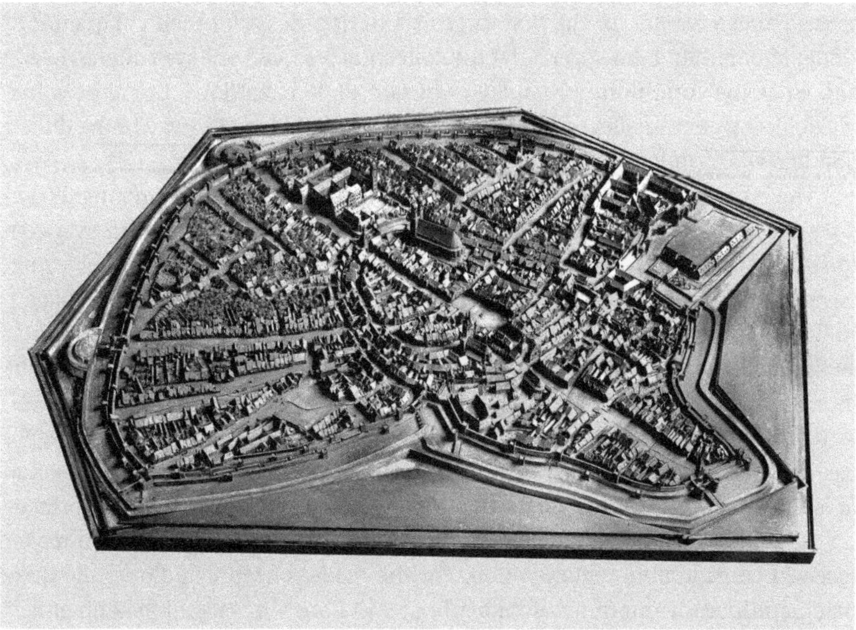

Fig. 10: Jacob Sandtner, Model of Munich, 1570, © Bavarian National Museum, Munich

plete the task of measuring what was to be carved in wood. In Ingolstadt, not even monasteries were exempt from the duke's spatial carte blanche.[45] This move signals a profound rupture with the habitual respect for clausura within Catholic Christianity. Spatial differentiations and property rights were equally disregarded, leveling the body politic for the purpose of surveying the terrain. Such a permit demonstrates the prince's commitment to this new political project, and the lengths he was willing to go in order to visualize his empowerment over his people and lands. The ducal permit also seems to hint at the importance of perception, and how he wanted these representations to be comprehensive and accurate.

Although the prince's subjects were made to cooperate, they benefited relatively little from the execution of the resulting plans. To be sure, a small number of visitors were able to view these marvelous objects, stored in Munich's newly

45 "[...]wo der [Sandtner], in Klöster und Hauser deshalb zu ersehen begert, wie es des Werkes Nothdurft nach thun muszt, dasz er jedes Orts eingelassen und ihm die Besichtigung nicht geweigert werde" (regarding Ingolstadt). Quoted after Reitzenstein, *Die alte bairische Stadt*, 8.

erected *kunstkammer* for the first three or four decades after their completion.[46] Under Maximilian I, however, after the collection was said to have suffered losses and since the conditions of display were said to be hazardous, the most valuable objects were transferred to the ducal *Residenz* and locked away in the duke's quarters where only the ruler had access to them.[47]

The creation of these models thus contains lessons about forging the territorial state in early modern Europe and Bavaria – a project that unfolded over centuries. In actuality, the dialectic of ducal elevation and the populace's subjection never succeeded to the degree that the models – with their clean-cut sense of controlled space – would suggest. The ideal city of the duke (a space and populace subject to the prince) and the city of the burghers (an urban community defined by its medieval charters and the right to self-government) continued to vie for power, status, and distinction throughout the early modern period. The rationally organized, unified territorial space embodied in the models served not as a depiction of reality, but rather as an icon for the subjection of Bavarians to the ruler-prince.

As with many things created to satiate a ruler's desire, the artisan-maker received considerable remuneration. For the model of Munich alone, the duke paid Sandtner the enormous sum of about 300 florins in several installments.[48] To mark the commission's completion, the model of Burghausen features a golden inscription, still visible today (fig. 9).[49] It celebrates the work as a crowning achievement of the cooperation between the patron, Duke Albrecht of the reunited "upper and lower Bavaria," and the model's maker, whose name appears toward the inscription's end:

> Anno Domini M.D.LXXIII. HAT DER DVRCHLEVCHTIG HOCHGEBORN FVRST VND HERR ALBRECHT PFA(L)ZGRAV BEY RHEIN HERZOG IN OBERN VND NIDERN BAIRN SEINER FVRSTLICHEN GNADEN SCHLOS VND STAT BURKHAVSEN WIE ES ZV DER ZEIT GESTANDEN IST DVRCH IACOB SANDTNER IN GRVNT LEGEN LASSEN.
> (In the year 1573, His Serene Highness Prince and Lord Albrecht, Count Palatine by the Rhine, Duke in Upper and Lower Bavaria, had Jacob Sandtner execute in profile his Princely Grace's Castle and Town of Burghausen executed in profile how it was at the time.)

46 There are indications that gifts provided access for select viewers of the Munich *kunstkammer* between 1578 and 1611. See Roth, *Der Anfang der Museumslehre*, 263. Johann Wolfgang Freymann payed Sandtner *6 kreuzer* in 1571 to see his model of Munich, probably in Sandtner's workshop. See Reitzenstein, *Die alte bairische Stadt*, 7.
47 Seelig, "The Munich *Kunstkammer*," 87.
48 Reitzenstein, *Die alte bairische Stadt*, 7. Ingo Schwab, "Zeiten der Teuerung: Versorgungsprobleme in der zweiten Hälfte des 16. Jahrhunderts," in *Geschichte der Stadt München*, ed. Richard Bauer (Munich: Beck, 1992), 166 speaks of 131 fl.
49 Other models probably also showed inscriptions. Only remnants seem to have survived. I was unable to inspect the evidence myself.

The inscription's final phrase – in the original text *in grunt legen lassen* – is replete with connotations. The literal translation is "to measure geometrically." Geographers and topographers used this term frequently in the sixteenth century, especially with regard to surveying and rendering urban environments in various media. Predecessors of these models in Augsburg and Nuremberg were described with the same formula, a fact signaling how the Bavarian models, early as their date of completion is, already partook of a nascent tradition of making urban models.[50] But *grunt* resonates more broadly in this particular context, connecting different dimensions of the endeavor. For one, *grunt* or "ground" emphasizes depth, thereby pointing to the artifact's plasticity, which is why I have rendered this part of the inscription as "to execute in profile." At the same time, in the sixteenth century, *grunt* also served as the German translation for the Latin *ratio* in the sense of a methodical treatise. As such, it was a magic word, frequently used to characterize the systematic foundations of knowledge, especially as they were used in the training of others.[51] As we will see, the term *grunt* is therefore apt to foreground the significant role given to manual expertise in the context of the new "vernacular science," to use Pamela Smith's coinage for early modern appreciation of artisan labor as the basis of scientific achievements.[52] With this inscription, Sandtner boldly declared himself a practitioner of an innovative art.

50 See Martin, "Stadtmodelle," 69. Quiccheberg had moved to Nuremberg as a boy and spent time in Augsburg before starting to work for Duke Albrecht, cf. *Der Anfang der Museumslehre*, 4–6, 279, 304–308, 310f. See also Reitzenstein, *Die alte bairische Stadt*, 8, with a similar inscription on a model of Ingolstadt, a smaller copy of the one in the Bavarian National Museum: "ANNO. 1571. IAR. HAT. HERZOG. ALBRECHT. DIES. LOBLICHE. STAT. DVRCH. IACOB. SANNDTER. IN. GRVNDT. LEGEN. LASEN. MIT. ALLEM. WIE. ES. ZVE. DISSER. ZEIT. GESTANDEN. IST. VND. HAT. DIESE. STAT. 5000. SCHRIT. VM. SICH. WARDT. BVRGENMAISTER. HERR. VLRICH. VISCHER." With its focus on the city and the mention of the mayor, it is probable that it was meant to be kept in Ingolstadt.

51 An example for this is the preface to Albrecht Dürer's "art of measurement" which is described as "the true foundation [*grund*] of all painting"; he also speaks of this treatise and his method as "a well-founded [*gründlich*] beginning" (*Vnderweysung der Messung*, Frankfurt am Main: Egenolff, 1536, A1v).

52 Pamela Smith, *The Body of the Artisan: Art and Experience in the Scientific Revolution* (Chicago: University of Chicago Press, 2004), 148, 237. On p. 148, the expression appears as "vernacular 'science.'"

Mastery through Models and the Lathe

We can better understand how early model making was simultaneously leveraged by elites, while also propelling the growth of manual expertise, if we briefly consider the parallel example of a related kind of craftsmanship: lathe turning. Sandtner was a lathe turner by trade. By his era, in the milieu of South German courts, turning had evolved to an activity deemed appropriate even for nobles.[53] Sixteenth-century technological innovations had made possible the manufacturing of oval and various other geometrical shapes. Products fresh off the lathe, whether of wood or of ivory, were highly prized for their material manifestation of applied geometrical theory. As objects *de luxe* of no immediate use, they were anything but household items. In the courtly milieu, they were often complexly-shaped pieces whose main purpose seems to have been the marvel they engendered. Quiccheberg, theorist and designer of Munich's *kunstkammer*, recommended that a *theatrum* or museum include a turning room in its layout,[54] and Duke William IV, father of Albrecht V, had already set up such a workshop at his Munich residence.[55] William V, Albrecht's son and successor, was the Bavarian duke who brought the most advanced practitioner of this art, Giovanni Ambrogio Maggiore, from Milan to Munich.[56] The rise of this craft was, like that of the three-dimensional city portraits, tied to the traffic of practical-scientific knowledge and its experts across the Alps.[57]

As with other innovative crafts, turnery was enveloped in secrecy. It required an expert hand able to master the complex interplay between movement and machinery; but turners, often protégés of the princes who employed them, shared

---

53 Klaus Maurice, *Der drechselnde Souverän:. Materialien zu einer fürstlichen Maschinenkunst* (Zurich: Ineichen, 1985). On p. 121, Maurice quotes from *Kurtzer Unterricht von der Dreh-Kunst*, published under the pseudonym Christian Drexelius but rendering the art of Johann Martin Teuber (1740). The preface summarizes the traditional frame of thinking about turnery: "The noble art of turning should prevail over other arts because its very origin is of God's hand. Let common people strive after other handcrafts, the art of turning is a work worthy only of the gods. When this was seen by the electors, princes and kings they decided to turn with the greatest of pleasure ..."

54 Quiccheberg, *Der Anfang der Museumslehre*, 256.

55 Dorothea Diemer, "Giovanni Ambrogio Maggiore und die Anfänge der Kunstdrechselei um 1570," in *Jahrbuch des Zentralinstituts für Kunstgeschichte* 1 (1985): 295–342, here p. 302.

56 Berndt Baader, *Der bayerische Renaissancehof Herzog Wilhelms V.* (Leipzig: Heitz, 1943), 265–267.

57 Georg Hoefnagel, one of the major contributors to Hogenberg's city atlas also painted at least the outside of one of the stacking boxes. See Diemer, "Giovanni Ambrogio Maggiore," 311f.

the secrets of their trade with patrons and their patrons' friends and relatives.[58] Emperor Maximilian I,[59] Duke Albrecht V,[60] William V, Maximilian I of Bavaria, and Emperor Rudolph II took an avid interest in a trade whose lathe-turned products filled beholders with awe over their beautiful, wondrous, and rare nature.[61] Turning the lathe eventually became a princely pastime and something of a craze,[62] spreading from the Wittelsbachs and Habsburgs to other courts across Europe.[63] As gifts, lathe-turned utensils became tokens of affection between rulers. Collectors, not surprisingly, sought to include lathe-turned objects in their collections. As a result, "displays of turning [became] an essential feature of princely collections by the late sixteenth century."[64] The courtly art of turnery thus operated as a "language of noble communication," as Klaus Maurice puts it in a seminal book on the subject.[65]

---

58 Maurice, *Der drechselnde Souverän*, 56 on the Dresden court and its employment of turners; Diemer, "Giovanni Ambrogio Maggiore," 307f. See also Helen Watanabe-O'Kelly, "The Management of Knowledge at the Electoral Court of Saxony in Dresden," in *Ways of Knowing: Ten Interdisciplinary Essays*, ed. Mary Lindemann (Boston: Brill, 2004), 53–65. See also *Princely Splendor. The Dresden Court 1580–1620*, ed. Dirk Sindram and Antje Scherner (Milan: The Metropolitan Museum of Art/Staatliche Kunstsammlungen Dresden, 2004). As a great courtesy, some of the trade's most advanced and cherished practitioners were sent from one court to the next to share their trade. (cf. Diemer, "Giovanni Ambrogio Maggiore"). As early as 1578, however, treatises also started to appear in print which published the knowledge of turnery with an elite audience of readers and book-buyers.

59 Emperor Maximilian I, patron of Dürer, is known to have been a lathe-turner. He also commissioned scale models. His lathe survives, see Maurice, *Der drechselnde Souverän*, 19. Maximilian owned a model of a fortified tower, the *Luginsland* Tower (Augsburg), see Antoine de Roux, Nicolas Faucherre, and Guillaume Monsaingeon, *Les plans en relief des places du roy* (Paris: A. Biro, 1989), 52, fn. 2, and Buisseret, "Modeling Cities," 125. See Martin, "Stadtmodelle," 71.

60 A goblet, possibly wrought by Albrecht V, is on display in the same hall of the Bavarian National Museum where the city models are on display today. See a photograph in Maurice, *Der drechselnde Souverän*, 59 (fig. 48).

61 These descriptive registers appear in a letter by Maria of Austria to Wilhelm V of Bavaria of January 9, 1575. See Diemer, "Giovanni Ambrogio Maggiore," 328: "den gannzen dag dar auf gefundert wies nur zu gen mues," "etwas seltzams," and "schon."

62 Diemer, "Giovanni Ambrogio Maggiore," passim.

63 Joseph Connors, "'Ars tornandi': Baroque Architecture and the Lathe," *Journal of the Warburg and Courtauld Institutes* 55 (1990): 217–236. Pamela Smith also mentions Franciscus dele Boë, Sylvius, a Dutch scientist who owned a turning machine and the Swedish general Carl Gustav Wrangel. The castle he had built for himself at the end of his life, Skokloster, contained a lathe room (finished in 1677). Cf. Smith, *The Body of the Artisan*, 236.

64 Walter S. Melion, "Love and Artisanship in Hendrick Goltzius's 'Venus, Bacchus and Ceres' of 1606," *Art History* 16 (1993): 60–94, esp. pp. 82–84.

65 Maurice, *Der drechselnde Souverän*, 16.

But what was at stake in the aristocratic display of artisanal skill? And how do such displays help us understand the related power dynamics at work in Renaissance elites' acquisition of models, objects that were likewise marvelous, geometric, and manually expert? To be sure, transformations and metamorphoses between separate realms of God's universe, between *naturalia* and *artificalia*, stood at the center of the *kunstkammer*.[66] Turnery also had moral implications, showing a prince as adverse to slothful behavior.[67] As an activity, turning the lathe was considered highly educational – teaching, among other things, the laws of mechanics – but was also deemed enjoyable and therapeutic.[68] What most attracted rulers to becoming craftsmen, however, was a sense of mastery over the material world. The ruler-turner could thus project an image of himself as not just a person who dominated his subjects, but as a creator of objects, a shaper of things of perfection and beauty. In the sixteenth century, such a notion conjured up associations with God as the first *artifex* and the mythical inventor of the trade. The art historian Walter S. Melion links this princely occupation with the perfection of the circle, reminiscent of God's creation (though oval-shaped objects stole the show above all other lathe-turned products).[69] In this symbolic context, machinery figured as "both metaphor and model."[70] According to Klaus Maurice, "[t]he machine was the model for any authoritarian order determined by a single individual" and a metaphor for the political order at large.[71]

Turning, with its multiple appeals for sixteenth-century princes and collectors, provides an intriguing lens to see how models in scale were understood. Models, like products off the lathe, aroused exceptional interest among cognoscenti. A thank-you note from Archduke Charles of Austria to his brother-in-law, William of Bavaria, exemplifies the mesmerizing possibilities these objects conveyed. Charles describes the gift as a "curious [also: rare] work of the lathe [*selzams draxlwerck*], the like of which" he had "never seen. Nor can I gauge

66 Horst Bredekamp, *The Lure of Antiquity and the Cult of the Machine* (Princeton: M. Wiener, 1995). Reviewers have remarked that this interest in transformations characterized early collections. Many of them were transformed into treasure collections in the seventeenth century. See Klaus Minges, "Die Sammlung als Medium des Weltbildes," *Kunstchronik* (April 1994): 229–235.
67 Echoing an earlier ideal, Karl Albert, Elector of Bavaria, provided instructions in 1733 for the education of his nephews, Maximilian and Clemens, in which turning is mentioned as possible leisure activity, as an alternative to playing pool. Friedrich Schmidt, *Geschichte der Erziehung der Bayerischen Wittelsbacher* (Berlin: Hofmann, 1892), 216.
68 On the last point, see Connors, "Ars tornandi," 225f.
69 Melion, "Love and Artisanship."
70 Maurice, "Der drechselnde Souverän," 140.
71 Ibid., 140f.

[*ausreiten*],"[72] he added, "how it got made." He consulted his own turner, a man named Hans, who did not tire of looking at this object and went on to discuss this marvel with his father, a turner himself. "In truth, I cannot look at it enough [myself]," admits Charles. "It seems so strange to me that it should have been turned."[73]

The object of admiration in question has not survived. But reading this letter puts us in a position to grasp one of the prominent specular responses to lathe-turned objects: incredulity. Such awe, bordering on disbelief, invited the gaze to linger, to go back, and to investigate the object's conundrum: the seeming impossibility of its existence.[74] "Turnery," to quote Joseph Connors, "is an art which delights in straining the limits of tool credibility."[75] Products off the lathe obfuscated the very conditions of their making, thus calling attention to how they were made. As a result, turned objects became the focus of intense scrutiny and the topic of extended conversations. Our letter points to a milieu of courtly curiosity, in which artisans were called in to debate the marvels of the lathe with nobles and rulers, many of whom were aspiring experts and practitioners themselves.[76] Turned objects promised to tie the recipient to the giver, and the maker to the viewer, through extensive engagement.

At first glance, such precious objects and scale models have little in common. Obviously, representations in relief are not themselves small-scale. But they do scale down the natural environment, and thus are in abundant company. Seeing *en miniature* became a modality highly treasured and often practiced among sixteenth-century elites. Thus viewed, city models took their place among other shrunken products of artisanal skill – such as miniature prints, boxwood carv-

---

72 The *Frühneuhochdeutsches Wörterbuch* lists the following explanations, among others, for *ausreiten*: "etwas ausrechnen, durch eine mathematisch-logische Operation herausfinden, feststellen" and "etw[as] der Größe e[iner] S[ache] entsprechend erkennen, ergründen, etw[as] vollständig ermessen" (*Frühneuhochdeutsches Wörterbuch*, vol. 2 (Berlin: de Gruyter, 1993), col. 1235.
73 Diemer, "Giovanni Ambrogio Maggiore, " 328 (document 4a).
74 Ibid.
75 Connors, "Ars tornandi," 223. See also Maurice, *Der drechselnde Souverän*, 8: "Unnatural forms began to take shape on the machines that were being developed, forms that could not possibly be worked by hand but could be made by machines, with multiple axes, in a crosswise, longitudinal and elliptical structure."
76 Intricately interwoven shapes, like the ivory *Contrefaitkugel* (1582), now in the Museo degli Argenti (Palazzo Pitti) in Florence were all the rage. On display in the Uffizii's *tribuna* after its opening in 1589, this gift of Duke William V of Bavaria to Duke Francesco I of Tuscany features a portrait of the giver's family hidden in one of the shapes. The *Contrefaitkugel* satisfied the demands for scopic connoisseurship and garnered the height of admiration. See Diemer, "Giovanni Ambrogio Maggiore," 296–301, 330.

ings, coral reef sculptures, coins, medals, jewelry, and the like – all refined and visually stunning *objets d'art* on display in the *kunstkammer*. These objects fed a certain microphilia. Tellingly, the sixteenth century saw the gradual introduction of the microscope into visual praxology – a scopic device whose advocates claimed that it unlocked whole new (smaller) worlds to the gaze.[77] City models, on the other hand, presented the familiar in miniature and on a different scale: by reducing the world, they made urban spaces accessible to experience in a new way.

Like lathe-turned objects, models occupied a central place in the communicative nexus between princes and experts or artisans in their service. The sixteenth century witnessed a vast literature on fortifications – a praxological discourse launched in German by the prolific artist-theoretician Albecht Dürer.[78] One of the earliest treatises in the wake of Dürer's advocates the use of models. Published in 1556, Reinhard Graf zu Solms argues that fortifying a place depended on a careful consideration of a particular site and its human resources. This treatise on warfare and fortifications unfolds in the form of a dialogue between an architect, a military expert, and a ruler. It is thus set in a textbook-like narrative frame that mirrors the courtly milieu described above: an architect, asked by a prince to study fortifications in Italy in order to adapt what he would find for his master's territory, turns to a military expert for advice. The expert then complicates the plan of using the most advanced military architecture by calling attention to the fallacy of copying fortifications not fit for the conditions of a particular locale. When the time is ripe to settle for a plan, the expert calls upon a carpenter to execute a three-dimensional model for the sake of the ruler's insight.

In this text, models occupy an elevated position. They embody the new relationship between rulers and the *experti* or artisans at court. As objects, they are said to guarantee that decision-makers, even if untrained in military architecture, will still acquire a basic understanding of how planned buildings will function. According to the author, drawings and similar two-dimensional devices are vulnerable to misrepresentations, as well as misperceptions, and therefore do not provide the secure grasp necessary for making non-experts see the utility of military structures. By contrast, three-dimensional renderings allow beholders to see the complexity of the matter while at the same time according potential patrons a pivotal role in the planning. As a result, they are not simply technical instru-

---

77 Catherine Wilson, *The Invisible World. Early Modern Philosophy and the Invention of the Microscope* (Princeton: Princeton University Press, 1995), 75.

78 Albrecht Dürer, *Etliche vnderricht zu befestigung der Stett / Schlosz / vnd flecken* (Nuremberg: n.p., 1527).

ments; they are vehicles of rhetoric and persuasion between princes (or rulers) and "professionals."[79]

For structures not yet built, models thus served the experts' need to communicate their architectural visions to rulers. In one of the benchmark treatises from the sixteenth century, Daniel Specklin's *Architectvra von Vestungen* (Architecture of Fortifications), models similarly appear at the nexus of conversations between military experts and rulers. Models work by "making evident" or, literally, by projecting a fortress before one's eyes (*vor augen stellen*).[80] The author also specifies how such models should be made: cut from pieces of limewood, glued together on a wooden base, and painted with watercolors.[81]

Models thus must be understood as strategic devices in communications between experts of various stripes and their patrons.[82] What in the sixteenth century was the domain of artisan-artists entrusted with a singularly responsible task would increasingly become an established professional expertise in the fol-

---

79 Reinhard Graf zu Solms, *Ein kürtzer Aufzug vnnd überschlag / Einen Baw anzustellen / vnd in ein Regiment vnd Ordenung zupringen / mit denen so darauff mit aller arbeit seyn wurden* (Cologne: Erben Arnold Birckman, 1556; Düsseldorf: Jacob Baethen, 1556), O2v-P3v. See Daniel Hohrath, *Die Kunst des Krieges lernen? Die Entwicklung der Militärwissenschaften zwischen Renaissance und Aufklärung* (Rastatt: Wehrgeschichtliches Museum 2003); Jan Lazardzig, *Theatermaschine und Festungsbau: Paradoxien der Wissensproduktion im 17. Jahrhundert* (Berlin: Akademie, 2007).

80 Daniel Specklin, *Architectvra von Vestungen / Wie die zu vnsern zeiten / an Stätten / Schlössern vnd Claussen / zu Wasser / Land / Bery und Thal / mit jhren Bollwercken / Caualiren / Streichen / Gräben vnd Läuffen mögen erbawet .. werden Jetzt aber auffs new ubersehen* (Strassburg: Lazarus Zetzner, 1608 [first edition, 1589; preface dated to 1599]), 5v/6r. See also, ibid., 18r/v, 19r/v (examples of Specklin's supposed communications with rulers).

81 Ibid., 6r: "alles von gutem / satten / weissen / Lindenholz / vnd ein Boden gemacht werden / in völliger grösse / Als der ganz Baw aussen vnd jnnen wird / darnach macht man widerumb ein Boden von holz / der im jungen Maßstab so dick / als der Boden / aufss Wasser ist / da man Bawen wird / darnach reißt man auff den vndern boden / wie der Baw sein soll / also reißt man den andern obern Boden auch / vnd schneid den auß / vnd leimt jhn darauff / darnach streicht man die Wasser mit einer Wasserfarben an / vnd die Böden mit jhrer farb / auch alle Gassen / Plätz / Kirchen darinn verzeichnet / Nachmalen macht man alle Bollwerck / Wähl / Mauren / Thürn / vnd streicht sie mit seim färblein an / die Wähl vnd Erden grün / ales was eckecht ist / muß sauber gemacht / woh es rund ist / gedrähet werden / die fensterle schwartz / vnd die dächlein roth angestrichen / von runden g(o)uffen knöpfflein / auff das was Thürn / Wachthäußlin / vnd ander ist gesetzt / deßgleichen außwendig der Lauff / Dachung vnd Boden / auch auffgeleimet / vnd mit farben angestrichen werden / wie an diesem durchschnit / mit Lit S im Kupfferblatt Num. 2 vngefährlichen zuersehen ist."

82 A similar point made by Isabelle Warmoes, "La collection des plans-reliefs français et la question de la représentation du relief chez les ingénieurs militaires (XVIIe–XIXe siècle)," in *Europa Miniature: Die kulturelle Bedeutung des Reliefs, 16.–21. Jahrhundert*, ed. Andreas Bürgi (Zürich: Verlag Neue Zürcher Zeitung, 2007), 115–126, here pp. 116f.

Fig. 11: Vigneux, Plan de Maastricht, ms 4 430, Bibliothèque de l'Arsenal, BnF, Paris

lowing centuries, model-making. Nowhere was this more evident than in France under King Louis XIV. During his reign (1643–1715), military experts amassed a collection of models of fortresses around France. In 1697, the year when an inventory was drawn up, the French king commanded over an impressive group of at least 144 scale models, complete with a staff to oversee their making and upkeep (fig. 11). This collection's very history parallels the political ascendancy of France over her neighbors; individual pieces were regularly updated until the Franco-Prussian War of 1870. A letter by Sébastien Le Prestre, Seigneur de Vauban (1633–1707), the most famous military architect of his time, gives ample evidence of the persuasive power he accorded models. In 1695, he asked to meet with the kingdom's controller general of finances, Claude Le Peletier, at the royal Tuileries, which housed the model of the town of Namur. Vauban hoped that the model itself could make the king's servant "realize, by *actually touching and seeing* them [*toucher au doigt et à l'oeil*], the [defensive] shortcomings of that town – there are many – and at the same time show you how [they] ... could be corrected."[83]

Two and a half centuries later, Roland Barthes coined the term "reality effect" to describe how a text, or in our case an object, effects an impression of being actual.[84] Such a concept is useful in distinguishing the models' appeal from other precious miniature objects: they were made for beholding; they were at the center of at times a secret knowledge production that involved the material world; they miniaturized the dimensions found of the known landscape; they were meant, above all, for the ruler and his helpers. In short, they were "marvelous," even if, by the seventeenth century, they had become decidedly less "rare." In numerous

---

83 Warmoes, *Musée*, 8; Roux et al., *Les plans*, 76: "Il y a un relief de Namur dans les Tuileries. Je vous demanderai la complaisance de le venir voir avec moi. Je vous ferai toucher au doigt et à l'oeil tous les défauts de cette place, qui sont en bon nombre, et à même temps apercevoir de quelle manière se pouvait corriger celui qu'on m'impute;
et vous verrez qu'il n'était corrigible qu'à de très grosses conditions de temps et de dépense. Ils se sont aperçus de celui-là parce que c'est celui par où ils ont été serrés de plus près. Mais il y en a bien d'autres, qui passent leurs connaissances, dont ils ne se sont pas aperçus. La plupart des gens répètent comme des perroquets ce qu'ils ont entendu dire à des demi-savants qui, n'ayant que des connaissances imparfaites, raisonnent le plus souvent de travers ... Engagez Mesgrigny et Filley de venir, cet hiver, à Paris et vous verrez de belles et savantes conférences, la vue sur le relief. Apparemment que M. le maréchal de Bouffles y sera aussi, qui pourra en prendre sa part; et cela vaudra bien la peine de l'aller voir." (October 6, 1695) On the 1697-inventory, see Nicolas Faucherre and Antoine de Roux, "Les plans en relief de Louis XIV, des outils de travail pour la construction de la frontière," in *Actes du colloque international sur les plans-reliefs*, 101–105. On the history of the collection, see Warmoes, "La collection des plans-reliefs français," 115–126.
84 Roland Barthes, "L'effet de réel," in *Œuvres complètes*, ed. Eric Marty, vol. 3 (Paris: Seuil, 2002), 25–32.

solicitations, Gottfried Wilhelm Leibniz (1646–1716) appealed to rulers to fund academic societies with access to "iconothecae ([that is] collections of engravings, plans, models, and paintings)" combined with libraries, gardens and similar collections.[85] His advocacy of such institutions of learning is driven by a theory of perception in which visual learning, the vibrant presence of things, and an ultimately God-like gaze further the human acquisition of knowledge: "although we have within us ideas of things remote from the senses, we nevertheless cannot pin down or devote attention to the knowledge of these things unless certain sensible marks approach them, such as names, characters, representations, analogies, models, links, and effects."[86] Such a concept can be traced back, among other things, to the pioneering work of sixteenth-century model-makers, and its eager reception (and subsidizing) by Europe's rulers.

The Politics of Urbanism

Importantly, models executed in scale thus make urban space experiential in a particular fashion. Unlike actual cities, models are devoid of what makes a city a city, the imprint of human life and the movement of people through urban space. To quote an ancient distinction, recently taken up by Richard Kagan, models show the city as *urbs*, from the Latin word for town (referring to the city's built environment), and not as *civitas*, the urban community.[87] Space as expressed in urban models typically drowns out the multitude of social relations encoded in actual cityscapes: ownership of buildings or lots, for instance, or areas defined

85 Gottfried Wilhelm Leibniz, "Denkschrift II," in *Leibniz und seine Akademie: Ausgewählte Quellen zur Geschichte der Berliner Sozietät der Wissenschaften*, ed. Hans-Stephan Brather (Berlin: Akademie der Wissenschaften, 1990), 77: "Zu allen diesen Wißenschafften dienen Bibliotheken, Iconothecae (oder Collectanea von Kupferstücken, Rissen, Bildungen, und Gemählden), Kunst- und Raritäten-Kammern, Zeug- und Rüst-Häuser, Gärten vieler Art, auch Thier-Behältnisse, und die grossen Wercke der Natur und Kunst selbsten."

86 Gottfried Wilhelm Leibniz, "Examen Religionis Christianae (Systema Theologicum)," in *Philosophische Schriften*, ed. Leibniz-Forschungsstelle der Universität Münster, vol. 4, C (Berlin: Akademie, 1999), 2387 (1686): "etiamsi ideas rerum a sensibus remotarum intus habeamus, non posse nos tamen in iis cogitationem defigere atque immorari cum attentione, nisi notae quaedam sensibiles accedant, ut vocabula, characteres, repraesentationes, similtudines, exempla, connexa, effectus." I thank Norma Goethe for having called my attention to this passage and her translation. See Horst Bredekamp, *Die Fenster der Monade: Gottfried Wilhelm Leibniz' Theater der Natur und Kunst* (Berlin: Akademie, 2004).

87 Richard L. Kagan, "*Urbs* and *Civitas* in Sixteenth- and Seventeenth-Century Spain," in *Envisioning the City*, ed. David Buisseret (Chicago: University of Chicago Press, 1998), 75- 107.

by specific human activities (the market, the court, the house, or the garden) or the work-related topography of the urban environment where different trades occupied different sections. The particular abstraction at play in city models thus veils the social makeup of urban spaces, turning them into a realm of pure representation. Devoid of human interaction and social signification, the city as model presents itself as an instrument of perception. Three-dimensional urban portraits are "conceptualized space," to quote Henri Lefebvre, quite distinct from the messiness of lived space.[88]

Sandtner's models were related to other projects of princely representation in Bavaria. Philip Apian's pioneering map of Bavaria (drawn between 1556 and 1558/1568) pursued a similar agenda of measuring and mapping the duke's territory.[89] (In the Bavarian *kunstkammer*, both of these seminal undertakings, the map of the duchy and the urban *maquettes* were exhibited in close proximity.[90]) Viewed in this context, the city models commissioned by Duke Albrecht V manifested a grand political project, the transformation of the duchy of Bavaria into a politically and religiously unified territory.[91] As Renate Eikelmann puts it, these endeavors "expressed the changed relationship which the ruler now had with his [lands]." For the first time, "these models enabled the unification of the Bavarian duchies to be registered with their material qualities by means of the new scientific methods of surveying."[92] Apian's and Sandtner's projects celebrated not only the political unity of Bavaria since 1505/1506, but also showcased the technologi-

88 Henri Lefebvre, *The Production of Space*, trans. Donald Nicholson-Smith (Oxford: Blackwell, 1991), 38.

89 Max Georg Zimmermann, *Die bildenden Künste am Hof Herzog Albrecht's V. von Bayern* (Strassburg: Heitz, 1895), 59–61; Reitzenstein, *Die alte bairische Stadt*, 5. Apian received the commission in 1556. He finished the original, monumental in size, in 1563, and published a smaller version in 1568. The gallery of maps in the Vatican and the Map Room in the Palazzo Ducale (or, as it is known today, Palazzo Vecchio) in Florence are different but comparable projects that intertwine innovative knowledge production, here with regard to mapping, and particular visions of rulership.

90 Seelig, "The Munich *Kunstkammer*," 84.

91 Cf. Ulrike Strasser, *State of Virginity: Gender, Religion, and Politics in an Early Modern Catholic State* (Ann Arbor: University of Michigan Press, 2004).

92 Renate Eikelmann, *Bayerisches Nationalmuseum: Handbook of the Art and Cultural History Collections* (Munich: Bayerisches Nationalmuseum, s.a.), 130f. The document which regulated succession for the duchy and mandated territorial unity for subsequent generations went back to 1506. This so-called *Primogeniturvertrag* was challenged briefly by the claims of Duke Ernst in 1554, however, at the beginning of Albrecht V's reign. One must suspect, therefore, that these conflicts were much on people's minds. Cf. Max Spindler, ed., *Handbuch der bayerischen Geschichte*, vol. 2 (Munich: Beck, 1967), 336.

cal advance of the new state and what those technologies made possible: a vision of ruler-centered statehood.

The models commissioned by Albrecht V were just one of his many efforts to advance the Duchy of Bavaria's cause. Above all, this grand project necessitated the creation of a ducal residence or capital city – a Munich that would be able to mirror his lineage's claims to political and aristocratic preeminence among Catholic rulers in the empire and beyond. Albrecht and the ducal administration therefore sought to transform the duchy's political center from a medieval town into a ducal residence.[93] In Munich, where the models were (and are) exhibited, the duke conspicuously undermined the magistrates' right to govern the city, seeking to take control of urban affairs. Albrecht also took steps to ensure a religiously uniform urban society. He forced non-Catholic residents to leave, among them some of the wealthiest burghers.[94] In 1567 – at a time when Quiccheberg had published his signature treatise, the building to house the ducal collection was built, and Sandtner was about to finish his first model, the duke demanded that the city employ undercover informers to spy on Protestant activities. Citizen status and work for the city had to be limited to people known to be avowed Catholics. Between 1569 and 1571, thirty-eight persons were expelled from the city for their Protestant leanings, exits prompted by the duke's intervention.[95] Increasingly, the ducal administration thus engaged in measures to enforce religious conformity among its subjects. Even the ducal cartographer and surveyor, the eminent Apian, was forced to leave the University of Ingolstadt on account of his religious beliefs.[96] Recipients of salaries from the ducal coffers were easy targets. In 1575, for instance, Sandtner was exhorted to stay with "the old and true Catholic religion" before he received payment of a yearly pension of 50 florins.

---

93 Critics have portrayed the dukes of Counter-Reformation Bavaria in often contradictory ways, as paragons of religious piety characteristic of the confessional state as well as art lovers who wrecked the duchy's finances through their lavish support for various arts, and the trail of enormous debts that their commissions and collectomania left behind. A focus on objects like Sandtner's city models may enable us to see how these two developments are in fact closely related.

94 Hans-Joachim Hecker, "Um Glaube und Recht: Die 'fürstliche' Stadt 1505 bis 1561," in *Geschichte der Stadt München*, 159f.

95 Cf. Strasser, *State of Virginity*, 17.

96 According to an "Instruction" about Albrecht's V education from 1541, Apian was one of the prince's teachers: "Dieweil es ain kurtzweilig Ding ist, auch sonnderlichn ainem fürsten nützlich unnd wol ansteet der Cosmographia unnd Geographia ainen verstanndt zu haben, solle der Apianus alle tag den Jungen Herrn Jn disen khunsten, auch rechnen unnd anderm ain stund lernen." Quoted from Schmidt, *Geschichte der Erziehung*, 6.

Unlike Apian, who left Bavaria for the University of Tübingen, Sandtner seems to have complied; the sum was paid.[97]

In this political, religious, and cultural context, urbanism emerged as an important vehicle for the new state. The state's power to reconfigure the built space became manifest in momentous construction projects. Duke William V, called the Pious, continued his father's endeavors, erecting buildings in the heart of Munich the likes of which had not been seen in the empire. Most notable was the palatial Collegium, home of the Jesuit Order. In its urbanistic dialogue with the ducal quarters to the northeast, it epitomized the alliance of secular power with early modern Catholicism. In turn, the façade of the Collegium's church, St. Michael, consecrated in 1597, features statues of Bavarian dukes, a veritable genealogical tree, including the prominently placed sculptures of Albrecht and William, shown with a large architectural model of the church (St. Michael became the burial place for the Bavarian House of Wittelsbach). To make way for the duke's ambitious construction, eighty-seven houses were razed.[98]

In this changing urban environment, modeled urban spaces had to be updated in order to maintain their claim on authenticity. For these city models could only fulfill their functions – as a technology of power, as a planning device, or as a quasi-cinematic tool – if they avoided discrepancies of reference. Of the models now on display in the Bavarian National Museum, only Munich, where the dukes had their residence, was reworked, at least once, probably in the early seventeenth century (fig. 10). The new fortifications, additions to the palace, and the Jesuit Collegium were updated – buildings that testified to the dukes' grand remodeling of their territory's seat of power.[99] That the other models were not altered likely reflects a related truth: that the impulse that led to the commissioning of the models – the impulse to visualize by means of a visual synecdoche a whole land – came to fruition most prominently in Munich. This formation of a politically and religiously united territory was riddled with complications, if not contradictions. Yet its culmination, if not fulfillment, were the models with their clean-cut abstraction from the social and legal realities of the day.

Bavaria's claim to political distinction found its architectural expression in, among other projects, the *kunstkammer* built near the Munich *Residenz* between 1563 and 1567 (and, since 1807, referred to as the *Münze* or Royal Mint). This was

---

97 Reitzenstein, *Die alte bairische Stadt*, 8: "d(er) alten wahren Catholischen Religion."

98 Reinhard Heydenreuther, "Der Magistrat als Befehlsempfänger: Die Disziplinierung der Stadtobrigkeit 1579 bis 1651," in *Geschichte der Stadt München*, ed. Richard Bauer (Munich: Beck, 1992), 205.

99 Eikelmann, *Bayerisches Nationalmuseum*, 131.

one of the first buildings erected in Europe to house a cabinet of curiosities or a museum – a design inspired by Quiccheberg, the *kunstkammer*'s ideologue. Executed by the architect Wilhelm Egkel, his was a Renaissance building – Munich's first – of four wings that enclosed an inner courtyard surrounded by three arcaded stories. The ground floor was reserved for the ducal stables while the large-windowed, sunny uppermost floor, visible on Sandtner's model of Munich, must have housed the dukes' collection.[100] The *kunstkammer* is where the city models were shown to a select few and where Quiccheberg's commanding vision of a universal collection, on display in an appropriate structure, became at least a partial reality. According to Arthur MacGregor, the objects were not locked away in cases or cupboards as in many contemporaneous cabinets of curiosities but rather exhibited openly, to "generate the utmost visual effect." If we follow his reconstruction, the models could be seen as an ensemble at the building's south-western corner, at the meeting point of two corridors, in close proximity to astronomical and other instruments. The visitors – whether aristocrats, scholars, or artists – who were given access to the collection upon request, could thus view the model of Munich and compare it to the city spread out before the windows (fig. 10).[101]

In his treatise, Quiccheberg typically describes the cabinet as a *theatrum*, a term that aptly captures the various layers of meaning at play in the production and reception of city models and similar objects.[102] At the time, *theatrum*, with its obvious reference to the stage, associated the world in its entirety. It gestures toward the nexus of microcosm and macrocosm, but it also designates the world as a moral stage for affects, vices, and virtures. Nowhere else but in the theatre, as Frances Yates contends, could the various, often contradictory Renaissance interests in the past and in the present, in antiquity and Christianity, be accommodated.[103]

100 The Antiquarium, also built by Egkel, followed between 1569 and 1571 to house the duke's collection of antiques – a building that, among other features, showed 102 painted vedute of places in Bavaria.

101 Arthur MacGregor, "Die besonderen Eigenschaften der 'Kunstkammer,'" in *Macrocosmos in Microcosmo*, 61–106, here pp. 65–70; Seelig, "The Munich *Kunstkammer*," 77. Among the men whose visits to the collection are testified are Abraham Ortelius, Georg Hoefnagel, Prospero Visconti, Duke Augustus the Younger of Braunschweig-Lüneburg.

102 On the title page, the word "theatri" sticks out. It is rendered in capital letters in a large font (see *Der Anfang der Museumslehre*, 35). According to Quiccheberg, the treatise was a preliminary work and would lead to a *theatrum sapientiae*, a "theatre of wisdom," which he never wrote.

103 Frances A. Yates, *Theatre of the World* (Chicago: University of Chicago Press, 1969); Lina Bolzoni, "Das Sammeln und die ars memoriae," in *Macrocosmos in Microcosmo*, 129–168; Paula

Significantly, the term *theatrum* connects Quiccheberg's treatise to other prestigious publishing projects: Theodor Zwinger's *Theatrum vitae humanae* (1565),[104] an enormous compendium of all human knowledge; Abraham Ortelius's groundbreaking *Theatrum orbis terrarum*, the first world atlas, published in 1570; the *Civitates orbis terrarum* – Braun's comprehensive city atlas, conceived as an urban companion piece to Ortelius;[105] and Jacques Besson's *Theatrum instrumentorum et machinarum* of 1578, a pioneering publication on engineering as well as the lathe.[106] Quiccheberg distinguishes his own from other large projects of his time, however, by taking their authors to task for using *theatrum* metaphorically. Their theatres were imagined, he contends; his, in contrast, evokes the notion of actual spaces with actual material objects.[107] In the fully sculpted object lies one of the dividing lines for Quiccheberg between a museum or *theatrum* in the metaphorical sense of the word and one in the true sense. Laying claim to both universality and plasticity nevertheless had a price: when it came to representing cities, his vision for the *theatrum* could only be realized through miniaturization. If not, one would have to deal with a museum of the world in the impracticable full scale, "the scale of *a mile to the mile*," to quote Lewis Carroll – whose fictional map in *Sylvie and Bruno Concluded* inspired Jorge Luis Borges's *On Exactitude in Science* (Del rigor en la ciencia), a short text about an empire whose cartographers produced the perfect but ultimately useless map in a size that equaled that of the empire itself.[108]

The vast horizon of Munich's *theatrum* is revealed, among other things, by the fact that the collection of cities on display in Munich's *kunstkammer* also

Findlen, "Die Zeit vor dem Laboratorium: Die Museen und der Bereich der Wissenschaft 1550–1750, ibid., 191–207, here p. 193.

104 Roth, *Der Anfang der Museumslehre*, 9, 15, 16, 272f. Zwinger's text is one of the few mentioned in Quiccheberg's own (p. 108). Zwinger and Quiccheberg knew each other since 1548 (p. 5).

105 The title varies. It also appeared as *Theatrum orbis civitatum*. At any rate, Braun uses the descriptor *theatrum* in the preface to the third volume (1581): "in diesem vnserm Theatro" (Braun, *Beschreibung*, vol. 3, (*)v.).

106 Maurice, *Der drechselnde Souverän*, 104 (figs. 7 and 8).

107 Quiccheberg, *Der Anfang der Museumslehre*, 106–109. One may think here of the anatomical theatre. Note that while in Basel he might have connected with the famous anatomist Felix Platter, cf. ibid., pp. 14f, 273. For Quiccheberg, who had travelled extensively in Italy, Giulio Camillo's theatre of memory provided an important model, ibid., 9f, 12, 25–34, 230, 241, 301f, and 111.

108 Lewis Carroll, *Sylvie and Bruno Concluded* in *The Complete Works* (London: The Nonesuch Library, 1939), 556 (emphasis in the original); Jorge Luis Borges, "Del rigor en la ciencia" (*El Hacedor*) in *Obras Completas*, vol. 2 (Barcelona: Emecé, 1989), 225.

included a model of Jerusalem.[109] Though unsigned, it was executed with the same finesse and on a scale similar to the other models. This Bavarian Jerusalem bears little resemblance to its actual topography, presenting a mere fantasy of the Holy City, a vaguely Near Eastern urban scenario with flat roofs. For the Munich court, a representation of Jerusalem in scale did not have to conform with the standard of verisimilitude imposed by the proximity of the seats of government rendered in relief to Munich. But the model enables the viewer a glimpse of a geographically distant and symbolically central location for Catholic Christians. The worldly and heavenly Jerusalem had anchored many medieval *mappae mundi*.[110] In Munich, it also enhanced the ducal collection on a temporal level; the model of Jerusalem pointed to Christian history and future salvation. The model's two palaces suggest that we are looking at the Holy City during the time of Christ, since the second temple is still intact and Herod's palace appears on an adjacent hill. In other words, the modeled Jerusalem provided a full-scale view of a past that had tremendous significance for the Christian believer and beholder.[111]

The princely collection was thus anything but an ornamental byproduct of grand political ambitions. As Paula Findlen reminds us, early modern cabinets of curiosities contained not only objects to gaze and marvel at; they were objects whose value lay in their usefulness.[112] The Munich *kunstkammer* lay at the very heart of Albrecht's self-fashioning as a Catholic ruler in the empire.[113] Regarding courtly cultivation of the arts, the dukes of Bavaria competed with the foremost rulers of Europe, emulating, among others, the Medici in their patronage.[114] The

109 The modelmaker was Lorenz Seelig, see Seelig, "The Munich *Kunstkammer*," 76–89 and *Macrocosmos in Microcosmo*, 68f. Documents testify that Sandtner built a model of Rhodes at the end of his life of which there are no further traces. (Reitzenstein, *Die alte bairische Stadt*, 10.) See above for the model of Rhodes, 1521.

110 Birgit Hahn-Woernle, *Die Ebstorfer Weltkarte* (Ebstorf: Kloster Ebstorf, 1987).

111 Reconstructions of ancient cities were also part of Georg Braun's multi-volume city atlas, a printing venture contemporary with the Bavarian collection of models (1572–1618). See, for instance, different reconstructions of the historic Jerusalem (i, 53; ii, 54; iv, 58/59) of which the one in the first volume has some resemblance to the Munich model. Ancient Rome (ii, 49; iv, 54/55) and Ostia (iv, 53) were also included. Georg Braun, *Beschreibung*.

112 Findlen, "Die Zeit vor dem Laboratorium," 195.

113 In the words of Uta Lindgren with regard to Duke Albrecht V: "afin d'avoir une image de sa souveraineté et la connaissance exacte de son pays, les représentations – cartes et plans-reliefs – revêtaient une importance primordiale." Uta Lindgren, "Les plans-reliefs de Bavière au XVIe siècle," in *Actes du colloque international sur les plans-reliefs au passé et au présent*, ed. André Corvisier (Paris: SEDES, 1993), 167–173, here p. 169.

114 While Albrecht V employed agents to buy ancient coins, gems, and sculptures for the ducal collection, Wilhelm V travelled himself to Italy, a grand tour *avant la lettre*, among other things,

two meanings of *repraesentatio*, that of political representation and that of rendition (in this case scientific), come together, however uneasily, in these objects

Approaching the semantics of city models means to make these three-dimensional portraits – with which many readers will be familiar – look a little less familiar. We have explored why such objects were produced and how they were understood in the sixteenth-century contexts for which they were created. In Munich's *kunstkammer*, the Bavarian cities *en miniature* functioned as a multiform technology of power for the ruler in the newly configured confessional state. Models such as these, with their uniform aesthetic code, served as planning devices, though we know little about their impact. We need not underestimate, however, the degree to which these same objects were able to generate viewing pleasure. The use of various materials, paints, and elaborate techniques to render sites exceeded what was called for in terms of practical utility. Relief models were therefore artifacts whose making positioned them as luxurious competitors in urban perspectivism. As fancy objects, they were "princely toys,"[115] apt to reflect on the authority of the ruler, the ruler as *artifex* and commander of his own realm. But they were also objects that called attention to the complicated processes that went into their making.

* * *

Early modern city models, I have argued, not only reflect but also shape relations between rulers and their subjects. How much so becomes evident when we set aside modeled spaces for the moment and approach sovereignty through the lens of political iconography.

In the frontispiece to Thomas Hobbes's *Leviathan* (1651), this crucible of political philosophy, the ruler towers over a terrain of fields, fortresses, settlements, and churches, minute in scale by comparison to his majestic body. This well-ordered, well-tilled, people-less land of plenty is an ideal space. Its inhabitants compose the king's garb, marking this image as a visual allegory of the body politic (fig. 12).

In a monograph on this iconic representation of the polity, Horst Bredekamp sees the difference in size between the king and the land as a sign of the ruler's elevated position (whose stature is larger than the sum of the individuals that

---

to buy relics. See Sigmund Riezler, "Albrecht V.," in *Allgemeine Deutsche Biographie*, vol. i [1875] (reprint: Leipzig: Duncker & Humblot, 1967), 234- 237, here p. 237; id., "Wilhelm V.," ibid., vol. 42 [1897] (reprint: Leipzig: Duncker & Humblot, 1971), 717–723.

115 Jean Meyer, "Le concept de plans-reliefs sous Louis XIV," in *Actes du colloque international sur les plans-reliefs au passé et au présent*, ed. André Corvisier (Paris: SEDES, 1993), 11–13.

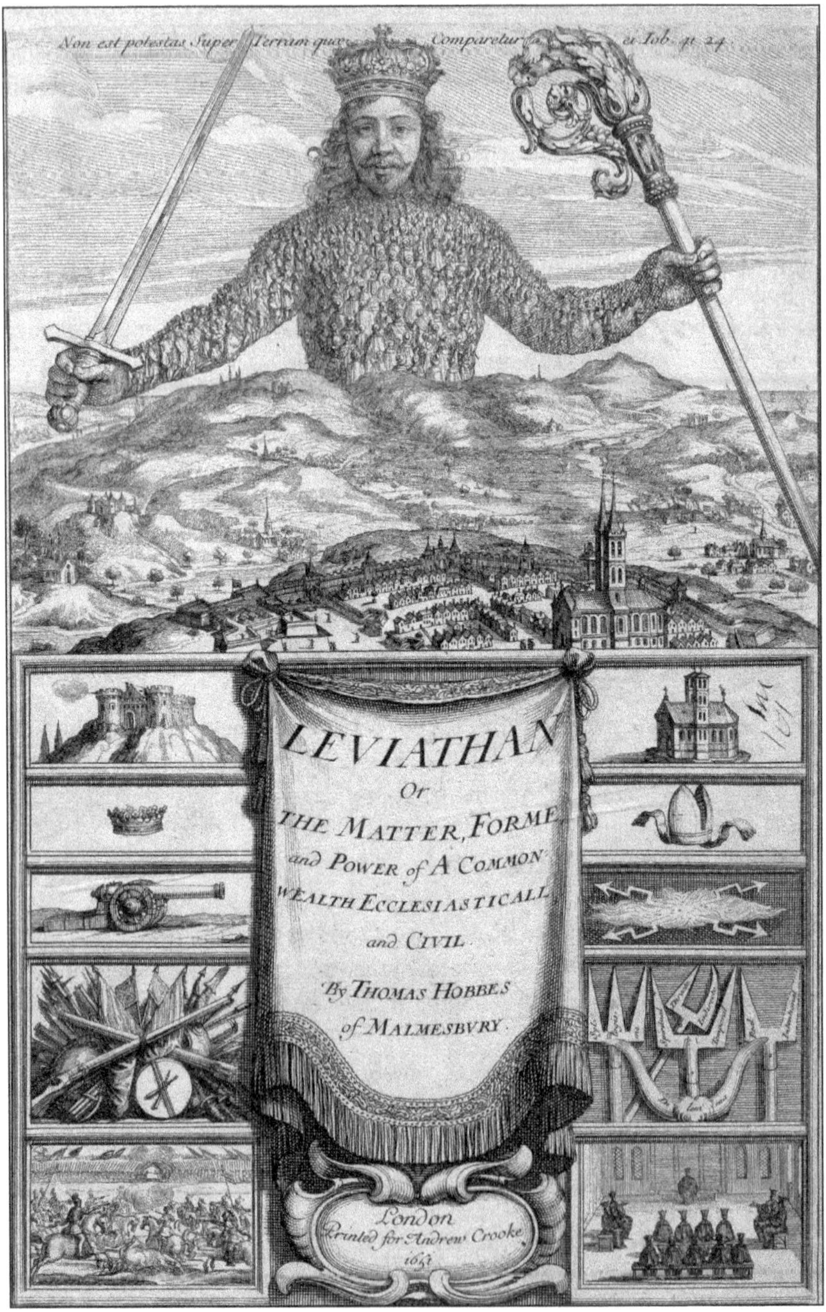

Fig. 12: Thomas Hobbes, Leviathan, 1651, frontispiece (Abraham Bosse?), © Trustees of the British Museum

comprise him).[116] If the sovereign is indeed a giant, as the treatise's title with its reference to a biblical monster suggests, then the scene in the foreground, the *Weltlandschaft*, represents the world as is, or rather as it could be if we only follow the treatise's vision: a flourishing and peaceful country where man is protected from his fellow man due to the sovereign's presence. This imagistic think-piece thus models socio-political relations regulated by scale, as do the city sculptures that were the topic of this chapter. (Photographs of a later age that depict political figures towering over three-dimensional renderings of buildings yet unbuilt seem to communicate similar, though more mundane, messages about a ruler's mastery over the social world via his mastery over scaled down spaces.)

What the rebus-like image that opens *Leviathan* has us imagine, in other words, are relations between subjects, the environs, and the ruler. It is telling therefore that in different versions of the same piece, the scenarios of subjection and empowerment vary in their affective valence, as a comparison of the treatise's early modern editions shows. Some frontispieces portray the king less as a menacing avenger than as a kind father.[117]

The manifold readings this image (and the treatise it inaugurates) invites revolve primarily around the sense of sight – the sense that Hobbes was keenly interested in: the political gaze, the gaze of foresight, and the fearful gaze that by "deterring destruction" holds violence among humans at bay.[118] "[T]here has been no philosopher or theorist of state before or since who so emphatically pursued visual strategies as core political theory," Bredekamp posits.[119] In fact, it is through the gaze that the Hobbesian ruler and his subjects bond. Whereas the peace that supposedly emerges from this bond is imagined to benefit the polity as a whole, the contract of everybody with everybody does not result in a universal gaze. As the famous image of 1651 has it, surveying the terrain is the sovereign's privilege, the sovereign gaze. Yet interestingly enough, there are different versions even as regards this crucial element. In a contemporary manuscript version of *Leviathan* the ruler's garb is made up of people who look out at the viewer.[120]

116 Horst Bredekamp, *Thomas Hobbes visuelle Strategien: Der Leviathan, Urbild des modernen Staates: Werkillustrationen und Portraits* (Berlin: Akademie, 1999); id., "Thomas Hobbes's Visual Strategies," in *The Cambridge Companion to Hobbes's 'Leviathan'*, ed. Patricia Springborg (Cambridge: Cambridge University Press, 2007), 29–60; id., "Staat," *Handbuch der politischen Ikonographie*, ed. Uwe Fleckner, Martin Warnke, and Hendrik Ziegler, vol. 2 (Munich: Beck, 2011), 373–380.

117 Bredekamp, *Thomas Hobbes visuelle Strategien*, 18–31.

118 Bredekamp, "Thomas Hobbes's Visual Strategies," 29.

119 Bredekamp, ibid., 30.

120 Bredekamp, *Thomas Hobbes visuelle Strategien*, 36–39.

Fig. 13: Anonymous, "The Burden of Nuremberg's Government," late sixteenth century, Stadtbibliothek Nuremberg, Grafikkasten Handzeichnungen groß, Nor. K. 6143

Whoever designed this intricate frontispiece must have done so in close collaboration with Hobbes. And if the image's author is indeed, as Bredekamp proposes, Abraham Bosse – an artist familiar with military themes and fortificatory science – it is even more likely that modeled spaces form an important visual intertext for gauging its meaning.[121]

A form of rule different from monarchic statehood is conjured up in a symbolic representation of Nuremberg's government from the late sixteenth century. Governing a free imperial city is captured here as a difficult balancing act with a seated senior magistrate carrying the modeled city (clearly recognizable as Nuremberg) as a burden on his shoulders, supported by a younger patrician to his right while a third is waiting in close proximity. The fall and destruction of Rome and Troy are cited in the accompanying text to remind the viewer that "vanity, self-interest, and counsel by the young" (*Hoffart Eigennutz vnnd Junger Rhat*) lead to disaster whereas perpetuating "severe punishment and good words" (*Hartte*

121 Bredekamp, *Thomas Hobbes visuelle Strategien*, 39–52. Bredekamp's attribution has largely been followed, see his "Thomas Hobbes's Visual Strategies," 52.

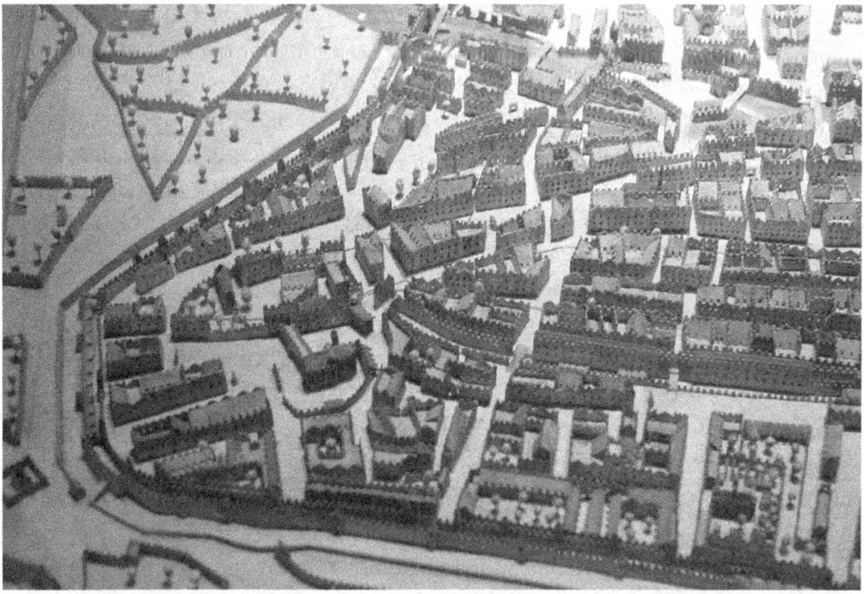

Fig. 14: Hans Sebald Behaim, Model of Nuremberg, 1540, 68.1 × 52.8 cm, detail (original in the Bavarian National Museum, Munich; copy by Sigmund Pfreundtner and Alfred Baumann, 1941/42), Stadtmuseum Fembohaus, Nuremberg (Photo: Author)

straf und gutewort) will secure the city's future prosperity. From Nuremberg, some of the earliest known city models survive or are known to have existed, predating this visual allegory of the magistrates' grip on the republic (fig. 13).

Whereas the Dukes of Bavaria initially allowed interested parties to visit their collection and the city models on display in Munich's *kunstkammer* in the spirit of aristocratic display, city councils like Nuremberg's showed themselves concerned with access to the information contained in three models that came into existence around 1540 – a time when new fortifications were planned for the city.[122] The councilors required from their makers – painters, printers, turners, carpenters, instrument-makers, and sculptors are among the professions known to have

122 Martin, "Stadtmodelle," 66–69. See also entry on Hans Beheim in *Allgemeines Künstler-Lexikon*, ed. Günter Meißner, vol. 8 (Munich: Saur, 1994), 294. The following entry from records of the council is quoted in this entry when Hans Beheim received 40 fl. for his product: "Hanns Behaim, maler, von wegen der Conterfectur Nürmberg, auf ein prêt gesetzt, mit allen heusern, gassen und anderem." The model was signed with the monogram HP. Whether the artist is identical with the painter by the same name (who specialized in miniature formats) is an open question.

executed such models in the sixteenth century – that they would not copy their design; the Nuremberg council thus strove to have control over the distribution of the spatial knowledge deemed sensitive to the city's security (fig. 14).

The sovereign's gaze as heralded by *Leviathan* looked different from beyond his realm's borders. A polemical image of Netherlandish origin depicts King Louis XIV of France and recasts this same gaze as a greedy, usurping one. In this composite image in the tradition of *Leviathan*, the absence of a subject and adulatory populace becomes a symbol of the vain glory of a ruler. This man of stone, fired up by devilish councilors (see the scene represented on the table cloth), no longer serves or protects a people. His military conquests – he has already laid one of his hands on yet another modeled place – leave him no other choice but to fortify his corporeal polity and rely on the protection offered by fortifications (fig. 15).

If we wish to seek modern examples of this tradition of using modeled places to figure the excessive violence of state power, we can see a potent image in Rudolf Schlichter's "Blind Power" (*Blinde Macht*) (fig. 16). The utterly destructive and ultimately self-destructive force of the modern state and war machine is given allegorical force in this prophetic image, a flaming indictment of National Socialism before the beginning of World War II from within Germany.[123] Painted in 1937, the year when several of Schlichter's works became part of the touring exhibit on "degenerate art," the canvas has a blind goliath in ancient military garb and encrusted with allegorical figures of deadly passions walk toward an abyss, leaving behind a people-less apocalyptic landscape of burning cities and devastation.

In this image, the artist draws on a wealth of iconographic sources reaching back among other inspirations to ancient Rome, the German Renaissance (Dürer, Altdorfer, Cranach), composite imagery in the tradition of the *Leviathan*-frontispiece, Goya's imagistic inventions, and traveling panoramas of natural disasters the artist encountered when growing up. It is a poignant meditation on the dangers of entrusting a sovereign with supreme power. What if the sovereign lacks sight or restraint? As in the polemical visual commentary on King Louis XIV, there are no people to be seen on this canvas. Only the traces of destruction attest to their former presence. Have the body politic and the ruler become one? Or has the people become victim to the ruler's insatiable destructive frenzy? Whatever the answer, this phantasmagorical goliath who towers above the world as if it were a model is running amok as an avatar of destructive rage.

123 Günter Metken, *Rudolf Schlichter: Blinde Macht: Eine Allegorie der Zerstörung* (Frankfurt am Main: Fischer, 1990).

Fig. 15: Anononymous, "L'habit usurpé," late seventeenth century, Koninklijke Bibliotheek, The Hague

Fig. 16: Rudolf Schlichter, “Blinde Macht” (Blind Power), 1937

Chapter Four

The problem with talking about models in our own era is, I posit, that models are replicas. They are, in other words, not the real thing; therefore models do not warrant our attention or critical gaze, or so the reasoning might go. They are considered toys, not in the sixteenth-century Bavarian sense of an urbanistic and educational tool for princes, but as a mere trifle, appropriate at best for children. "It is the simulacrum that is the truth," is the epigraph that Jean Baudrillard once attributed to a book in the Old Testament in order to direct our attention to "the real" as a strategy – the real in quotation marks, in which simulacra reign supreme. As Baudrillard has it, today simulacra no longer reference the real. Yet the history of making models and the history of building ruins – the two themes that intersect in the chapter that follows – tell the story of how these vehicles of "the real" require particular references in order to be meaningful.[1]

In the eighteenth century, history became an ever more potent intellectual force, relied upon in Europe's increasingly elaborate efforts to grasp what seemed to be an increasingly complex world. Both built ruins and models, as we will see, contributed to History's rise. Marveling at these vehicles' realism was part of the city model, as it emerged in the Renaissance. But now verisimilitude as a standard began to be introduced into new areas, namely into replicating the time-worn monuments of the past. The power of History as well as power in history was perhaps nowhere more apparent than at the scene of destruction, the always-looming underside of an eighteenth-century belief in historical progress. In the age of reason, intense debates focused on the question of why empires, especially the Roman Empire, had declined. In this sense, modeled or built destruction regularly touched on the theme of power.

But where history became overtly produced, its artifice had to disappear. After all, the copy that is best is the one that does not communicate its own status as a copy. When the exploration of the world as historical established itself more firmly in the nineteenth century, these artifacts that had fed the historical imagination of previous generations were relegated to the attic of the history of History. One may detect a certain anxiety about History's own status in these efforts to make its constructedness disappear from view. Even "the most progressive thinkers of the age could not ... afford the luxury of conceiving historical knowledge in general as a problem," writes Hayden White.[2] *Amidst these urgent debates about the authentic past, it is easy to forget the actual past. So let us immerse ourselves in the late eighteenth-century, let us wander in the gardens, let us experience the artifice of their built ruins and try to comprehend the power of artificiality.*

---

1 Jean Baudrillard, *Simulacres et simulation* (Paris: Galliée, 1981).

2 Hayden White, "The Irrational and the Problem of Historical Knowledge in the Enlightenment," in *Irrationalism in the Eighteenth Century*, ed. Harold E. Pagliaro (Cleveland, OH: Press of Case Western Reserve University, 1972), 303–321, here p. 318.

Schwetzingen's Built Ruins

> "How is a ruined child different from a ruined castle?" (Thomasina to Septimus)
> Tom Stoppard, *Arcadia* (1993)[1]

In December of 1764, a young Englishman visited the recently completed Villa Albani in Rome, eager to study its superb collection of antiquities.[2] "I observed in the garden which is but small an artificial ruin" of a temple, he noted in his diary: "Small and without taste in itself, it appears ridiculous in Rome. Perhaps all imitations of this [artificial] kind are ill judged."[3] This aside, by the traveler who would author *The History of the Decline and Fall of the Roman Empire* (1776–1788), contrasts conspicuously with the enthusiasm the same Edward Gibbon heaped on ruinous remains of actual ancient sites during his grand tour. In his writings, Gibbon recorded a vision of the past brought to life by the sight of the city's many ruins – an epiphany that inspired, or so Gibbon claimed retrospectively, one of the most celebrated modern ruminations about the ancient past.[4] The eighteenth century, as we will see, witnessed an unprecedented popularity of ruins across

1 Tom Stoppard, *Plays Five: Arcadia, The Real Thing, Night & Day, Indian Ink, Hapgood* (London: Faber and Faber, 1999), 21.

2 Johann Joachim Winckelmann, the German art critic, arrived in 1765 to catalogue the collection that would profoundly shape his own influential ideas about the art of the ancients.

3 *Gibbon's Journey from Geneva to Rome: His Journal from 20 April to 2 October 1764*, ed. Georges A. Bonnard, (London: Thomas Nelson, 1961), 237.

4 *Gibbon's Journey*, ibid., 235: "Depuis le Pons Milvius j'ai etè [sic] dans un songe d'antiquitè" (After [arriving in Rome at] the Ponte Milvio I have been in a dream of antiquity.) Gibbon authored his *diarium* in French until his arrival in Rome on October 2, 1764, when he seems to have been so consumed by the experience that he ceased writing it. The following entries are few and sketchy by comparison, and the author switches to English (see previous quotation and footnote). For a retrospective account of his exposure to Rome, see *The Autobiography of Edward Gibbon, Esq.* (New York: Turner and Hayden, 1846), 164: "But, at the distance of twenty-five years I can neither forget nor express the strong emotions which agitated my mind as I first approached and entered the *eternal city*. After a sleepless night, I trod, with a lofty step, the ruins of the Forum; each memorable spot where Romulus *stood*, or Tully spoke, or Caesar fell, was at once present to my eye; and several days of intoxication were lost or enjoyed before I could descend to a cool and minute investigation." Ibid., 169: "It was at Rome, on the 15th of October, 1764, as I sat musing amidst the ruins of the Capitol, while the bare footed friars were singing vespers in the temple of Jupiter, that the idea of writing the decline and fall of the city first started to my mind. But my original plan was circumscribed to the decay of the city rather than of the empire." Citing this passage, a recent editor of Gibbon's *The History of the Decline and Fall of the Roman Empire* commented: "There are good reasons for believing that it did not happen quite like that" (see ibid., vol. 1, ed. David Womersley [London: Penguin, 1994], xix).

European culture. What had been for previous generations (including those who made the first city models) a passing interest became a means of defining a broad gamut of affective scenarios and intellectual themes. In Gibbon's time, ruins were said to move and mobilize, if not intoxicate (to use Gibbon's descriptor), though few ruin-gazers have left a tome equal to his as testimony to the palpable effects of ruins on the human psyche.

By comparison, Rome's faux garden ruins elicit only a passing comment. Structures such as the one in the villa's garden call forth less the venerator of the ancients than the arbiter of a modern taste gone awry.[5] Gibbon's ridicule was emblematic of the judgment of connoisseurs, dilettantes, and antiquarians who espoused the late eighteenth-century's growing thirst for evidentiary historical truth – a concern whose corollary was disdain for historic mimicry. Yet the triumph of historicism – as espoused by Gibbon and as echoed by generations of historians thereafter – leaves us with nothing but a distorted view of an eighteenth-century imaginary that actually found great value in built ruins, even in places like Rome where the real things offered themselves for inspection.

As we look closer, we will see that historical authenticity and reconstructive history were far from opposites, as standard narratives about history as a "new science" would suggest. To the contrary, built ruins were one of the ways in which a thirst for historical evidence manifested itself. In the words of Peter Fritzsche, during the late eighteenth and early nineteenth centuries, ruins "were increasingly regarded as the sites of particular and knowable historical events."[6] While Fritzsche's comments aim at authentic ruins, they pertain to built or artificial ruins as well. As connectors to a time and place long gone, ruins, whether actual or artificial, helped to stimulate and shape notions of the past. (As cultivators of connection, these built ruins are quite similar in purpose to the German rubble models after World War II, except that those models concerned a history that was not distant at all.) For these reasons and more, as we will see, built ruins are anything but "garden follies."

---

5 The building, an almost complete temple, is a work by Carlo Marchiono. See Reinhard Zimmermann, "Ruin," in *The Dictionary of Art*, vol. 27 (London: Macmillan, 1996), 323f. For a critique of an "artificial ruin" in England from the first half of the eighteenth century, see David R. Coffin, *The English Garden: Meditation and Memorial* (Princeton: Princeton University Press, 1994), 37.

6 Peter Fritzsche, *Stranded in the Present: Modern Time and the Melancholy of History* (Cambridge: Harvard University Press, 2004), 101. A similar point in Reinhard Zimmermann, *Künstliche Ruinen: Studien zu ihrer Bedeutung und Form* (Wiesbaden: Reichert, 1989), 7. See also Andrea Siegmund, *Die romantische Ruine im Landschaftsgarten: Ein Beitrag zum Verhältnis der Romantik zu Barock und Klassik* (Würzburg: Königshausen & Neumann, 2002), 75–79.

The spectacular garden landscape of Schwetzingen in Germany and other gardens explored below remind us that historicity and destruction were part and parcel of the impressions these sculpted environments imparted to their visitors. Ruinous sites of the eighteenth century reverberated with invocations of nature's destructive forces and violent political conflict alike; eighteenth-century landscape designs brimmed with ideas about naturalism, history, education, and archeology. This chapter will thus seek to uncover a way of experiencing the past that to us is not readily accessible: an engagement with the past as artifice, evidence, and affect.

Fascination with Ruins

Ruins only gradually generated interest as ruins. To return to the site of our previous exploration, at the beginning of the sixteenth century, ancient edifices exerted their symbolic power not so much because of their current, crumbling incarnation, but on a secondary level, as example and analogue.

In a passage from Albrecht Dürer's "aesthetic excursus" (written 1512; published 1528), ruins help to illuminate the concept of divinely inspired artistry:[7] Even in its time-worn physical state, the Renaissance artist and theorist states, ancient architecture unmistakably reveals its greatness. Ruins are said to be impressive despite their ruination, not because of it. To be sure, Dürer's *drümer* (rubble) are no mere debris. Dürer regards this "rubble" as the artist's analogue and a simile of the artistic self. Thus he awards rubble the respect that travelers, artists, and scholars alike would later attach to the word "ruins." The "new Apelles" from Nuremberg was among the first Renaissance artists engaged in what was a momentous effort to establish painting as *ars*, the artist as God's messenger – literally, a genius – and the inventions of great artists as unique.[8] As a theorist of the visual arts and of the artist, Dürer detects God's presence amidst the "rubble." Divine agency is manifest not in having brought about the ruination of Roman splendors (*bracht*); rather, the work of God in its marvel is evident *even*

7 Albrecht Dürer, "Der ästhetische Exkurs," in *Schriftlicher Nachlaß*, ed. Hans Rupprich, vol. 3 (Berlin: Deutscher Verein für Kunstwissenschaft, 1969), 293: "Des sehen wir exempel bey der Römer zeyten, da sie in jrem bracht waren, was bey jnen gemacht ist worden, der drümer wir noch sehen, der gleychen von kunst in vnsern wercken yetz wenig erfunden wirdet."

8 This is the context in which the Dürer passage appears. The "splendor" of Roman ruins is said to be an analogue to an artist whose sketch, executed in one day, is superior to the work of another artist that took a full year.

though ancient buildings lie in tatters. Roman ruins are thought to transcend their crumbling state.

In contexts other than as testimony to the grandeur of the ancients, ruination could carry markedly different connotations. The remains of a stone building visible in the background of Michael Ostendorfer's woodcut of the Beautiful Madonna of Regensburg tell a different story, for instance: that of the violent expulsion of the city's Jewry and the destruction of their synagogue in 1519. For anybody willing to question whether such acts against imperial law pleased God, the events seemed to dissipate all doubt: During the synagogue's demolition a worker was injured but regained his health the next day. To commemorate this supposed Christian triumph, a chapel was built to which the ruins in the background serve as antitype (fig. 17).[9]

Fig. 17: Michael Ostendorfer, Pilgrimage to the Beautiful Madonna of Regensburg, woodcut, 1520, detail, © Trustees of the British Museum

9 Hans Belting, *Likeness and Presence: A History of the Image before the Era of Art*, trans Edmund Jephcott (Chicago: University of Chicago Press, 1994), 453–457. Albrecht Dürer owned this woodcut and added a note of disapproval.

The story of ancient ruins' rise to visual focus and fame since the Renaissance has usually been cast as one of discovery.[10] This narrative heralds Italians as the early proponents of ruins. Invocations of the grandeurs of Italian antiquity ushered in a search for actual remains of the Roman Empire. Starting in the fourteenth and fifteenth centuries, Italian humanists, antiquarians, architects, and artists increasingly sought out the presence of ancient monuments as revealing elements of their own past, portraying them in a variety of discourses and media. Giovanni Dondi dall'Orologio, Filippo Brunelleschi,[11] and Giuliano da Sangallo[12] went on quests to survey ancient remains for useful knowledge about building techniques, architecture, and history. Small groups crystallized around these activities – communities that included practitioners of both the *artes mechanicae* and the *artes liberales* (similar to the joining of mathematic theory and artisanal craft seen in sixteenth-century Bavaria). The painter and printmaker Andrea Mantegna investigated "the very ruination of ancient art" in an intellectual milieu of scholars and artists centered in Padua.[13] To be sure, Italian soil readily yielded coins, ceramics, sculptures, and other objects to treasure-seekers who collected, circulated, and sold them (as well as described, copied, published, and commented upon them). Yet ruins were different from other relics of the treasured ancient past in that at least in their entirety, they were exempt from the practices of exchange and plunder common among scholars.[14] The remains of ancient Roman architecture had to be appreciated (and were despoiled) *in situ*.

What is obliterated in this story – of excavating the past as discoveries of the previously forgotten, unknown, or underappreciated – is the fact that the nature of the past changed in the process of exploring its material remnants. The material past became a place that even in its fragmented state should, the logic went,

10 Cf. Jacob Burckhardt, *The Civilization of the Renaissance in Italy*, trans. S. G. C. Middlemore (London: Penguin Books, 1990), 123–129; Roberto Weiss, *The Renaissance Discovery of Classical Antiquity* (Oxford: Basil Blackwell, 1969), 59–72 and passim; Leonard Barkan, *Unearthing the Past: Archaeology and Aesthetics in the Making of Renaissance Culture* (New Haven: Yale University Press, 1999); Anthony Grafton, "The Ancient City Restored: Archaeology, Ecclesiastical History, and Egyptology," in *Bring out Your Dead: The Past as Revelation* (Cambridge, Mass.: Harvard University Press, 2001), 31–61.
11 Ross King, *Brunelleschi's Dome: How a Renaissance Genius Reinvented Architecture* (New York: Penguin Books, 2000).
12 Giuliano da Sangallo, *Il Libro di Giuliano da Sangallo: Codice Vaticano Barberiniano Latino 4424*, ed. Christian Hülsen (Leipzig: O. Harrassowitz, 1910).
13 Lawrence Gowing, "Mantegna," in *Andrea Mantegna*, ed. Jane Martineau (Milan: Electa, 1992), 3. Mantegna's intellectual and artistic milieu was the theme of the Paris exhibition, *Mantegna 1431–1506*, ed. Giovanni Agosti and Dominique Thiébaut (Paris: Musée du Louvre, 2008).
14 Despoiling of ruins, see Barkan, *Unearthing the Past*, 34–36.

be scouted for information as well as seen, experienced, or touched. The possibilities of physical exploration were a departure from an approach in which the ancient past existed primarily as a written phenomenon. Petrarch's Rome was above all a literary invocation, woven out of fragments "to effect a reconstruction or resurrection of the city."[15] Writers embedded the spoils of ancient quotations into novel compositions, enabling erudite readers to reset old parts into new poetic wholes, a foretaste of a full revival of antiquity.

Epistemologically, poetic texts were thought to "arouse something akin to sensual perception."[16] Accordingly, literary texts reveal a profound joy in the past's materiality. Francesco Colonna's novel, the *Hypnerotomachia Poliphili* (1499), figured the search for the material splendors of antiquity through an erotic plot.[17] Tellingly, however, Polia's passionate reverie in a ruined temple occasions Poliphilo's exploration of epitaphs, i.e. written messages.[18] Even in the case of the *Hypnerotomachia* with its stunning illustrations, where images and texts work in tandem, textual knowledge is accorded a privileged place in bringing the ancient world to life for the sake of the present.[19] But the marked preference for the textual among these early humanists gradually eroded. Across the sixteenth century, just as the city models were inaugurating a new means of conceptualizing sovereignty, the Roman past acquired a sensory and visual profile for those interested in extracting or exercising its lessons.

Ruins became agents of exchange in increasingly common pictorial concoctions that sought meaningful links between concerns of the present and a long-ago age: ancient motifs were paired with Christian iconography, factual depic-

---

15 Alison Cornish, "Embracing the Corpse: Necrophilic Tendencies," in *Dead Lovers: Erotic Bonds and the Study of Premodern Europe*, ed. Basil Dufallo and Peggy McCracken (Ann Arbor: University of Michigan, 2006), 60.

16 Gregor Vogt-Spira, "Senses, Imagination, and Literature: Some Epistemological Considerations," in *Rethinking the Medieval Senses: Heritage, Fascinations, Frames*, ed. Stephen G. Nichols, Andreas Kablitz, and Alison Calhoun (Baltimore: The Johns Hopkins University Press, 2008), 55.

17 Francesco Colonna, *Hypnerotomachia Poliphi: The Strife of Love in a Dream*, trans. Joscelyn Godwin (London: Thames & Hudson, 1999).

18 Colonna, *Hypnerotomachia*, 236–271.

19 Johannes Helmrath, "Die Aura der Kaisermünze: Bild-Text-Studien zur Historiographie der Renaissance und zur Entstehung der Numismatik als Wissenschaft," in *Medien und Sprachen humanistischer Geschichtsschreibung*, ed. Johannes Helmrath, Albert Schirrmeister, and Stefan Schlelein (Berlin: de Gruyter, 2009), 99–138. See also Giuseppe Olmi, "Die Sammlung – Nutzbarmachung und Funktion," in *Macrocosmos in Microcosmo: Die Welt in der Stube: Zur Geschichte de Sammelns 1450 bis 1800*, ed. Andreas Grote (Opladen: Leske & Budrich, 1994), 169–189, here pp. 173f.

Fig. 18: Plate, maiolica, sixteenth-century Italy, Museo Civico d'Arte Antica a Palazzo Madama, Torino (Photo: Author)

tion with historical fantasy, human bodies with stones.[20] Whether we look at an actual edifice or at a painting, as ruins-gazers we get a taste of a temporal-spatial expanse – a pictorial chronotope in which both space and time become manifest.[21] Ruins are the visual form that allows for encounters between time and space in evocative simultaneities.[22]

20 Siegmund, *Die romantische Ruine*, 47f.

21 M. M. Bakhtin, "Forms of Time and of the Chronotope in the Novel," in *The Dialogic Imagination*, ed. Michael Holquist (Austin: University of Texas Press, 1981), 84–258.

22 See Lynn Hunt, *Measuring Time, Making History* (Budapest: Central European University Press, 2008) on the fact that "modern conceptions of time seem to require spatial representation" (4).

To be sure, in their multifarious presence, visual representations of ruins were not subservient to the reins of one semantic master. To the *inventores* of such imagery, ruins were motors of dynamic visual relations. They prompted the viewer to consider the connections between different elements – images of man and ruined edifices, mythology and architecture, nature and humanity, self and antiquity. Ruins came to function as membrane between a historically vague but eminent past and immaterial reflections. Thus they provided artists with a visual idiom whose applicability was vast.

What has characterized the fascination with ruins since the Renaissance was their tremendous versatility. Looking across the representations of the last four centuries, it is often impossible to state with any degree of exactitude why ruins were chosen as a particular signifier other than that they signified potently. Examples from a vast repertoire of material evidence – Christmas crèches, china, furniture, stove designs, wall papers, jewelry, etc. – point toward a growing visual constituency that was intrigued by ruins and a great aesthetic appeal among this expanding viewership. At times, their use was merely symptomatic of a sensibility, a matter of design more than of symbolism. The ruins depicted thus frequently border on the ornamental. Their appeal lay above all in the vast semantic fields they seem to have unlocked – fields including bucolic peace and death. Ruins invoked a visual mythology whose variations allowed the gaze to wander freely through the erudite *imaginaire*. Reminiscences about art, architecture, literature, history, philosophy, and the self – probably then as now – are fair game in the ensuing play of ideas (fig. 18).

As ancient civilizations renewed their spell over European intellectuals, however, authentic remains of ancient buildings, though high in demand, were hard to come by, especially north of the Alps. The solution was perhaps inevitable: if we cannot get to the originals, then build a copy. The "building" of destroyed or decayed structures, housed in evocative settings, therefore catered to an intelligentsia with an avid desire to stimulate a visual encounter with antiquity. (One of the oldest such ruins, though no longer extant, dates to the sixteenth-century Italian Renaissance.[23]) Critics like Gibbon notwithstanding, faux ruins were eagerly erected, and landscape gardens became the favorite setting for them. As instigators of reflection, garden ruins drew on many modes of engagement and layers of meaning-making that had accrued during the history of their appreciation – among them religious meditation, solitude, vanity, and moral or personal reflections. And by the eighteenth century, they also contributed to an imaginary

23 Sabine Eiche, "Francesco Maria II della Rovere's *Delizia* in Urbino: The Giardino di S. Lucia," *Journal of Garden History* 5 (1985): 154–183.

in which book knowledge and familiarity with ancient monuments among the educated reinforced and intensified the past's after-echo.[24]

Landscapes lent themselves to aesthetic experimentation with ruins for many reasons. Gardens figured as *Gesamtkunstwerke* at the seams of nature and art. According to writers, critics, and garden theorists, landscaping brought together different areas of knowledge, disciplines such as botany and agriculture, as well as various branches of art – painting, sculpture, and architecture. Not unlike the genre of city models, landscaped gardens offered visual effects from multiple perspectives. But these sculptures could be walked not merely around, but also through; they invited open-air strolls in an excerpt of nature refigured to enhance appreciation not just of the natural world, but of the world made by man.[25]

As early as 1728, Batty Langley, the English architect, recommended the use of ruins in his *New Principles of Gardening.*[26] Others, his colleague William Chambers among them, were soon to follow. Chambers provoked controversies among garden aficionados by recommending Chinese scenarios – including ruins – as an antidote to the perceived dullness of the English garden.[27] Thomas Whately, another garden critic, distinguished between historical and "fictitious ruins," according the latter a lesser effect. Yet he conceded that even if the "impressions are not so strong, [...] they are exactly similar" in that both authentic and artificial ruins activate the imagination.[28] In his *Observations on Modern Gardening* (1770) ruins figure as merely one accent element among others, such as farmhouses, monuments, sculptures, or temples. By dint of these various structures, so the reasoning ran, landscapes perceived to be uniform would gain in visual appeal.

Varietas had long been a treasured feature of prose style, and a "variety" of visual effects, as described by Langley and Whately, now emerged as an ideal for landscapes with open-air sceneries. Within a wide spectrum of proposals for the improvement of landscape gardens especially in England, ruins were thought to function as particularly potent attractions for the eye. In fact, garden views were

---

24 Peter Geimer, *Die Vergangenheit der Kunst: Strategien der Nachträglichkeit im 18. Jahrhundert* (Weimar: VDG, 2002).

25 In *What Gardens Mean* (Chicago: University of Chicago Press, 1998) Stephanie Ross offers an account of the intersection of art and gardening in the eighteenth century (passim).

26 Batty Langley, *New principles of gardening: or, The laying out and planting parterres, groves, wildernesses, labyrinths, avenues, parks, &c. after a more grand and rural manner, than has been done before ...* (London: A. Bettesworth et al., 1728).

27 David Porter, *Ideographia: The Chinese Cipher in Early Modern Europe* (Stanford: Stanford University Press, 2001), 155–184.

28 Thomas Whately, *Observations on Modern Gardening, Illustrated by Descriptions* (London: Payne, 1770), 132.

made to resemble painted tableaux. Langley recommends that ruins be "viewed with one Eye through our Hand, or a piece of Paper roll'd up, so as to look through the same, you will behold its agreeable Effect with abundance and Pleasure," cutting from view other attractions or sights.[29] In general, parks encouraged the visitor to walk the paths and to be drawn by the eye, to follow the seduction of vistas and to rest at intervals.

It was believed that ruins in particular would arrest both the visitor's gaze and motion. As surprise effects, ruins were thought to be useful for making a visitor linger, and for eliciting a range of responses. Whether visible from afar or concealed from sight, whether ruins were part of a garden tableau or fully accessible to a spectator's investigation, such features invited visitors to slow their movement. The wanderer was expected to respond with curiosity, to stroll in their direction, mull over the scene, investigate the remains, and ruminate over their form or meaning. "At the sight of a ruin," writes Whately in *Observations on Modern Gardening*, "reflections on the change, the decay, and the desolation before us, naturally occur."[30]

Built ruins mount time in its plasticity – an invented past that could be seen, approached, touched, and treaded on – making time experiential. This sensual encounter or confrontation with time unfolded with a visitor's perambulation through space.[31] At best, a slowdown of movement in the present paved the way for opening oneself to the wide expanse of time, the broad possibilities for reflection. Yet these garden ruins were successful only, some garden critics warned, if they were erected in places whose well-chosen location made these edifices seem "probable."[32] Ruins thus functioned as connectors, interconnecting places as well as temporal layers in a locale that often invoked the memory of other, distant locales in Italy or elsewhere. If a ruin was built properly, movement through space would be choreographed to the viewer's inner reflections. But, interestingly enough, specific responses were not prescribed in the relevant

29 Langley, *New Principles of Gardening*, xv. This practice is reminiscent of the much-cited use of the Claude-glass (named after the landscape painter Claude Lorrain), a colored glass that allowed the beholder to frame particular landscapes as if they were a painting.
30 Whately, *Observations*, 155.
31 Cf. Gilles Clément, *Le jardin en mouvement* (Paris: Pandora, 1991); id., *Le jardin en mouvement: De La Vallée au Parc André Citroën* (Paris: Sens et Tonka, 1994).
32 Carl August Boettiger, *Reise nach Wörlitz 1797*, ed. Erhard Hirsch, 8th ed. (Berlin: Deutscher Kunstverlag, 2000), 66, quoting William Gilpin's *Observations relative chiefly to picturesque beauty made in the year 1776 in the Highlands of Scotland*. See also Friedrich Ludwig von Sckell, *Beiträge zur bildenden Gartenkunst für angehende Gartenkünstler und Gartenliebhaber*. Reprint of 2nd ed., Munich 1825 (Worms: Werner, 1982), 36.

garden treatises. Spatial movements were to stimulate "movements of the soul," a term the German garden critic Christian Cay Laurenz Hirschfeld adapted from eighteenth-century ideas of perception. The garden's hoped for effects were clear, however, even if the emotional or intellectual particulars were not.[33]

In many and unforeseeable ways, ruins therefore contributed to a deepening of the landscape experience, provoking a resonance in the individual. They were meant, in the words of one German poet, as "Denkmale" (monuments) or occasions to reflect; ruins were memorials that invited thinking, ensnaring the ruin-gazer into their spell.[34] Ruins thus served as stimuli and intensifiers, apt to heighten the haunting echo of an affect-inducing landscape.

Analogy and comparison were the mental processes thought appropriate for appreciating ruins.[35] Such an activity allowed for a never-ending supply of connections across geographic spaces and historical times. Garden visitors could draw references between what could be seen and what remained invisible. Ruins allowed for positioning one's own life in relation to history, for instance. They stimulated one's memories, be they memories of texts, images, or travels. Intriguingly, this comparative mode of thinking accommodates but does not require moral judgment. Ruins were thus believed to be replete with associations and affects, while lacking a sententious lesson or epimythium. To use a phrase coined by David Porter, ruins instilled a sense of "sublime alienation" in their beholders.[36] In fact, when entering a landscape with ruins, we often believe that we are entering a realm which transcends the personal and the ephemeral.

By the mid-eighteenth century, ensembles with ruins had become common elements of English-style landscape gardens, an established form of landscaping both in England and on the continent. As an architectural type harking back to antiquity, the country villa provided the appropriate setting for a nod to the imperial European past. English landscapers in particular experimented assid-

---

33 Christian Cay Laurenz Hirschfeld, *Theorie der Gartenkunst* (Leipzig: M. G.Weidmanns Erben and Reich, 1779–1785). See vol. 1, 155f.

34 Friedrich von Hardenberg-Novalis, *Das dichterische Werk, Tagebücher und Briefe*, vol. 1, ed. Richard Samuel (Munich: Carl Hanser, 2004), 475: "Den Montag, wo wir nach Halle fuhren und unterwegs in Dessau das Georgium [villa with extensive landscape garden near Dessau] besahen, hatt ich zuweilen einen hellen Gedanken." (1797)

35 Cf. Walter Benjamin, *The Origin of German Tragic Drama*, trans. John Osborne (London: Verso, 1998), 178: "Allegories are, in the realm of thoughts, what ruins are in the realm of things." On this book and Benjamin's conception of allegorical ruins, see Jane O. Newman, *Benjamin's Library: Modernity, Nation, and the Baroque* (Ithaca: Cornell University Press, 2011), 11, 138–184.

36 Porter, *Ideographia*, 178.

uously with ruinous structures, providing architectural models with a European cachet.[37]

Early modern pleasure gardens in Europe had first and foremost been places of courtly display. As the loci of court festivities, such as fireworks, theatrical performances, and music-making, these often enclosed grounds had much in common with the theatre as a foundational form for political, aesthetic, and cultural engagement in Renaissance, Baroque, and Enlightenment Europe – an engagement in which the court fashioned itself in the image of a well-ordered, ideal society. Yet the mode of appreciation that eventually emerged with the picturesque garden was decidedly less collective and more solitary. While visitors might have been guided in their viewing experience by artistic-literary canons or by guidebooks for a sculpted garden, the dominant mode of reception was individual immersion or immersion in small groups. Appreciating the garden fancy is thus comparable to tourism and its paradoxical claim that the way we have an authentic experience is to replicate the activity of others.

Like the tourist, garden visitors were not generally all by themselves. Often, they were accompanied by like-minded souls – fellow travelers or friends. Companionship was said to enhance the outdoor experience. When in 1797 Carl August Boettiger set forth in writing his visit to the gardens of Dessau-Wörlitz, he first delivered a sketch of the congenial troupe of travelers – five men and a girl, the ten-year old daughter of one of them – who accompanied him on this outing.[38] Shared appreciation is also suggested by the *vedute* that were disseminated in large print runs and that instructed visitors on how to move through a garden. Silence or at most well-measured conversations among friends was considered appropriate. Actual crowds were thought to be a nuisance, though for Boettiger the presence of other visitors, at least in one instance when those others were at a distance, made his own experience all the more memorable: "One enjoyed twice, since one enjoyed with hundreds [of other visitors]" (*Man genoß doppelt, denn man genoß mit Hunderten*).[39] Gardens thus invoked larger collectives, instantiating an understanding of the social as a collective of individuals.

---

37 Coffin (*The English Garden*, 31–56) provides an overview.

38 Boettiger, *Reise*, 16. For his guidebook of Rome, Stendhal invented a company, see his *Promenades dans Rome* (Nendeln: Kraus Reprint, 1968); translated by Haakon Chevalier as *A Roman Journal* (New York: Orion Press, 1957), xix. In his widely disseminated guidebook of Rome, Augustus Hare recommended: "Those who wish to fix the scenes and events of Roman history securely in their minds will do best perhaps to take them in groups." See his *Walks in Rome*, 20th ed. (London: Paul Kegan, 1913), 14.

39 Boettiger, *Reise*, 67. In this case, it is important to note that Boettiger appreciated the other visitors from a distance. When his own group took a gondola ride together with a company of

Simulating ravishes of time in a new building posed and continues to pose severe challenges to the architect. When Langley discusses the question of precisely how to integrate ruins into gardens he is forthright in advocating built ruins as opposed to the flatness of *trompe l'oeil* ruins paintings. *New Principles of Gardening* offers inspiration for ruinesque garden designs by means of illustrations of a vaguely Italianate vintage with ruins. Yet only one of them is an actual garden view; the others were capriccios featuring ruins. For all his emphasis on the need for three-dimensional structures, the author devotes little thought on how to transform these highly evocative representations into solid buildings.

While Langley remained silent on the problem of how to recreate the contingencies of time in architectural form, the landscape designers who followed his and the call of others to create ruins became acutely aware of the difficulties of the task at hand. "It is indeed very difficult to make [ruins] delude and make one believe that the ravages of time and not art or violent causes had created this destruction" (*Allein es ist sehr schwer, sie so erscheinen zu machen, daß sie täuschen und glauben lassen, der Zahn der Zeit und nicht die Kunst oder andere gewaltsame Ursachen hätten diese Zerstörung hervorgebracht*), writes Friedrich Ludwig von Sckell in 1818, summing up his life-long efforts in this regard.[40] He proceeds to give detailed advice as to the selection of building materials, the choice of an appropriate site, the mode of construction, and similar such questions, offering a very clear plan for ways of building that simulate destruction. An architect entrusted with such a project, he claims, needs to gain expertise in actual ruination as well as in the painterly impact of the overall design *in situ*. He explicitly warns garden planners against first erecting and then demolishing buildings in order to produce the desired naturalistic effect.[41] Building destruction thus required a superior *conceptor* versed in both landscaping and the arts. At the same time, Sckell conceded that individual elements of a consciously ruinous structure would have to be treated extensively in order to visually approximate the workings of time.[42]

Given the exigencies of the endeavor, as outlined by one of its foremost practitioners, it is hardly surprising to find that the critic Hirschfeld took a stance against building ruins: "It will always remain more difficult for the garden artist

strangers, he was much annoyed by the expression of enthusiasm by one of his fellow travelers (ibid., 65f).

40 Sckell, *Beiträge*, 36.

41 Whether such a practice was common, is hard to assess. An example in Coffin, *The English Garden*, 45.

42 Sckell, *Beiträge*, 36–38.

to imitate ruins so that its illusion is satisfactory. Since so many attempts, even under the guidance of connoisseurs, have failed, one would be well-advised, to recommend discontinuing them entirely."[43] Garden planners did not take his advice, evidently, so that many of the gardens Hirschfeld reported on in his five-volume *Theory of Garden Art* included ruinous structures.

To the cultural critic, landscape gardens promise immediacy of access, as if, were one equipped with an archive in the form of landscape and the requisite discourses, one could easily uncover the experience of eighteenth-century garden lovers. In truth, even if still extant, gardens have evolved over time. Critics need to cull the history of specific gardens as well as of general garden appreciation from a variety of sources: theoretical treatises, guidebooks, travelogues, maps, vistas, and archeological findings – all with their own limitations. An analysis needs to be carefully compiled from different pieces of a historical puzzle. Like treatises on landscaping, the discussion of principles of garden architecture therefore needs to be grounded in the specificity of particular gardens – gardens such as Schwetzingen.

Arcadia on the Rhine

During his reign, Carl Theodor, Elector of the Palatinate (r. 1742–1799), embellished his summer residence in Schwetzingen near Mannheim, Germany, on a grand scale with a landscaped park. This "magic garden," as the poet Daniel Schubart quipped,[44] included both geometrical designs with wide-ranging perspectives and "parties sauvages dans le style de la nature" (wild parts in the natural style) featuring a series of theatre-like garden scenes that came into existence over the course of the elector's rule, including a Temple of Apollo, a bath-

43 Christian Cay Laurenz Hirschfeld, *Theorie der Gartenkunst* (Stuttgart: DVA, 1990), 150: "Schwerer bleibt es immer für den Gartenkünstler, Ruinen auf eine vollkommen täuschende Art nachzuahmen; und weil so viele Versuche selbst unter den Händen der Kenner misslingen, so möchte man fast veranlasst werden, ihre Fortsetzung lieber abzurathen, als zu empfehlen." The English translation of this opus is incomplete, see Christian Cajus Lorenz Hirschfeld, *Theory of Garden Art*, trans. Linda B. Parshall (Philadelphia: University of Pennsylvania Press, 2001). On Hirschfeld's fluctuating but influential opinions on ruins, among other topics, see Urte Stobbe, *Kassel-Wilhelmshöhe: Ein hochadeliger Lustgarten im 18. Jahrhundert* (Berlin: Deutscher Kunstverlag, 2009), 104–109, 137f, 151–157.

44 Quoted after Bärbel Pelker, "Sommer in der Campagne – Impressionen aus Schwetzingen," in *Hofoper in Schwetzingen: Musik – Bühnenmusik – Architektur*, ed. Silke Leopold and Bärbel Pelker (Heidelberg: Winter, 2004), 9–37, here p. 13.

Fig. 19: Johann Michael Zeyher, "Beschreibung der Gartenanlagen," 1809, Water Castellum, Copperplate

house, a Chinese bridge, a mosque, and similar attractions.[45] Among them is the so-called Roman water *castellum*,[46] an ensemble the court architect Nicolas de Pigage erected around 1779 (fig. 19).

Arches flank a multistory structure that immediately is the focus of the visitor's eye. From the center cave of this crumbled building, itself arched, springs a rivulet, feeding a small lake. As a terminus building at the garden's northern edge, the "water castellum" doubles as a gate, controlling the flow of water,

45 The best introduction to the park and its history, see Ferdinand Werner, "Der Garten der kurfürstlichen Sommerresidenz Schwetzingen," in *Lebenslust und Frömmigkeit: Kurfürst Carl Theodor (1724–1799) zwischen Barock und Aufklärung*, ed. Alfried Wieczorek (Regensburg: Pustet, 1997), 63–72. See also Dieter Hennebo and Alfred Hoffmann, *Der architektonische Garten: Renaissance und Barock* (Hamburg: Broschek, 1965), 361–369.

46 A variety of descriptions circulated for this structure already in the eighteenth century: "ruine," "ruines," "Wasserleitung ruine," "le Bâtiment et l'Aqueduc des ruines," For an introduction, see Saskia Dams, *Der Englische Garten im Schwetzinger Schlossgarten: Der Tempel der Botanik und das römische Wasserkastell mit Aquädukt und Obelisk* (Munich: Grin, 2001).

though this technical function becomes evident only when the visitor climbs the stairs to the *castellum*'s top. From the lookout, one's gaze is free to wander inside and outside the garden.[47]

What kind of a structure is the "water castellum"? As reminders of a long-gone past – whose remains supposedly reach into the present – artificial ruins are often promiscuous structures, simultaneously invoking a plethora of architectural models and past moments; this is also the case here.[48] Is it a military building? Is it a water sanctuary (as hinted at by the water-themed reliefs on its façade)? The ensemble arrests one's gaze, a riddle set in stone. This commanding architectural scenario skillfully transposes the *castellum*'s mix of architectural references into a highly evocative setting. The theatre-like quality of the scene is highlighted by a frontality that embraces the visitor within its semicircular layout.[49] Referencing aqueduct, bridge, gate, a classical *castellum*, and triumphal arch at the same time,[50] the site confounds visual expectations. Whereas there are a number of ancient buildings that have been cited in the literature as precursors, the "water castellum" models an architectural composite – a virtuoso capriccio rendering impossible a ready assignation of architectural type, function, or meaning.

The contingencies of time are prominently on display. The stone (trass), the broken reliefs, the chipped surfaces, and the heaps of rocks underneath the arches (which, we assume, once formed the aqueduct) all stage the workings of time. In its ruined evocation the building is asymmetrical yet strongly suggestive of a symmetry that one suspects "once" was there. Some of the horizontal surfaces appear as though they originally (one of the many terms that verge on meaninglessness when we talk about fabricated ruins) were to serve as basins for plant growth; a hallmark of actual ruins across Europe were overgrown bushes, vines, and weeds. De Pigage and his assistants would have encouraged a similar impression of overgrowth. Similarly, the arches to the south of the castle reach into a thicket of bushes and trees. The base of the obelisk at the scene's center is lined with a careful arrangement of stones that suggest a halted movement. The well seems to have broken through the stone, announcing nature's victory over

---

47 Hirschfeld, *Theorie der Gartenkunst*, vol. 5 (Leipzig: Weidmanns Erben, 1785), 546f: "Auf einem Thurm, der zu ihnen [den Ruinen] gehört, hat man eine schöne Aussicht in die umliegende Landschaft."

48 A good example would be the ruins in Ludwigslust of 1788 which combines Roman features with elements that remind the viewer of a medieval castle ruin.

49 The back of the "water castellum" is not accessible.

50 See also the three reliefs by Konrad Linck with representations of water nymphs and a Roman river God.

human ambitions (though the reliefs on the building's outside with their invocation of water belie such an interpretation).[51]

The effect is, to quote a contemporary description of this ensemble, "painterly."[52] Indeed, with its stacked spatiality and multiple frames, the "water castellum" forges a scene of surprising depth through simulating the workings of time and other strategies; not accidentally, there is no single viewpoint from which the "water castellum" can be fully appreciated. The "water castellum" is "a theatre in nature" – a pendant to the actual theatre just to the east of this built ruin, which served the court during the summer months at Schwetzingen since 1753.[53]

As a concept derived from the garden literature of the time, "painterliness" provides an apt frame through which to view artificial ruins. In the case of the "water castellum," the *mise-en-scène* is reminiscent of one of the most cherished and frequently painted Italian landscapes, the Campania.[54] Yet the Schwetzin-

---

51 The Greek and Roman god Poseidon, depicted on one of the reliefs, was also known as "earthshaker." His anger was said to cause earthquakes and as god of water and the sea he was said to be responsible for floods. See Benjamin Hederich, *Gründliches Mythologisches Lexikon* [1770] (Darmstadt: Wissenschaftliche Buchgesellschaft, 1986), 1709–1722, here col. 1722; William Smith, ed., *A Dictionary of Greek and Roman Biography and Mythology* [1880] (London: Tauris, 2007); *Der neue Pauly: Enzyklopädie der Antike*, ed. Hubert Cancik and Helmuth Schneider (Stuttgart: Metzler, 2001), vol. 10, 201–206, here col. 201f.

52 Hirschfeld, *Theorie*, vol. 5, 546; Sckell, *Beiträge*, 38: "malerische[] Wirkung" (painterly effect); Johann Michael Zeyher and G. Roemer, *Beschreibung der Gartenanlagen zu Schwetzingen: Mit 8 Kupfern und einem Plane des Gartens* (Mannheim: Benderische Buchhandlung, 1809), 38; Johann Michael Zeyher and J. G. Rieger, *Schwezingen und seine Garten-Anlagen* (Mannheim: Schwan und Götz [1826]), 127.

53 Monika Scholl, "Das Schwetzinger Schloßtheater – Der Idealtypus eines Sprech- und Musiktheaters des 18. Jahrhunderts," in *Theater um Mozart*, ed. Bärbel Pelker (Heidelberg: Winter, 2006), 83–101; Hans-Joachim Scholderer, "Bühne und Maschinerie des Schwetzinger Schloßtheaters," in *Hofoper in Schwetzingen*, 155–176; Monika Scholl, "Bretterbude? Neue Erkenntnisse zur Baugeschichte des Theaters," ibid., 251–303. The garden installations, including the artificial ruins, were possibly also used as stage sets, see Annette Frese, "Bühnengestaltung für die Sommerresidenz: Typologie der 'Decorationes,'" ibid., 181–246, here pp. 190f (artist either Giuseppe Quaglio or Lorenzo Quaglio).

54 As many eighteenth-century collections, Elector Carl Theodor's collection of graphic art and paintings included works by Claude Lorrain, Salvatore Rosa, and similar such artists. See Holm Bevers et al., eds., *Zeichnungen aus der Sammlung des Kurfürsten Carl Theodor* (Munich: Staatliche Graphische Sammlung, 1983). For the history of the collection, see Karl Ludwig Hofmann, "Die kurpfälzische Gemäldegalerie in Mannheim – von der Fürstensammlung zur Bildungseinrichtung," in *Lebenslust und Frömmigkeit*, 239–243. Carl Theodor traveled through the Campania on his way to Pompeii and Herculaneum on his second trip to Italy in 1783. Freiherr Stephan von Stengel who kept a diary of this trip praised the fertility of these paradise-like lands while criticizing a lack of diligence, freedom, and justice, see Stephan von Stengel, *Der Kurfürst Karl*

gen ensemble also subverts an approach to ruins as based on bucolic landscape paintings. Approaching the scene through the lens of painterliness risks identifying the scenery exclusively with an iconography of melancholic reflection of a long-gone past. However, as a lens, the frame of "painterliness" more readily accommodated the historical than garden theorists of the time posited. Ruinous props built in German landscape gardens during the second half of the eighteenth century did not simply instantiate garden theory. Their material remains often narrate processes, processes of decay and destruction. The Roman "water castellum" can therefore be viewed as an architectural essay in history, the history of destruction (fig. 20).

When in 1825 one of the creators of Schwetzingen, Friedrich Ludwig von Sckell, reflected on the principles of gardening, he stated authoritatively: "Fire and war make ruins also out of new buildings. Such ruins are not what I am referring to here, and art also should not emulate them" (*Durch Brand und Krieg werden auch neue Gebäude in Ruinen verwandelt; allein solche Ruinen warden hier nicht gemeint, und diese darf auch die Kunst nicht nachahmen.*)[55] This was not to say, however, that *old* or seemingly old buildings should not have reminded viewers of the destruction wrought by fires and wars of the past. For those in the know or for those who subscribed to the publications of the Palatine Academy of Sciences, the scene held a deeper meaning.[56] It marked the site of a past that had been unearthed and could now be visited. During the construction of the arboretum near the site chosen for the *castellum*, human remains and ancient objects were discovered in the ground. In fact, this was the second time an archeological dig had been executed on garden grounds. Some years earlier, tombs had been discovered, excavated, and interpreted as those of fallen Roman and German soldiers.[57] On the very grounds of the garden, a battle between Roman and Germanic forces was thought to have taken place. A savvy academician culled a passage from the chronicles of Ammianus Marcellinus, the historian of late antiquity, that lent credence to an otherwise undocumented battle between Emperor Valentian I and Germanic soldiers in the year 368 (though the fact that women were amongst the buried should have raised doubts about the accuracy of the assertion).[58] A plaque

---

Theodor in Rom: Tagebuch seiner zweiten Romreise, ed. Günther Ebersold (Mannheim: Palatium, 1997), 94.

55 Sckell, *Beiträge*, 36 (translation, H.P.)

56 The obelisk is a work by Joseph Anton Pozzi.

57 Wiltrud Heber, *Die Arbeiten des Nicolas de Pigage in den ehemals kurpfälzischen Residenzen Mannheim und Schwetzingen* (Worms: Wernersche Verlagsgesellschaft, 1986), 583.

58 Johann Casimir Häffelin, "Entdeckungen einiger Altertümer in den kurfürstlichen Lustgärten zu Schwetzingen," *Rheinische Beiträge zur Gelehrsamkeit*, vol. 1 (1777): 89. Cf. Ammianus Marcel-

Fig. 20: Water Castellum, Schwetzingen, detail (Photo: Author)

with the elector's name and an inscription was mounted to mark the site and remind visitors of the war and death that once occurred there.[59] Printed guides to the garden from the early nineteenth century make these associations explicit. Their author, Johann Michael Zeyher, called attention to the park's ancient past. He even described and re-interpreted the archeological finds on the backdrop of a long-winded discussion of burial customs among the ancients. Importantly, he framed visits to the garden within an extensive commentary on Schwetzingen's and the territory's histories.[60] In Schwetzingen, the past was not only knowable. It also was somewhat authentic, even if this same antiquity was remembered through artificial ruins. It is worth remembering in this context that some of the age's built ruins made use of extant architectural remains or featured spolia to heighten their factual appeal.[61] Strange as it may seem, historical hindsight and staged scenes invoking the past were no opposites.

To be sure, Schwetzingen had lain within the orbit of the Roman Empire and, as a result, the Rhine valley offered archeologically fertile ground. One of the main charges of the Mannheim Academy, founded in 1763, was to prepare a comprehensive historical, archeological, and geographical encyclopedia of the Palatinate.[62] Under the aegis of the elector, provincial archeology and similar academic pursuits played a key role in presenting this territory as a place privileged both by its rich history at the crossroads of civilizations and by the state of the art scientific endeavors used to bring this same history to new life. "That the Romans lived in these regions is shown by the monuments which time has

---

linus, *Ammianus Marcellinus*, trans. John C. Rolfe, vol. 3 (Cambridge, Mass.: Harvard University Press, 1956), 66 (xxvii, 10, 7). The editor of this modern edition notes with regard to the place name Solicinium: "perhaps Schwetzingen, near Heidelberg," though most historians of today would not agree.

59 Zeyher, *Beschreibung der Gartenanlagen zu Schwetzingen*, 73; Zeyher, *Schwezingen und seine Garten-Anlagen*, 105: "Martis et Mortis Romanor[um] ac Teutonum Arca Urnis et Ossibus Instrumentisque aliis An. MDCCLXV de detecta" (In the year 1765, the fields of war and death of Romans and Germans were unearthed because of weapons, urns, bones and other objects). See Michael Hesse, "Tempel, Themen, Aquädukte: Antikerezeption in den Schwetzinger Parkbauten," in *Der Pfälzer Apoll*, 175–181, here p. 180.

60 Zeyher, *Beschreibung der Gartenanlagen*; Zeyher, *Schwezingen und seine Garten-Anlagen*. Even if there is much overlap, the two editions vary significantly in structure, illustrations, and wording.

61 Zimmermann, *Künstliche Ruinen*, 162–170, 225 (Weimar, 1784).

62 Claudia Braun, "Kurfürst Carl Theodor als Denkmalpfleger," in *Lebenslust und Frömmigkeit*, 347–352; Rosmarie Günther, "Die kurpfälzische Akademie der Wissenschaften," in *Der Pfäzer Apoll: Kurfürst Carl Theodor und die Antike an Rhein und Neckar*, ed. Max Kunze (Ruhpolding: Rutzen, 2007), 39–48.

not yet destroyed," as Zeyher, the garden's director, pointed out in his guidebook.[63]

Clearly, with the "water castellum," we are not in peaceful Elysium anymore. We are in Arcadia, that myth-laden landscape of ancient Greece and, in Roman literature, the pastoral playground of shepherds, fauns, and the god Pan. Fittingly, a life-like faun sculpture in a grove near the "water castellum" may have transported visitors precisely to this enchanted, long-lost place whose *imaginaire* informed so many eighteenth-century landscape scenes. Yet in one respect, Arcadia was conceived of as a realm whose temporal troubles resembled our own: Death wielded power even there.

Et in Arcadia ego, an inscription that first appeared on seventeenth-century Arcadian-themed paintings by Guercino and Nicolas Poussin, originally designated just that. As the German art historian Erwin Panofsky reminds us in a hauntingly beautiful essay, the inscription should have been understood as "Death wields power even here," before the quotation was haplessly reconceived as the emphatic "And I lived in Arcady, too."[64] The message imparted by De Pigage's ensemble differs from the moralizing message of a mere *memento mori* ("be mindful of [your imminent] death"). At stake is not exclusively a reminder of the term-limits on all life, including one's own, but rather the historical past with its knowable death and destruction. As Panofsky has us note, the famous second version of Poussin's painting *Et in Arcadia ego*, now in the Louvre, presaged this turn away from *vanitas*-symbolism and to introspection of a different kind, a "mellow meditation on a beautiful past."[65] The figures gathered around the stone sarcophagus, two of them tracing its inscription, seem to take an intellectual interest in their disturbing discovery: the presence of mortality in the midst of Arcady. It is as if the personages represented in this painting, widely known at the time through prints such as Bernard Picart's (fig. 21), modeled responses to the marvels of landscaped gardens, especially ruins. After all, they gather in front of this monument with a sense of curiosity, seemingly involved in a discussion; what is a sarcophagus in this composition could also be some other ancient remain or a ruin – all the more since eighteenth-century built ruins often invoked tombs.[66]

63 Zeyher, *Beschreibung der Gartenanlagen*, 3: "Daß übrigens die Römer in diesen Gegenden gewesen sind, beweisen die Denkmähler, welche die Zeit noch nicht zerstört hat."
64 Erwin Panofsky, "'Et in Arcadia Ego': Poussin and the Elegiac Tradition," in *Meaning in the Visual Arts: Papers in and on Art History* (Chicago: University of Chicago Press, 1955), 295–320.
65 Ibid., 313.
66 Zimmermann, *Künstliche Ruinen*, 106–111.

Fig. 21: Bernard Picart after Nicolas Poussin, "Le souvenir de la mort au milieu des prosperitez de la vie" – The memory of death in the midst of the affluence of life, print © Trustees of the British Museum

Neither the mythological past nor the past of Roman history was merely "beautiful," as Panofsky suggests. Remembrance of things past did not lay to rest the menace of death, demise, and destruction. As is evident with the "water castellum," the potential for disaster retained a powerful presence even if relegated to a historical moment like a battle in antiquity. Suggestions of violent events in the past were useful precisely in bringing this past to life by drawing the spectator into an affecting theatre of history. In other words, when it came to the moderns' connections with the ancients, a historically trained gaze complemented the references to ancient Gods and myths visibly entrenched in the same park.

Historical claims required accuracy of reconstruction. Fittingly, details of the Roman "water castellum" – from the arches to the cornices to the architraves, etc. – betray an intimate understanding of Roman architecture, or at least of the publications of Piranesi, one of the foremost experts on the subject.[67] Nicolas de

67 Hesse, "Tempel, Themen, Aquädukte," 178.

Pigage, the "water castellum's" architect, had embarked on a professional tour of Italy in 1767 and 1768 – a *Bildungsreise* whose expenses were covered from the coffers of the elector.[68] Carl Theodor himself followed the path of his architect when, during the winter of 1774/1775, he went on the first of two whirlwind grand tours for spiritual and educational improvement; no surprise, Rome was his destination.[69] In addition to the region's rich historical past, De Pigage's built ruins therefore conjured up memories of travels for the prince and his architect.

Yet in the eighteenth-century Palatinate, electoral ruins also imparted historical and political meanings beyond the region's deep history reaching back to the times of the Roman Empire – associations that were hard to escape. Heidelberg castle, the electorate's former seat of rule, had been laid to ruin during the Palatine War of Succession when French troops invaded an already war-ravished territory (1689 and 1693); it had only been patched thereafter – a fact that made the residence's move to Mannheim all the more attractive. Then as today, the castle's hollow Renaissance façade hovers high above the river valley as if a reminder of the transitoriness of political grandeur and courtly splendors.[70] Drawing on the images of Apollo, the god of the muses (Apollo Musagetes), Elector Carl Theodor crafted the iconography of his rulership not only in emulation of the "Sun King" Louis XIV (Apollo was the God of the Sun), but also in the image of Apollo Palatinus. He wanted to be seen as a restorer of the Palatinate to its former magnificence under Frederick V, the elector crowned King of Bohemia – an event that had unleashed the Thirty Years' War.[71] Meditations on a ruinous past therefore

68 Annette Frese, "Nicolas de Pigage 1723–1796: Leben und Werk," in *Hofoper in Schwetzingen*, 247–250. Note that De Pigage became a member of a prestigious academy of architects in Rome, San Luca.

69 Günther Ebersold, "Die Italiensehnsucht des Kurfürsten," in *Lebenslust und Frömmigkeit*, 231–235; Reinhard Stupperich, "Carl Theodors Romreisen 1774/1775 und 1783," in *Der Pfälzer Apoll*, 17–24; Karl J. Svoboda, *Eine kurfürstliche Winterreise nach Italien: Die Reise des Grafen von Veldenz alias des Kurfürsten Carl Theodor von der Pfalz von Mannheim nach Rom im Jahre 1774/75* (Ubstadt-Weiher: Regionalkultur, 1998).

70 When Leopold Mozart visited Schwetzingen in 1763 to have his two wunderkinder, Wolfgang Amadeus and Maria Anna (Nannerl), perform at court, the family went on an overnight excursion to visit Heidelberg. Mozart père compared Heidelberg to their home town Salzburg and commented on "the collapsed towers and walls in the castle that can be marveled at in wonderment" (die eingefahlenen Thürn und Mauern im Schloß, die mit erstaunen anzusehen sind"). See Bärbel Pelker, "W. A. Mozart zu Besuch in der Kurpfalz," in *Theater um Mozart*, ed. B. Pelker (Heidelberg: Winter, 2006), 59–82, here p. 63. Mozart returned twice to the Electorate, 1777–1778 and 1790 (when he visited the park at Schwetzingen again, a possible source of inspiration for "The Magic Flute.")

71 Apollo Palatinus was not only the title of a homegrown Apollo; the description also had ancient resonances (Apollo on the Palatin). Cf. Martin Spannagel, "Carl Theodor als pfälzischer

also called upon the visitor to appreciate a relatively peaceful present that would potentially extend into a happy future: where once war and destruction reigned, human life and the arts flourish once again.[72]

Indeed, the garden of Schwetzingen had a predecessor on the bastions of Heidelberg castle whose fame in humanists' programmatic descriptions perpetuated its image long after the garden itself had disappeared. Its successor garden in Schwetzingen obliquely references Heidelberg's "Hortus Palatinus" – a term that could be translated either as "The Palace's Garden" or as "Garden of the Palatinate."[73] As the virtual center of the electoral lands, Carl Theodor's summer residence in Schwetzingen corresponded visually with the territory's outer edges. On a clear day, the visual axis through the castle's central archway extends from the marshes of the Rhine where the summer residence is located toward the Palatinate's other centers. One can detect the mountains above Heidelberg in the east and near Neustadt, another administrative center, in the west. In fact, the elector had gone to considerable length in order to reinforce these connections. When a forest was found to obstruct the sovereign's free-roaming gaze across his territory, trees were forcibly razed – a sign for the contradictions inherent in Carl Theodor's enlightened rule.[74] Visual axes thus centered this territory in the prince's summer residence, a symbolic bringing together of the land whose infrastructure the elector had done much to renew. By diplomatic means, Carl Theodor pursued a political vision of a vast state along the Rhine. And his passion for building ruins, roads, and a state found its apex in the garden of Schwetzingen where political aspirations and cultural ambitions converged, a landscape to represent the elector's prominence as a ruler who exhibited a respect for the past while plotting a political future that never came to be.[75]

Apoll, der Palatin und die arkadische Vorgeschichte Roms," in *Der Pfälzer Apoll*, 25–29. Apollo Palatinus was also the title given to Carl Theodor in an edition of Aesop's fables, published by François-Joseph Terrasse Desbillons in Mannheim in 1789, equipped with an image of the Temple of Apollo in Schwetzingen. See Hermann Wiegand, "Zwei geistige Antipoden am Hof Carl Theodors – Voltaire und Desbillons," in *Lebenslust und Frömmigkeit*, 159–168.

72 Zimmermann, *Künstliche Ruinen*, 183f.

73 Hennebo/Hoffmann, *Der architektonische Garten*, 77–84; Reinhard Zimmermann, *Hortus Palatinus: Die Entwürfe zum Heidelberger Schlossgarten von Salomon de Caus, 1620* (Worms: Wernersche Verlagsgesellschaft, 1986); Lili Fehrle-Burger, *Die Welt der Oper in den Schloßgärten von Heidelberg und Schwetzingen* (Karlsruhe: G. Braun, 1977).

74 Zeyher, *Beschreibung der Gartenanlagen*, 21f, 58. Zeyher, *Schwezingen und seine Garten-Anlagen*, 121.

75 Characteristically, a portrait of this potentate and patron of the arts, especially of music – Mannheim boasted Europe's premier orchestra in this period – shows him standing in front of the Temple of Apollo in Schwetzingen. Painting by Johann Peter Hoffmeister, Carl Theodor c.

The workings of destruction on the grounds of this landscape park are even more evident in another artificial ruin De Pigage built for Carl Theodor in the same landscape garden in 1787–1788 (fig. 22).[76] Clearly, one ruin per garden was no longer sufficient to feed a growing craze for ruin props. When construction work on this second project began, however, the elector had already moved his court from Mannheim to Munich, after he had succeeded the last Bavarian Wittelsbach prince. A letter of 1787 by De Pigage speaks of this project as "a very agreeable surprise for Our Most Serene Master," Carl Theodor ("une surprise bien agreeable [sic] pour Notre Sérénissime Maitre").[77]

The genesis of the site, to the extent that it is known, sheds light on discussions among eighteenth-century garden literati. After his visit to Schwetzingen, the garden critic Hirschfeld reported on plans for an Egyptian scene opposite the already finished Mosque, complete with a tomb vault and mummies – a project he proceeded to ridicule as out of character with the structure's immediate context, the Rhine valley. If executed, this monument to Pharaoh Sesostris, like Carl Theodor a prolific builder, would have provided a commentary on the ruler of the Palatinate in a historical guise. Importantly, however, the plan bespeaks a continuing thirst for an array of historically specific ensembles. Possibly in response to Hirschfeld's barb at an outlandish garden scene, the plan was never executed.[78]

1770, Reiss-Engelhorn-Museum, Mannheim, Germany, Kunst- und Stadtgeschichtliche Sammlungen (see Ralf Richard Wagner, "Arkadien auch in Schwetzingen?" in *Hofoper in Schwetzingen*, 47). See also the portrait bust of Carl Theodor in Roman guise after Giuseppe Cerachi, c. 1789, cf. *Der Pfälzer Apoll*, 11, 31. "L'Arcadia conservata" or "Errettetes Arcadien" (Arcadia Restored) of 1775 – an opera with music by Niccolò Jommelli and the Mannheim composer Ignaz Holzbauer on a libretto by Mattia Verazi was staged in front of the Apollonian "theatre de verdure" (nature theatre) in the park at Schwetzingen, only a short walk from the "water castellum." See also Silke Leopold, "Opernrepertoire des Schwetzinger Schloßtheaters," in *Hofoper in Schwetzingen*, 140–143. The production celebrated the convalescence of the elector from a life-threatening disease. In a travel diary of 1783, the electoral administrator Stephan von Stengel used Arcadia to describe Carl Theodor's reign, see Von Stengel, *Der Kurfürst Karl Theodor in Rom*, 129: "Carl Theodor, unter deßen sanfter wohlthätiger Leitung die Musen sich schon längst in der Pfalz arkadischen Gefilden versammelt hatten." On landscape gardens of the period as decidedly political project, see Stobbe, *Kassel-Wilhelmshöhe*, 137–157.

76 Sckell co-operated with De Pigage on the execution, if we follow Sckell's own claim. Sckell had traveled to England and was intimately familiar with the latest in garden design.

77 Heber, *Arbeiten*, 655. The fact that De Pigage who had traveled to England in 1776 (where he met his collaborator Sckell, also travelling for the elector) uses the term "surprise" in this context shows how in tune he was with the garden discourse of the time.

78 In his guides to Schwetzingen, Zeyher criticizes Hirschfeld for having misinterpreted the site – a further indication that Hirschfeld's publications were very influential. See his *Beschreibung der Gartenanlagen*, 55f., and *Schwetzingen und seine Garten-Anlagen*, 117–119.

Fig. 22: Johann Michael Zeyher, "Schwezingen und seine Garten-Anlagen" [1826], Temple of Mercury

What was erected instead entered the record as the Temple of Mercury, though the tower-like building in fact resembles a tomb structure more than a temple.

Meticulously contrived elements of decay and destruction pervade the scene. Sandstone blocks carefully cascade down the slope of the hill atop of which the temple sits (fig. 23). Artificial cracks cover its façade, suggesting an unstable structure at risk of crumbling. Holes dot the floors and ceilings; the belvedere on top is only partially covered. The Temple of Mercury communes with the surrounding landscape and the open skies. Its name is apt, with the building serving as a connector between the divine and the human spheres (among other obligations, Mercury served as the messenger god). Yet this contact zone was conceived not as a harmonious encounter but as a violent tremor. The visitor daring to climb the seemingly crumbling tower moves away from the human sphere of the garden's ground and up towards the divine, thus becoming part of this sublime architectural scene (fig. 24).

Fig. 23: Temple of Mercury, Schwetzingen (Photo: Author)

Fig. 24: Temple of Mercury, Schwetzingen (Photo: Author)

As one of the last buildings to be completed in Schwetzingen, the Temple of Mercury resonates with other garden structures. Not accidentally, the temple offers the highest observation deck from which the garden can be appreciated panoramically. Though positioned at the garden's southern edge, it is visible from afar yet also offers extensive vistas, or at least it once did, since nineteenth-century reforestation has made it difficult to fully grasp the web of visual dialogues that were formerly at play. The building's fragmented cupola resonates with the distant Temple of Apollo as well as with the Mosque's roof, a structure in plain view from the site. Such resonances were intentional – notwithstanding the critique of Hirschfeld who criticized the "water castellum," among other reasons, because its proximity to the Temple of Botany disrupted the illusionism of both respective spectacles.[79] Much to the chagrin of Hirschfeld, who favored notions of an enhanced indigenous landscape, in Schwetzingen visual threads connected a vast and universalizing gardenscape, not a series of isolated garden tableaux.

As I have argued, architectural invocations of a malleable past were one strategy among many that were intended to prompt the garden visitor to ruminate. But the resonances of staged material demise with historical associations that reverberate through eighteenth-century landscaped parks could not easily be contained, not least since ruination touches on the contingency of political rule itself. Modern interpretations of Schwetzingen would at times prefer to impart a sententious message from visual resonances between different ensembles. But this and other landscaped parks lack closure because they do not exclude other interpretations.[80] The echoes between the "mythical views of sovereignty" on full display and visions of power in ruins never cease to unsettle.[81] This interplay was rooted in variations on one and the same theme: power – power to make an imprint on the surroundings as well as power that envisioned a new era or imagined its own limits.

To conjure up a concept – whether of a word or a thing – through its *contrarium* or opposite is a well-known trope, irony.[82] For the purpose of my argument, irony can be defined as a relation that exposes a difference. In the case of built or imagined ruins, connections could span space and time, interlacing that which is perceptibly distinct, though rarely collapsing this difference entirely. Put differ-

79 Hirschfeld, *Theorie*, vol. 5, 546.

80 Cf. Claus Reisinger, *Der Schloßgarten zu Schwetzingen* (Worms: Wernersche Verlagsanstalt, 1987).

81 Martha Feldman, *Opera and Sovereignty: Transforming Myths in Eighteenth-Century Italy* (Chicago: University of Chicago Press, 2007), 278.

82 Dilwyn Knox, *Ironia: Medieval and Renaissance Ideas on Irony* (Leiden: Brill, 1989), 9 and passim. The formulation originates with the *Rhetorica ad Alexandrum*.

ently, the illusionistic impulse that fed the craze to build perfect ruins could never quite drown an awareness of their artificiality. In the intermediate realm constituted by irony, the fascination with ruins thrived. Irony might be in the eye of the beholder. But for those willing to see, ruins intimated a rich nexus of relations, including those between the palace and the ruins in the palace's garden, geometrical gardens and gardens in a natural style, ruins artificial and ruins authentic.[83]

In other words, built ruins incite visual comparison – a way of seeing I have coined as comparative specularity in a different context, the rubble models. Viewed through this lens, the Schwetzingen ruins may even have figured as a commentary on the orphaned Palatinate whose ruler now resided far away and rarely came to visit his park.

To pick a different example, in *Sanssouci*, the summer residence King Frederick II of Prussia erected near Potsdam after 1745, visitors cannot escape the dialogue between an ensemble of artificial ruins – the wall of an amphitheatre, a pyramid-shaped tomb, temple columns (1748) – and the royal apartments. The design of the *cour d'honneur* (where visitors would have arrived) to the north of the building with its curved double row of columns is interrupted in order to provide an unimpeded and emphatic vista onto the "ruins hill." Located in the distance on a hill, the ruins are positioned above the residence and in perceptible dialogue with it. This "ruins hill," to be sure, expresses a profound appreciation for Roman architecture and alludes to its eighteenth-century kin, neoclassicism. To those in the know, these ruins may even have reminded viewers of the limits of royal power: The ruins ensemble surround a water basin from which the garden's spouts should have been fed, if only the king's engineers had succeeded in pumping up water from a nearby river to the hill overlooking *Sanssouci*.[84] But more generally, one cannot help but wonder how to relate ruins and residence in this case. Are we to associate Frederick's rule with a revival of the ancients? Are we to associate Frederick's Prussia of the present with the Roman past? Does the ruins ensemble simply serve to enhance the king's grandeur? Or do these ruins also function as a reminder that in the future Prussia's political and military departure would be

83 Here, my use of the trope is akin to the ironic mode which Hayden White has diagnosed for Enlightenment historiography. See Hayden White, *Metahistory: The Historical Imagination in Nineteenth-Century Europe* (Baltimore: The Johns Hopkins University Press, 1973), Chapter One, esp. pp. 65–69.

84 Stobbe, *Kassel-Wilhelmshöhe*, 87; Hans-Joachim Giersberg, *Schloss Sanssouci: Die Sommerresidenz Friedrichs des Großen* (Berlin: Nicolai, 2005), 143.

reduced to nothing but historical memories and ruined remains? Importantly, such readings do not exclude one another.[85]

As we have seen, the eighteenth-century fascination with ruins as a sublime idiom on the plain of history pre-dated the French Revolution and its aftermath. The complex semantics of ruins – their potency, their irony, their referentialiy – was not caused by the French Revolution or the period's historical ruptures. Instead, ruins and rumination on ruins offered a lens to reflect on the age's political, social, and cultural upheavals. Insights into an ever changing world stimulated the comparative gaze, as evident in a wide array of contemporary work. We can cite the twin canvasses Hubert Robert painted of the Louvre's Grand Gallery, one with a view of a projected art gallery (*Projet d'Aménagement de la Grande Galerie*) and paired with a second "imaginary view" of the same corridor *en ruines* in which the vault opens to a dramatic sky, not unlike Schwetzingen's Temple of Mercury (*Vue imaginaire de la Grande Galerie en ruines*, both 1796).[86] Or, to pick an equally striking example, a 1830 watercolor by Michael Gandy that depicts a cutaway view of the Bank of England – John Soane's signature building – as if "in ruins."[87] Infallibly and without the aid of counterparts, ruins contain their own *contraria* or opposites. They conjure up contrasts and correspondences across time and space. What may distinguish ruins from other potent signs then is, among other features, the fact that comparative specularity ekes out a living not only *between* a ruin and something else but also *within* the ruin itself.

85 In Kassel, under the rule of Landgrave William IX, the projected chateau (Weissenstein, now Wilhelmshöhe), high above the city of Kassel but below the monumental sculpture of Hercules on top of the hill, was originally projected to be designed as a ruinous prop. Much like in Schwetzingen, artificial ruins, among them an aqueduct (1788–1792) and a medieval castle (1793–1801), came to adorn this landscape garden. See Stobbe, *Kassel-Wilhelmshöhe*, 140, 145, 170–173. As a prince and future ruler, William IX inhabited an artificial medieval castle near Hanau (Wilhelmsbad, ibid., table 18).

86 Hubert Burda, *Die Ruine in den Bildern Hubert Roberts* (Munich: Fink, 1967), 172. In addition to producing a vast visual archive of ruins and garden scenes, Hubert Robert oversaw the design of gardens.

87 John Wilton-Ely, *Piranesi, Paestum & Soane* (London: Azimuth, 2001), 61. Wilton-Ely writes on Soane: "When in the throes of profound disillusionment with his sons' failure to meet his expectations and also deeply hurt by professional censure from the Royal Academy, in 1812 he wrote a profoundly ironic description of his house as if reduced by predatory Time to a mysterious Piranesian ruin ..." See also Christopher Woodward, *In Ruins* (New York: Pantheon, 2001), 160–176.

Miniature Ruins

The building of garden ruins, like the building of the earliest city models, was not exclusively a manifestation of princely passions and aristocratic display.[88] During the later eighteenth century, landscape gardens constituted a surprisingly permeable sphere of engagement attracting a wide swath of the educated classes. Sovereignty, as Martha Feldman argues, "points in different ways: initially toward the monarch who reigns supreme among all his subjects ... but increasingly toward self-determining groups and their ideals, or the ideals of the citizen who is no longer subject but sovereign himself."[89] (The project of a national theatre in the German language, a short-lived yet significant enterprise in eighteenth-century Electoral Mannheim and Munich, had arisen from a similarly mixed milieu of burgher associations and aristocratic circles.[90]) Indeed, in the small universes of German principalities, nascent civil society accommodated a variety of practitioners, and horticulture was only one example of a range of cultural pursuits shared across social and professional stations.[91] It is therefore highly relevant that princely gardens became publicly accessible spectacles already during the Enlightenment – spaces where different classes gathered.[92] During the 1780s, Carl Theodor, by that time only rarely in residence, opened his pleasure-grounds in Schwetzingen to visitors. Travelers came in droves, and social groups were said to mingle on the garden's grounds.[93]

In fact, "Enlightened entertainment," offered a particular kind of education, and "allowed for the legitimate indulging for the eyes," according to Barbara

88 Cf. Carl Georg, Duke of Mecklenburg, *Garten und Landschaft gestern und heute: Zur Geschichte der Gefühle in der Natur* (Haigerloch: PES-Edition, 1984).
89 Feldman, *Opera and Sovereignty*, 39.
90 Stephan Pflicht, *Kurfürst Carl Theodor von der Pfalz und seine Bedeutung für die Entwicklung des deutschen Theaters* (Reichling: Ehresmann Verlag, 1976).
91 Isabel V. Hull, *Sexuality, State, and Civil Society in Germany, 1700–1815* (Ithaca: Cornell University Press, 1996).
92 Stobbe, *Kassel-Wilhelmshöhe*, 73–91 and passim.
93 Elisabeth Szymczyk-Eggert, "' ... sogar wäre es mir lieb, wenn Ihr Schwetzingen besuchtet,'" in *Gärten der Goethezeit*, ed. Harri Günther (Leipzig: Edition Leipzig, 1993), 149, with a quote from the "Besuchsordnung" of 1787: "einem jeden Aus- und Einheimischen ohne Unterschied des Standes den freyen Zutritt in den Schwezinger Herrschafftlichen großen Lust-Garten wie vorher mildest zu gestatten." Note the term "wie vorher," as before. Zeyher, *Beschreibung der Gartenanlagen*, 30, includes a description where the presence of the ruling family did not impede groups of people from taking pleasure in the garden.

Stafford.[94] The underlying motivation of garden ruins – to urge reflection – had not changed, but the seriousness of this activity was able to include a sense of pleasure that any educated person was capable of appreciating. The vast and celebrated garden landscape erected by Count Franz von Anhalt-Dessau during his reign (1764–1817), the enlightened ruler of a tiny principality near Prussia, was never fenced in. These gardens were neither a space for garden follies nor mere leisure grounds; they were pedagogically motivated amelioration projects for the public's education. Needless to say, they included a great numbers of ruins, intended to move, instruct, delight, and shock.[95]

For those searching out more ruins and unable to build a ruin, the growing eighteenth-century market for luxury goods offered a less expensive option: the acquisition of scale models. Miniature renderings of ancient monuments were first sold to travelers on the grand tour to Italy. Elector Carl Theodor bought a superb and precious replica of Emperor Trajan's Column in Rome, for instance, on his second trip to Italy in 1783.[96] From the nexus of antiquarians, art dealers, and artisans came the idea to replicate the aura of ruins quasi-industrially. Inspired, among other things, by elaborate crèches (nativity scenes) produced in eighteenth-century Italy (including some in which the crèche showed meticulously made ancient ruins, a feature of Nativity scenes since the Renaissance), and soon fashionable across Europe, Giovanni Altieri, Agostino Rosa, Antonio Chichi, Carl May, and other artisans began to manufacture a variety of ancient sites – but ruins above all – in scale.[97] Tombs, triumphal arches, a range of temples, the Colosseum, as well as the Pantheon were for sale to customers willing to spend the considerable amounts such artifacts cost.[98] This range of products (which, with few exceptions, were all Roman sites) mirrored the long-standing recom-

94 Barbara Maria Stafford, *Artful Science: Enlightenment Entertainment and the Eclipse of Visual Education* (Cambridge, Mass.: MIT Press, 1994), 73.

95 The literature on Dessau-Wörlitz is vast, an excellent introduction in Norbert Eisold, *Das Dessau-Wörlitzer Gartenreich: Der Traum von der Vernunft* (Cologne: DuMont, 1993); Kulturstiftung Dessau Wörlitz, ed., *Unendlich schön: Das Gartenreich Dessau-Wörlitz* (Berlin: Nicolai, 2005).

96 Francis Haskell and Nicholas Penny, *Taste and the Antique: The Lure of Classical Sculpture, 1500–1900* (New Haven: Yale University Press, 1981), 47: "the replica (two meters tall) with silver gilt figures on a lapis lazuli ground, begun in 1774 and signed in 1780 by Luigi Valadier" (illustration, p. 51). See also *Der Pfälzer Apoll*, 34–36. Stephan von Stengel left a description of the artwork and its sale to the elector, see Stengel, *Kurfürst Karl Theodor in Rom*, 128f.

97 Werner Helmberger and Valentin Kockel, eds., *Rom über die Alpen tragen: Fürsten sammeln antike Architektur* (Landshut: Arcols, 1993), passim; Peter Gercke et al., *Antike Bauten in Modell und Zeichnung um 1800: Vollständiger Katalog der Korkmodelle und der Sonderausstellung 1986* (Kassel: Staatliche Kunstsammlungen, 1986).

98 Kockel, "Rom über die Alpen tragen," in *Rom über die Alpen tragen*, 24.

mendations of authors and tour guides of the must-see sites in Rome.[99] But by offering bridges and locks in model form, they also appealed to experts interested in the feats of ancient engineering. Available in different sizes or as a series – a savvy sales formula developed by Chichi and emulated by others – agents sold models to connoisseurs from all across Europe. Starting around 1770, collections of models were placed on display in Gotha, St. Petersburg, Schwerin, Aschaffenburg, Munich, Kassel, and Darmstadt, among other places. A London commercial exhibition is documented as early as 1776.[100] In Paris, an "architectural museum" is known to have opened its doors in 1806; its main attraction was an array of modeled ruins, a total of 76 pieces.[101]

Carl May (1742–1822), a pastry cook in the service of the archbishopric of Mainz for most of his life, became the most prominent sculptor of such objects north of the Alps.[102] His product range comprised 43 known models, some of them produced in a variety of sizes, the majority of which – 37 – represented ancient buildings, practically all of them ruins (fig. 25).[103]

Built garden ruins and scale models of ruins originated from the same imaginary. This is, however, not only a story of genesis and mutual influence, the question why modeled ruins made visual sense to viewers in the decades before and after 1800. This inter-text also pertains to the many correspondences between what was on display inside buildings and what could be visited *en plein air*, between art collections and garden architecture, between villas and their surroundings – correspondences that were the building blocks of a historically informed gaze.[104]

---

99 The product range of model-makers included the Temple of Paestum, Campania, near Naples. On models of medieval sites see below.

100 Ibid., 20.

101 Kockel, "Rom über die Alpen tragen," 19–20 (ill. 20). As the illustration demonstrates, these models were exhibited in combination with *vedute* of the sites.

102 Werner Helmberger, "Carl Joseph May (1742–1822): Hofkonditor und Korkbildner," in *Rom über die Alpen tragen*, 63–89.

103 Ibid., 67f.

104 In *Sanssouci*, the many paintings and reliefs of landscapes or allegories with ruins in the royal apartments, executed 1746–1747, resonated with the ensemble built on a hill under the skies (1748). In *Ludwigslust*, an eighteenth-century residence of the Counts of Mecklenburg-Schwerin, the models and paintings of ruins as well as other images within the chateau corresponded in an oblique way with the realm of the garden with its built ruin (1788). Another example is the *Luisium* garden near Dessau where a dialogue was forged between a built ruined archway in the garden and the villa's Pompeii room with its invocation of an eruption of Mt. Vesuvio through a series of color paintings and other scenes of ancient sites. The nearby garden of Wörlitz contained a miniature Vesuvio set up for theatrical performances of an eruption, complete with a

While a variety of materials were used to build these artifacts – wood, stone, dried plants, wire, etc. – their surfaces consisted mainly of cork. On a practical level, the lightness of cork meant that these intricate objects could be shipped easily (as had been the case with the cork model of the city of Florence for a Medici pope Vasari described) – a fact that agents advertized to their potential clients.[105] What is more, the suggestive quality of the material with its porosity and warm coloration was intrinsic to their appeal. Cork was perceived to magically replicate the appearance of time-worn stone buildings.[106] As an organic material used to render stone, cork mediated between the realms of nature and art, a relation that had motivated many early modern scientific and artistic inventions. More so, to the eyes of a historically minded viewership, cork imaged the imprint of time. It was therefore the perfect material to feed the eighteenth-century historicist-artistic enterprise, a narration of the past that tempted viewers to simultaneously forget about and delight in the simulation at its core.

Frances Haskell and Nicholas Penny once opined that eighteenth-century "travelers who flocked to Italy agreed that the reality far surpassed the copies on which they had been brought up."[107] Such a statement sounds persuasive today, when the studying of models is typically an affair of little import – because they are *copies*, after all; but surprisingly, such doubt and condescension was not an opinion frequently expressed at the time.[108] When Johann Wolfgang Goethe narrated his arrival in the Eternal City in 1786, he described his first exposure to ancient marvels as a transformative encounter with sites which he had known since childhood, much like Edward Gibbon had in 1764.[109] But *pace* Gibbon, he did so without belittling the various media in which he had first experienced these

---

replica of the villa owned by William Hamilton near Naples and an amphitheatre. For the latter see *Der Vulkan im Wörlitzer Park*, ed. Kulturstiftung Dessau Wörlitz (Berlin: Nicolai, 2005).

105 Helmberger, "May," 67f.

106 In an anonymous essay on these models, the author praises the models' "heavenly magic" (Kockel, "Rom über die Alpen tragen," 24).

107 Haskell, *Taste and the Antique*, xiii.

108 Kockel ("Rom über die Alpen tragen," 24) quotes an English traveler who in 1783 expresses doubts about the model's effect since the buildings' greatness cannot be fully appreciated in this form.

109 Johann Wolfgang Goethe, *Italian Journey*, trans. W. H. Auden, Elizabeth Mayer (London: Penguin, 1962), 129: "All the dreams of my youth have come to life; the first engravings I remember ... I now see in reality, and everything I have known for so long through paintings, drawings, etchings, woodcuts, paster casts and cork models is now assembled before me." Id., *Italienische Reise*, in *Werke: Hamburger Ausgabe*, vol. 11, ed. Erich Trunz (Munich: Beck, 1988), 126: "Alle Träume meiner Jugend seh' ich nun lebendig; ... seh' ich nun in Wahrheit, und alles, was ich in Gemälden und Zeichnungen, Kupfern und Holzschnitten, in Gips und Kork schon lange gekannt,

Fig. 25 : Round Temple in Tivoli, Model by Carl Mary 1792/1814, columns: 18,3 cm, Schlossmuseum, Aschaffenburg (Photo: Bayerische Verwaltung der Staatlichen Schlösser, Gärten und Seen)

ancient sites – drawings, etchings, engravings, paintings, and cork models. Quite the opposite, in fact: he was emphatic about the experience of these unspeakably beautiful sights in replication as in the original. These representations were thus an indispensible means to make the most of one's traveling experience; they could serve as both preparation and souvenir. Without such exposure, the informed immersion would simply not have been equally profound, useful, or memorable.

In 1800, an essay published in Germany dignified cork models (whose dissemination had already spawned a lively promotional discourse) with a technical term, "Phelloplastik" or phello-sculpture, derived from the Greek words for cork

steht nun beisammen vor mir." It is certainly no accident that this extensive list culminates in cork models.

and sculpture.[110] Whether used to prepare or to commemorate a trip, whether one set them up as table pieces or as academic objects of study, critics regarded them as full of potential uses and possibilities. If displayed ornamentally on tables during dinner festivities, for instance, these models were presented as if they had the power to elevate the evening's conversations to a higher level of erudition.[111] Such sculptures became all the rage, celebrated by contemporary commentators above all for their naturalist qualities. As a three-dimensional medium, not unlike the sixteenth-century excitement over city models, these models were said to be superior to prints and drawings.[112] Many critics promoted them as objects whose visual appeal equaled that of the originals they represented, eliding their considerable inaccuracies, instead presenting them as faithful replicas in miniature form.[113] One edge they had over their real-life competitors, it was said, was that models isolated the site in question from visual distraction. They provided scopic control which could not so easily be achieved *in situ*. These objects thus incited and instantiated the sovereign's gaze we encountered in the previous chapter with regard to the city models for sculpted ruins. Repeatedly, contemporary German discourses mention that no detail would escape one's studious gaze. These laudations went as far as claiming that in the future timely and costly travels to Italy would no longer be necessary for architects in training: "One believes oneself to stand in front of" the monuments, or so the argument ran.[114] Approached from these panegyrics, a visit to the actual sites was not so much a moment of fulfillment but harbored the risk of disappointing the traveler.

---

110 The term was taken up in an encyclopedia of 1816, see Helmberger, "May," 63.

111 Kockel, "Rom über die Alpen tragen," 24, quotes an 1800-essay: Such models have "alle Monumente des Alterthums, ohne den Ort seine Zierde zu rauben, transportabel gemacht und die Mittel der Möglichkeit, an ihrer Bewunderung Theil zu nehmen, den Kunstsinn durch Anschauen und Vergleichen zu schärfen, wahren Kunstgeschmack zu verbreiten und den Begriffen von architektonischen Kunstwerken mehr Klarheit, Deutlichkeit und Bestimmtheit zu geben." See also Helmberger, "May," 80.

112 Essay on models from 1800 as quoted in Helmberger ("May," 74).

113 A particularly telling early description of 1779 is quoted in Kockel, "Rom über die Alpen tragen," 11: "Man kann nichts täuschenderes sehen. Alles ist bis auf die geringste Fuge, den kleinsten Stein, das kleinste Graßplätzchen und Schutthaufen ausgemessen, und dargestellt ..." A similar description, not without irony, by the playwright August von Kotzebue: "Man kann sich nichts treueres denken. Er hat alle Steine wirklich gezählt, bei ihm ist keiner mehr, und keiner weniger als in der Natur. Fast möchte ich behaupten, er hat auch die Grashalmen und Blätter gezählt, die auf den Ruinen wachsen. Nicht genug! er hat jeden dieser Millionen Steine so gewissenhaft nachgebildet, als ob er ein Portrait kopierte." In a notice of 1794, Carl May's models were praised along the same lines (quoted in Helmberger, "May," 64).

114 Kockel, "Rom über die Alpen tragen," 11: "Man glaubt davor zu stehen."

Only over time, however, did models begin to approximate the standards of well-measured authenticity hailed by their admirers. Carl May, for one, never set foot on Italian soil. Like other sculptors working in the same vein, he relied on eclectic information – a variety of publications and other scale models. Actual measurements were hampered mainly by limited access to the relevant sites or the fact that phello-sculptors lacked the equipment necessary to measure precisely. The resulting distortions notwithstanding, the model-makers supplied their products with miniature scales and signed them, sometimes using the confidence-inspiring epithet "architect." Claims to faithful representation were sometimes just that, mere claims, though these same claims instigated corrections and improved standards. Between 1802 and 1830, Domenico Padiglione systematically documented archeological excavations in Pompeii via scale models designed to preserve a record for posterity.[115] Over the course of twenty-two years (1790–1812), Carlo Lucangeli worked on two elaborate models of the Colosseum made of wood and with claims to architectural accuracy, one in its ruined state *and* a reconstructive model – another instance of comparative specularity.[116] It is emblematic of the changing expectations that Carl May's son and successor, Georg May, an engineer by profession, travelled to Italy in order to perfect his father's product line and to expand the repertoire of buildings. The verisimilitude that had inspired the making of city models gradually also became the historicist's passion.

What had been a sideline for his father, models of German medieval monuments, became more of a focal point in his generation. During the Napoleonic wars, especially after the *Empereur*'s conquest of the German lands, the Middle Ages acquired urgent political and cultural significance as a national past. Germans now began to look to the medieval period for visions of cultural renewal and cultural grandeur. In 1816, the future king of Bavaria, Louis I, commissioned Carl May to work on a model of Heidelberg castle – a collaborative project between father and son with Georg gathering the data and Carl modeling (fig. 26). The prince's interest in what May called this "most beautiful German ruin" derived not merely from its associations with German Romanticism but, as Valentin Kockel argues, also from its genealogical appeal for a Wittels-

---

115 Kockel, "Rom über die Alpen tragen," 21f.

116 Cianluca Schingo, "I modelli del Colosseo," in *Sangue e Arena*, ed. Adriano La Regina (Milan: Electa, 2001), 105–115; and Cinzia Conti, "Il modello ligneo dell'Anfiteatro Flavio di Carlo Lucangeli: Osservazione nel corso del restauro," ibid., 117–125. The models were celebrated in contemporary publications, see Charles Lucangeli, *Modèle qui offre la restauration du Colisée de Rome* (Rome: Salvioni, 1827).

Fig. 26: Carl and Georg May, Cork model of Heidelberg Castle, 1816–1829 (base: 323 × 320 cm; scale ca. 1:56), formerly Bavarian National Museum, Munich (Photo: Beringer)

bach prince.[117] Heidelberg thus serves as a reminder of how particular ruins and models accommodated a variety of fascinations and interpretations.

The collection of information about a vast castle complex with an architectural history spanning centuries required enormous surveying efforts. As a result, its making took years and was completed by Georg May only in 1829.[118] Once finished, this scale model was put on display in Aschaffenburg and then in Munich where it went up in flames in one of the 1944 air raids on the city. If the plans to rebuild Heidelberg castle that were vigorously discussed in Wilhelmine Germany had in fact been carried out,[119] the Mays' model would have become an important repository of information about the castle's prior existence as an edifice in

117 Kockel, "Das Heidelberger Schloß: Ein Korkmodell von Carl und Georg May, angefertigt 1816–1829, zerstört 1944," in *Rom über die Alpen tragen*, 91–117.

118 Scale 1:56, measurements at the base 323 × 320 cm.

119 Manfred F. Fischer, "Heidelberger Schloss," in *Geschichte der Rekonstruktion: Konstruktion der Geschichte*, ed. Winfried Nerdinger (Munich: Prestel, 2010), 339–342.

ruins – not unlike the Treuner model of Frankfurt after the old city's destruction in March of 1944.

* * *

Ruins, actual and artificial, were catalysts of an imaginary about the past. They were felt to make experiential something that eludes our grasp, time. They invited us to linger. They mobilized viewers through affective scenarios that allowed them to imagine a time when what was now ruined (or seemed to be) was complete; they allowed viewers to imagine forward to their own demise or to compare their own time with the past. Ruins triggered modes of comparative specularity across time. They thus contributed to a larger early modern European tendency to see the material world in historical terms.

By virtue of one site above all, Schwetzingen, we have explored the proliferation of ruins as well as the dissemination of a ruins imaginary among many viewers around 1800. What had interested only a few humanists, artists, and antiquarians in the sixteenth century increasingly involved more viewers, most prominently the nobility and the "middling sort." A variety of media – painting, prints, models, and architecture, to name but the most common ones – stimulated and satisfied a hunger for ruins as visual emblems. Ruins became local, ruins became moveable, and ruins décor became domestic. Ruins could be visited close to home when built ruins in landscape gardens transported invocations of ancient sites to northern locales. While most of the ruins imaginary around 1800 revolved around classical ruins, non-classical, especially medieval, ruins with their more local associations also started to attract attention.

At the same time, during the late eighteenth century, scale models of ruins became something of a fashion. Within the plethora of media forging images of ruins, scale models were distinguished from their counterparts *in situ* by the fact that they offered complete visual control. In a competitive field where viewers brought knowledge to such simulacra, these objects increasingly also became marvels of accuracy. The position high above the models that we saw with regard to the sovereign subject since the sixteenth century was now instantiated by those who surveyed and ruled the past as it touched on the present. But the "scientific" history practiced by historicists since the nineteenth century has submerged the memory of these vehicles of the historical imagination with their rich affective facture, though they continue to be made and shown.

Chapter Five

Models of destruction are situated at the intersection of two ways of seeing, the sovereign gaze and the ruins gaze: Rubble models image the effects of violence in history within visual conditions similar to the ones created for the sovereign or ruler. Yet the relation of the two visual modes is an uneasy, if not paradoxical, one. Ruins have the potential to raise one's awareness of the flow of time or trouble the temporal layers that separate one's present from the past or the future. Conversely, the sovereign gaze distances us from the conditions on the ground, and lifts the observer, if only for a moment, into a simulated viewpoint defined by unmitigated visual access and comprehensiveness. In short, a sovereign position leads to bodily and emotional composure, whereas the ruins gazers may become aware of themselves as historical subjects within a web of relations circumscribed by time and place. Yet these two gazes converge in that they ensnare the viewer with their invitation to measure or compare, to situate oneself or define others, to analogize or ruminate.

Indeed, visions of ruined cities from a perspective high above the devastation pervade the photographic, cinematic, and other records from the Second World War's immediate aftermath. But we should not delude ourselves. Not everybody was looking or was looking as intently as we might surmise, let alone looking in the same way. Reporting from a visit to Germany, her former homeland, in 1950, Hannah Arendt wrote, "[a] lack of response is evident everywhere, and it is difficult to say whether this signifies a half-conscious refusal to yield to grief or a genuine inability to feel."[1] This refusal to take in the panorama or appreciate the particulars also surfaces in Billy Wilder's film comedy, A Foreign Affair *(1948) – in this case with regard to non-Germans visiting the war-scarred Germany. The opening sequence captures a US delegation, as their airplane begins its descent into Berlin – an ironic intertext with Leni Riefenstahl's "Triumph of the Will" that had Hitler flying through the clouds to a Nazi party rally held in Nuremberg* (Triumph des Willens, *1935*). *As endless strips of monotonous shells of the city's buildings pass by the aircraft's windows, the passengers, a fictitious Congressional delegation, respond in radically different ways to the ruins of the Reich's former capital spread out underneath. Some delegates are looking with great curiosity, calling attention to "the pesthole down below" or rehearsing figures such as the amount of explosives dropped on the city, while another traveler is entirely absorbed in recording the vastness of the destruction on film. Flying above the derelict Berlin inevitably triggers responses – opinions, reflections, and debates about Germany's political future among them. The sovereign gaze is, here and elsewhere, a gaze that is thought to be critically dis-*

1 Hannah Arendt, "The Aftermath of Nazi Rule: Report from Germany," *Commentary* 10 (1950): 342.

cerning; it is the gaze of the actual or supposed expert. Yet Congresswoman Phoebe Frost of the same delegation chooses not to look down; in fact, she demonstrably takes off her glasses and lectures her distracted fellow politicians on their delegation's true duties, namely to look into the moral conduct of US soldiers stationed in Berlin. Once on the ground, she will be the one to go and see for herself in fact. Her refusal to accept the summary but distorted view offered to the committee by the US representatives ultimately allows her to come to an independent judgment that will transform her character permanently.

Arendt once stated that, unlike in making art, man is free but not sovereign in acting politically, that is he or she is able to act yet unable to know the conditions or consequences of one's actions.[2] *This brief observation touches on the possibility that certain vehicles of the imagination have the potential to catapult humans into a sovereign position, if only for a moment, allowing beholders "to see the world" from an elevated perspective – a shift both empowering and potentially distancing that is worthy of our attention.*

---

2 Hannah Arendt, *Denktagebuch: 1950 bis 1973*, ed. Ursula Ludz and Ingeborg Nordmann (Munich: Piper, 2002), 82.

From Rubble to Ruins in Heilbronn and Elsewhere

> This then, I thought, as I looked round about me, is the representation of history. It requires a falsification of perspective. We, the survivors, see everything from above, see everything at once, and still we do not know how it was.
> (Das also, denkt man, indem man langsam im Kreis geht, ist die Kunst der Repräsentation der Geschichte. Sie beruht auf einer Fälschung der Perspektive. Wir, die Ueberlebenden, sehen alles von oben herunter, sehen alles zugleich und wissen dennoch nicht, wie es war.)
> W. G. Sebald, *The Rings of Saturn*[1]

Seeing the bombed-out German cities as ciphers began not after Germany's defeat but with their destruction during the war. When, in late October 1943, parts of Kassel were reduced to ashes by Britain's Royal Air Force, Joseph Goebbels, the Reich's propaganda minister, hastened to give meaning to the remains. In his speech of November 5, 1943 – two weeks after the fatal attacks – Goebbels recast human suffering, death, and loss as a sacrifice for a better future. "When the few still extant bells in Germany will ring in victory, you will march through this city's fields of rubble in happiness," he told his audience. "You will view these ruins as pledges and guarantors of victory. You will stand still in front of every house and say: we have sacrificed this house, too, for victory."[2] Note how buildings, here used as signifiers of victorious sacrifice, mask the lurid destruction that many in the audience must have witnessed first-hand. Note also, how the terminology proceeds from "rubble" to "ruins": rubble designates the vastness of destruction and ruins their transformation into symbols.[3]

---

1 W. G. Sebald, *The Rings of Saturn,* trans. Michael Hulse (New York: New Directions, 1999), 125; id., *Die Ringe des Saturn* (Frankfurt am Main: Fischer, 1997), 151f.

2 Joseph Goebbels, *Goebbels-Reden*, vol. 2: *1939–1945*, ed. Helmut Heiber (Düsseldorf: Droste, 1972), 259–285, here p. 285: "wenn einmal die wenigen in Deutschland noch vorhandenen Glocken den Sieg einläuten werden, dann werden auch Sie beglückt durch die Trümmerfelder dieser Stadt marschieren ... Sie werden diese Ruinen als die Unterpfänder und die Garanten des Sieges betrachten. Sie werden dann vor jedem Haus stillstehen und werden sagen: auch dieses Haus haben wir für den Sieg geopfert." On the question who attended the event, see ibid., 259, n. 1. See also Werner Dettmar, "Kassel im Luftkrieg," in *Leben in Ruinen: Kassel 1943–1948 im Gedenkjahr der Stadt Kassel zur Erinnerung an ihre Zerstörung am 22. Oktober 1943*, ed. Christina Coers-Dittmar and Alexander Link (Kassel: Jonas Verlag, 1993), 11–22.

3 Similar arguments also surface in the 1945-new year speech Adolf Hitler delivered on the radio: "dereinst als Abschluß dieser Zeit auch die deutschen Städte sich wieder aus ihren Trümmerhaufen erheben werden zu neuen Plätzen deutscher Städteherrlichkeit. Der nationalsozialistische Staat wird mit seinr Energie und Tatkraft alles das, was heute der Zerstörung verfällt, in wenigen Jahren neu errichten." (Quoted in Domarus, *Der Untergang*, 16f).

Such visionary, if not millenarian, statements about the nation's future (statements made in the face of egregious deprivation, loss, and suffering) would have been difficult to uphold without the work of ridding cities struck from the air of a major attack's disastrous effects, when dead bodies piled up in the streets and, in the words of a Kassel NS official, "the scenes that take place in front of the uncovered corpses, are horrifying."[4] Restoring order in cities hit from the air and the control of access to ruined neighborhoods in bombed out-cities absorbed increasing energies within the Nazi state as the air war over Germany intensified.[5]

Post-war discourses, as we have seen in the case of Frankfurt, continued to shape the meaning of the mountains of rubble in Germany's devastated urban centers. For years after the war, the complete removal of the debris that covered the cities of defeated Germany was a distant prospect. Just as the rubble (and its emerging corollary, ruins) was omnipresent, these piles of dust, stone, and other materials ascended to the status of omnipresent signifiers. They were deployed in a variety of media in order to capture the vastness and totality of the destruction. Within Germany and in discourses about Germany, rubble and ruins also helped to determine which pasts, presents, and futures were usable. In this context, the terms, with their particular inflections, invoked a war-induced dereliction, as authors struggled to produce accounts of what distinguished the sights of the ruined cities of post-war Europe from the ruins of the past.

In an essay of 1946, the year the Treuner brothers built the model of Frankfurt's ruined old city (fig. 27), the French writer Elsa Triolet (1896–1970), an observer at the Nuremberg Trials, conjured up a panoramic view of Nuremberg in rubble. In this context, she coins a phrase, "model ruins" (*ruines modèles*) which remakes the city, and its seemingly endless heaps of debris, into an image ready for visual consumption as well as a description of an exemplary situation. In Triolet's account the remains of this medieval city lack all focus or beauty.[6] Unlike the romance of ruins built in landscape gardens, and of authentic ruins flocked to in Rome or elsewhere, she states, these are the remains of what was only yesterday a city but had become an enormous, inhabited graveyard. The memories of the

4 Letter of the NSDAP Kreisleitung, October 25, 1943, to the mayor of Kassel, Schimmelpfennig: "Das Bild ist erschütternd und die Scenen, die sich vor den unbedeckten Leichen abspielen, sind schauderhaft." (Kassel, Stadtmuseum) On the air raids in Kassel and reactions to the events in Nazi Germany, see Jörg Arnold, *The Allied Air War and Urban Memory: The Legacy of Strategic Bombing in Germany* (Cambridge: Cambridge University Press, 2011), 30–59.

5 As the devastations progressed, large-scale plans, never realized, took shape to resettle Germans to the countryside. See Gutschow, "Hamburg," passim.

6 Other observers had a different response, speaking of the beauty of the scenes of devastation. See Chapter Two.

conflagrations that caused Nuremberg's ruination were all too fresh; the mind could not roam sentimentally.

And yet, as we emerge from our explorations of sixteenth-century city models and eighteenth-century model ruins, we cannot avoid the implications of Triolet's term, and the metaphoric miniaturization implicit in it – in an article published in the very year when the Treuners sculpted their "Plastic Sketch." Model, as metaphor and simile, brought the vastness of devastation into focus and into the realm of comprehensibility. Similarly, she compares the ruined cityscape to a basket that had been dropped, hinting at the human agency behind the disaster. She emphasizes semantic equivalencies between material ruin and political collapse. "Model ruins" allow her to imbue the rubble with judgments in a warning against what she, a Communist, saw as a rising wave of anti-democratic sentiments in a Europe on the brink of the Cold War. Presented thus, Triolet's Nuremberg constitutes a vast but daunting ground for political action, and the ruined cityscape sets the scene for a global political crisis in the making, which roils beneath the surface of the Nuremberg Trials' humanitarianism.[7]

It is in this context of multiform post-war representations of loss and devastation that our new, and now familiar, representational form emerged in Germany: three-dimensional miniature cities in ruins. Miniatures, in whatever form or medium, skew the rules that ordinarily govern how observers encounter the world, opening up novel horizons of perception. When destruction is miniaturized, as it is in the rubble models, these enigmatic vistas of destruction bring the monumentality of miniatures into focus. By changing conventions of seeing or imagining, the reader is granted an immediacy of perceptive access, one marked by simultaneity rather than a sequence of impressions as in a documentary film. Without suspending the everyday, miniaturization thus works in the *irrealis* or 'as if' mode. If we follow Susan Stewart, the grand theorist of the miniature, their "smallness" stands in an inverse relation to the responses they occasion: minia-

7 Elsa Triolet, "Der Prozeß tanzt" (7. Juni 1946), in *Der Nürnberger Lernprozess: Von Kriegsverbrechern und Starreportern*, ed. Steffen Radlmaier (Frankfurt am Main: Eichborn, 2001), 251–267. Triolet is also the author of *L'inspecteur des ruines* (Paris: La bibliothèque française, 1948) – a novel which emplots similar themes in a narrative allegory. Set after the end of World War II in Paris and unnamed ruin of a town in Germany, the protagonist, a former resistance fighter who had been imprisoned in Germany and has lost everything, including his identity, becomes hired as a dealer in a scheme to turn rubble, debris, and detritus into monetary gain; as the business scheme sinks into the rubble and moral ruin, the image of a new society shines forth in which unhappiness and "ruins become the exception" (*The Inspector of Ruins*, trans. Norman Cameron, New York: Roy Publishers, [1953], 225).

Fig. 27: Robert and Hermann Treuner, "Plastic Sketch," Frankfurt, 1946, Historisches Museum (Photo: Author)

tures have the potential to generate an excess of meaning – as we will see, it is this potential that is at the heart of their appeal.[8]

Here we will excavate the semiotics of scale; we will parse the signs offered by the genre of ruins that exploded from the rubble of World War II. As mentioned at the beginning of our study, there are ten known models in Germany: Frankfurt (1946), Hamburg (ca. 1950), Hannover (ca. 1951; exact dates for the complete model is unknown), Kassel (1955), Heilbronn (1960), and Münster (ca. 1966) in the two decades after the end of the war, and, after a hiatus of twenty years, Bielefeld (1985), Würzburg (1989), Trier (2001), and Pforzheim (2000-, unfinished). These intriguing three-dimensional renderings of bombed-out cities vary in many details, but are joined by their foundational elements. They each provide glimpses of war's destruction and devastation, offering themselves to their viewers as instruments of *Verlustbewältigung* or coming to terms with the

8 Susan Stewart, *On Longing: Narratives of the Miniature, the Gigantic, the Souvenir, the Collection* (Durham: Duke University Press, 1993).

Fig. 28: Model of Hannover 1945, detail (Photo: Author)

terrible loss of life, suffering, and the urban dereliction wrought by the air raids.[9] They may enable us to come to terms with a violent past by forging a visual echo, and thus a memory, of the bombings. Importantly, the models have often been presented in public as open signifiers; many were originally or are on view in publicly accessible spaces with little verbal explanation to accompany them. If presented thus, they accommodate a variety of gazes and forms of engagement, as I will demonstrate for one particular city, Heilbronn.

My discussion of Heilbronn's *Ehrenhalle* (Memorial Hall; literally: Hall of Honors) with its city models will use the architectural context of an urban memorial to elucidate the semantic potential of relief models between 1945 and the mid 1960s for the commemorations of the air raids during the first twenty years after the end of the war. Such miniatures are mobile monuments. They have occasionally been moved, as we saw with the Frankfurt rubble model, and set up in

9 This term, with its echo of "Vergangenheitsbewältigung" (coming to terms with the past), is heuristically valuable. I am aware of the contradictions that continue to trouble the deployment of "Vergangenheitsbewältigung" with its problematic suggestion, among other things, that one can ever bring to a close the memory of Nazi atrocities.

various or changing contexts. That the *Ehrenhalle* has changed little since it first opened its doors calls for an analysis of the spatial experience within which the models functioned and function. In the case of Heilbronn, an *in situ*-investigation can be complemented by archival records about the memorial's planning that open a window on the political and aesthetic contexts that birthed the memorial and its city models. We will then survey other such models, in order to gauge the genre and its history of display, especially as regards a second period of commemorating the air raids over German cities, from the mid-1980s onward when the historical recovery of the air raids gained ground.

An analysis of how ruined urban spaces have been displayed as models in city halls and museums in the decades since 1945 challenges the assumption that post-war Germany evaded representing the air raids altogether. Whereas W. G. Sebald and Jörg Friedrich among others centered the recent debate over the air raids on the notion of a repressive hypothesis, I seek to widen our lens by focusing on the intertwined realms of memory, history, and representation as they have unfolded between 1945 and the present.

Modeling Urban Destruction

The fixity of models stands in marked contrast to what they represent. The Latin word *ruina* means collapse, or rather collapsing – in other words a process. The medium of a three-dimensional model alongside the contingency of actual destruction – with its shifting piles of rubble, its unstable façades in perpetual danger of collapse, the omnipresence of dust and ash, not to mention stench and vermin, and the plant growth or animal life that quickly emerge in the wake of attacks from the air – form an arresting material paradox. Through an intensive and laborious process, these model-makers make a permanent image of something impermanent (fig. 28).

Scale models make urban space experiential in a particular fashion: city models, as I have argued in an earlier chapter, are vehicles of surveying and planning. Unlike actual cities, they are devoid of the imprint of human life; they may be exacting in their details, but their features are generic – roadways, fountains, houses, façades – little changed from the standards set by their sixteenth-century prototypes. But a model takes on a distinct meaning once it references a bombed-out city rather than an inhabited place. Models freeze moments in time, or rather artificially recreate them, transforming these moments into objects ready for visual investigation, both within time and outside of it. They seek to capture a city's moment of greatest devastation, but their precise reference point in time is often either elusive or unstated, at least until the 1980s, as we will see below, when new standards of accuracy were brought to bear on the making of such models. Indeed modeled stasis transcends a specific moment in time so that it is difficult for the observer to resist the impulse to fall into an extended meditation, as was the effect of the built ruins in landscape gardens.

Dagmar Barnouw has observed that for the US war photographer Margaret Bourke-White "the fascination of the photograph was the distance that allowed her to see only one-dimensional shapes forming intriguing patterns undisturbed by human fears and hopes."[10] Oft-reproduced images of German cities after the end of hostilities regularly evoke the vast emptiness of hollow spaces that, the viewer knows – the architectural skeleton of a city is recognizable after all – once teemed with life. Due to the sheer amount of destruction, the past survives only in its ruinous reflection. Hardly anyone appears to tell the disaster's story. If there is somebody present, it is in the form of observers of the vast desert of devastation, who magnify the spectacle of destruction by their detached shadow-like presence; they are too small for us to identify with, and certainly too small to actually do anything about all that devastation.

Another common "observer" in post-war photographs are the silent stone sculptures that survived the inferno unharmed, like the allegorical figure of *Güte* (benevolence) who looks out over Richard Peter's iconic shot of the ruined city of Dresden. Like much German post-war photography of Germany's urban destruction, this and similar shots betray religious overtones – even if the Dresden image was not shot from a church tower but from city hall and the sculpture in question is not an angel but an allegorical figure.[11]

We should note that such photographs of depopulated cities stand in marked contrast to other iconic glimpses of World War II: emaciated concentration camp survivors, staring at the camera from behind barbed wire, and the piles of corpses

---

10 Dagmar Barnouw, *Germany 1945: Views of War and Violence* (Bloomington: Indiana University Press, 1996), 101.

11 "Dresden nach der Zerstörung am 13.2.1945: Blick vom Rathausturm nach Süden," Sächsische Landesbibliothek, Abteilung Deutsche Fotothek. See Susanne Vees-Gulani, "'Phantomschmerzen': Durs Grünbeins 'Porzellan' und neue Wege in der Literatur über den Luftkrieg," in *Luftkrieg: Erinnerungen in Deutschland und Europa* (Göttingen: Wallstein Verlag, 2009), 277–296, here pp. 277f. See also David Crew, "Building or Bodies? Using Photographs of the Bombing of Dresden, 1945–1975," talk presented at the German Studies Association, September 18, 2003. With gratitude to David Crew for having shared this paper with me. For a similar example see the photograph rendered in Jörg Arnold, *The Allied Air War and Urban Memory*, 5: "Magdeburg in Mourning." There is a different kind of photo that foregrounds survival; yet they often did not achieve iconicity. Cf. *Die Hamburger Katastrophe vom Sommer 1943 in Augenzeugenberichten*, ed. Renate Hauschild-Thiessen (Hamburg: Verein für Hamburgische Geschichte, 1993).

discovered after the liberation of the camps.[12] These images of emaciation and death shock us with flesh – the bodies here are teeming, abundant, but marked by experiences that defy the imagination. The city images look completely different, and yet the absence of people leads us to a similar place: a sense of human loss that exceeds the imagination. As in post-war photography, models of devastated cityscapes function like a synecdoche for the people who once lived there and the urban space that continues to exist only insofar as it is enshrined in personal memory or historic documentation. Absences invite interpretive pirouettes – acts that give meaning and fill the void. Therein lies one of the many appeals of seeing ruins, be they real remains, or built ruins, or artifacts like models.

Questions as to "Who bombed and why?" cannot be answered through these objects. Like the victims of the bombings, the agents of destruction are absent. Notably, some of the exhibits surrounding the rubble models feature no factual account of the loss. Even in exhibits with extensive historical narratives, the text of the exhibits frequently evade the question of whether the attack was justified, favoring a descriptive mode instead when the unfolding of an aerial attack and its consequences are presented to the visitor. The destruction of Kassel, for example, was not only the result of the Allied attacks. Once the air raids over German cities had started, Nazi officials seized the opportunity to wipe clean the urban slate, making way in some neighborhoods for projected reconstructions in a National-ist Socialist future that never came. There is no mention of this, however, in the extensive exhibit surrounding the model in the city's history museum.[13]

When cities in ruins are presented as models, the horrors of destruction are masked by renderings that generate a silence of, as is often remarked, eerie beauty. As I suggested, the pictorial conventions can be traced back to the visual code used to represent ruins since before the built ruins of eighteenth century Europe. The lasting impact of this code has imbued the tension between absence and presence, and between past and present with nostalgia and desire. As we have seen with the faux ruins in Schwetzingen and elsewhere, even an artificial invocation can provoke yearnings for or a contemplation of a different place in time.[14] Invocations of classic ruinous beauty, therefore, are more multivalent than a mere emphasis on their picturesque qualities conveys. However obliquely,

12 Brink, "Secular Icons," passim. See also Ulrike Weckel, *Beschämende Bilder: Deutsche Reaktionen auf alliierte Dokumentarfilme über befreite Konzentrationslager* (Stuttgart: Franz Steiner, 2012).

13 Information from Sascha Winter, email January 29, 2003.

14 For an introduction, see Michael S. Roth, *Irresistible Decay: Ruins Reclaimed* (Los Angeles: The Getty Research Center, 1997); Midas Dekkers, *The Way of All Flesh: A Celebration of Decay*, trans. Sherry Marx-Macdonald (London: Harvill, 2000).

images of ruins since the Renaissance have gestured toward the often-disastrous events that turned once flourishing settlements into deserted heaps of stone – a perception that gained new poignancy in the post-war context.[15]

Importantly, the rubble models (as well as many war memorials) testify to a code of aesthetic restraint in the rendering of human suffering. In the aftermath of war, many artists chose to register the effects of the air raids, whether in word or in image, by hiding suffering from plain view. Taking pictures in bombed out-cities had been a punishable, though rarely enforced, offense in Nazi Germany and certain neighborhoods were declared no-go zones during the war and thereafter.[16] Of the salacious photographs taken during the air war, many were published only recently. The ones that appeared at the time primarily had the purpose to alarm viewers about atrocities committed by Germany's enemies. The visual code that emerged in the defeated Germany focused on "dead cities," in the words of the critic Mike Davis;[17] they rarely showed either harrowing scenes or the life that persisted and re-emerged amongst the urban rubble. In the few German publications that depicted the horror in the wake of aerial attacks, the breach of etiquette was evident and, at least in some cases, politically motivated. Some photographs published shortly after the war sought to raise awareness about Nazi crimes, whereas the photograph of stacked corpses from Dresden appeared in 1953 as part of a campaign against the Western allies as perpetrators.[18]

The exceptions prove the rule for three-dimensional artwork as well. When Alfred Hrdlicka's (1928–2009) sculpture in memory of "Operation Gomorrah," the devastating air raid on Hamburg in 1943, went up in 1986 – part of an only partially completed four-part counter-sculpture to a 1936 military monument – the

---

15 See, for instance, Hans Vogel, *Die Ruine in der Darstellung der abendländischen Kunst* (Kassel: K. Winter, 1948). In Stanley Kramer's 1961 film *Judgment at Nuremberg*, when Dan Haywood (Spencer Tracy) arrives in the city where he is to serve as judge in one of the war trials, a similar point is made visually, as the camera documents a drive through bombed-out Nuremberg and seizes on a ruins capriccio that adorns the villa of a former Nazi official, his temporary home. On the nexus of ancient ruins and contemporary historical events in the Renaissance, see also my "Self-Portrait with Ruins: Maerten van Heemskerck, 1553," *The Germanic Review: Literature, Culture, Theory* 86 (2011): 262–276.

16 Ralf Blank, "Review of Jörg Friedrich's *Brandstätten: Der Anblick des Bombenkriegs* (2003)," H-Soz-u-Kult, October 22, 2003 <http://hsozkult.geschichte.hu-berlin.de/rezensionen/2003-4-044>. For Hamburg, see a document cited in Niels Gutschow, "Hamburg: The 'Catastrophe' of July 1943," in *Rebuilding Europe's Bombed Cities*, ed. Jeffry M. Diefendorf (Basingstoke: Macmillan, 1990), 114–130, here p. 118.

17 Mike Davis, *Dead Cities, and Other Tales* (New York: New Press, 2002).

18 Gilad Margalit, *Guilt, Suffering, and Memory: On German Commemoration of the German Victims of WW II* (Bloomington: Indiana University Press, 2010), 173.

sculptor offended this code of aesthetic restraint by graphically invoking collapsing buildings, disfigured bodies, and a corpse.[19] In other words, to gaze in the wake of the air raids was mostly predicated on gaining a measure of distance.

The first rubble models were built for those viewers who had lived through the air raids and their children. Germans who survived the war would have confronted these models in the lobbies of city halls or public exhibitions. With the exception of the rubble model of Frankfurt, the plaster, or wood, or plastic of these models had not touched the actual debris or devastation; instead, they promised to propel the viewer into a position distant from the disaster itself but in plain view, a panoramic perspective rather than an immersion on the ground. Such material, spatial, and temporal distancing – viewers know that the model had been made *after* the devastation – brought with it the hope of leaving behind the all-absorbing reality of the catastrophe, inviting instead a readiness to enter into a communal, and abstracted, vision of loss.

Representations of communal loss serve many functions. One is the hortatory dimension of ruined cities, evident for example in the exhibition "Never forget!" (*Niemals vergessen!*) that opened in Vienna's *Künstlerhaus* in 1946, after more than a year of planning. The exhibition was an antifascist manifesto – organized primarily by Austria's left – meant to pave the way for a new society. Though as Wolfgang Kos argues, it was dated by the time its doors opened – because of its heavy reliance on a pre-1934 pictorial repertoire and political propaganda – 260,000 visitors saw it in only fourteen weeks. On entering they were confronted with a large-scale but flat panorama of the bombed-out Vienna beneath a dramatic painted sky, the city's landmark cathedral helpless among the ruins. Hitler's spectral presence in the clouds of smoke glossed the panorama's title, *Bilanz des Krieges* or "Balance of the War," indicting National Socialism and the *Führer* for the disaster. Urban devastation figured here as a complex symbol of social, political, and moral ruin as opposed to the vaguer notions generated by the rubble models.[20]

During the German (or Austrian, for that matter) *Wiederaufbau*, or Reconstruction, the rhetorical force of panoramas and models acquired a specific edge. In the immediate post-war years, as throughout their history, ruins referenced a multi-layered temporality. In the particular case of rubble models, this temporal-symbolic nexus relied on absences, namely by obfuscating the specifics of

---

19 Malte Thiessen, *Eingebrannt ins Gedächtnis: Hamburgs Gedenken an Luftkrieg und Kriegsende 1943 bis 2005* (Hamburg: Dölling und Galitz, 2007), 304–311.
20 Wolfgang Kos, "Die Schau mit dem Hammer," in *Eigenheim Österreich: Zu Politik, Kultur und Alltag nach 1945* (Vienna: Sonderzahl, 1994), 7–58, here pp. 22–24.

individual guilt or collective entanglements within an all-encompassing cipher of urban disaster. To be sure, they were reminders of a fraught past in that they show destruction, even if they remain reticent about its causes. At the same time, however, in the context of post-war Europe, the presence of rubble operated as an appeal for its removal. In another installation in "Never forget!," the ruined city formed the backdrop for a heroic appeal to the future, in the form of a stone mason and his female companion working amidst the carnage of some of Vienna's most famous buildings.[21] Urban ruins conjured up the construction worker, who became a figure central to the imaginary of the late 1940s and the 1950s. These valiant men and women seemed to encapsulate a vague promise to remove Europe's fraught past along with the rubble.[22]

In the wake of defeat and devastation, exhibitions, construction exhibits (*Bauausstellungen*) in particular, were popular vehicles in appealing to citizens for support in the countless rebuilding efforts of the urban infrastructure. The first of these exhibits opened its gates in Berlin as early as 1946; other cities across Germany followed suit.[23] Wherever they were inaugurated, such exhibitions mobilized visitors in a variety of ways for the unprecedented tasks at hand: one would first encounter extensive statistical data on the damages to the built environment and then the far-reaching plans, solutions, or efforts made to address the community's needs. At the 1949 German construction exhibit (*Deutsche Bauausstellung*) in Nuremberg, for instance, a room dedicated to the war-induced destruction – a section entitled "chaos" – contained not only extensive information on the material losses but also offered a theatre-like prospect with an assemblage of painted ruins in a brick frame (as if one were to look through a damaged fire wall), evoking "Nuremberg's night of horrors on January 2, 1945" (*Die Schreckensnacht Nürnbergs am 2. January 1945*); approximately 300,000 people came

---

21 Wolfgang Kos, "'Zukunftsfroh und muskelstark': Zum öffentlichen Menschenbild der Wiederaufbaujahre," in *Eigenheim Österreich: Zu Politik, Kultur und Alltag nach 1945* (Vienna: Sonderzahl, 1994), 59–150.

22 "Frankfurt oder Bonn?" *Rhein-Neckar-Zeitung*, June 30, 1949, see Thomas Bauer, *"Seid einig für unsere Stadt": Walter Kolb – Frankfurter Oberbürgermeister 1946–1956* (Frankfurt a.M.: Waldemar Kramer, 1996), 70. A 1947 exhibit in Magdeburg, East Germany, entitled "Magdeburg Is Alive" (*Magdeburg lebt*), featured a "chamber of horror" with rather abstract evocations of conflagration and ruination in the context of an exhibit dedicated to the large sweep of the city's history, see Arnold, *Allied Air War and Urban Memory*, 64–67.

23 Winfried Nerdinger, *Architektur der Wunderkinder: Aufbruch und Verdrängung in Bayern 1945–1960* (Salzburg: Anton Pustet, 2005), 106. On the twentieth-century history of construction exhibits in Germany, see Johannes Cramer and Niels Gutschow, *Bauausstellungen: Eine Architekturgeschichte des 20. Jahrhunderts* (Stuttgart: Kohlhammer, 1984).

Fig. 29: Rubble Relief, Hamburgmuseum (Photo: Author)

to see the displays.[24] Let us remember that Frankfurt's rubble model was created for a 1946–1947 construction exhibit in the state of Hesse (although not much is known about its displays).[25] Similarly, the origins of the models of Hannover are linked to *Constructa* (1951) – a fair meant to serve as an international forum for the modern city.[26]

In Hamburg, the creation of the "rubble relief" (*Trümmerpalette*), now in the Hamburg Museum, goes back to the year 1950 when the city launched its first long-range development plan after the war's end (fig. 29). It had its counterpart in a relief that rendered the then current state of urban affairs and was regularly updated until the mid-1970s to reflect changes and additions to Hamburg's cityscape (though some of the buildings one can make out were in fact never built).

---

24 Ibid., 106–109.

25 Kristina Vagt, *Politik durch die Blume: Gartenbauausstellungen in Hamburg und Erfurt im Kalten Krieg (1950–1974)* (Hamburg: Dölling & Galitz, 2013), 120f.

26 Stadtarchiv Hannover, kps 392; Staatsarchiv Hamburg 321-3 I 1497; *Constructa Bauausstellung 1951 Hannover 3. Juli bis 12. August*, ed. Die Verbände und Organisationen der Bauwirtschaft, Bauwissenschaft und Baukunst (Hannover: Deutsche Messe- und Ausstellungs A.G., [s.a.]). See also Cramer/Gutschow, *Bauausstellungen*, 213–222.

Both reliefs were exhibited in tandem in the so-called Hamburg Pavillon at the International Garden Exhibit (1953) – an event that, like the *Constructa*, sought to issue a vigorous statement about West Germany's re-integration into the concert of European nations. Ironically, this exhibit was located on grounds previously used for military parades, now transformed into gardens, where flowers from all over the world bloomed. This show thus sought to signal the country's return to peace, democracy, and internationalism. With their fashionably curvy shapes, the reliefs were offset against one another in a display dedicated to Hamburg's war damages and urban efflorescence. Remarkably, the hall or pavillon featured a gallery from where visitors could gain an elevated perspective on how to gauge the state of urbanism in the city.[27] One of the rare newspaper reports to comment on viewers' responses to the models appeared in the context of this exhibit. As urban sculptures, they were said to incite people caught up in the exigencies of everyday life to ruminate on their recent life trajectories, as well as those of their community (fig. 30). "People have passionate discussions in front of these maps [sic]," the journalist stated, adding that in the process "the horrors of the bombing nights come alive again, the wild fury of war, whose destructions were malicious and senseless and who transformed a [once] flourishing city into a crater landscape."[28] Note how the use of an allegorical figure veils viewers' own participation or experience in the war. But, inevitably, the journalist's mention of the "inferno" of the recent past calls forth its opposite, wonderment over the urban life that had already emerged or was about to emerge from the rubble.[29] This example of comparative seeing, the fact that, like in Hamburg, representations of urban ruins were habitually paired with invocations of the (re)built city in the decades after 1945, thus found its corollary in an emotional narrative that

27 Werner Hebebrand, "Hamburg-Pavillon unterrichtet über eine schaffensreiche Zeit," in *Handbuch Internationale Gartenbauausstellung Hamburg 1953* (Hamburg: Hanseatische Druckanstalt, 1953), 94f. For the exhibit in Vienna (see below), boxes the size of 200 × 150 × 50 cm were made to transport the panorama models to Austria.

28 [], "Zwei Karten," *Hamburger Echo*, July 21, 1953: "Die Menschen diskutieren leidenschaftlich vor diesen Karten. Das Grauen der Bombennächte wird wieder lebendig, die wilde Furie des Krieges, die sinnlos und mutwillig zerstörte, die eine blühende Stadt in eine Kraterlandschaft verwandelte ... Und die Menschen dieser Stadt, von denen viele durch das Inferno der Vernichtung gegangen sind, können es selber kaum fassen, daß die andere Karte der Rechenschaftsbericht einer großartigen Aufbauarbeit ist. Die Allmacht des Tages läßt ihnen sonst kaum Zeit, darüber nachzudenken, einen einzigen Gedanken daran zu verschwenden, daß sich ihre Vaterstadt, ihre Heimat wieder aus den Trümmern erhoben hat und daß Hamburg wieder das Antlitz einer lebensvollen, zukunftsfrohen Stadt trägt." I am grateful to Kristina Vagt and Sandra Schürmann for having shared this article with me.

29 Ibid.

promised redemption from far-reaching destitution. The visual cues in the exhibit as well as the two-partite account in this news report reinforced a highly patterned storyline about two moments said to be inextricably entangled, 1945 (not 1933 or 1939) and the present.

At the time, comparative seeing was meant above all to validate a future on the backdrop of a damaged past. But, given the open-ended nature of comparing visuals, be they graphs, photographs, or models, this type of specularity through juxtapositions could also accommodate different views. Such an approach may have become more common after 1960, when criticism of inhospitable post-war cities intensified. Books such as Wolf Jobst Siedler's 1961 *Die gemordete Stadt* (The City That Was Killed),[30] a collection of essays first published in the same year as Jane Jacobs's *The Death and Life of Great American Cities*,[31] and Alexander Mitscherlich's 1965 *Die Unwirtlichkeit unserer Städte* (The Inhospitability of Our Cities)[32] heralded a change in public opinion that was to gain traction in subsequent years. These published manifestos for a humane urbanism ushered in a broad re-assessment of urban renewals in post-war Germany and elsewhere. Interestingly enough, Siedler first professed his love for the old in an ironical mode – after all, the shortcomings of the pre-war city seemed all too apparent in 1961. In light of mounting evidence for the bleakness of urban modernism, however, viewers were increasingly persuaded by a vision that favored the old over the new.[33]

Comparative seeing therefore also may have contributed to new contexts for the rubble models other than pride in the rebuilt cities they seem to initially have been intended to promote. The second wave of commissioning such models after 1985 (or the reconfiguration of post-war exhibits in museums) had them function less in a progress narrative (as had been the case between 1946 and 1966) but in a historical progression that could also accommodate ambivalence toward, if not rejection of, the new. At any rate, in the context of comparative specularity, a widely held argument took hold that the rebuilding in fact equaled a second destruction, possibly even more extensive than the air raids of World War II.[34]

---

30 Wolf Jobst Siedler and Elisabeth Niggemeyer, *Die gemordete Stadt: Abgesang auf Putte und Straße, Platz und Baum* (Berlin: Siedler, 1993; first 1961, 1978).
31 Jane Jacobs, *The Death and Life of American Cities* (New York: Random House, 1961).
32 Alexander Mitscherlich, *Die Unwirtlichkeit unserer Städte: Anstiftung zum Unfrieden* (Frankfurt am Main: Suhrkamp, 1965).
33 Siedler, *Die gemordete Stadt*, 3 (preface 1961).
34 On this notion and its dissemination, see the preface to the 1978 and 1993-editions of Siedler's *Die gemordete Stadt*.

Due to the popularity of construction exhibits in post-war Germany, the city of Hamburg sponsored a number of small displays of scale models at various locations around the city between 1956 and 1962.[35] Through these shows, the population could survey individual buildings or developments before they went up. At a time when the city's efforts to meet the demands of post-war society were ongoing, such exhibits catapulted viewers forward in time to a place where futures were at hand and arrived quickly.[36] A document from Hamburg's construction department that encourages the mounting of small construction exhibits for the benefit of the urban population cites a conversation that supposedly took place between a five-year old boy and his mother in front of a model on display – a conversation much reflective of widespread hopes to restore the supposedly damaged social and gendered order together with the reconfiguration of the built environment. "Oh, mother, what is this?" the boy asks and receives the following answer: "This is how Hamburg will be. Father can explain this to you."[37] From 1953 onward, the rubble models were used as a means against the forgetting that the authorities feared was an almost inevitable outcome of their own success in renewing the city. What had been accomplished under adverse conditions by those who had survived the war was commemorated so that the citizenry would be grateful for what local governments had achieved with stunning speed.[38] In a similar vein, a synthetic exhibit in Hamburg portrayed the city's "new face" – to cite the title of a photo contest held for ordinary citizens in 1960.[39] Interestingly enough, the 1966 exhibit "Hamburg Builds" (*Hamburg Baut*) – note the present tense – took place at a construction site, shortly before its completion, of a pedestrian tunnel near the rebuilt central train station. Once again, the city government showcased the "rubble relief" (*Trümmerpalette*) or "damage model" (*Schadensmodell*) as well as the updated relief of the rebuilt city (together with many photographs), juxtaposing utter destruction with the city that emerged in its place. But the goal was more

---

35 Staatsarchiv Hamburg, 321-3 I 104, 105, 106, and 118.

36 Spiro Kostof, *The City Assembled: The Elements of Urban Form Through History* (Boston: Bullfinch, 1992), 262, reprints two models of the same so-called Grindelberg-area in Hamburg, a relief model of an urban neighborhood "in rubble" and after reconstruction – images taken from Kurt Hoffmann, Rudolf Lodders, and Albrecht Sander, *Die Hochhäuser am Grindelberg* (Stuttgart: Julius Hoffmann, 1959). This suggests that "rubble models" were occasionally used to render subsections of cities. Like in other cases, the relief of the ruined and the rebuilt neighborhood were paired.

37 Staatsarchiv Hamburg, 321-1 I 104 (July 7, 1958).

38 See, for instance, Hebebrand, "Hamburg-Pavillon," 94. This aspect also surfaces in the speeches of mayors who opened construction exhibits in Hamburg and elsewhere.

39 Staatsarchiv Hamburg, 321-1 I 116.

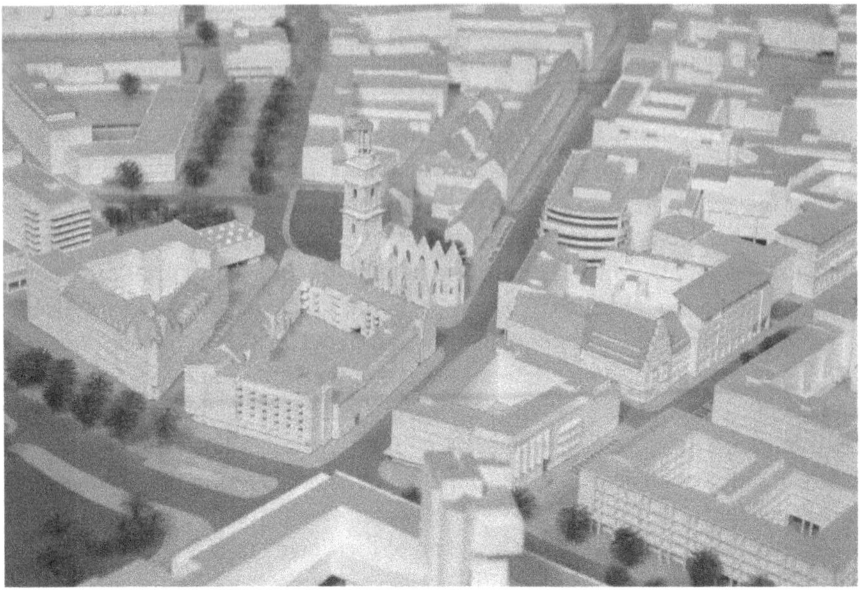

Fig. 30: Hannover Today, Model, detail (Aegidienkirche in ruins) (Photo: Author)

ambitious this time. "Hamburg Builds" purported to chart the entire evolution of urban building and rebuilding since 1945. Infallibly, the models were chosen as a setting for Mayor Herbert Weichmann's opening speech.[40]

Though most of the construction exhibits targeted primarily a local audience, some, like Hamburg's aforementioned International Garden Exhibit, reached a wider public; approximately 4,000 people attended the opening event alone.[41] Yet these local efforts also ushered in the exchange of experience via exhibitions among European cities that had faced large-scale bombings, thus forging alliances between cities across the continent.[42] After the success of Hamburg's 1966 exhibition, "Hamburg Builds" – with ca. 130,000 visitors in two months – the city government was invited to showcase its urban revival in Vienna's city hall in

40 Staatsarchiv Hamburg, 321-3 I 1270. The text on the wall started with 1945 and an accounting of "rubble" whose removal, it was said, inaugurated a period of new beginnings. See Staatsarchiv Hamburg, 321-3 I 108. In the discussion leading up to the exhibit, the head of Hamburg's construction department, Meyer Helwege, explicitly stated that he wished to see no swastikas or hands raised for the Hitler salute.

41 Vagt, *Politik durch die Blume*, 103.

42 Staatsarchiv Hamburg, 321-3 I 1271.

1968, for instance – an exhibit that, once again, included the "rubble relief" and its counterpart, the model of the city at present, among sixteen other construction or architectural models.[43] Such exhibits even brought together cities that had found themselves in enemy camps not long before or were, as in the following case, located on different sides of the Iron Curtain.[44] In 1966, West Germany was invited to display its post-war urban renewal in three Soviet cities – Leningrad, Kiev, and Moscow: "Modern Architecture in the Federal Republic of Germany" (*Moderne Architektur in der BRD*). In exchange, a show on the Soviet Union was to travel to three German cities – Hamburg, Cologne, and Munich – the following year, fifty years after the Russian Revolution. This was the first major event under the umbrella of a 1959 agreement on cultural exchange between the two countries (whose realization had been delayed by the building of the Berlin Wall). To great fanfare, three of Hannover's city models, including the model of the levelled 1945 city, travelled to the Soviet Union, among architectural models of schools, theatres, and museums from various places across Germany; the local press reported repeatedly about the technically demanding transfer, setup, and presentation, complete with an accompanying soundtrack and a technical staff on site.[45] To be sure, construction exhibits avoided a reckoning with a past that remained divisive, possibly within West Germany but definitely beyond its borders. Instead, they foregrounded technical expertise, architectural solutions, and issues in urbanism. Triumph over urban dereliction apparently offered fertile grounds for social, cultural, and political rapprochement. Yet in a competitive climate between capitalism and communism, these exhibitions also were meant to showcase economic resilience and technical advance, if not superiority.

Since the war, public presentations of ruins models have tended to couple an image of the city at its worst with one of the rebuilt city that took its place (as in Hannover, Hamburg, Kassel, and Heilbronn). While such juxtapositions are also used in museums – where the model of destruction sometimes is paired with a model of the city at an earlier stage (seen in the history museums of Frankfurt, Trier, Münster, and Pforzheim, though the different models were not always created as pairs) – this arrangement seems to have emerged in city halls, where they highlighted a civic administration's efforts to restore the built environment.

---

43 Staatsarchiv Hamburg, 321-3 I 111.

44 Cf. Jack Masey and Conway Lloyd Morgan, *Cold War Confrontations: US Exhibitions and Their Role in the Cultural Cold War* (Baden: Lars Müller, 2008).

45 [kl], "Hannover geht nach Moskau," *Hannoversche Allgemeine Zeitung*, March 9, 1966; [Pa.], "Hannoversche Stadtmodelle sollen sechs Monate lang russisch reden," *HAZ*, June 7, 1966; [kl], "Überstunden für Hannover," *HAZ*, July 13, 1966. On the preparations for the exhibit, see Staatsarchiv Hamburg, 321-3 I 1269.

Fig. 31: Model of Hannover 1945, City Hall (Photo: Author)

Hannover's City Hall, completed in 1913 in a commanding Neo-Renaissance style and one of the few buildings to survive the air raids, provides a grand setting for an impressive group of city models whose origins went back to the 1951 *Constructa*. In its monumental central court, four models are on display, each of them 4,50 × 5,50 m: Hannover 1689, Hannover 1939, Hannover 1945 (fig. 31), and today's Hannover (regularly updated).[46] As these models move us through four centuries of the city's life, they seek to project an arc of gratifying progress. The rubble model is still astounding, and yet the devastation seems a momentary blip in

46 Intensive research in Hannover's *Stadtarchiv* has generated little information on their origins and history. What is known is the following: Rudolf Hillebrecht, who oversaw the city's post-war construction department, is credited with having had the idea for commissioning these models (ca. 1948). Some parts of them were shown at the Constructa, a construction exhibit, in 1951 (See Helmut Knocke and Hugo Thieler, *Hannover: Kunst- und Kultur-Lexikon* [Hannover: Schaefer, 1994], 185.). Up to 12 modelmakers and graphic artists were on the city's payroll (the last of them went into retirement recently) to create and update the models which took more than ten years to complete. (Conrad von Meding, "Eine Stadt steht Modell," *Hannoversche Allgemeine Zeitung*, March 16, 2007.) I thank Holger Horstmann from the Hannover city archive for his invaluable assistance, and Margarita Paßiel for having shared information on the model with me.

Hamburg and other city hall displays. Ironically, since the model of Kassel's post-war rebirth was constantly updated, it became so worn that it has been relegated to storage and the model of Kassel in ruins is now on display in the local history museum while the model of Kassel rebuilt is not.[47] These counter-models rely on modes of presentation that date back to the Renaissance,[48] but in the context of post-war Europe, one is strongly led to believe, they were intended to inspire pride in the quick pace of reconstruction and the re-emergence of civic urbanity after large-scale devastation.

Still, visitors were (and where the original setting is preserved, like in Hannover, are) left to their own impressions to make sense of these cities' urban histories and their urban destruction in exhibits put up between the 1950s and the 1970s, after which point some of the models on public display in cities were moved into museums.[49] Loss in these city hall commemorations is figured largely as a contemplative experience. This is nowhere more in evidence than in Heilbronn, where no accompanying exhibit and little information interrupts or, rather, frames one's encounter with the rubble models. Without contextual commentary, rubble models are likely to reinforce existing narratives, rather than challenge or transform them. And in the immediate post-war decades, that existing narrative tended to be the transformation of rubble into ruins, and with it individual suffering into collective loss. To examine this interpretive pattern in greater detail, we turn to Heilbronn.

---

47 Kassel Stadtmuseum, Information from Hermann Wegener, June 2003. The model, first on display in city hall (1953), was then exhibited in the museum on the history of Kassel after 1983. The current exhibit opened its doors in 1993.

48 Etienne du Pérac, *I Disegni de le ruine di Roma e come anticamente erono* [1574], ed. Rudolf Wittkower, 2 vols. (Milan: Pizzi, 1963); also as id., *Le antiche rovine di Roma nei disegni di du Péarc* (Milan: Pizzi, 1990). Cf. Margaret M. McGowan, *The Vision of Rome in Late Renaissance France* (New Haven: Yale University Press, 2000), 40f, 118f. See also the sixteenth-century print by an unknown artist that shows a reconstruction of the Colosseum (*Theatrum sive Coliseum Romanum*) in which the viewer can look into the building, reprinted in *Vedute di Roma nel 1500*, ed. Cecilia Canetti et al. (Rome: Dino Audino, 1990), n. 40. For the pairing of poetic images of ancient and modern Rome, see Rodrigo Cacho Casal, "The Memory of Ruins: Quevedo's 'Silva' to 'Roma antigua y moderna,'" *Renaissance Quarterly* 62 (2009): 1167–2003.

49 Wolfgang Steinweg, *Das Rathaus Hannover*, ed. Fremdenverkehrsverein, 3rd ed. (Hannover: Benatzky, 2003), 6: "Die vier Stadtmodelle … in der großen Halle sind für den Besucher der erste Anziehungspunkt; hier erhält er zugleich auf anschauliche Weise einen Überblick über das Wachsen, Sterben und Neuerwachen der Großstadt Hannover."

Shaping Public Commemoration

In Heilbronn, the memorial hall (*Ehrenhalle*) commemorating the city's staggering losses opened its gates to the public on December 4, 1963. The opening came nineteen years after the city's devastating attack; in the words of a local historian, "6530 citizens and the old center had to die" in a single air raid.[50] (By the end of the war, the population of Heilbronn had decreased from 74,214 in 1939 to 46,350 in 1945.)

Hailed by one observer as one of the most beautiful such memorial spaces in Germany when it first opened,[51] the hall – which contains, as we will see, a funereal mosaic, three carefully chosen photographs, and three city models – came into being after an animated debate among politicians, experts, and residents between the years 1959 and 1963. The debate, as elsewhere in Germany, revealed the high stakes in honoring the country's war dead and its numerous other losses. Controversial issues that had surfaced in Frankfurt when Benno Elkan's un-realized monument to the "unknown civilian victim" of the air raids divided the public in the early 1950s bore a remarkable similarity to the ones debated in Heilbronn: these issues centered on the politics, aesthetics, and financial costs of representing loss and devastation, both within the defeated nation and in material form. Unlike in Frankfurt, however, the project was not destroyed by this controversy. Though just a few years after Elkan's final defeat, the memorial hall at Heilbronn emerged at a moment of growing distance to the catastrophe, a moment of increasing urban confidence; with selective input from Heilbronn's citizens, and with a firm hand, the mayor and city council were able to speedily realize the memorial building. Heilbronn's *Ehrenhalle* projected the devastation of the recent past into the very heart of the city's post-war present. It provided a space for mourning but, just as important, for the transfiguration of mourning into a means for the community to look forward.[52]

---

50 Peter U. Quattländer, *Heilbronn: Planung des Wiederaufbaues der Altstadt: Dokumentation zur Ausstellung des Stadtplanungsamtes 1994* (Heilbronn: Stadtarchiv Heilbronn, 1994), 19. On human losses in Heilbronn, see Susanne Lachenicht, "Mythos Trümmerfrau? Trümmerräumung in Heilbronn 1945–1955," in *Heilbronnica 2: Beiträge zur Stadtgeschichte* (Heilbronn: Stadtarchiv, 2003), 319–360, here pp. 324f.

51 [tz], "Eine würdige Gedenkstätte für die Toten des Zweiten Weltkriegs," *Heilbronner Stimme*, November 30, 1963, n. 277, 9.

52 Werner Föll, *Chronik der Stadt Heilbronn*, vol. 10: *1970–1974* (Heilbronn: Stadtarchiv, 1999). This is not to say that all over Germany the reticence that had prevented Frankfurt from erecting a monument to the air war waned in these years. Whether a monument dedicated to the air war's effects on individual cities could be realized in post-war Germany continued to depend on local

Fig. 32: Heilbronn, New City Hall, Courtyard (Photo: Author)

As a first step, the city government designated a centrally located space to house the memorial, thereby anchoring the subsequent discussion spatially. The architect Rudolf Gabel created a so-called "cube of silence" within the shell of an eighteenth-century mansion adjacent to Heilbronn's city hall complex (built between 1954 and 1959), formerly the city's archive (fig. 32).[53] This architectural sculpture, with its two rows of windows harking back to the old building, its boxy spaciousness inside, and its modulated sonar-ocular interior, eloquently speaks of a past that has been radically transfigured.[54] To go from the 1950s courtyard

political configurations as well as the initiative of individuals and associations. An interesting example of a discussion, see Christian Groh, "'Was Pforzheim angetan wurde!' Erinnerungsorte und Denkmäler zum Luftkrieg," in *Luftkrieg: Erinnerungen in Deutschland und Europa*, ed. Jörg Arnold, Dietmar Süß, and Wolfram Thießen (Göttingen: Wallstein, 2009): 183–199. See also Thießen, *Eingebrannt ins Gedächtnis*, 226–235.

53 On the memorial's history, see Helmut Müller, "'Kubus der Stille': Die Ehrenhalle am Kieselmarkt im Rathaus," *Heilbronner Stimme*, November 30, 2000, 4. The first usage I encountered in the relevant files of Heilbronn's archive was in [if], "Muß Trauer klassisch sein?" *Heilbronner Stimme*, August 25, 1962, 13.

54 Interestingly enough, the "Ehrenhalle" has been used for rallies and exhibitions by a variety of groups, including political parties, anti-Fascists, and an association of German soldiers; see

Fig. 33: Heilbronn, Ehrenhalle, façade, detail (Photo: Author)

into the cube requires passing through an ornate but war-scarred Rococo façade of red sandstone with a ruined relief of an eagle, the city's crest, emblematically resplendent above the entrance below a window; as a free imperial city, Heilbronn marshaled the same heraldic bird as the Holy Roman Empire, though since the eighteenth century it had been differentiated from the imperial eagle (fig. 33). The vast hall that opens up beyond the massive doors envelops the viewer in a space of whiteness, little adorned, where sounds from the outside recede and the light is muted.

In 1959, the city held a public competition for a monument to commemorate its war losses in this historically layered space within the former archive building. Fifty-four entries were submitted, many of them indebted to the sculptural language of Christian iconography; the proposals abounded with angels, bells, and crosses. These submissions were ranked by a team of experts and exhibited for the public between December 1959 and January 1960. The first prize went to a relief-like sculpture invoking a mass of abstract corpses arranged across a wall below a simple wooden cross.[55] The city parliament (*Gemeinderat*) chose to ignore the awards, however, and instead opted to preserve the striking interior of the reconstructed edifice. They argued that a large indoor sculpture would compromise the beauty of the "cube of silence"; they also felt that a figural solution to the problem of creating a memorial would mar the space's integrity and its compelling void. Instead, in September of 1961, the city contacted Karl Knappe (1884–1970), a renowned Munich-based artist who had been barred from his professorship under the National Socialist regime and who after the war helped design a church interior in Hiroshima (1955–1963).[56] Knappe proposed just the simple, non-figural solution the parliament sought: a wall of large slabs of conglomerate stones (*Nagelfluh*), in a range of different hues, anchored by a commemorative inscription (quoted in full and interpreted below), lines of crosses, and a sun. The

---

"Gedenken an die Toten der Kriege," *Heilbronner Stimme*, August 29, 1964, n.199; Kachelmus, "Gedenkfeier für die Opfer des Dritten Reiches," *Heilbronner Stimme*, November 20, 1975, 17; *Heilbronner Stimme*, June 4,1975, 16; Jürgen Becker, "Totengedenken in der Ehrenhalle," *Heilbronner Stimme*, March 24, 1997, 15.

55 Gerlinde Martina Aurich-Klepsch. See Dieter Brunner, "Kunst am Bau im Heilbronn der 50er Jahre," in *Heilbronn und die Kunst der 50er Jahre: Das Kunstgeschehen der 50er Jahre in Heilbronn*, ed. Andreas Pfeiffer (Heilbronn: Städtische Museen, 1993), 97.

56 Karl Knappe had lost his professorship at Munich's Technical University in 1933 – a chair he had held since 1930 – as an artist defamed as "culture bolshevik" (*Kulturbolschewist*). In 1955–1963, he designed artwork for the Peace Memorial Church in Hiroshima, Japan. On Knappe, see Galerie Günther Franke, *Gedächtnisausstellung Karl Knappe* (Munich: Galerie Günther Franke, 1975). Like Elkan, Knappe had designed several war monuments after World War I.

Fig. 34: Heilbronn, Ehrenhalle, Interior shot with model of Heilbronn 1945 (Photo: Author)

composition had an immediate appeal, as it was reminiscent of a monumental tombstone and a war cemetery (fig. 34).

The artist's sculptural language is expressly routed through the material. In fact, Knappe claimed that the material itself – the enormous slabs of stone – guided him in the creation of a sculpture that resembled a mosaic made up of large elements. The expressiveness of the work of art is therefore not predicated on the sculptor's formal will triumphing over an unyielding stone but is, in his own description, "ornamental."[57] In the midst of Knappe's work, a delegation of the city's decision-makers visited the artist's studio in Munich: Would such a solution really give an idea of the horrors of the air raids? Would it conflict with the architectural space and its Rococo encasing? In brief, would such a monument be effective in engendering reflection (*Besinnung*)? Certain critics lamented that the monumental wall was unaffecting or "in need of explanation" (*erklärungsbedürftig*)[58] – in other words, too abstract. Whereas Elkan's proposal for a monument to the "unknown citizen" and victim to the air raids had been criticized for its all too figurative idiom, now abstraction emerged as a source of criticism (though for politicans and decision-makers abstraction may have held connotations as the apogee of Western art that was pitted against socialist realism, even if for local artists and exhibitions this was a minor theme).[59] In response, political representatives proposed what was now a four-century old solution: city models. They would provide an antidote to abstraction. The concreteness of the models, as usual, was turned to as an aid to rumination.

Two of the three models already existed when Knappe's monument design was in discussion; the government had commissioned their making in the mid-1950s, in the midst of the city's adamant effort to rebuild, and they were on display in the New City Hall. Yet their move next door, and their inclusion in the solemn space of the *Ehrenhalle* did not go without discussion. It was feared that their presence, in whatever form, would interfere with the hall's stark design and contemplative purpose. Despite these reservations and questions, three relief models and three photographs depicting the disaster and its aftermath were incorporated into the *Ehrenhalle*. Ultimately, the model of the city in 1939 was set

57 Heilbronn, Stadtarchiv, Zeitgeschichtliche Sammlungen, Ehrenhalle: [hf], "Um die Gestaltung der Ehrenhalle," *Neckar-Echo*, May 17, 1962, 4. See also Karl Knappe, *Das Gesetz heisst Wand – der Ausweg Plastik* (Stuttgart: Verlag KG, 1950). The artist's manifesto circulated among decision-makers in Heilbronn.

58 "Künstlerisches Experiment bis zum letzten Stein," *Heilbronner Stimme*, May 17, 1962, 3. The question of a sculpted relief surfaced repeatedly during the debate; Knappe was known to have designed reliefs in other contexts.

59 See exhibition catalogue *Heilbronn und die Kunst der 50er Jahre* cited above.

next to a model of the city in 1960 (fig. 37); a few feet apart from these models, the model of Heilbronn's "zero hour," in close proximity to the three photographs: the city in flames, a woman moving in front of hollowed out buildings, and chalk signs that went up in the ruined Heilbronn after the attack with people providing information about their whereabouts or searching for survivors. The multiple losses of World War II were thus situated in a wide-ranging urban-historical nexus; the models radiated outward and into the city, its history, and its changing post-war cityscape (figs. 35 and 36).

Fig. 35: Heilbronn, Ehrenhalle, Heilbronn 1945 (Photo: Author)

A modeled city's dialectic invocation of presence and absence depends, at least in part, on the materials from which it is made. Just like Knappe's stones, the various materials for city models enable different sculptural and interpretive possibilities, and generate different viewing experiences. Since the Renaissance, most city and fortification models were constructed out of wood as the primary material; some of which were then painted to create varying effects. In the last several decades, such models have typically been rendered in plastic. Both plastic and wood are capable of depicting the colorful details that lend them an aura of the authentic. These models read like reality; the ensuing models feel like shrunken versions of cities that we could actually walk in. First it was thought that a model of the destroyed Heilbronn should be cast in bronze or metal and dramatically illuminated by a spotlight from the ceiling. The three models that went up, however, for reasons lost to the historical archive, are made of unpainted plaster. They are uniform in tone, so that the details of these very different cityscapes recede into an overall impression.[60]

Plaster models have a long history – a history that continues to this day. As part of its collection, the *Musée des Plans-Reliefs* in Paris owns an early modern sculpted bastion executed in plaster. Unlike in Heilbronn, however, some of its surfaces were painted so that the model resembles three-dimensional architectural renderings made of materials other than plaster.[61] The heyday of plaster models seems to have been the mid-twentieth century, however. Between 1933 and 1937, the archeologist Italo Gismondi (1887–1974) and the model-maker Pierino di Carlo (1906–1992) collaborated on a large model of Rome during the reign of Emperor Constantine in the early fourth century, produced for a 1937 exhibition – the Augustan Show of Roman Culture (*Mostra Augustea della Romanità*) – sculpted in the commanding scale of 1:250, and enhanced by the well-tempered application of paint. After the collaborators resumed their work in the post-war period – a work that would not come to a halt until 1982 – this model has been a, if not the, centerpiece of the Museum of Ancient Civilization in Rome, an artistic-artisanal showpiece *and* a catalyst of knowledge about antiquity.[62] Like in Fascist Italy, where Mussolini showered words of praise over the Gismondi/Di Piero-model, plaster was also a favorite material to render architectural projects in Nazi Germany. The modeled vision of the Third Reich's imagined post-war future, a Berlin renamed Germania, was executed in unpainted plaster, just like other models of ideologically motivated urbanistic models from the same period.[63]

---

60 By contrast, in 1964 Karl and Emma Weingand finished a colorful model of Heilbronn around 1800 (Stadtarchiv Heilbronn).

61 The Hannover models mentioned above also originally used plaster as a material in their creation, see Conrad von Meding, "Eine Stadt steht Modell," *Hannoversche Allgemeine Zeitung*, March 16, 2007. On a nineteenth-century model of Jerusalem executed in painted plaster, see Andreas Kaplony, "Das Zürcher Jerusalem-Modell aus dem Jahr 1846," in *Europa Miniature: Die kulturelle Bedeutung des Reliefs, 16.–21. Jahrhundert*, ed. Andreas Bürgi (Zürich: Verlag Neue Zürcher Zeitung, 2007), 149–164, here p. 150 (plates 24–27).

62 Valentin Kockel, "Rekonstruktion als Rezeption: Die Rekonstruktion antiker Stadtbilder und ihre Verbreitung," in *Geschichte der Rekonstruktion: Konstruktion der Geschichte*, ed. Winfried Nerdinger (Munich: Prestel, 2010), 96–113, here pp. 105–107; James E. Pecker, "Italo Gismondi and Pierino Di Carlo: 'Virtualizing' Imperial Rome for 20th C. Italy," *American Journal of Archeology* 112 (2008) <http://www.ajaonline.org/sites/default/files/01_Packer%20RvArt.pdf>.

63 See, for instance, Bundesarchiv Bild 146-1983-018-03A, "Germania," Modell "Große Halle."

Plaster is a material replete with associations, from bodily imprints or death masks to makeshift objects designed to help in the process of artistic creation. Importantly, it is a material that enthralls with its modesty – a theme to which I will return. After all, plaster does not call attention to itself; it has little value in and of itself, transcending its own materiality and hinting at the immateriality of meaning-making, if not the metaphysical.[64] Not accidentally, the whiteness of unpainted plaster is reminiscent of eighteenth- and nineteenth-century collections of classical sculptures, copies that allowed students and artists across Europe to gain first-hand experience with ancient art. In consonance with Johann Joachim Winckelmann's (1717–1768) momentous conception, these sculptures were more than art; their beautiful form held the promise of physical, social, and national renewal in a post-classical age.[65]

In Heilbronn, arguably, the use of plaster for the three city models accesses still different connotations. The very same material invokes not historical continuity but above all absence. Indeed the even texture and color – an off-white – may remind us of how futile it is to attempt to recover what is lost.[66] The visual amalgamation of the models – the old Heilbronn, Heilbronn in ruins, and post-war Heilbronn – provokes a melancholic engagement with a present that cannot disentangle itself from the past. The models' uniform appearance thus works against the representational risk of miniature forms, which is that they will assume the triviality of toys.

The impact of rubble models builds on a concatenation frequently found in commemorative texts, historical characterizations, and other descriptions of the air war's effects on cities: the report of the numbers of lives lost combined with figures or data on the level of destruction, be it the amount of rubble, the percentage of destruction, or similar such information. These figures, whose accuracy was and is difficult to ascertain, despite all the post-war efforts to measure loss and map destruction, abound in post-war discourses. One result of the figures' omnipresence is that these discourses have forged an intimate connection between the loss of lives and material loss.[67] It is no surprise then that near the Heilbronn rubble model was a stand that held a book with a complete list of the

64 Monika Wagner, "Gips," in *Lexikon des künstlerischen Materials: Werkstoffe der modernen Kunst von Abfall bis Zinn*, ed. M. Wagner (Munich: Beck, 2002), 106–113.

65 Alex Potts, *Flesh and the Ideal: Winckelmann and the Origins of Art History* (New Haven: Yale University Press, 1992).

66 One of the problems of modeling in plaster is that other materials cannot easily be integrated into its fabric.

67 As Thiessen shows, this concatenation can be traced back to war-time propaganda, see *Eingebrannt ins Gedächtnis*, 56.

names of all known war dead from Heilbronn; the visitor was thus encouraged to gauge the magnitude of human loss or search for the names of Heilbronners who perished, alongside a consideration of the city's physical loss.[68]

In Heilbronn, there is a remarkable absence of paratexts, be it captions or plaques (from the time of the hall's opening). This "authorless" mode of presentation is common in images and memorials of the war in Germany and across the world.[69] Authorless verses, mosaic, and photographs are offered as "catalysts of memory," and these constituent parts – images without context, verses without poets – can become local icons, open to the interpretive needs of each individual imagination.[70] Just as canonical photographs of destroyed cities in Germany, whether in books or in public exhibits, circulated frequently without captions that would have identified what was seen or when and where they were taken, the photographs on display in Heilbronn, conspicuous in their lack of artistry, are presented without titles, dates, or their photographers' names. The wall's sculptor in turn set his own example of "artlessness." Given the magnitude of Heilbronn's losses, Knappe theorized that the artist's persona ought to be subordinate to the materials as well as the setting, organizing his artistic process accordingly and communicating reverence, respect, and resilience in humility. Similarly, the local poet whose verses conclude the commemorative inscription goes unacknowledged.

This elision of explicit authority is also found in the models. Though their makers' names are noted as Karl Schenkel and Fritz Bissinger, the small plaques on each table of display are quite unlike Jacob Sandtner's proud proclamation of his authorship centuries earlier in re-creating the Bavarian cities in limewood. In Heilbronn, urban "sculptures" *sans* artist came to match a memorial wall *sans* sculptor. The reduction of paratextual or authorial frames obfuscates the memorial's genesis, emphasizing instead the site's transparency, a site ready for inscription.[71] By conspicuously displaying authorial restraint, it imparts a message onto the viewer to do likewise, thus modeling a proper response to loss.

---

68 Rolf Palm, ed., *Heilbronner Kriegs-Opfer 1939–1945* (Neckarsulm: Industrie- und Handelskammer, 1994). Similar volumes exist for other cities. The book is no longer on location but available upon request in city hall. The "cube of silence" and the city hall are connected through a door.

69 Cf. Cornelia Brink, "Secular Icons: Looking at Photographs from Nazi Concentration Camps," *History and Memory* 12 (2000): 135–150.

70 Brink, "Secular Icons," 146.

71 Note the resonance this lack of paratext has with the ways that W. G. Sebald uses photographic images throughout his oeuvre, and also in *Air War and Literature*.

Fig. 36: Heilbronn, Ehrenhalle, detail (Photo: Author)

It is the models that mediate between the collective dimension of the memorial and an appeal to the individual or small groups. In that sense, the fact that their makers are identified by name makes sense in the hall's overall choreography. The visitor, having entered through the hall's main gate, is first dwarfed by the monumentality of the mosaic wall one encounters opposite the entrance. After walking into the room, lingering, and turning around, you come to stand above miniatures before you, and you then can re-immerse yourself in the actual city.[72] The emotional journey of the *Ehrenhalle* is thus from a larger-than-life

72 In Nazi Germany, plaster models of Albert Speer's designs for the projected future Berlin (Germania) were occasionally mounted not at the usual table but at chest height. Such displays invariably communicated grandeur – in other words, they instilled an affective response different from the sovereign gaze associated with these models since the Renaissance (Chapter Three), making even this miniature form seem monumental. For film footage, see Artem Demenok's *Welthauptstadt Germania* (Dokumentation, 52 min., ARTE/RBB, Germany 2004). For descriptions, see Albert Speer, *Inside the Third Reich: Memoirs*, trans. Richard and Clara Winston (New York: Macmillan, 1970), 132–133, 139, 149, 152, and 159. This edition includes two photographs by Heinrich Hoffmann of models mounted in this way, one of the 'Haus der Kunst,' Munich, 1933 (following p. 133), and one of the projected triumphal arch for Berlin from 1939 (following p. 286). See also Stephen D. Helmer, *Hitler's Berlin: The Speer Plans for Reshaping the Central City*

mourning to a melancholic mastery, a visual command over the environment that does not deny loss but rather perpetuates a recognition of the losses.

The act of viewing inevitably touches on the issue of the viewer's agency. Installations of the models in Heilbronn follow the convention of display since the first sixteenth-century city models; the visitor is invited to assume the standard bodily position above the modeled city – what, in a radically different context, Mary Louise Pratt called the "monarch of all I survey"-posture.[73] The bird's-eye-view above the display tables, covered by glass, draws the viewer into the model's minutiae, arresting the gaze and inviting inspection; as we look we circle around the model, taking possession by looking. As I have argued earlier, city models in high relief interpellate the planner, the geometer, and the worker – something underlined by the brief factual information provided along with the Heilbronn models on the changing downtown topography, the number of plots as well as other numerical information. In this particular setting, the models also call forth the local citizen – the spectator who inevitably had insights or sentiments about the city that had been lost to the bombs, or about the quick pace of recovery much in evidence outside the hall.

Every citizen of Heilbronn had been called upon by the National Socialist regime to clear the city of approximately 1,500,000–1,700,000 cubic meters of rubble immediately after December 4, 1944, and then again by the US military government following the end of the war (when members of the former Nazi party and other NS organizations were required to perform extended public service).[74] To be sure, not everybody had removed rubble. Despite the frequent reference to "rubble women" among post-war Germans, in Heilbronn only the Nazi city government, and not the post-war government, called upon women for mandatory removal work. Interestingly enough, this labor was called *Ehrendienst*, or "honorary service," in NS Germany as well as in post-war Germany – a name for the unpaid labor performed that resonates with the name for the memorial, *Ehrenhalle*.[75] This process of ridding the city of rubble provided an imaginary basis for the post-war community.

(Ann Arbor, MI: UMI Research Press, 1985), 24, 109 as well as figs. 28, 29, and 46 (photographs taken between January and July 1941).

73 Mary Louise Pratt, *Imperial Eyes* (New York: Routledge, 1992), 204f.

74 Quattländer, *Heilbronn*, 29f.

75 Diefendorf, *In the Wake of War*, 24; Lachenicht, "Mythos Trümmerfrau," 326–355. On the emergence, history, and critique of the myth of "rubble women," see Elizabeth Heinemann, "The Hour of the Woman: Memories of Germany's 'Crisis Years' and West German National Identity," *American Historical Review* (1996): 354–395; Nicole Kramer, "Ikone des Wiederaufbaus: Die 'Trümmerfrau' in der bundesdeutschen Erinnerungskultur," in *Luftkrieg: Erinnerungen in*

Fig. 37: Model of Heilbronn 1960, Ehrenhalle, detail (Photo: Author)

In the models, the debris encountered at close range by the generation of rubble women and rubble men was recast in a whitened, veiled, and somewhat distant mode. Indeed what is most striking about this memorial is its restraint, evident in the sparse wording of the inscription (as we will see below), the few photographs, and the spare uniformity of the unpainted plaster city models. They constitute but a moderate concession to the desire for visual anchors that had surfaced in the debate mentioned earlier leading up to the 1963 opening. It is as if the firestorm that swept through the city in 1944 had extinguished practically everything in its wake, so that the space's iconoclastic whiteness in this Protestant city now bears witness to the bombs' aftereffects. Restraint, to be sure, characterizes the memorial's aesthetics, and its vernacular modernism. Yet restraint also characterizes the hall's kinesthetic effect on the visitor's movements within the cube. He – and I am choosing the male pronoun advisedly – is likely to slow his pace or halt for a moment when confronted with the funerary wall, or when his steps echo through the hall. Indeed the "cube of silence" seeks to actively induce a mode of reflection (*Besinnung*) in the visitor: "[This] work of art is not sad. It forces [one] to be quiet," in the words of a journalist at the time.[76] These church-like effects are accentuated at night when on occasion light shines forth from the twelve candelabras mounted on the walls (fig. 36).

As Frank Biess reminds us, "anti-intensity" was a conscious post-war response to what was widely seen as the emotional excess of the NS regime.[77] To be sure, aesthetic restraint found expression in Heilbronn's post-war urbanism, with its synchronized roof lines and homogeneous blocks that went up on the rubble lots (of which there remained hundreds as recently as 1957) (fig. 37).[78] The

---

Deutschland und Europa, ed. Jörg Arnold, Dietmar Süß, and Malte Thießen (Göttingen: Wallstein, 2009): 259–276. On the term "honor" that belonged to the standard vocabulary in the Nazi commemoration of air raid victims, see Arnold, *The Allied Air War and Urban Memory*, 87; Gregor, *The Haunted City*, 164. One citizen, Rudolf Brauch, in a letter to Mayor Meyle of February 21, 1962, stated explicitly that one should not speak of *Ehrenmal* – loosely to be translated as a monument honoring the victims – but of *Mahnmal* or memorial, which is, he said, what the artists have designed (Heilbronn, Stadtarchiv, Zeitgeschichtliche Sammlungen, Ehrenmal).

76 [tz], "Eine würdige Gedenkstätte," 9: "Das Kunstwerk ist nicht traurig [referring to the mosaic]. Es zwingt nur zum Stillesein."

77 Frank Biess, "Feelings in the Aftermath: Toward a History of Postwar Emotions," in *Histories of the Aftermath: The Legacies of the Second World War in Europe*, ed. Frank Biess, Robert G. Moeller (New York: Berghahn, 2010), 34.

78 Quattländer, *Heilbronn*, 32 and passim. See also the architecture discussed in *Heilbronn und die Kunst der 50er Jahre*, 21–37. Joachim Hennze speaks of an "austere design without compromise" (*kompromißlos nüchterne Gestaltung*) with regard to the new station buildings in Heilbronn and Pforzheim (ibid., 24). On the general discussion, see Diefendorf, *In the Wake of War*, 63; on

theme of restraint also resonated through contemporary discussions among the monument's planners. Other than in the memorial's sparse imagery, a preference for aesthetic diminuendos surfaced most symptomatically with regard to the proposed use of gold appliqué on the memorial wall, which caused some commotion among the representatives involved in the planning. While the building's façade was red, the hall's interior was suffused with black, grey, and, above all, white, a color code associated with mourning, loss, and possibly purification, from which gold accents departed dramatically. The question for the memorial's planners in city hall was how to impart a glimmer of hope to the spectator without interfering with the contemplation of loss. Originally, Knappe had wanted to frame his tapestry of stones with pilasters tinged in gold, but these were deemed inappropriate. The planners eventually compromised on traces of gold that now adorn the wall's upper right corner; they are suggestive of an evening sun, but also connote a cautious sense of light, warmth, and a future, as does the inscription's poem, which invokes metamorphosis through loss.

This aesthetic-architectural code of restraint and its affective calibration aimed to bestow a well-measured sense of orientation and direction on the spectator. We can see this sense of direction in the three models, with their progression from 1939 to 1960 (casting 1945, the model set apart, as the disaster without precedent), even though its historical narrative is anything but precise; the 1939 model, for instance, contains a replica of Heilbronn's synagogue, a large signature building, despite the fact that it had fallen victim to the arson attack of November 10, 1938 (not November 9, like in most other German cities) – as if the pre-war city had been an intact community.[79] The cautiously optimistic look forward possibly betrays a certain anxiety about the risk of its opposite, the angry look back. This is not far-fetched, especially if we think of commemorations of the Dresden

---

the example of Würzburg, see Jörg Paczkowski, *Der Wiederaufbau der Stadt Würzburg nach 1945*, 2nd ed. (Würzburg: Ferdinand Schöningh, 1995), 76–81 and passim. Paczkowski is particularly perceptive about the turn to medieval models as one source of inspiration for post-war reconstruction which resonates with my own analysis, though in Heilbronn, Emil Beutinger, the city's first post-war mayor explicitly excluded "copying of [architectural] styles" in a statement issued on March 8, 1946 (Quattländer, *Heilbronn*, 34–37, here p. 35).

79 The same could be argued for the painted ruins and rubble-scenes by artists from or working in Heilbronn, see Annette Ludwig, "Zwischen Krieg und Wirtschaftswunder: Künstlerische Reflexionen in der Nachkriegszeit," in *Heilbronn und die Kunst der 50er Jahre*, 38–53, and Siegfried Simpfendörfer, "Nah und fern – das Thema der Landschaft in der Kunst der 50er Jahre: Eine Collage," ibid., 54–67. Simpfendörfer argues: "Es wird deutlich, daß das nationalsozialistische System nicht nur die Städte vernichtete, sonder auch die Fähigkeit der Menschen, auf die Folgen angemessen zu reagieren" (58).

raids held in the German Democratic Republic during the 1950s, when the regime cast the Allies as perpetrators in order to rally its citizens and stir up nationalist resentment against the Western powers. In Heilbronn, by contrast, the memorial, ever so cautiously, exudes a sense of a forward-looking political outlook.

Survival in the rubble was an express concern for those who had lived through the catastrophic attack of December 4, 1944. When Heilbronners commented on the design for Heilbronn's memorial hall, with its models devoid of humans and its funerary wall, they often invoked memories of the life that continued, or sprang up, in the midst of the urban wasteland after the air raid – memories they wanted to pass on and see represented in the memorial, be it as a sign of hope or as a measure of historical accuracy. Not accidentally, Knappe spoke of the life-like fabric of the conglomerate stone he used for his wall-composition, linking his monumental composite tombstone with the lives and deaths of those commemorated. Some Heilbronners wanted the memorial to incorporate the handwritten signs that went up after the attack – many chalked on stones or remaining walls – informing loved ones and friends of their survival, but this proved impossible because of their ephemeral quality. By the early 1960s, when the planning of the *Ehrenhalle* entered its final phase, no signs of this kind could be found, so to include them would have required their re-creation. But one of the *Ehrenhalle*'s three photographs – of this wasteland graffiti – reminds the visitor of these traces in the midst of the city's dead zone; not accidentally, it is the last of three images, part of the memorial hall's restrained re-affirmation of life in the post-war city.[80]

Individual *Besinnung* in this church-like memorial – aided by its multiform dialogue between a wall, three photographs, and the three city models – is only one mode of memorializing the city's darkest (and according to some, most meaningful) hour. Not only is the *Ehrenhalle* community-oriented in its central location and its architectural symbolism of a layered past, its interior – the cube – and the square on its outside are configured as a ready stage for commemorative events and political gatherings. In Heilbronn as well as in other German communities, both in the West and the East, the post-war decades were replete with urban rituals, commemorative events, and festivities.[81] Many a German community reg-

---

80 I read the three photographs from left (the disaster) to right (well after the disaster).

81 For Heilbronn, see some suggestions in *Heilbronn und die Kunst der 50er Jahre*, 101, 116–126. Also, Jörg Arnold, "Beyond Usable Pasts: Rethinking the Memorialization of the Strategic Air War in Germany, 1940 to 1965," in *Memorialization in Germany since 1945*, ed. Bill Niven and Chloe Paver (New York: Palgrave Macmillan, 2010), 26–36, here pp. 29, 31. For the Federal Republic of Germany, to my knowledge no comprehensive studies have been undertaken. Materials and discussion in various publications by Malte Thiessen, especially his magisterial study of

ularly commemorated the most devastating attacks from the air with church services or public ceremonies, held at mass graves in cemeteries[82] or at venues such as the *Ehrenhalle*. At first sight, citizens' gatherings, orchestrated as they were, bear some resemblance to the rallies held in National Socialist Germany. Upon closer inspection, however, they appear to have been governed by the same post-war culture of affective restraint that pervaded the *Ehrenhalle* as a built space.

Post-war associations and rituals of commemoration were important vehicles for the political formation of the population as citizenry after 1945.[83] Our investigations into post-war memorial cultures have been almost entirely national in their focus; as a result, we have largely overlooked the role of local, communal rituals in forging a sense of belonging in civic populations confronted with scarcity of housing, large-scale loss, and the disruptions caused by post-war migrations.[84] Only recently have local studies begun to provide a corrective; preliminary investigations into small mnemonic communities have revealed institutional, political, and cultural dynamics particular to specific locales that are not,

---

Hamburg's memorial culture over the post-war decades, *Eingebrannt ins Gedächtnis*, 146–154, 165f, 223, and passim. See also Heide Hammel, *Und neues Leben blüht aus den Ruinen: Der kulturelle Wiederaufbau in Pforzheim 1945–1949* (Heidelberg: verlag regionalkultur, 2003), frontispiece. See also Robert G. Moeller, "The Politics of the Past in the 1950s: Rhetorics of Victimisation in East and West Germany," in *Germans as Victims*, 26–42, 234–239; Gregor, *The Haunted City*, 135–207. In the German Democratic Republic, huge civic squares were created to accommodate political gatherings. See, for instance, the Altmarkt in Dresden: Jürgen Paul, "Reconstruction of the City Centre of Dresden: Planning and Building during the 1950s," in *Rebuilding Europe's Bombed Cities*, ed. Jeffry M. Diefendorf (Basingstoke: Macmillan, 1990), 170–189, here p. 176. See also Jeffrey Herf, *Divided Memory: The Nazi Past in the Two Germanys* (Cambridge, Mass.: Harvard University Press, 1997).

82 In *Pforzheim 23. Februar 1945 Der Untergang einer Stadt*, 25, an undated photo (early 1960s?) of the annual commemorative "Trauerfeier" to the dead lost to the air raid on February 23, 1945 prefaces other illustrations of Pforzheim before and after the attack ("Jedes Jahr am 23. Februar versammeln sich viele hundert Pforzheimer zur Trauerfeier an der Gedenkstätte auf dem Hauptfriedhof"). See also Matthias Meinhardt for Dresden ("Der Mythos vom 'Alten Dresden' als Bauplan: Entwicklung, Ursachen und Folgen einer retrospektiv-eklektizistischen Stadtvorstellung," in *Städte aus Trümmern: Katastrophenbewältigung zwischen Antike und Moderne*, ed. Andreas Ranft and Stephan Selzer [Göttingen: Vandenhoeck & Ruprecht, 2004], 172–200, here pp. 187–190).

83 Christian Groh, "Remembering the Air War: Public Debate and Remembrance of the Bombing of Pforzheim," Conference Paper, German Studies Association, Pittsburgh, 2006. I thank Dr. Groh for having shared his paper with me.

84 See Alexander Renz, *Chronik der Stadt Heilbronn*, vol. 6: *1945–1951* (Heilbronn: Stadtarchiv, 1995), xxx-li.

at least not entirely, reducible to the nation's trends.[85] In fact, the *Ehrenhalle*'s 1950s Neo-Renaissance courtyard with its Italianate fountain that prefaces the "cube of silence" is a nod to the early modern heyday of communalism south of the Alps – evidence of the "self-centredness," that is the localism, "of post-war West-German memory cultures" within communities as well as a hopeful sign – set literally in stone – for the vibrancy of this communalism and this community in the post-war world.[86]

The urban community invoked in post-war commemorations – the same community that the *Ehrenhalle* was built to honor – was one in which political and social consensus was privileged over the expression of social or other distinctions.[87] What is more, what Jürgen Habermas calls the "representative publicness" was constituted by these commemorations, and governed the design of memorial spaces like the *Ehrenhalle* that turned communal loss into a basis for the polity.[88] According to Robert G. Moeller, "[o]ne of the most powerful integrative myths of the 1950s emphasized not German well-being but German suffering; it stressed that Germany was a nation of victims, an imagined community defined by the experience of loss and displacement during the Second World War."[89] These and similar narratives often found their most poignant expression at the local level.

85 Thießen, *Eingebrannt ins Gedächtnis*; Gregor, *Haunted City*; Malte Thiessen, "Das kollektive als lokales Gedächtnis: Plädoyer für eine Lokalisierung von Geschichtspolitik," in *Geschichtspolitik und kollektives Gedächtnis: Erinnerungskulturen in Theorie und Praxis*, ed. Harald Schmid (Göttingen: V&R unipress, 2009), 159–180; id., "Die 'Katastrophe' als symbolischer Bezugspunkt: Städtisches Gedenken an den Luftkrieg in der BRD und der DDR," in *Die Weltkriege als symbolische Bezugspunkte: Polen, die Tschechoslowakei und Deutschland nach dem Ersten und Zweiten Weltkrieg*, ed. Natali Stegmann (Prague: Masarykův ústav a Archiv, 2009), 91–108; Janina Fuge, Rainer Hering, Harald Schmid, eds., *Das Gedächtnis von Stadt und Region: Geschichtsbilder in Norddeutschland* (Hamburg: Dölling und Galitz, 2010).

86 Gregor, *Haunted City*, 3.

87 See Alexander Renz, *Chronik der Stadt Heilbronn*, vol. 7: *1952–1957* (Heilbronn: Stadtarchiv, 1996).

88 Jürgen Habermas, *The Structural Transformation of the Public Sphere: An Inquiry into a Category of Bourgeois Society*, trans. Thomas Burger (Cambridge, Mass.: MIT Press, 1989).

89 Robert G. Moeller, *War Stories: The Search for a Usable Past in the Federal Republic of Germany* (Berkeley: University of California Press, 2001), 6. See also ibid., 13: "In the public memory of the 1950s, only a handful of Germans appeared as perpetrators, the overwhelming majority were victims, and no one was both: guilt and innocence were mutually exclusive." See also id., "War Stories: The Search for a Usable Past in the Federal Republic of Germany," *American Historical Review* 101 (1996): 1008–1048; id., "Remembering the War in a Nation of Victims: West German Pasts in the 1950s," in *The Miracle Years: A Cultural History of West Germany, 1949–1968*, ed. Hanna Schissler (Princeton: Princeton University Press, 2001), 83–109.

Fig. 38: Heilbronn, Ehrenhalle, detail (Photo: Author)

The inscription on the memorial wall, jointly authored by teachers and local ministers at the city's bequest, indicates as much in its linkage of different strands of human loss, with soldiers topping the list:

> *Wir gedenken* unserer Toten aus dem Zweiten Weltkrieg 1939–1945.
> *3435* Gefallene und Vermisste,
> Unserer Opfer aus den Bombenangriffen auf unsere Stadt
> *7137* Männer, Frauen und Kinder.
> Der *405* Verfolgten, die um ihrer Rasse, ihres Glaubens und ihrer Überzeugung willen ihr Leben verloren.
>
> In Brand und Sturz, im Schwinden und Werden, Über Särge und Wiegen wölbt hoch die Gnade ihr Zelt. Aus der Toten Gedächtnis erwachse der Wille, das Gute zu wirken, dem Frieden der Erde zu dienen.
>
> (*We commemorate* our dead from the Second World War 1939–1945.
> *3435* soldiers fallen or missing in action,
> Our victims as a result of the air raids on our city
> *7137* men, women and children.
> The *405* persecuted who lost their lives because of their race, their religion or their beliefs.

> In conflagration and downfall, in vanishing and becoming, over coffins and cradles, mercy vaults her tent. May the will to do good [and] to serve peace on earth result from the commemoration of the dead.)[90]

In this inscription the details of the past have been subsumed in a sense of all-encompassing loss. That past is reduced to a mention of the dates of the Second World War in Europe – significantly, the memorial begins in 1939, and not in 1933, with the coming to power of National Socialism – a choice that further emphasizes the purity of loss, avoiding a sense of the reader's potential involvement in or responsibility for that loss. The differences between the groups of dead citizens listed are underplayed, and there is not a whiff of accusation. No mention of National Socialism, fascism, Germany, or the Allies gestures toward the reasons why we mourn (though the damaged eagle on the crest above the main gate could well be read as a muted commentary on the state of the nation, despite the crest's local connotations, or the ways in which Heilbronn's own fate was imbricated in the nation's). This vision of loss as the basis for communal identity does not distinguish between perpetrators and victims; it does not call for honoring particular groups of victims or survivors, or comparing different forms of suffering. It constitutes the community as a gendered space whose symbolic center is occupied by the decidedly male figures of the soldier and the city planner. Not surprisingly, first drafts of the inscription had failed to include a reference to the annihilation of Jewish life and those persecuted for their faith or belief.

The correspondence between the phrase *wir gedenken* – "we commemorate" – the numbers of the dead, and the sun, all of which are tinged in gold, is highly suggestive of a narrative of urban salvation from the rubble (fig. 38). In this scenario, the victims figured as the reference point from which communal resurrection would result. This subtle use of color also incorporated the war dead into the community, all the more if we connect these tinges of gold with the courtyard that envelops the *Ehrenhalle*, which is embedded with strands of light blue and gold tiles. Amidst the dominant white, these colors are part of a carefully designed symbolic choreography in which Heilbronn's re-emergence from the rubble is interlaced with a vaguely circumscribed but powerfully invoked sense of loss – a loss whose cause is ignored or assumed to be known, but whose possibilities for rebirth are celebrated.

Heilbronn's *Ehrenhalle* was part and parcel of a consensus-oriented communalism whose contours permeated the political culture of the early Federal Republic, a built manifesto for the "foundational myth" (Malte Thiessen) of the

90 The italics designate words rendered in gold.

post-war city with its community of residents united in a sense of loss and the task of beginning anew. From this vantage point, the memorial complicates a standard assumption about post-war German memory culture. Available research has posited a "rigid separation" between familial-communal and national forms of commemoration.[91] Germans who had lived through the war typically presented themselves as victims, so the story goes, in personal narratives – shared mostly in private settings – centered on the war, the bombings, or dislocation after 1945. By contrast, communal memorials such as the *Ehrenhalle* alluded to German victimhood only obliquely, though the term appears in the description. But as we immerse ourselves further in the *Ehrenhalle*, and as we explore the many ramifications of the city models it contained, we see how spaces like the one in Heilbronn may have moderated between different forms of remembrance.[92] The mixture here of public and private, of individual and communal, cautions us against an exclusive emphasis on this separation between personal and familial war memories on the one hand and the ritual memory of the community on the other. While it is important to acknowledge the gulf that separated the public and private spheres of World War II commemoration in post-war West Germany, their co-existence also was ripe with encounters, negotiations, and confrontations.

In the visitor's movement through the *Ehrenhalle*, memories, stories, or anecdotes may have been remembered in the mind rather than expressed aloud. In other words, the *Ehrenhalle* was a forum for the affirmation of responses to loss rather than an outlet for them. Quasi-liturgical spaces such as this conditioned the visitor for a measured comportment and, at best, moderate participation.

91 Vera Neumann, *Nicht der Rede wert: Die Privatisierung der Kriegsfolgen in der frühen Bundesrepublik: Lebensgeschichtliche Erinnerungen* (Münster: Westfälisches Dampfboot, 1999), 337.
92 Dorothee Wierling, "Generations as Narrative Communities: Some Private Sources of Public Memory in Postwar Germany," in *Histories of the Aftermath*, 102–120. On German victim narratives and their persistence, see Harald Welzer, "Krieg der Generationen: Zur Tradierung von NS-Vergangenheit und Krieg in deutschen Familien," in *Nachkrieg in Deutschland*, ed. Klaus Naumann (Hamburg: Hamburger Edition, 2001), 552–571, esp. p. 565; Regina Mühlhauser, "Vergewaltigungen in Deutschland 1945: Nationaler Opferdiskurs und individuelles Erinnern," ibid., 384–408; Klaus Naumann, "Der Bombenkrieg: Deutsche als Opfer – ihrer selbst?" in *Der Krieg als Text: Das Jahr 1945 im kulturellen Gedächtnis der Presse* (Hamburg: Hamburger Edition, 1998), 33–71; Moeller, *War Stories*; Andreas Huyssen, "Air War Legacies: From Dresden to Baghdad," in *Germans as Victims*, 181–193, 265f. On the rise of victim narratives as a form of social recognition in the 20th c., see Klaus Günther, "Ein Modell legitimen Scheiterns: Der Kampf um Anerkennung als Opfer" (185–247) and Ophelia Lindemann, "Opfergeschichten: Paradoxien der Anerkennung zwischen Erzählen und Zuhören," in *Strukturwandel der Anerkennung: Paradoxien sozialer Integration in der Gegenwart*, ed. Axel Honneth, Ophelia Lindemann, and Stephan Voswinkel (Frankfurt am Main: Campus, 2013), 249–273.

Approached thus, the "cube of silence" potentially functioned as (to borrow Pierre Nora's phrase) a "realm of memory" and also a tomb of memories. The *Ehrenhalle* became an architectural receptacle in which memories were validated at the same time that they were enshrouded, if not enshrined, in silence. The result was a vision of an urban collective forged from past sufferings, steeled by the promise of a better future, whose individuals shared a code of restraint forged in a response to the devastating past. Memorials such as this were spaces erected to anchor memories and emotions at the same time as these same memories and emotions were kept from view. Importantly, such restraint is different from repression. Rather, this space and its icons allowed for, if not encouraged, "remembering selectively,"[93] remembering collectively, and remembering stereotypically – three characteristics of the commemoration of the air raids. These formulations in fact remind us of the concurrence of representation and taboo in W. G. Sebald's 1999-essay *Air War and Literature*. As I have argued in the introduction, Sebald's essay reflects rather than ruptures a post-war dialectic of commemoration that has oscillated between the poles of silencing and remembering the air raids.[94]

Mediation between the public and the private mnemonic spheres also characterizes the political process by which the *Ehrenhalle* came into existence. City officials and journalists called upon residents to participate in the creation of "their" monument; the entries to the competition were publicly displayed, and residents were asked to evaluate them. In addition, local records testify that whether invited or not, some residents participated in the discussions leading up to the *Ehrenhalle*'s opening in 1963. Nevertheless, the mayor, political representatives, and experts held the reins in the decision-making process. They ultimately provided the artists with the space in which to pursue an authorless art thought appropriate for coming to terms with the city's war losses, an art that would help its population. The monument that opened its gates to the public thus reflected Mayor Paul Meyle's (1948–1967; DVP, a liberal party in Germany's southwest) vision of the *Ehrenhalle* as a space expressing simultaneously the "horrors of war and destruction" (*Grauen und den Schrecken des Krieges und der Zerstörung*) as well as "the nonetheless, the courage to live, and gratitude for having survived"

93 Moeller, *War Stories*, 16. For mechanisms of coping with the burden the war placed on individuals and families through discourses and recourse to cliched narratives, see the excellent study by Neumann, *Nicht der Rede wert*.

94 Cf. Hermann Lübbe, "Der Nationalsozialismus im politischen Bewusstsein der Gegenwart," in *Deutschlands Weg in die Diktatur: Internationale Konferenz zur nationalsozialistischen Machtübernahme im Reichstagsgebäude zu Berlin*, ed. Martin Broszat et al. (Berlin: Siedler, 1983), 329–349, esp. 334f.

(*das Trotzdem zum Ausdruck kommen, der Mut zum Leben und die Dankbarkeit, mit dem Leben davongekommen zu sein*).[95]

Neil Gregor has reminded us powerfully of the competing interests and memories that stood at the heart of West German society; insistence on consensus worked against the tensions that pulled this society apart. Heilbronn's post-war community, constructed not through the lens of the memorial, as I have done in the preceding pages, but from the political archive would be a history with radically different contours: a community marked by the presence of American troops (who oversaw a POW camp as well as a Displaced Persons camp), impassioned debates over rebuilding, the delights and pains of economic expansion as well as the arrival of so-called guest workers around the time of the memorial's opening to hint at some of the tensions in the urban fabric between 1945 and 1963. The notion of a collective predicated on loss thus reflected anything but an affective reality, but rather a political vision offered to the memorial's visitors by a paternalistic order. It is a vision of belonging together in suffering that is highly meaningful in its own right.[96]

From Commemoration to Historicization

Today, rubble models have largely ceased to speak without verbal assistance. As more and more survivors of World War II pass away, fewer viewers will have experienced, or remember, the air war. As new models have been built, their audience – and thus their purpose – is unavoidably different. Rubble models of the last three decades are no longer produced, like the one in Heilbronn, to incite reflection and meditation in the first generation of post-war Germans. As the decades pass, personal narratives of destruction will no longer be available from family members, one of the key modes of disseminating knowledge on the air raids in the immediate post-war period. As a result, new contexts and new forms of presentation have emerged in exhibitions and museums, at times incorporating models originally made for city halls. While they no longer perform largely as miniature monuments in civic contexts, rubble models have not been shelved

95 Letter of Paul Meyle to G. Martina Aurich-Klepsch, the winner of the competition, February 1, 1962, cited in Dieter Brunner, "Kunst am Bau im Heilbronn der 50er Jahre," in *Heilbronn und die Kunst der 50er Jahre*, 98.

96 The same communalism that inspired the building of the *Ehrenhalle* has eroded since. This may be why what once was hailed as one of the most beautiful memorial spaces comes across not only as a monument to the war's losses but also as a monument for post-war communities' vibrancy that has itself receded into the realm of the past.

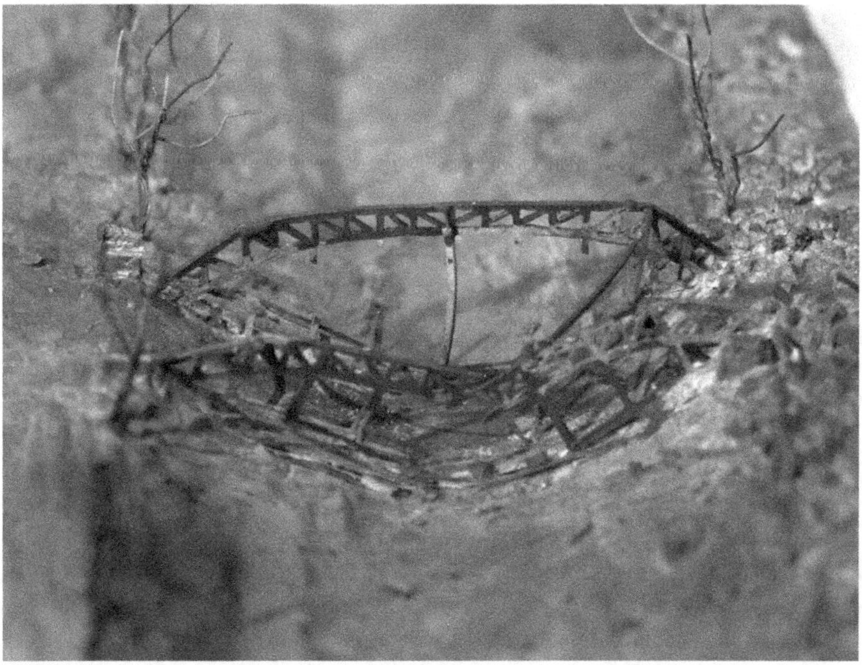

Fig. 39: Goethe-Bridge, Pforzheim, detail of model (Photo: Marco Keller /Nicolai Knauer)

as a genre. Instead, the models made in the last thirty years – for Bielefeld, Würzburg (where two versions of the same model are on display in a memorial *and* a museum), and Pforzheim – have been commissioned for local history exhibitions to inform about the air war.[97] In the case of Pforzheim, for instance, the model-makers stress the widespread ignorance of young residents about the city's demise – a knowledge without which today's cityscape can barely be understood – as motivating their meticulous research and reconstruction.[98]

These changes would not have the same impact, however, if the historiography on National Socialist Germany had not changed as fundamentally as it has

97 The most extensive account of this change in memory culture in Thießen, *Eingebrannt ins Gedächtnis*, 243–457. See also Ute Frevert, "Perspektivenwechsel: Die NS-Vergangenheit in den achtziger Jahren," in *Geschichtsvergessenheit – Geschichtsversessenheit: Vom Umgang mit deutschen Vergangenheiten nach 1945*, ed. Aleida Assmann and Ute Frevert (Stuttgart: Deutsche Verlags-Anstalt, 1999), 258–271.
98 Interview of July 25, 2006.

over this same period, from "a past in which Germans were victims" to one "in which Germans had committed crimes," to introduce a formula coined by Robert G. Moeller.[99] Yet this shift in both historiography and mentality has stimulated poignant questions as to how to approach historical moments like the air raids in which Germans can be understood as victims and not perpetrators – the same question that troubled critics in Frankfurt's contentious post-war debate about how to properly memorialize. What is more, a wave of recent and highly visible publications since the 1990s – including, most prominently, W. G. Sebald's *Air War and Literature* and Jörg Friedrich's *The Fire* – has moved the air war center stage in popular historic interest. The ensuing debates on the air raids have created additional motivation for museums to upgrade or introduce new exhibits on the topic.

Built initially in public settings for post-war viewers and originally displayed with little commentary, scale models of bombed-out cities have subsequently been turned into vehicles of knowledge production. As didactic tools in exhibition contexts, the models with their evocative material presence thus continue to play a role in shaping perceptions and a public memory of the air raids. None of the exhibitions surveyed for this study – museum exhibitions where rubble models are on display – tackle the question of whether and how the estimated 400,000 people lost to the Allied attacks over Germany can be understood as victims. In the museums where the everyday experience in the bomb shelters is highlighted, as is the case in Kassel or Hamburg, the air war as *Alltagsgeschichte*, it would seem, disrupts the all-encompassing notion of loss that informed the viewing of rubble models in the immediate post-war decades. Most verbally explicit exhibits, however, rely on extensive factual information and a detailed narrative of the events leading up to an individual city's catastrophe, leaving the overarching questions about the ethics and justice of the attacks to the visitor.

The example of the *Ehrenhalle* demonstrates above all the importance of immediate spatial contexts for comprehending the referential prowess of rubble models. Context is similarly crucial with models made for or now exhibited in museums. Within treasuries devoted to a city's extended past, the rubble models gain potency amongst a museum's collections in its entirety, and simultaneously enhance the meanings of the rest of the collection. In Frankfurt, for instance, the rubble model was originally placed in the lobby of the now defunct 1972 Historical Museum, so visitors had to pass by this evocative reminder of the city's greatest urban disaster on their way to other museum exhibits. By reminding museum-goers of various war-induced urban losses, every other object is imbued with a new

99 Moeller, *War Stories*, 177.

value: all of them escaped the bombs and firestorms. They become not just historical objects, but relics, having survived the unprecedented ravages of world war.

At times, the placement of rubble models confuses the line between memorials and historical exhibitions. When models are on display in museums they allow for, if not encourage, comments and, at times, even debate among museum-goers, at least compared to the ways that imposing memorials like the *Ehrenhalle* in Heilbronn moderate responses. This is what I witnessed in Frankfurt's History Museum in 2003 when a visitor took the model as an occasion to tell a group of friends from abroad about his boyhood memories of an air raid on the city which he witnessed from afar.

As a result, historical exhibits that include rubble models, set up with plenty of room to roam about them, still have not divested their memorial functions entirely. In Münster's city museum, opened in 1979, an impressive model of the city in ruins (built ca. 1966) is accorded its place in a chronological presentation of the city's development. Among the museum's more than twenty city models, the one showing Münster at the end of World War II stands out. While chronologically earlier models feature bright, uplifting reds and greens, this one is in shades of brown, connoting dirt, detachment, and, ultimately, what has to be left behind.[100] In fact, in a few recent historical exhibits, the link between city modeling and the urban population hinted at for Heilbronn and elsewhere has been marshaled for a very specific purpose: these models are accompanied by a request for contributions, mobilizing the public to cover the costs of modeling a city in ruins.[101]

In Würzburg, two models of the city finished in 1989 are displayed in two formats – small, of the city center, and large, Würzburg as a whole – the smaller one as part of a commemorative exhibit in city hall and the larger one in the local history section of an internationally recognized regional museum (*Mainfränkisches Museum*). Both exhibits document the city's demise on March 16, 1945, when a bomber fleet of the Royal Air Force set the city ablaze, dropping approximately 982 tons of markers, explosives, and incendiary bombs during a raid that lasted seventeen minutes. The resulting fire-storm reached temperatures between 1000

---

100 See *Münster im Modell: 25 Jahre Verein Münster-Museum e.v.* (Münster: Stadtmuseum Münster, 2003). The scale – 1:1000 – has the effect that the degree of destruction is rendered schematically for individual buildings.

101 In Würzburg in 1984, a mayor's initiative (Klaus Zeitler), issued in the year before the forty-year anniversary of the city's near annihilation, resulted in a conscription by which most of the 412,000 Deutschmarks projected to be needed for building a miniature replica of the "dead city" were raised through donations. In Pforzheim, civic associations provided much of the funding for an unfinished rubble model.

Fig. 40: Würzburg, Grafeneckart, Memorial (Photo: Author)

Fig. 41: Würzburg, Model, detail (Photo: Author)

and 2000 degrees Celsius, turning the city into an urban inferno. 5000 people perished. In 1998, the exhibit, after having been installed in one of the city's oldest structures, a tower now part of the city hall complex, was moved to the renovated tower's ground floor with its vaulted ceiling and Renaissance gate: a centrally located, meticulously preserved architectural gem to house a historical exhibit on the city's demise for tourists and residents alike.[102] Independent of the locus of display for either model, however, in a city hall or in a museum, ample commentary frames the models (fig. 40).

Starting four decades after the war's end, concerted efforts at historical accuracy – research enabled in part by previously inaccessible military archives in the UK and the US – and naturalistic effects in model-making were marshaled to reach out to post-war generations without first-hand knowledge of the attacks or memories of their aftermath. To build the destroyed Würzburg forty years later, the model-maker Friedrich Schuller relied on a systematic survey of various

102 On this particular air raid, see Domarus, *Der Untergang des alten Würzburg*; Hermann Knell, *To Destroy a City: Strategic Bombing and Its Human Consequences in World War II* (Cambridge, Mass.: Da Capo Press, 2003).

records: city plans, cadastre data, Allied photographs, films, drawings, and eyewitness accounts. The city's construction department both prepared and oversaw the process from 1985 to 1989. Since most of the photographs of the ruined city are in black and white, the model's careful coloration had to be meticulously reconstructed from the extant information, the work of Rainer Krämer-Guille. Composed of durable, painted plastic, the Würzburg models set a new standard for the three-dimensional rendering of destruction, topped only by the more recent Pforzheim rubble model and its even more meticulous reconstruction of devastation (figs. 39; 41).

The recent models in Würrzburg and Pforzheim, along with being occasions for intensive research on the air raids, are innovative, among other things, in that they portray not a vaguely defined moment in time (as did the earlier models in Frankfurt, Kassel, and Heilbronn) but a particular date – in the case of Würzburg, March 22 and March 24, 1944, when US reconnaissance planes took extensive aerial photographs of the devastated cityscape that had been almost obliterated a week earlier. Such temporal precision reflects the painstaking efforts at approximating historical accuracy instead of the summary view modeled in earlier rubble reliefs. Ironically, what prompted the mayor's desire to have Würzburg's urban catastrophe rendered so precisely was a trip to Frankfurt; the city's delegation was inspired by the rubble model's inaccurate but evocative portrayal of the *Altstadt*'s destruction (although a Würzburg paper reported a similar such plan as early as 1947).[103]

For Pforzheim's rubble model in the making, Marco Keller and Nicolai Knauer equally survey all available data, collecting an unprecedented database that is brought to bear on computer-generated images that then allow producing matrices of plastic replicas in scale. As far as possible, they proceed house by house, constructing the cityscape piece by piece, as it were. One section or module – of ten such modules completed in 2006 – requires on average 1,000 hours of work; when the model grows to include suburban neighborhoods, 600 hours are estimated for completion. Two details shall convey an idea of this model's exacting standard of accurate rendering – reminiscent of the historicist models of

103 [jes], "Auferstanden aus Ruinen: Das Modell des zerstörten Würzburgs," *Würzburger katholisches Sonntagsblatt*, March 13, 2005. The author claims that the idea of the rubble model surfaced for the first time in an article in the 1947-*Stadtanzeiger*. Subsequently, in the fall of 1951, this idea was taken up by Max von Freeden, director of the *Mainfränkisches Museum* in Würzburg, who proposed three models of the city: 1500, 1750, and 1945. See also Stadtarchiv Würzburg, Vbl, Jul 18, 1984; Vbl June 10, 1988; Vbl, March 17, 1987. A model of Würzburg 1525 was completed in 1967 (Franz Seberich). Cf. Franz Seberich, *Das Stadtmodell 'Würzburg um 1525' im Mainfränkischen Museum* (Würzburg: Freunde Mainfränkischer Kunst und Geschichte, 1968).

ancient buildings from the late eighteenth and early nineteenth century. From the photographic record of the Allied post-February 23 reconnaissance mission over Pforzheim, the model-makers concluded, on the basis of the shadows cast by sunlight, that the tracery of the Castle Church's Gothic windows survived the attacks on the building's southern side, whereas they had collapsed on the north, and thus they are rendered thus in the model. It is Keller's and Knauer's goal to get as close as possible to the city's demise with their urban relief of destruction. When eye-witnesses viewed part of the model and challenged its accuracy with regard to one detail, claiming that a particular oriel had been obliterated by the raid, the model-makers could cite one photograph where it had survived in the first hours or days after the attack. Between 2001 and 2006, new modules were presented to the public in the presence of school classes and the press, making the model's completion a task that involves the local public.[104]

The specific features of rubble models become particularly evident when we compare them to other kinds of models. The resurgence of ordinary life in the aftermath of destruction is the focus of a diorama of Halberstadt created between 2000 and 2005.[105] At roughly 7 square meters, this model (scale 1:87) by Dieter Janietz condenses a multi-year period between April 8, 1945, the date of the aerial attack, and 1950, when the roof truss of St. Martini went up in a central part of town, a date and event chosen by the model-maker. The model is populated with colorful figurines busy in the midst of heaps of rubble and shells of buildings: Some workers remove debris, others raze what remains of buildings, while a train carries the wreckage away.[106] Building activity has resumed; a medieval statue of Roland in front of city hall is freed of its protective mantle of brick; some people are using public transportation; and a shepherd grazes a flock of sheep near St. Martin's church. This vision of the immediate post-war years – as a return to work and normalcy in the midst of dire devastation – overshadows the period's political changes. The formation of the German Democratic Republic of which Halberstadt was part is manifest only in a public billboard along one of the passable streets reading *Frauen in der Nationalen Arbeitsfront eine Macht im Friedenskampf* (Women in the National Workers' Front – a force in the fight for peace)

---

104 All data in this paragraph from an interview with Nicolai Knauer and Marco Keller on July 25, 2006.

105 Alexander Kluge, "Der Luftangriff auf Halberstadt am 8. April 1945" [1977], in *Chronik der Gefühle*, vol. 2: *Lebensläufe* (Frankfurt am Main: Suhrkamp, 2000), 27–82; id., *Der Luftangriff auf Halberstadt am 8. April 1945* (Frankfurt am Main: Suhrkamp, 2008). Cf. Werner Hartmann, *Halberstadt brennt: Eine Dokumentation über Halberstadt im Luftkrieg insbesondere über die Zerstörung der Stadt am 8. April 1945* (Halberstadt, 1990) [first version 1967].

106 Klaus Scherff, *Trümmerbahnen* (Stuttgart: transpress, 2002).

and in the presence of the *HO* or *Handelsorganisation*, the city's first state-run department store, which opened its doors in Halberstadt in 1950. (The *HO*, incidentally, was razed after re-unification, during the years when this diorama was in the works.)[107] Built more than five decades after the end of the war and based on archival materials, the Halberstadt diorama – a populated scene in small scale as opposed to the model's abstract rendering of space – captures an idyllic community in the midst of urban ruination.

Though no rubble model was made in the German Democratic Republic, the country's end in 1990 spawned forms of remembering the immediate post-war past that are comparable to those in West Germany. In this sense, the air war over Germany has become part of a public memory that potentially unites all Germans on both sides of the former border separating the two Germanies.[108] Accordingly, an association of citizens in post-reunification Halberstadt sponsored a relief model in sculpted bronze, erected on a stele in front of city hall and dedicated to the rubble women who cleared the city (fig. 42). Unlike the models we have seen so far, this relief may be touched and felt.[109] In a city whose demise Alexander Kluge captures as a human catastrophe during which capitalist society's dysfunction became evident in the most glaring manner, in turn, the memory of the air raid has settled into its sentimental, material, and tactile representation.

The stasis of urban portraits in rubble becomes apparent, particularly if we compare them to models of urban disasters other than the carpet bombings of German cities. At the *Museum of London*, for instance, "The Great Fire Experi-

107 Since 2008 exhibited in Städtisches Museum im Spiegelschen Palais, Halberstadt, where it was first shown in an exhibit commemorating the museum's one-hundred-year anniversary (2005) and between 2006 and 2008 in Martini Church. It is a loan from the modelmaker and owner, Dieter Janietz. See *100 Jahre Geschichte: 1905–2005: Das Museum – Die Stadt – Die Halberstädter*, ed. Günter Maseberg (Halberstadt: Veröffentlichungen des Städtischen Museums, 2005), 291. This information is based on an interview with Mr. Janietz, September 22, 2008.

108 Bill Niven, "Introduction: German Victimhood at the Turn of the Millennium," in *Germans as Victims: Remembering the Past in Contemporary Germany*, ed. B. Niven (New York: Palgrave Macmillan, 2006), 1–25. See also Jeffrey K. Olick, "What Does It Mean to Normalize the Past? Official Memory in German Politics since 1989," in *States of Memory: Continuities, Conflicts, and Transformations in National Retrospection*, ed. Jeffrey K. Olick (Durham: Duke University Press, 2003), 258–288.

109 Klaus Neumann, "Lange Wege der Trauer: Erinnerung an die Zerstörung Halberstadts am 8. April 1945," in *Luftkrieg: Erinnerungen in Deutschland und Europa*, ed. Jörg Arnold, Dietmar Süß, and Malte Thießen (Göttingen: Wallstein, 2009), 203–220, here p. 215. The monument is of 2005. Neumann reports that a call for such a monument dedicated to "rubble women" was published in a local paper as early as 1970 (ibid.).

Fig. 42: Halberstadt, Relief (Photo: Author)

ence," an installation on the city's devastating fire of 1666, combines models, lighting effects, sounds, and a recorded narration of the disaster to create a sense of the fire's spread and the destruction left in its wake.[110] The model of the Great Fire of Hamburg (1842), on display in the Museum of the History of the City of Hamburg (now Hamburg Museum), similarly attempts to depict the unfolding of the destruction rather than focus exclusively on its aftermath. In the Imperial War Museum's "Blitz Experience," currently in storage, the visitor sits in a simulated London air raid shelter that, once the door is closed, shakes under the impact of the bombs. A museum brochure describes how "[a]ppropriate sights, sounds and smells evoke for visitors a sensation of being caught in the bombing of London during the Second World War."[111] The shelter is exited into a scene of a ruined street, where museum goers are accompanied out by uniformed museum staff equipped with flashlights. Strikingly, stories of human loss are relegated to the

---

110 See <www.museum-london.org.uk/Molsite/learning/features_facts/tudo r_stuart_london1.html>.

111 *Imperial War Museum* (London: Imperial War Museum, 2000), 22f (with photograph of the ruined streetscape that visitors encounter upon leaving the air shelter).

words spoken by the guide. Reenactment in a museum is a dusty affair in this case, arguably less immediate than its promise. In Germany, where the air war did not end in victory but in defeat, no equivalent seems to exist; there, one's release from the packed bomb shelter does not mirror the uplifting sentiments citizens of the UK harbored in 1945, when after the many war-induced losses, the war concluded with an Allied victory.[112]

Another model of devastation is a pedagogical fiction about a catastrophe that, though anticipated or feared, never happened. In 1960, the predecessor to what is now the *Federal Academy for Crisis Management, Emergency Planning, and Civil Defense* (Akademie für Krisenmanagement, Notfallplanung und Zivilschutz) in Bad Neuenahr commissioned a model of Bonn – then the capital of the Federal Republic of Germany – to depict various forms of destruction after an atomic strike on the city's Kennedy Bridge. Since it was presumed that the capital's downtown would be utterly destroyed, it is not included in the model, which depicts instead Bonn's northern suburbs, where survival would supposedly have been possible.[113]

In Bielefeld's *Historisches Museum*, set up in a former factory in 1994, the visitor encounters a 1985-model of the city *in* – rather than *after* – World War II (fig. 43).[114] The viewing experience is quasi-cinematic. Installed in an upright sloping position at the end of a room, bounded by lockers from a factory on one side and machinery on the other, the model, protected only by a railing, can be approached at close range, as if from a low-flying aircraft. An actual bomb hung from the ceiling adds to the dramatic quality of the presentation. The cinematic effect is further heightened by the color photographs attached to the railing and arranged to look like film stills. Strangely, this exhibit turns the visitor into a pilot. Whether one imagines flying an Allied or a German warplane, the installation counters a narrative of mere victimhood while simultaneously conveying the feeling of a world turned upside down. Also disorienting is the use of materials, which ruptures the standards of modeling that have dominated the previous centuries: here damage is highlighted through the application of paint while buildings that survived intact are mere wooden blocks. Destruction, in

112 Compare a reference to a comparable installation in a 1993-exhibition in the Museum für Hamburgische Geschichte, see Thiessen, *Eingebrannt ins Gedächtnis*, 320.

113 Bodo-Michael Baumunk and Gerhard Brunn, eds., *Zentren, Residenzen, Metropolen in der deutschen Geschichte* (Cologne: DuMont, 1989), 431 (no photograph). The model is now held at the *Haus der Geschichte* in Bonn. It has only been shown in the context of special exhibits (1989; 1999). Wolfgang Kreutzer was kind enough to send me a digital photograph.

114 The model is of ca. 1985 (Modellbauwerkstatt der Stadt Bielefeld).

Fig. 43: Bielefeld, Historisches Museum (Photo: Author)

other words, is more strikingly rendered. The city's ruins seem to be more real than the buildings that survived the raids. This difference may be meant to guide the viewer toward assessing what and how much was destroyed. But the exhibit also ironically reflects and ruptures conventional modes of display for modeled urban spaces; Sandtner's sixteenth-century models of Bavarian cities were mounted on tables to ensure scopic control, and this has been the preferred mode of display since, though the height of such tables vary and stimulate different viewing experiences. At any rate, if the Bielefeld exhibit serves as an inspiration for future museum designs, then the rubble model's miniature monumentality has come to its historic end and new modes of installations will beckon museum visitors to follow their allure.

* * *

In the displays we have surveyed, meticulously crafted scale models of ruined cityscapes translated the chaos of "rubble" into the focus of "ruins." They summon a variety of other representational genres, the city model, the diorama, and ruins imagery among them. Yet in bringing together these various representational codes, these models have generated a tradition of their own.[115] We have seen the various ways, since the sixteenth century, that models have been produced: not only to please aesthetically but to survey the realm, particularly a territory's fortifications, to plan military campaigns, and to impress onlookers in a sort of specular containment policy. An analytic focus on rubble models brings to the fore the artifice that is part and parcel of the cultivation of both memories and histories. Rubble models convert catastrophic events into spectacle by turning human and other loss into a material object from which traces of human life have been excised, thus enabling the gaze to rest without exposing the viewer to the risk of voyeurism that hovers over photographic records of human disaster. Ultimately, the rubble model is a vehicle of the historical imagination, reflecting a suffering that can only be experienced in fragments and from afar. The scale of these monumental miniatures is predicated on distance that is at once material, temporal, and spatial. As monument-like objects, they translate disasters into miniature, seeking to convert individual sufferings into an image of comprehensive material loss: "We, the survivors, see everything from above, see everything at once, and still we do not know how it was."

115 The most recent model, Pforzheim, currently under construction, has, like the one in Würzburg, been inspired by its ancestor, the Frankfurt "rubble model," though the tradition of modeling is so widespread in Germany that no particular inspiration seems to have been necessary to motivate the making of a particular model.

How to exhibit models? We have looked at their use in Germany across a wide range of eras, and we are about to take our investigation even further afield. Clearly, city models, even models of urban destruction, have a history. But do models also have a future?

For centuries, as I have noted through a series of exemplary analyses, models have thrived in exhibits that can best be described as instructional. Whether they show us the workings of a machine, the structural design of a building, or the built fabric of a whole city or a section thereof, we look at models as a means to learn. In a way, we are at risk of seeing right through them in order to perceive something else. This demonstrative quality is the prime reason why models have been deemed useful. In short, exhibitions frequently capitalize on models' ability to propel the viewer to a position of understanding, mastery, and difference in perception, whereas models' own status as objects enters our view only as an afterthought.

Photographs and postcards of modeled spaces are emblematic in that regard. Through camera angle, zoom, and details, these images dwell on the 'as if,' as if what we are seeing were an actual space. They give insight and pleasure through their invitation to misread the scene – an exercise in "sweet deception" that Johann Michael Zeyher saw at work in the imitative ruins of Schwetzingen's park. For many architects of the mid-twentieth century, such photographs served as an important vehicle for promoting buildings yet unbuilt in magazines. Only if we look closely, we discover that the spaces are sculpted and the façades of cardboard. In other words, as a rule, models are locked into a perpetual and uncritical present. Such images are paradoxical, as Davide Deriu points out, because they suture what he calls the "evidentiary force of photography" to the "fantasy world of models."[1]One could also say that models have a promiscuous presence; they simultaneously exist in more than one register.

Remembering who built models, who commissioned them, and remembering what we know about the history of their existence over time therefore works against conventional modes of appreciating models. Doing so conspicuously would mean to dispense with the aura of self-evidence that has enveloped these objects and their displays.

To be sure, curators have started to exhibit models in innovative ways. Coloring, lighting, and positioning can challenge conventional modes of viewing models at table height – a form of engagement known to have existed since the Renaissance. At the same time, contemporary artists are exploring the evocative poten-

---

1 Davide Deriu, "Transforming Ideas into Pictures," in *Camera Constructs: Photography, Architecture and the Modern City*, ed. Andrew Higgott and Timothy Wray (Burlington, VT: Ashgate, 2012), 159.

tials of working with replicas, miniatures, and dioramas. One may think here of Michael Dreher who constructs scale models of historical sites such as his Republic of Free Wendland (2000), the 1980 camp of the anti-nuclear protest movement in Germany: a miniature, peopleless monument to an ephemeral space of communal politics, executed in monotonous brown and black hues – a model whose enigmatic presence incites questions about where the activists have gone. Seeking to countervail the deceptive stillness, if not melancholic calm, of miniature sculptures (Dreher's as well as that of the rubble models), another artist, Matthias Schmeier, creates dioramas of confrontations. These works include scenes from the history of environmental politics in Germany or from the recent war in Bosnia – everything meticulously rendered on the basis of extant photographic records. These works seem to urge us to consider the contingencies of history: What would happen if we moved the figurines to replay the moment and change the historical outcome? In yet another example of the use of models at the interface of history, memory, and art – The Shape of Things to Come (1999–2004) by Jake and Dinos Chapman – the artists created a phantasmagoric scene of a massacre with hundreds of miniature figurines: a dark vision that draws on the artistic registers of the apocalypse, of wars, and of history (some actors in the scene wear swastika armbands) that aims at confounding temporal layers and shocking viewers.

By contrast, Thomas Demand's photographs of monumental models seek to avoid the ludic associations at work in Dreher's and Schmeier's sculpted spaces. In 2006, he created a naturalistic set of a grotto from bits of paper. Its only record is the photographs he took; the life-size model itself was destroyed once the photographic images were taken. Demand's model images are nothing if not perfect, though they are always mediated. In his book Model Studies of 2011, the same artist zooms in on the haunting material frailty of models by offering mysterious camera close-ups of miniature architecture.[2] On the most basic level, such mediations and remediations between different registers, dimensions, and media seek to shake up our usual ways of seeing. In fact, models have had an underappreciated presence in the visual arts ever since artists of the Russian and German avant-gardes started to use them during the 1920s as an end in and of themselves in order to lend wings to the political, social, and aesthetic imagination. It is precisely this "in-between-ness" that artists' models exploit to great effect. With their expansive temporal reach into possible or impossible futures, they hover between sculpture and image, architecture and experiment, art and non-art, assertion and brittleness.

Cross-fertilizations between artistic creations on the one hand and historical reconstructions on the other hand may help to shape our engagement with models.

---

2 Thomas Demand, *Model Studies* (London: Ivorypress, 2012).

I have claimed that the modeling of inhabited spaces has a history that is meaningful to the genre as we know it. I have noted that city models have a multiform presence. But such models may also have a future. From the vantage point of Cyber City – the evanescent digital worlds accessible from our computers (like in the model of virtual Alt-Frankfurt*) – we can gauge and appreciate models' material presence and their mediality anew. Models are agents in mediating the world for us via the comfort of scale. Their diminutive size offers up manageable versions of complex, even troubled human spaces, from the bombed out cities of post-war Germany to the sociopolitical complexities of early modern Munich to the space we will now consider, the remains of Hiroshima.*

Epilogue

Scaling *Hiroshima*

(... *A man's voice, flat and calm, as if reciting, says:*)
HE: You saw nothing in Hiroshima. Nothing.
(... *A woman's voice, also flat, muffled, monotonous, the voice of someone reciting, replies:*)
SHE: I saw *everything. Everything.*[1]

These are the first words spoken in one of the most celebrated movies of post-war cinema, Alain Resnais's *Hiroshima mon amour* (1959), based on a script by the novelist Marguerite Duras. Uttered by dispassionate voices, this exchange launches the film as an exposition on the art of seeing. The multiple associations of the entwined bodies on screen (that we have seen before we hear these words), their discontinuous montage, and the glaring visual contrasts incite viewers to become aware of themselves as viewers. How can we approach, how could we see, and what would it mean to see Hiroshima?

In the film, we encounter the city in the hustle and bustle of post-war development. This "new Hiroshima" – the name of the hotel where the French female protagonist resides – is the place where her love affair with a Japanese architect fades in and out of the plot. It is here where the female lead has come in order to act in a movie about peace, though we get to see only parting shots of its making. As the theme of this film inside the film illustrates, Hiroshima in the 1950s figures also as a powerful conduit to the past. It is a place that lives through the echoes of one of the greatest disasters in human history. There, on August 6, 1945, the United States Air Force dropped the first atomic bomb in history – a strike that wiped out approximately 80,000 lives, a third of the city's population, in a second.

As the present-day plot of *Hiroshima mon amour* begins its descent into the emotional abyss of the violent past, the opening sequence recapitulates all that the nameless and paradigmatic woman *has* seen. The movie offers us flashes of her vantage point, as if we are to judge for ourselves whether she indeed saw everything or nothing there is to see about Hiroshima. What she has seen is certainly horrible.[2] But how could one person see *everything* there is to see about Hiroshima?

---

1 Marguerite Duras, *Hiroshima Mon Amour: A Screenplay by M.D.: For the Film by Alain Resnais*, trans. Richard Seaver (New York: Grove Press, 1961), 15. Marguerite Duras, *Hiroshima mon amour: Scénario et dialogue* (Paris: Gallimard, 1960), 22: "Une voix d'homme, mate et calme, récitative, annonce: LUI 'Tu n'as *rien* vu à Hiroshima. Rien.' *A utiliser à volonté. Une voix de femme, très voilée*, mate *également, une voix de* lecture récitative, *sans ponctuation, répond* : ELLE 'J'ai *tout* vu. *Tout*.'"

2 Resnais used footage that would not have been commonly available at the time. See Abé

The camera guides us through first a hospital and then a museum – places the French actress visits in order to understand Hiroshima. Here, we get to survey the imprint of the past catastrophe onto the present narration. In the museum, the camera records the tables, the photographs, and the *sammelsurium* or miscellany of objects exhibited, as visitors circulate through the space. One of the shots from the museum sequence captures the destroyed city. It is Hiroshima in the wake of the attack. From an elevated angle, we notice the empty shells of a few damaged buildings; they protrude from a cityscape that is almost entirely flat, rubbled to dust. As we glimpse at the destruction and try to comprehend this overwhelming site, we see a railing that runs along the lower edge of the frame. We notice captions jutting out from the cityscape; each paper slip gives the name of one of the wrecked buildings. We perceive that the landscape that surrounds this scene of devastation is painted. We eventually come to realize that what the camera has canvassed is a relief model. As the camera continues to survey this haunting image of a city, we see children gazing down at the hollowed out Hiroshima in quiet curiosity (figs. 44 and 45).

In this characteristic tracking shot, the director first presents an urban vista of destruction and then proceeds to decode it as a museological form.[3] Moving between close-up and wide angle, reconstruction and deconstruction, representation and rupture, is emblematic of the dual vision of *Hiroshima mon amour* – a film that injects a good measure of skepticism into the images we see on screen.[4] "The reconstructions have been made as authentically as possible," the female voice insists, reminding the viewer of the simulated reality both on display and on screen.[5]

Mark Nornes, *Japanese Documentary Film: The Meiji Era through Hiroshima* (Minneapolis: University of Minnesota Press, 2003), 183–219. See also his *Forrest of Pressure: Ogawa Shinsuke and Postwar Japanese Documentary* (Minneapolis: University of Minnesota Press, 2007).

3 This repeats the cinematic move encapsulated in the opening sequence, described above in the first paragraph, with its disquieting simultaneity of images of bodies in pain and images of bodies in amorous embraces that are only with cinematic time parsed apart when the reader recognizes the two humans as a couple.

4 Cf. Martin Jay, *Downcast Eyes: The Denigration of Vision in Twentieth-Century French Thought* (Berkeley: University of California Press, 1993), 459–469. Resnais and French New Wave Cinema does not figure in this account which sheds light on ocular skepticism, though these films might have themselves inspired new modes of seeing.

5 *Hiroshima Mon Amour*, 18; *Hiroshima mon amour*, 25: "Les reconstitutions ont été faites le plus sérieusement possible."

Figs. 44 and 45: Alain Resnais, "Hiroshima mon amour" (1959), film stills

Our exploration of rubble models in particular, and city models in general, has been animated by a critical impulse akin to Resnais's. I believe these models are worthy of a second glance. Doing so means going against the grain of this genre of objects. If successful, models conventionally make viewers forget the models' status as vehicles of what it is they model. In that sense, *Hiroshima mon amour* provides a critical counterpoint. The banality of the modeled object brings to the fore the many constraints implied in capturing a human catastrophe that exceeds our representational grasp. By suturing together glances of Resnais's film, modeled representations of destruction, and Hiroshima's memory-scape, here we will touch on commonalities and differences in the efforts of Japan and Germany to come to terms with large-scale destruction and losses that exceed our imagination. In so doing, we will seek a means to more fully grasp the complications of approaching a disastrous past in modeled form.

The main hall of the museum in Resnais's film functions as a depository of individual objects tied to the victims and survivors; each of the displayed relics, from the misshapen bicycle to the streaks of hair lost after the attack, is framed by written descriptions and visual records. Unlike the student's lunchbox whose contents turned into coal, unlike the shadows of vanished humans, as well as the myriad traces of tragic, painful, and deadly experiences on display in the same museum today, a city model is evidently not a document from the past. As we have seen again and again, a model is a document of the present, a reconstruction of the past that serves our needs today. Constructed after the event, a three-dimensional recreation forges a panoramic picture of the past, frozen in time, for the present, a present that is itself elusive since it inevitably vanishes with the progression of time. Like memories, such an object cuts through several temporal layers. It invokes memories of a city that once was as well as reflections on the urban entity that has come to emerge in its place, a space the visitor has traversed in order to enter the museum where the model offers itself for the beholder.

In the context of *Hiroshima mon amour*, models, in a way, are like films; they are made, and the filmic narrative with its images and voice-overs is made so as to not have us forget their constructedness. They tie the representations of the past to the present moment in which they are being seen. Significantly, the presentation of the museum's model is part of a filmic sequence that surveys various modes of simulation, reconstruction, and reenactment. After the glances the viewer gets of the museum, its visitors, and the model of Hiroshima after the attack, we are exposed to excerpts from a Japanese feature film on the nuclear bombing of Hiroshima, somewhat crude images of a human tragedy that are themselves then superseded by documentary footage.

Fig. 46: Model of Hiroshima After the Blast, 1:1000, Peace Memorial Museum (Photo: Author)

Though much of Resnais's film centers on constructedness, the model of a bombed Hiroshima was not a mere set piece; built sometime in the decade after the bombing, it is the rare case of a model akin to Germany's rubble models. This exceptional instance allows us to revisit some of our foundational arguments through a different lens. A large-scale model of the devastated cityscape of Hiroshima has been a feature of the display in the city's Peace Memorial Museum from its opening in 1955. The museum's archive contains no information on what inspired its making. In Hiroshima, as in many German cities, the model's commissioners and makers remain in the shadow of an object built to render the aftermath of a horrific event. We do know that the first model was transferred to the museum from the exhibit at the A-Bomb Memorial Hall (Moto-machi), an exhibit opened in 1949 and predicated on the personal collections found, gathered, and eventually organized in the wake of the city's demise. Since that transfer, the "panorama model"[6] has been deemed such an asset to the Peace Memo-

6 In order to differentiate this comprehensive model representing all of Hiroshima after the attack from the two city models of Hiroshima's Nakajima neighborhood mentioned below, I am calling this model of destruction a "panorama model." In most contexts, I refrain from calling

rial Museum's exhibition that it was remade in its entirety and improved several times, namely in 1958, 1969, and in 1991.[7] In the current exhibit, the model on display measures 5.5 meters in diameter. Mounted at low height, it shows, at a scale of 1:1000, an area that extends in a radius of 2,750 m from the hypocenter – the point where the bomb exploded – marked on the model by a red object hung from the ceiling (fig. 46). As visitors gaze over the wide and open spaces of the model, they capture a glimpse of a devastated cityscape very different from the German examples we have seen. In the case of Hiroshima, like in other Japanese cities, the built environment consisted mostly of wooden structures. "[T]here were not even the mountains of rubble of German towns; the wooden structures had gone up in flames and smoke, leaving the ground covered with black dust and spent embers," writes Kenzo Tange, architect of the Peace Memorial Museum in which the model stands.[8] With these words, Tange describes post-war Tokyo, a city devastated not by one nuclear attack but by a series of conventional air raids with even higher losses of life during the attacks (Hiroshima victims, of course, also died *after* August 6, 1945) (fig. 47). Nonetheless, his remarks are relevant for Hiroshima whose wood structures also burned after the bombing, a fact which accounts for the empty space in the model.

Since the East Building of the Peace Memorial Museum with its additional exhibition space opened its doors to the public in the early 1990s, two other scale models have been incorporated into the museum's collection. They show the Nakajima-neighborhood of Hiroshima, at a scale of 1:200 and with a diameter of 3.35 m – the section of the city closest to the hypocenter. This tip of land between two arms of the Ota River once was one of the city's most lively neighborhoods and has been transformed into the Peace Memorial Park after 1949. Like some of the models at memorial sites in Germany, these 1993 models are set up dialogically, the first representing the neighborhood before the bombing, and the second depicting the obliterated neighborhood. They are thus an instance of comparative specularity, that is a "before and after," seeking to capture the sudden disappearance of urban fabric, history, and life, and conjuring up a

---

it a "rubble model" in order to call attention to the different effects the air war had on Japanese cities and their modeled representation; such effects are discussed below.

7 According to staff members, the first rectangular-shaped panorama model was brought to the museum from the A-Bomb Memorial Hall. It was replaced with the model we see in Resnais' film, a round model, probably created for the Hiroshima Restoration Exposition, with pictures of mountains painted on the bordure.

8 Quoted in Paulo Riani, *Kenzo Tange* (London: Hamlyn, 1969), 7. The text is not dated or footnoted. It was probably written for Riani's publication.

Fig. 47: Monument in Memory of Victims of the Tokyo Air Raids and in the Pursuit of Peace (2001), Tokyo (Photo: Author)

third, the space's commemoration in today's Peace Memorial Park (figs. 48, 49, and 50).

Models of destruction recommend themselves as emblems of the catastrophes in their entirety. Abé M. Nornes has expounded on how photographers of atomic devastation stitched together photographic stills into what he calls "atomic 'cinemascope,'" an attempt to master the vast scene of destruction compositionally.[9] This panoramic view is precisely what these Japanese models and their German equivalents afford. Positioned in the middle of a room, a model allows the visitor to circle around the entire perimeter of the scene; we can literally see the devastation from every angle, choose the perspectives that captivate us most, and survey the damage at our own pace. The hint of an "omniscient viewpoint" or sovereign gaze must have been particularly powerful for the Japanese public, who for decades had very little access to the filmic record of their cities' destruction.[10]

9 Nornes, *Japanese Documentary Film*, 191.
10 Nornes, ibid.

Figs. 48-49: Models of Nakajima neighborhood before and after August 6, 1945, 3.35 m, 1:200, Hiroshima, Peace Memorial Museum (Photos: Author)

Fig. 50: Model of Nakajima-neighborhood, 3.35 m, 1:200, Hiroshima, Peace Memorial Museum (Photo: Author)

In Hiroshima, as in the German cities where rubble models are on display, models have shaped the memory of the attack. Interestingly, the museum has repeatedly singled out the panorama model as a signature object. On the covers of brochures, photographs show visitors bent over scale models, contemplating their lessons. The museum's archive contains many photographs with the models serving as a foreground and reference point for the celebrities, luminaries, and statesmen who have visited the museum since 1955. Over the years, Marilyn Monroe, Gustav Heinemann, Olof Palme, Pope John Paul II, and others have been photographed towering over these urban sculptures of destruction. In such pictures, the visitors and not the victims are in focus. No human sufferings jar the record of an official visit to the museum. Instead, such photographs show visitors taking in the scene of destruction, often visibly assisted by experts who exploit the object's educational potential.

Despite these photographs' focus on viewing, the models' representational frame all too often vanishes from sight, unlike in Resnais's film. Information about the model such as origin and make is occluded in favor of their verisimilitude and their putative comprehensiveness; they are objects whose mediality is rarely captured in words. Relief models scale down a vast area into measured three-dimensional space. The models thus rely on our desire to understand, to see "the big picture," and offer us a potentially comforting view. But as we have seen in Germany, that desire goes hand in hand with abstraction, if not distortion.

In Hiroshima as in some German cities, the visitor is invited to compare the photographic record with the models of destruction. Such comparative inspection will find the models elucidating but also lacking. The model of the destroyed Nakajima-neighborhood does not replicate the devastation with exactitude, for instance. There are noticeable discrepancies between the photographs and the three-dimensional reconstruction on display in the same room.[11] If we adduce the "science documentary" shot by a Japanese film team in late 1945 (*The Effects of the Atomic Bomb on Hiroshima and Nagasaki*), this difference becomes even more palpable.[12] What appears as a relatively flat surface in the model, tinged in a monotonous grey hue, was in fact an intricate texture of the past, an abundance of echoes of the city that once was. Needless to say, the explosion, conflagration, and radiation obliterated the urban scene.[13] But that transformation may not have been as radical as the model would have us believe. The documentary footage shows us how the rubble and dust contained traces of the city, its buildings, and their residents. When recreated post factum, the scene of destruction proves elusive. The model distances, offering us a vast overview instead.

As accounts by A-bomb survivors make evident, such a synthetic view would have been hard to come by immediately after the attack. The impossibility of a sovereign gaze or panoramic perception was apparent when survivors, for days after the attack, seemed confined to narrow circles of perception, blinded, disoriented, or incapable to comprehend what had happened. John Hersey's influential 1946 *Hiroshima*, an account of six lives before, during, and after the attack, has the city as a whole enter the stage only on August 18, 1945, twelve days after the bombing:

> the houses on the outskirts of the city, standing but decrepit, with broken windows and disheveled tiles; and then, quite suddenly, the beginning of the four square miles of reddish-brown scar, where nearly everything had been buffeted down and burned; range on range of collapsed city blocks, with here and there a crude sign erected on a pile of ashes ...; naked tress and canted telephone poles; the few standing, gutted buildings only accentuating the horizontality of everything else (the Museum of Science and Industry, with its dome stripped to its steel frame, as if for an autopsy; the modern Chamber of Commerce Building, its tower as cold, rigid, and unassailable after the blow as before; the huge, low-lying, camouflaged city hall; the row of dowdy banks, caricaturing a shaken economic system); and

---

11 This concerns the embankment around the bridge.

12 Nornes, *Japanese Documentary Film*, 191–219, here p. 193.

13 The Peace Memorial Museum in Hiroshima featured an exhibit on the making of the film in spring of 2009.

> in the streets a macabre traffic – hundreds of crumpled bicycles, shells of streetcars and automobiles, all halted in mid-motion.[14]

Hersey's description literally guides us through the destruction, beginning on the "outskirts" and then moving closer and closer to the "scar" of the bomb. The passage has a cinematic quality, as if we are watching a scene pass before our eyes or as if we were standing above the city. The description, like so much writing about war's devastation, seeks to make meaning: the jump to metaphors – "macabre traffic," the museum's dome stripped "as if for an autopsy" – and the jump to symbolic interpretation – the destroyed banks "caricaturing a shaken economic system" – all seek to compare the scene to something more familiar, all seek to make sense out of the incomprehensible. The rubble model, I believe, is an extension of this impulse to survey and comprehend.

As we have seen, the rubble model lifts us off the ground, away from the overwhelming presence of destruction, as in Hersey's description, and into a more comfortable position above it all. If we are above the scene of devastation, we feel ourselves immune to the harm we might or might have experienced at ground level. The model transforms us into an observer, whatever we were before laying our eyes on this object. And the comfort of the observer's distance may precisely be what was and is desired in the exhibit. Compared to the complete loss of orientation as remembered by survivors of the attack, visitors to the museum command this geometrically conceived urban space from an elevated position, as if we flew a reconnaissance plane after the bomb had been dropped.[15] They get interpellated as seers of everything there supposedly was to see about Hiroshima as a built space after the attack.

The impact of the exhibit has been a cause of continuous concern for the Peace Memorial Foundation, the organization entrusted, among other tasks, with overseeing the museum. From the outset, the organization committed itself not only to informing visitors about the destructive force of the A-bomb but to promoting world peace. Yet how should one shake up the visitor? How to approach an event that Abé Mark Nornes has called "an event beyond human experience"?[16] How to build a cognitive bridge to an ever more distant event? How does one

---

14 John Hersey, *Hiroshima* (New York: Knopf, 1946), 88. The text was first published in *The New Yorker*. Marguerite Duras quotes Hersey.

15 See Robert Jay Lifton, *Death in Life: Survivors of Hiroshima* (New York: Random House, 1967), 29.

16 Abé Mark Nornes, "Cherry Trees and Corpses: Representations of Violence from WW II," in *The Japan/America Film Wars: World War II Propaganda and Its Cultural Contexts*, ed. A. M. Nornes and Fukushima Yukio (Chur: Harwood, 1994), 148.

respond to visual and historical literacies that are in constant flux? How to appeal to different audiences, from Japan and abroad? How to respond to the "memory shift" in Japan where the visual representation of the war has become a bone of contention in debates over a usable past for the nation, a nation moving away from the exigencies of the post-war order?[17]

In the context of today's museum, as much as in the museum shown in Resnais's film, the panorama model works in tandem with other objects, displays, and installations. Since the museum's last restructuring, photographs, material traces of human suffering, and a life-size reconstruction of "Big Boy," as American soldiers named the bomb, surround the model, targeting the visitors' senses from a variety of angles. In the Peace Memorial Museum's main hall, objects, images, and texts that speak of or reflect the experiences of the victims and the survivors abound. Such material contexts, as we have seen, have also become a common sight in German history museums across the last three decades, though they are, as a rule, much less comprehensive.

Yet in Hiroshima, the section with the panorama model also includes an installation that has no equivalent in Germany. It shows humans immediately after the explosion, as the world around them has gone up in flames. Positioned opposite the scale model, this diorama with its life-size mannequins radiates the red color of fire into the exhibit. Whereas the scale model invokes the loss of life through humans' sheer absence from the scene of destruction, this installation seeks to graphically bring people back into the frame. Three figures with shattered physiques and in tattered clothes march through carefully arranged debris toward the visitor, as if they had lost all orientation, looking for help. Even such an evocation of human suffering with its direct appeal to the viewer pales, of course, in comparison to when we seek to imagine the impossible, the actual experience. The installation reduces the stench, the sounds, the heat, and the ruin of a radiated world to a discrete three-dimensional moment, a moment that may be jarring, but one from which we can easily turn away, as our gaze flits to the competing displays in the same room. Amidst this abundance of installations and displays, we are reminded of the inadequacy of every single element in the museum's presentation in approximating this catastrophic event – a point made also by *Hiroshima mon amour*.

---

17 Julia A. Thomas, "Photography, National Identity, and the 'Cataract of Times': Wartime Images and the Case of Japan," in *American Historical Review* 103 (1998): 1475–1501; Carol Gluck, "The 'End' of the Postwar: Japan at the Turn of the Millennium," in *States of Memory: Continuities, Conflicts, and Transformations in National Retrospection*, ed. Jeffrey K. Olick (Durham: Duke University Press, 2003), 289–314.

The memorial landscape of Hiroshima offers revealing commonalities and differences to the memorialization of the air raids on German cities. In Germany, we have seen that commemorating the air raids has often been a local affair. Yet by 2013 only one German city has instituted a museum on its destruction, as Hiroshima did in 1955, intended to serve as a built manifesto against war and nuclear arms.[18] The air raids over Germany have entered the national historiography and public debates with great force only recently, and this entry, as I have shown, has been contested, not least because, according to some critics, such a thematic focus risks to undo a consensus by presenting Germans, the perpetrators, as victims. In the German context, only the city of Dresden may have name recognition similar to Hiroshima in conjuring up the horrors of the air raids, nationally and internationally – a hierarchy of international anti-war commemoration that Dresden and Magdeburg acknowledged by presenting themselves in the 1980s as the German equivalents of Hiroshima and Nagasaki.[19] These efforts at constructing parallels notwithstanding, Hiroshima's demise has consistently had a prominent place in the national *and* international historical imagination since August 6, 1945 (and films like *Hiroshima mon amour* have played their own part in bringing this about).

Exceptional events, like the first atomic bomb used in warfare, tend to stimulate exceptional responses. On the fourth anniversary of the first atomic bombing, the Japanese Diet passed the "Law for the Construction of the City of Hiroshima for the Commemoration of Peace." Hiroshima, a military port, became the city of peace. "The people of Hiroshima have decided in unison to put themselves on the side of peace and to show that to the world. The physical appearance of the town where the people of Hiroshima will live shall be a monument to perpetual peace."[20] The creation of a memory-scape in the first city hit by an atomic bomb was part of this post-war urge to commemorate the past and instigate peace.

Like in Germany, ruins and representations of war ruins have become catalysts of commemorations. Ruins, whether modeled or actual, speak of many things. As we have seen, they speak of catastrophic events in history. But what

---

18 The first city to do so was Hamburg. On September 1, 2013 – the anniversary of Nazi attack on Poland, not the anniversary of the most devastating attacks on Hamburg in July 1943 – the city opened an exhibition dedicated to the air war's experience near the tower of St. Nicolai whose ruins have served as a memorial since 1977. See Frank Keil, "Schrecken und Hoffnung," *Die Zeit*, July 4, 2013, 18.

19 Jörg Arnold, "'Nagasaki' in der DDR: Magdeburg und das Gedenken an den 16. Januar 1945," in *Luftkrieg: Erinnerungen in Deutschland und Europa*, ed. J. Arnold, Dietmar Süß, and Malte Thießen (Göttingen: Wallstein, 2009), 253.

20 Riano, *Tange*, 8.

associations do ruins evoke in the case of Japan? We should consider that Japan has not seen the many modes of engagement with ancient Roman sites and modern ruins that has captivated the European imagination. It is a country where wooden buildings predominated until the Meiji period, when Western building techniques took hold. In Japan, the renewal of historically significant buildings at regular intervals rests on meticulous documentation of a given structure and expert rebuilding (kaitai-shuri) and the ritual rebuilding of shrines.[21] However, as a result of decidedly modern catastrophes such as the earthquake which flattened Tokyo in 1923 (the so-called Great Kanto Earthquake), the air raids between 1941 and 1945 and other effects of the "Great Asian War," scarred physical environments have entered into Japan's cultural frame with novel force during the twentieth century.[22] Somewhat ironically, the ruins of large Western-style buildings commemorate the wartime destruction of Japanese cityscapes. In Hiroshima, it is the Hiroshima Prefectural Industrial Promotion Hall – a bold European design by the Czech architect Jan Letzel opened to the public in 1921 – that now serves as the city's landmark of ruination; in Nagasaki, it is Urakami Cathedral.[23]

Like in Europe, post-war Japanese cinema circulated highly evocative images of physical devastation. One may cite the dilapidated structure that serves as a backdrop for Akira Kurosawa's *Rashomon* (1950), or the same director's glimpses of a blighted cityscape in *Stray Dog* (1949). In Kenji Mizoguchi's *Ugetsu monogatari* (1953), set during the sixteenth-century civil wars, a ruined and haunted manor house oscillates between a war-driven vision of plenitude and an index of the brutalities of war. Not unlike Wolfgang Staudte's *Murderers Among Us* (Die Mörder sind unter uns; 1946), the first German post-war film, or Roberto Rossellini's *Germany Year Zero* (Germania Anno Zero; 1948), the cinematic imagination of Japanese film after 1945 mirrors moral quandaries in material fragmentation.[24]

---

21 Niels Gutschow, "Wiederaufbau, Neubau und Rekonstruktion in Asien: Zur Kontinuität von Objekt und Ritual in Nepal, Indien und Japan," in *Geschichte der Rekonstruktion: Konstruktion der Geschichte*, ed. Winfried Nerdinger (Munich: Prestel, 2010), 36–47. See also the same catalogue, pp. 192–197.

22 A park in Sumida, a ward within Tokyo, features several memorials to commemorate disasters that struck Tokyo, among them a museum commemorating tthe 1923-earthquake with a large collection of paintings on the city's ruins.

23 The cathedral was rebuilt in 1980. Photographic shots of Nagasaki in the wake of August 9, 1945, frequently focus on this cathedral. A part of its structure that remained after the blast has been moved as a monument to Peace Park. In the cathedral, the visitor will find glass windows with renderings of the destroyed building; a display of arranged ruined remains outside the church reminds visitors of its destruction.

24 Eric Rentschler, "The Place of Rubble in the *Trümmerfilm*," in *Ruins of Modernity*, ed. Julia

The most iconic modern war ruin in Japan, and arguably the world, is the Hiroshima's A-Bomb Dome, a short walk from the Peace Memorial Museum and its scale models. Resnais's *Hiroshima mon amour* capitalizes on the ruined edifice in a number of stills. The two models of the Nakajima-neighborhood are in fact exhibited under the vault of a scaled-down replica of the same dome. The former Hiroshima Prefectural Industrial Promotion Hall resonates, with local, national, and international audiences alike, as a visual allegory of warfare in the nuclear age. Its hollow façades and imposing cupola are close to where the bomb exploded; no human in the building at the time of the bombing is known to have survived the attack. During the post-war era, this reminder of an unsettling past was saved from destruction. That these ruins have become as recognizable as they are is not least the effect of *Hiroshima mon amour* and the internationally renowned mangas by Keiji Nakazawa, *Barefoot Gen* (1973–1985), among other representations.

Kenzo Tange, the visionary architect, actually designed the Peace Memorial Museum (1955) to provide an architectural frame for the ruined A-Bomb Dome (fig. 51).[25] As one approaches the Peace Memorial Park along Peace Boulevard,[26] the new post-war thoroughfare on which the Peace Memorial Museum is located, one can make out the dome in the distance, framed by the fragile but elongated bar of the museum's main hall, elevated on piers.[27] "[E]verything was ... left in rough concrete, so that nothing can divert attention from the objects on display," Tange said about his design. Yet this "rough concrete" also assures that we are not distracted from the landscape of destruction outside of the museum.[28] The museum building demarcates the park's memory-scape from the city that surrounds it. At the same time, visual axes, such as the one which points to the ruined A-Bomb Dome mentioned above, establish temporal reference points, evoking a web of

Hell and Andreas Schoenle (Durham: Duke University Press, 2010), 418–438; see also Johannes von Moltke, "Ruin Cinema," in the same volume, 395–417.

25 Alfred Altherr, *Three Japanese Architects/Drei japanische Architekten* (Teufen: Arthur Niggli, 1968).

26 Originally named Hundred-Meter Road; the public chose its current name.

27 These *piloti* are inspired by Le Corbusier. But they also reference Japanese wooden frame houses, elevated above the ground, a typical example of the amalgamation of different traditions in Tange's work. See Kenzo Tange, *Katsura: Tradition and Creation in Japanese Architecture* (New Haven: Yale University Press, 1972), 18 (on the Ise Shrine). On visual axes in Japanese architecture, see ibid., 38: "Japanese architecture ... is an architecture of vistas, of continuity, of perspective."

28 Kenzo Tange, *Architecture and Urban Design 1946–1949*, ed. Udo Kultermann (New York: Praeger Publishers, 1970), 17f.

Fig. 51: Hiroshima, Peace Memorial Museum (architect: Kenzo Tange) with the former Hiroshima Prefectural Industrial Promotion Hall in the distance (Photo: Author)

relations connecting the old and the new, references to the atomic past and the viewer's present.

In a far-reaching urbanistic vision unprecedented in the history of modern Japanese architecture, Tange originally sought to center Hiroshima's new "urban core" in the dome's ruined remains.[29] Peace Memorial Park is the now-uninhabited space where once lay the heart of Hiroshima; the expanse with its various monuments and gardens, poignantly conjures up the losses of August 6, 1945. Yet if Tange's plan for Hiroshima had been realized fully, the Peace Memorial Park would have found a pendant in a civic forum across the river featuring a children's library, sports facilities, and other community buildings.[30] This "three-dimensional urban design" of remarkable complexity, to use Tange's words, thus anchored his urbanism in a ruined building as an epitome of a painful past

29 David B. Stewart, *The Making of a Modern Japanese Architecture: From the Founders to Shinohara and Isozaki*, 2nd ed. (Tokyo: Kodansha International, 2002), 164–177. "Urban core" was the theme of the 8th CIAM in 1951 (*Congrès Internationaux d'Architecture Moderne*) which Tange attended. The plan was anticipated in his master plan for Hiroshima of 1946, before he entered the competition for the Peace Memorial Park.
30 Stewart, *The Making of a Modern Japanese Architecture*, 174.

(something we have seen, though in a more modest form, regarding Heilbronn in Germany).[31] Like in Frankfurt, though on a more grandiose scale, the cityscape that emerged in Hiroshima after 1945 responded in manifold ways to the devastation that lay at its origins. A nexus of new urbanism, model-building, ruins-gazing, and political re-orientation emerged in Hiroshima as well as in many German cities in the wake of defeat, and the commemorated past was enshrined in order to provide a foundation for post-war society. Tellingly, the male lead in Resnais's film is an architect (though we get to see none of his buildings).

Resnais follows Tange in that *Hiroshima mon amour* deploys the same dialogue between the museum and the dome as a visual anchor between the temporal layers stripped bare in the film. The anti-illusionist film-maker Resnais thus reflects his own dual vision in Tange's "double-edged vision of past and present, East and West."[32] In fact, the camera dwells on the ruins of the Hiroshima Prefectural Industrial Promotion Hall in a series of stills.[33] But *Hiroshima mon amour* also deflects the building's centrality in another scene that juxtaposes the dome with a white, scaled-down reproduction, a model, striking in its patent artificiality: It is a prop paraded around by professional peace activists. In this disorienting moment, the cheap reproduction appears larger than the original building in the frame's background (fig. 52). Throughout the film, as we have seen, *Hiroshima mon amour* thrives on confrontations between originals and copies, documentary footage and filmic reconstructions, reminiscences and reenactments.[34] To be sure, such juxtapositions call attention to the film's own artifice. What is more, these contrasts rupture conventional modes of viewing.[35] Visual counterpoints of this kind expose imperfections and distortions to plain view. But in the context of Resnais's filmic language such dialogic configurations resist the validation of

31 Stewart, *The Making of a Modern Japanese Architecture*, 171 (published 1985–1986).
32 Stewart, *The Making of a Modern Japanese Architecture*, 164. See also Tange, *Katsura*, passim on the mixing of different aesthetic languages.
33 In *Night and Fog* (*Nuit et Bruillard*) of 1955, a film on the death camps of Nazi Germany, Resnais settles on ruins in a closing sequence, while Michel Bouquet speaks the following words, authored by Jean Cayrol: "With our sincere gaze, we survey the ruins as if the old monster lay crushed beneath the rubble" (Criterion Collection, 2003). German translation by Paul Celan. Ruins as a resting point are all the more important since Resnais composed the film as a form of constant movement.
34 On Resnais's access to this footage, see Nornes, *Japanese Documentary Film*, 216.
35 Max Ophuls's last film, *Lola Montès* (1955), might have served as an inspiration for Resnais in using scale models. In this film, much celebrated by the *auteurs* of the French New Wave cinema, small-scale theatrical props, architectural, and other models visualize the narrative emplotment of Montez's life as based on a filmic economy of scale.

Fig. 52: Alain Resnais, "Hiroshima mon amour" (1959), film still

auratic authenticity over imitative replicas.[36] What emerges from these cinematic reflections is rather a difference of degree: all images of Hiroshima, including the film's own, are open to the charge of inadequacy.[37] The viewer is urged to realize that words as well as images, or models for that matter, are partial, slippery, and ultimately deficient in light of the disaster.

36 Here my interpretation differs from Mary Caruth who in her "Literature and the Enactment of Memory (Duras, Resnais, *Hiroshima mon amour*)" writes: "I would suggest that the interest of *Hiroshima mon amour* lies in how it explores the possibility of a faithful history in the very indirectness of this telling." See her *Unclaimed Experience: Trauma, Narrative, and History* (Baltimore: Johns Hopkins Press, 1996), 25–56, here p. 27. For an interpretation more akin to my own, see Kyo Maclear, "The Limits of Vision: 'Hiroshima Mon Amour' and the Subversion of Representation," in *Witness and Memory: The Discourse of Trauma*, ed. Ana Douglass and Thomas A. Vogler (New York: Routledge, 2003), 233–247, 326.

37 This stance is all the more remarkable since some of the original footage in the film was not commonly available to film audiences in 1959.

Daringly, the plot of *Hiroshima mon amour* stitches together two tragedies that occurred in the final days of the war, an attack from the air that obliterated a Japanese city and a personal story experienced in France – tragedies of a vastly different scale. The presence of scale models throughout *Hiroshima mon amour* may well reflect this fundamental asymmetry at the core of the script. To be sure, scale is one of the foundational problems for any narrative, historical or not. Yet this problem is especially acute for narrations which take on the weight of History, especially when this history revolves around a disastrous event that annihilated the lives of many.[38] Whereas we view echoes of the devastations wrought by the atomic bomb in the film's opening sequence, we learn about the woman's personal tragedy only as this cinematic essay unfolds: she once had a lover, a German soldier stationed in the provincial town of Nevers during the occupation of France. The film explains that this lover was killed a day before the liberation of France that then resulted in shame and public humiliation for her and her family; French women in sexual relationships with Germans during World War II were considered collaborators. Memories of this phase in the protagonist's life were extremely painful, we eventually learn; she sealed them off for many years, until they are unleashed by her encounter with a foreign lover in Hiroshima.[39] The rapprochement between the vastly unequal tragedies of Nevers and Hiroshima on the grounds of memory remains fleeting, however. It is a connection consummated most conspicuously in the act of naming: "Hi-ro-shi-ma. That's your name,"[40] she says to the Japanese lover, and he in turn names her "Nevers." These are the last words spoken in the movie, words suggesting a closure, if only momentary, as well as a new beginning.

The difficulties, if not impossibilities, of capturing mass destruction by means of representation has become the center of gravity for studies on collective memory; not surprisingly, the Holocaust has become this literature's vanishing point.[41] It has been claimed that in *Hiroshima mon amour* Resnais, who

---

38 Recently, historians have started to think about issues of scale more explicity, see Sebouh David Aslanian, Joyce E. Chaplin, Ann McGrath, and Kristin Mann, "How Size Matters: The Question of Scale in History," *American Historical Review* 118 (2013): 1431–1472.

39 Chiori Miyagawa's play, "I Have Been to *Hiroshima Mon Amour*," first performed in 2009, counterpoises the film's asymmetry, that is the French actress having a story and the Japanese architect as a mere listener to her story, though we know he has a story as well. See Steven McElroy, "Answering a Movie and a Nuclear Horror," *The New York Times*, May 10, 2009, Arts 9 and Wilborn Hampton, "The A-Bomb Revisited, From Below," *The New York Times*, May 21, 2009, C4.

40 Duras, *Hiroshima Mon Amour*, 83; Duras, *Hiroshima mon amour*, 124.

41 Dominick LaCapra, *Representing the Holocaust: History, Theory, Trauma* (Ithaca: Cornell University Press, 1994); id., *Writing History, Writing Trauma* (Baltimore: Johns Hopkins University

also directed a film on the death camps, *Night and Fog* (Nuit et Bruillard; 1955), issued a similar caveat. After all, this feature film resulted from Resnais's refusal to make a documentary about Hiroshima.[42] Shoshanna Felman singles out *Hiroshima mon amour* among other films as a work that can "instruct us in the ways in which testimony has become a crucial mode of our relation to events of our times – our relation to the traumas of contemporary history."[43] But the film does not get mired in the dilemmas of representing great disasters, or its own status as testimony, but rather stages the elusiveness of the past as time passes and survival asserts itself – a story of which the models are part when children (who because of their age could not have witnessed Hiroshima's devastation) glance at its reconstructed ruinscape.[44]

What is more, powerfully intoxicating as personal memories of pain and shame are in *Hiroshima mon amour*, they do not seem to secure companionship, not even between two lovers. In this tale memories do not connect, they separate.[45] While the male lover revels in becoming a witness to *Nevers*'s revelation of a repressed past, his female counterpart is pulled toward an all-absorbing moment that she resists to relinquish in full. She remembers in an "inner monologue"; she speaks in "soliloquy," even though her lover is in the room.[46] Ultimately, she insists on the potential of forgetting in the very moment of remem-

---

Press, 2001); *Witnessing the Disaster: Essays on Representation and the Holocaust*, ed. Michael F. Bernard-Donals and Richard R. Glejzer (Madison: University of Wisconsin Press, 2003); *Trauma and Cinema: Cross-Cultural Explorations*, ed. E. Ann Kaplan and Ban Wang (Hong Kong: Hong Kong University Press, 2004); E. Ann Kaplan, *Trauma Culture: The Politics of Terror and Loss in Media and Literature* (New Brunswick, N.J.: Rutgers University Press, 2005); Marianne Hirsch, *The Generation of Postmemory: Writing and Visual Culture after the Holocaust* (New York: Columbia University Press, 2012); and Michael S. Roth, *Memory, Trauma, and History: Essays on Living with the Past* (New York: Columbia University Press, 2012).

42 John Francis Kreidl, *Alain Resnais* (Boston: Twayne, 1977), 54.

43 Shoshanna Felman, "Education and Crisis, Or the Vicissitudes of Teaching," in *Testimony: Crises of Witnessing in Literature, Psychoanalysis, and History* (New York: Routledge, 1992), 5.

44 Cf. Anthea Buys, "*Hiroshima Mon Amour* and the Necessity of Oblivion," *English Studies in Africa* 52 (2009): 50–60.

45 In a note added to the film's "synopsis," a summary not included in the English translation, Duras responds to viewers who had assumed that the female protagonist would stay in Hiroshima, despite her saying she won't, when asked by her lover. The author does so by disavowing knowledge about what happens after the film ends; she claims not to know: "Certains spectateurs du film ont cru qu'elle 'finissait' par rester à Hiroshima. C'est possible. Je n'ai pas d'avis. L'ayant amenée à la limite de son refus de rester à Hiroshima, nous ne nous sommes pas préoccupés de savoir si – le film fini – elle arrivait à transgresser son refus" (Duras, *Hiroshima mon amour*, 16, n.).

46 Duras, "Synopsis," in *Hiroshima*, 15f (not included in the English translation).

bering, consumed by a sense of power over her past.[47] Translating personal memories into a shared memory, if only between two people, is thus exposed as a fragile endeavor, a problem Maurice Halbwachs once situated at the heart of his sociological approach to memory.[48] How then to stitch together by means of commemoration cities, cultures, and nations?

My reading of Resnais's film therefore puts critical pressure on claiming *Hiroshima mon amour* directly as a visual meditation on history and trauma. The film casts a glaring light on the tangential, the ephemeral, and the banal that have both enabled and disabled "communication across traumatic and cultural boundaries," to quote Mary Caruth in her enlightening essay on the joint project of Duras and Resnais.[49] City or rubble models with their simulated qualities offer a visual emblem for this tension. To be sure, they are somewhat beautiful. As such they issue an invitation to engage and see. But they also toy with the trivial. In other words, they are indispensible.

Ultimately, *Hiroshima mon amour* resists an answer to the question raised at its outset, whether an infinitely painful past is knowable. To be sure, one cannot see everything; the woman's statement is excruciatingly naïve. Her visit to Hiroshima, to the museum, and its pain-staking reconstructions, the model of Hiroshima in the wake of the attack among them, is a form of enlightened tourism at best. At the same time, the forbidding "nothing" that her counterpart posits she has seen, also misses the mark. As long as we are alive and able to see, we cannot help but see. After all, we have seen *something*. In the process of seeing, we may learn something about what it is to see. At one point, Nevers insists,"*I think looking closely at things is something that has to be learned.*"[50] Though offered with nonchalance, this comment is a kernel we must consider. As we hear the female protagonist proffer these words, the camera fades out into a black screen; the beginning of a new sequence invites us to do precisely that – to look closely at what we see.

Looking closely, whether at models or movies, means to understand seeing as an activity of the intellect.[51] Looking closely in the sense of my argument means to look with an eye to the deep history of seeing. If we adopt such a stance, we can begin to understand particular kinds of seeing as having been instigated by or

---

47 Duras, *Hiroshima Mon Amour*, 124; Duras, *Hiroshima mon amour*, 83.

48 Maurice Halbwachs, *On Collective Memory*, trans. Lewis A. Coser (Chicago: University of Chicago Press, 1992).

49 Caruth, *Unclaimed Experience*, 49.

50 *Hiroshima Mon Amour*, 28; *Hiroshima mon amour*, 41: "tu vois, de bien regarder, je crois que ça s'apprend."

51 Horst Bredekamp, *Theorie des Bildakts* (Berlin: Suhrkamp, 2010).

revolving around particular objects – objects such as models – seeing as an activity with a historical memory, and an activity that is itself significant as an agent of change: "In this way, the past falls into ruin and vanishes only in appearance."[52]

52 Halbwachs, *On Collective Memory*, 39.

In Conclusion

My parents were relocating. As they sorted through their household, I was to receive one of only two objects salvaged from the rubble of my maternal grandparents' bombed-out house: a pair of old-fashioned serving spoons in silver. One of them bore marks from the devastating air raid on my home town, the other did not. I had set my eyes on the spoon with its indelible spots; my mother was adamant that I should take the unblemished piece. To be sure, she may not have wanted to part with this relic for memory's sake. But although, as far as I can remember, neither spoon ever made it to our dinner table, all she talked about at that moment was their use value, not their potential as memorabilia. Despite this momentary disagreement, her memories connected us – two generations in post-war Germany – more so than she ever realized or acknowledged. My wish to own the "wounded" spoon that is now part of my household was, in a way, itself a tribute to my mother, as is this book.

When growing up, I was transfixed by my mother's stories about the past, her experience on March 18, 1945, among them (fig. 53).[1] In her telling, she escaped being buried alive in the cellar of a sixteenth-century house only by a stroke of luck and the helping hands of a soldier. Nonetheless, when we drove in my parents' car through the narrow street where the family home had once stood, stuck in late afternoon traffic, my mother would sometimes exclaim that not enough bombs had fallen in the war (implying that otherwise the town's remaining medieval streets would be wider, allowing us to move on, though this was left unsaid).

The multiple, conflicting sentiments she harbored in regards to the air raid on Bad Dürkheim have stayed with me. My mother was both remarkably unsentimental and very emotional about the disaster that struck our small town in the West of Germany during the last days of World War II. Yes, hers were tales of loss. Their occasional retellings bespoke a deep attachment to the wounds the past had inflicted on her life. But hers also was a story of liberation, renewal, and a half-hearted desire to forget. For someone whom the Nazi state had categorized as a half Jew, the bombs of that fateful day heralded the impending arrival of American troops, and with them freedom from oppression, though not, at least not immediately, from homelessness and destitution. My mother's father, whose

1 Josef Kaiser, *"Gemeinsames Schicksal – gemeinsame Arbeit!" Zur Wiederentstehung des demokratisch-politischen Lebens in Bad Dürkheim nach dem Zweiten Weltkrieg* (Neustadt a.d. Weinstrasse: Neue Pfälzer Post, 1987), 11–13. In a town of ca. 9,500 inhabitants, 285 died as a result of this raid. 530 residential buildings had been partially or entirely destroyed. 9,000 cubic meters of rubble had to be removed.

Fig. 53: Bad Dürkheim, Night of March 18, 1945 (Photographer unknown; family-owned photo)

commitment to my grandmother never seems to have wavered, despite pressures to divorce her on "racial" grounds, derived a lesson from his family's survival, or so the story went. After Germany's defeat, he went into politics in order to build a new and democratic society so that the Nazi past would not repeat itself in the country's future. As mayor from 1946 until his death in 1960, he oversaw the town's rise from the rubble with its new squares and widened streets.

My family's experiences, like many stories about a war's impact on people's lives, are both typical and exceptional. As a young baby-boomer, I grew up with stories about the violent end of one era and the hardships of beginning anew, even if the setting for passing on select tales about the recent past to the next generation was always within the family, not with strangers. (Could I ask her now, my mother would disapprove of my sharing these reflections with you.) Thinking back to my mother's and my grandmother's vivid narratives reminds me of how personal an endeavor this book has been. The air war over Germany, its commemoration, and the urban communities that emerged from the rubble – themes that reverberate through its pages – originated with the tales they shared with me. Its writing may be said to exemplify a "sense of a living connection" (Eva Hoffman) that has become known as "postmemory" – that is a memory that "*can* be transferred to those who were not actually there to live an event," in the words of Marianne Hirsch.[2]

2 Marianne Hirsch, *The Generation of Postmemory: Writing and Visual Culture after the Holocaust* (New York: Columbia University Press, 2012), 3. See also her chapter (with Leo Spitzer), "Testimonial Objects," ibid., 177–199.

This is, however, not the only reason why this project has led me on a risky path. Writing the essays that, taken together, make up this book required me to learn a new language, how to verbalize the visual, and embark on an intellectual journey beyond my comfort zone: thematically, chronologically, geographically, and disciplinarily.

If we seem to know one thing it is that small objects don't matter much. Explaining my fascination with miniature cities to family, friends, and colleagues, I encountered a bevy of reactions: giggles, raised eyebrows, puzzled looks, even concern. Why investigate objects as insignificant and self-evident as a city model? I never developed an easy answer to such signs of discomfort with the direction my academic interests had taken. Sure, when people issued these challenges, I emphatically stated that small things *do* matter. With *Miniature Monuments*, I want to put critical pressure on widely held assumptions about what matters and what does not in the construction of memories and histories. No doubt, the very fact that models, models of cities in particular, are often taken for granted makes them intriguing objects to write about. They are, as the title of my book has it, monuments that have escaped our attention because of their miniature size and their supposed legibility. Apparently, some things need to be small in order for them to exude an aura of being easily graspable. Conversely, "[c]olossal size confounds comprehension," as Darcy Grimaldo Grigsby asserts (through a reference to Immanuel Kant).[3]

In archives and museums, I encountered an additional layer of resistance against my *Miniature Monuments*: Some experts found it hard to warm up to the idea that I researched not the horrors of the bombings themselves but exhibitions to make these events come alive after 1945. Rest assured, by focusing on a vehicle picturing a "moment" in history like a scale model of a bombed-out city I am not saying that there is nothing left to research about these disasters from the air. Rather, my focus on small things takes comfort from the thought that whatever medium of memory-making we choose we engage in an activity that is akin to scaling and resizing. No amount of insistence on the traumatic nature of the events will prevent this from happening.

Since you have picked up *Miniature Monuments*, you may not share the opinion that scale models don't matter. You may have always been or, better still, have become a model enthusiast. Ultimately, what I want to impart in these final pages is the following: This book is an exercise in the history of seeing. In the

3 Darcy Grimaldo Grigsby, *Colossal: Engineering the Suez Canal, Statue of Liberty, Eiffel Tower, and Panama Canal: Transcontinental Ambition in France and the United States during the Long Nineteenth Century* (New York: Periscope, 2012), 131; see also p. 17.

preceding chapters, I have explored what this object lets us see, what it hides from view, and why one would create it in the first place. Let me quickly recapitulate some of the relevant perspectives: Three-dimensional models provide the viewer with an elevated vantage point, something I call the sovereign gaze; they exhibit and at the same time disavow the considerable knowledge that goes into the making of three-dimensional renderings of urban spaces; the rubble models seek to provide glimpses of disasters that are captured, or one could also say modified, for the sake of a distanced viewing; finally, by functioning within the framework of a visual rhetoric of ruins, such models incite what I have termed comparative specularity, that is they invite comparisons to what was before and what came after the destructions.

As the recent theorist of models, Reinhard Wendler, has it, models thrive in the lively interstices between mental and material processes defined by their being *of* something and *for* something. What rubble models purport to show is deceptively simple. They are three-dimensional renderings *of* a city in a state of dereliction. At the same time, their often elusive temporality, their questionable historicity, and their enigmatic void remind us that they are more complex than such a straightforward description suggests. Artifice is part of their appeal: "Everything guaranteed unnatural and everything exactly like nature," as Siegfried Kracauer quips about the props kept at the cinematic city or dream factory where many Weimar movies were shot.[4]

What rubble models are *for*, by contrast, is harder to determine. Even if equipped with captions, exhibitions, and other contexts that guide the beholder, they are signifiers whose meanings are difficult to pin down. The fact that they accommodate a spectrum of viewers' responses made them particularly useful objects in the wake of war when the memories were fresh and communities had an interest in skirting differences as to what was to be commemorated. As Grigsby writes perceptively, "miniature invites fantasy."[5]

But what are the limits to the models' openness as signifiers? There is, to be sure, the weight of the object's genre, its generic qualities, and the comfort of appreciating them within the long history of making or viewing city models – a history that, in the case of Europe, leads back to the Renaissance. Viewed thus, city models, and rubble models of urban spaces are no exception in that regard, are instruments of modernity *par excellence*. They were, at least initially, tools to make people look forward in time. Yet as these mobile signifiers were moved

4 Siegfried Kracauer, "Calico-World: The UFA City in Neubabelsberg," in *The Mass Ornament: Weimar Essays*, trans. Thomas Y. Levine (Cambridge, Mass.: Harvard University Press, 1995), 281.
5 Grigsby, *Colossal*, 159.

about from one exhibit to another or as they started to shine within museum displays, it becomes apparent that they also occupy the other side of modernity's infatuation with the future: History. They afford the viewer the illusion of a look back in time. Put differently, they are reminders of a past that many may have wanted to forget and that others feared would be forgotten all too quickly (in fact, my mother held both of these contradictory, positions in one person). Approaching these objects then through Wendler's theorizing of the artists' *modello* and of scientific models, these fluid functions for makers and viewers do not come as a surprise. They are part and parcel of the model-ness of models.[6]

But are these miniature and somewhat mobile models also monuments? Through their sheer size and placement in space, monuments seek to convey certainty. Often erected in a brittle present and for an uncertain future, they commemorate social or political upheavals in retrospect. One of the earliest theorists of models and monuments, the fifteenth-century humanist Leon Battista Alberti, captures their prowess as threefold. The rubble models are a piece of artless art with a stunning presence (*ornamentum*); they incite the polity to remember a past the local commissioners considered meaningful (*memoria*); and they want to provide guidance for the future (*bonae mores*).[7] Viewed thus, the rubble models are in fact monument-like. Whereas their miniature size may camouflage to some degree their character as monuments, these models invite us to assess the agency of a genre as a catalyst of remembering collectively. As Dietrich Erben has it, monuments are paradoxical.[8] And as such, they are generative.

Miniature Monuments makes the case that an analysis of visual objects benefits from a deep history of seeing. This is why, in the previous chapters, I have interlaced the early modern with the modern: Sandtner's sixteenth-century model of Bavarian cities with Frankfurt in rubble, as the Treuners sculpted it in 1946. Historical narratives, as I imagine them, are not simply about adding pre-histories to the object under consideration. Writing in this vein means to bring a deep historical sensitivity to representations of twentieth-century disasters: the resonances of church architecture in the midst of post-war memorials,

6 Reinhard Wendler, *Die Rolle der Modelle in Werk- und Erkenntnisprozessen* (Ph.D., Humboldt University, 2008); id., *Das Modell zwischen Kunst und Wissenschaft* (Munich: Fink, 2013).

7 Leon Battista Alberti, *L'architettura: De re aedificatoria*, trans. Giovanni Orlandi (Milan: Il Polifilo, 1966), vol. 2, 649–699; id., *On the Art of Building in Ten Books*, trans. Joseph Rykwert, Neil Leach, and Robert Tavernor (Cambridge, Mass.: MIT Press, 1988), 238–257 (vii.16 – viii.4). See also Book Two, Chapter One, on his recommendation that the architect "not only use drawings and sketches but models of wood or any other material" (*On the Art of Building*, 33f).

8 Dietrich Erben, "Denkmal," in *Handbuch der politischen Ikonographie*, ed. Uwe Fleckner, Martin Warnke, and Hendrik Ziegler, vol. 1 (Munich: Beck, 2011), 235.

like in Heilbronn, or the tussle between rubble and ruins, when most ruinologists have categorically divided the engagement of the distant past from the visual echoes of recent catastrophes. "[T]he very persons most intensively engaged in the study of the premodern past are conditioned to overlook in important ways its relationship to the present."[9] As Brad S. Gregory knows, this statement can easily be turned on its head. Modernists often fail to see their histories connected to a deeper past. This erasure is especially common, it would seem, when the events that shook the twentieth century are under discussion – tragedies whose forceful resonances in the present tend to absorb, if not outright flatten, the long expanses of historical time stretched out before us. If I succeeded in delivering an example for an interlaced cultural history, I have achieved much.

My hope is that in having written such an entangled history – that is a history whose connections go beyond what is conventionally considered as belonging together – there are gains, despite the considerable risks. The rest is for you to see.

9 Brad S. Gregory, *The Unintended Reformation: How A Religious Revolution Secularized Society* (Cambridge, Mass.: Harvard UP, 2012), 8f. See also Daniel Lord Smail, "History and the Telescoping of Time: A Disciplinary Forum," *French Historical Studies* 34 (2011): 1–6.

Bibliography

Archives

Bundesarchiv
Hauptstaatsarchiv Wiesbaden
Institut für Stadtgeschichte, Frankfurt am Main
Peace Memorial Museum, Hiroshima
Sächsische Landesbibliothek – Staats- und Universitätsbibliothek Dresden, Abteilung Deutsche Fotothek
Staatsarchiv Hamburg
Stadtarchiv Bad Dürkheim
Stadtarchiv Hannover
Stadtarchiv Heilbronn
Stadtarchiv Würzburg

Periodicals

Bildende Kunst
Frankfurter Allgemeine Zeitung
Frankfurter Neue Hefte
Frankfurter Neue Presse
Frankfurter Rundschau
Frankfurter Zeitung
Freiburger Nachrichten
Hamburger Echo
Hannoversche Allgemeine Zeitung
Heilbronner Stimme
New York Times
Rheinische Beiträge zur Gelehrsamkeit
Der Ruf
Würzburger katholisches Sonntagsblatt
Die Zeit

Print Publications

Adamo, Sergio. "Constructing an Event, Contemplating Ruins, Theorizing Nature: The Lisbon Earthquake and Some Italian Reactions." In *European Review* 14 (2004): 339–349.

Adorno, Theodor W. *Briefe an die Eltern 1939–1951.* Frankfurt am Main: Suhrkamp, 2003.

Agosti, Giovanni, and Dominique Thiébaut, eds. *Mantegna 1431–1506.* Paris: Musée du Louvre, 2008.

Alberti, Leon Battista. *L'architettura: De re aedificatoria*, trans. Giovanni Orlandi. Milan: Il Polifilo, 1966.

—. *On the Art of Building in Ten Books*, trans. Joseph Rykwert, Neil Leach, and Robert Tavernor. Cambridge, Mass.: MIT Press, 1988.

Altherr, Alfred. *Three Japanese Architects/Drei japanische Architekten*. Teufen: Arthur Niggli, 1968.

Ammianus Marcellinus. *Ammianus Marcellinus*, trans. John C. Rolfe, vol. 3. Cambridge, Mass.: Harvard University Press, 1956.

Applegate, Celia. *A Nation of Provincials: The German Idea of Heimat*. Berkeley: University of California Press, 1990.

Arendt, Hannah. "The Aftermath of Nazi Rule: Report from Germany." In *Commentary* 10 (1950): 342–352.

—. *Denktagebuch: 1950 bis 1973*, ed. Ursula Ludz and Ingeborg Nordmann. Munich: Piper, 2002.

—. *Essays in Understanding 1930–1954*, ed. Jerome Kohn. New York: Harcourt Brace, 1994.

Arnold, Jörg. *The Allied Air War and Urban Memory: The Legacy of Strategic Bombing in Germany*. Cambridge: Cambridge University Press, 2011.

—. "Beyond Usable Pasts: Rethinking the Memorialization of the Strategic Air War in Germany, 1940 to 1965." In *Memorialization in Germany since 1945*, ed. Bill Niven and Chloe Paver. New York: Palgrave Macmillan, 2010, 26–36.

—. "'Nagasaki' in der DDR: Magdeburg und das Gedenken an den 16. Januar 1945." In *Luftkrieg: Erinnerungen in Deutschland und Europa*, ed. J. Arnold, Dietmar Süß, and Malte Thießen. Göttingen: Wallstein, 2009, 239–255.

Arnold, Jörg, Dietmar Süß, and Malte Thießen, eds. *Luftkrieg: Erinnerungen in Deutschland und Europa*. Göttingen: Wallstein, 2009.

Aslanian, Sebouh David, Joyce E. Chaplin, Ann McGrath, and Kristin Mann. "How Size Matters: The Question of Scale in History." In *American Historical Review* 118 (2013): 1431–1472.

Assmann, Aleida. "1945 – Der blinde Fleck der deutschen Erinnerungsgeschichte." In *Geschichtsvergessenheit – Geschichtsversessenheit: Vom Umgang mit deutschen Vergangenheiten*, ed. Aleida Assmann and Ute Frevert. Stuttgart: Deutsche Verlags-Anstalt, 1999, 97–138.

—. *Der lange Schatten der Vergangenheit: Erinnerungskultur und Geschichtspolitik*. Munich: Beck, 2006.

Assmann, Aleida, and Ute Frevert, eds. *Geschichtsvergessenheit – Geschichtsversessenheit: Vom Umgang mit deutschen Vergangenheiten*. Stuttgart: Deutsche Verlags-Anstalt, 1999.

Assmann, Jan. *Religion und kulturelles Gedächtnis: Zehn Studien*. Munich: Beck, 2000.

Atze, Marcel. "' ... und wer spricht über Dresden?' Der Luftkrieg als öffentliches und literarisches Thema in der Zeit des ersten Frankfurter Auschwitz-Prozesses 1963–1965." In *W. G. Sebald: Politische Archäologie und melancholische Bastelei*, ed. Michael Niehaus and Claudia Öhlschläger. Berlin: Erich Schmidt, 2006, 205–217.

Atze, Marcel, and Franz Loquai, eds. *Sebald: Lektüren*. Eggingen: Edition Isele, 2005.

Auslander, Leora. "Beyond Words." In *American Historical Review* 110 (2005): 1015–1045.

Austin, Dan, and Sean Doerr. *Lost Detroit: Stories behind Motor City's Majestic Ruins*. Charleston, SC: The History Press, 2010.

Baader, Berndt. *Der bayerische Renaissancehof Herzog Wilhelms V.* Leipzig: Heitz, 1943.

Baak, Bernhard. *Zerstörung, Wiederaufbau und Verwaltung der Stadt Kleve: 1944–1957*. Kleve: Boss, 1960.

Bahnsen, Uwe, and Kerstin von Stürmer. *Die Stadt, die sterben sollte: Hamburg im Bombenkrieg, Juli 1943*. Hamburg: Convent, 2003.

Bakhtin, M. M. *The Dialogic Imagination*, ed. Michael Holquist. Austin: University of Texas Press, 1981.

Bakhtin, M. M. "Forms of Time and of the Chronotope in the Novel," trans. Michael Holquist. In *The Dialogic Imagination*, ed. Michael Holquist. Austin: University of Texas Press, 1981, 84–258.

Baldoli, Claudia, Andrew Knapp, and Richard Overy, eds. *Bombing, States and Peoples in Western Europe 1940–1945*. London: Continuum, 2011.

Barkan, Leonard. *Unearthing the Past: Archaeology and Aesthetics in the Making of Renaissance Culture*. New Haven: Yale University Press, 1999.

Barker, Ralph. *The Thousand Plan: The Story of the First Thousand Bomber Raid on Cologne*. London: Chatto & Windus, 1965.

Barnouw, Dagmar. *Germany 1945: Views of War and Violence*. Bloomington: Indiana University Press, 1996.

—. *War in the Empty Air: Victims, Perpetrators, and Postwar Germans*. Bloomington: Indiana University Press, 2005.

Bartetzko, Dieter. *Denkmal für den Aufbau Deutschlands: Die Paulskirche in Frankfurt am Main*. Königstein im Taunus: Karl Robert Langewiesche Nachfolger, 1998.

Barthes, Roland. "L'effet de réel." In *Œuvres complètes*, ed. Eric Marty, vol. 3. Paris: Seuil, 2002, 25–32.

Baudrillard, Jean. *Simulacres et simulation*. Paris: Galliée, 1981.

Bauer, Thomas. *'Seid einig für unsere Stadt': Walter Kolb – Frankfurter Oberbürgermeister 1946–1956*. Frankfurt am Main: Waldemar Kramer, 1996.

Baumunk, Bodo-Michael, ed. *Zentren, Residenzen, Metropolen in der deutschen Geschichte*. Cologne: DuMont, 1989.

Beeby, Thomas H. "Rudolf Schwarz and Mies van der Rohe: The Form of the Spirit." In *Constructing the Ineffable: Contemporary Sacred Architecture*, ed. Karla Cavarra Britton. New Haven: Yale School of Architecture, 2010, 82–95.

Behringer, Wolfgang, and Bernd Roeck, eds. *Das Bild der Stadt in der Neuzeit: 1400–1800*. Munich: Beck, 1999.

Belting, Hans. *Likeness and Presence: A History of the Image before the Era of Art*, trans Edmund Jephcott. Chicago: University of Chicago Press, 1994.

Benda-Beckmann, Bastiaan Robert von. "Eine deutsche Katastrophe? Deutungsmuster des Bombenkriegs in der ost- und westdeutschen Geschichtswissenschaft." In *Luftkrieg: Erinnerungen in Deutschland und Europa*, ed. Jörg Arnold, Dietmar Süß, and Malte Thießen. Göttingen: Wallstein, 2009, 297–311.

Bendix, Werner. *Die Hauptstadt des deutschen Wirtschaftswunders: Frankfurt am Main 1945–1956*. Frankfurt am Main: Waldemar Kramer, 2002.

Benjamin, Walter. *The Origin of German Tragic Drama*, trans. John Osborne. London: Verso, 1998.

Bernard-Donals, Michael F., and Richard R. Glejzer, eds. *Witnessing the Disaster: Essays on Representation and the Holocaust*. Madison: University of Wisconsin Press, 2003.

Beutler, Ernst. "An Goethes hundertundzwölften Todestage, dem 22. März 1944, starb auch das Haus seiner Kindheit, starb die Stadt seiner Jugend" (1944/45). In *Goethe im Urteil seiner Kritiker: Dokumente einer Wirkungsgeschichte Goethes in Deutschland*, vol. 4, ed. Karl Robert Mandelkow. Munich: Beck, 1984, 258–260.

Bevers, Holm, ed. *Zeichnungen aus der Sammlung des Kurfürsten Carl Theodor*. Munich: Staatliche Graphische Sammlung, 1983.

Biess, Frank. "Feelings in the Aftermath: Toward a History of Postwar Emotions." In *Histories of the Aftermath: The Legacies of the Second World War in Europe*, ed. Frank Biess and Robert G. Moeller. New York: Berghahn, 2010, 30–48.

—. "Histories of the Aftermath." In *Histories of the Aftermath: The Legacies of the Second World War in Europe*, ed. Frank Biess and Robert G. Moeller. New York: Berghahn, 2010, 1–10.

Biess, Frank, and Robert G. Moeller, eds. *Histories of the Aftermath: The Legacies of the Second World War in Europe*. New York: Berghahn, 2010.

Blank, Ralf. "Kriegsalltag und Luftkrieg an der 'Heimatfront.'" In *Das Deutsche Reich und der Zweite Weltkrieg*, vol. 9/1: *Die Deutsche Kriegsgesellschaft 1939 bis 1945; Politisierung, Vernichtung, Überleben*, ed. Jörg Echternkamp. Munich: Deutsche Verlags-Anstalt, 2004, 357–461.

—. "Zerstört und vergessen? Hagen, das Ruhrgebiet und das Gedächtnis des Krieges." In *Luftkrieg: Erinnerungen in Deutschland und Europa*, eds. Jörg Arnold, Dietmar Süß, and Malte Thießen. Göttingen: Wallstein, 2009, 162–182.

Boehling, Rebecca. "*Stunde Null* at the Ground Level: 1945 as a Social and Political *Ausgangspunkt* in Three Cities in the U.S. Zone of Occupation." In *Stunde Null: The End and the Beginning Fifty Years Ago*, ed. Geoffrey J. Giles. Washington, DC: German Historical Institute, 1997, 105–128.

Boehnke, Heiner, et al., eds. *Hr – 50 Jahre Rundfunk für Hessen*. Frankfurt am Main: Insel, 1995.

Böll, Heinrich. "Bekenntnis zur Trümmerliteratur." In *Essayistische Schriften und Reden*, vol. 1, ed. Bernd Balzer. Cologne: Kiepenheuer & Witsch, 1979, 31–34.

Boettiger, Carl August. *Reise nach Wörlitz 1797*, ed. Erhard Hirsch, 8th ed. Berlin: Deutscher Kunstverlag, 2000.

Bolzoni, Lina. "Das Sammeln und die ars memoriae." In *Macrocosmos in Microcosmo: Die Welt in der Stube: Zur Geschichte des Sammelns 1450 bis 1800*, ed. Andreas Grote. Opladen: Leske & Budrich, 1994, 129–168.

Borges, Jorge Luis. "Del rigor en la ciencia" (*El Hacedor*). In *Obras Completas*, vol. 2. Barcelona: Emecé, 1989.

Bosselmann, Peter. *The Representation of Places: Reality and Realism in City Design*. Berkeley: University of California, 1998.

Boer, Pim den, Heinz Duchardt, Georg Kreis, and Wolfgang Schmale, eds., *Europäische Erinnerungsorte*, 3 vols. Munich: Oldenbourg, 2012.

Bott, Gerhard, ed. *Nürnberg 1300–1550: Kunst der Gotik und Renaissance*. Munich: Prestel, 1986.

Boym, Svetlana. *The Future of Nostalgia*. New York: Basic Books, 2001.

Bradford, Ernle. *The Shield and the Sword: The Knights of St. John*. London: Hodder and Stoughton, 1972.

Braun, Claudia. "Kurfürst Carl Theodor als Denkmalpfleger." In *Lebenslust und Frömmigkeit: Kurfürst Carl Theodor (1724–1799) zwischen Barock und Aufklärung*, ed. Alfried Wieczorek. Regensburg: Pustet, 1997, 347–352.

Braun, Georg, and Frans Hogenberg. *Beschreibung und Contrafactur der vornembster Stät der Welt*, 6 vols. 1572–1618. Reprint, ed. Max Schefold. Plochingen: Müller & Schindler, 1965–1970.

—. *Civitates orbis terrarum: 'The Towns of the World,' 1572–1618*, 6 vols. 1572–1618. Reprint, ed. R. A. Skelton. Cleveland: World Publishing Co., 1966.

Bredekamp, Horst. *Die Fenster der Monade: Gottfried Wilhelm Leibniz' Theater der Natur und Kunst*. Berlin: Akademie, 2004.

—. *The Lure of Antiquity and the Cult of the Machine*. Princeton: M. Wiener, 1995.
—. "Staat." In *Handbuch der politischen Ikonographie*, eds. Uwe Fleckner, Martin Warnke, and Hendrik Ziegler, vol. 2. Munich: Beck, 2011, 373–380.
—. *Theorie des Bildakts*. Berlin: Suhrkamp, 2010.
—. *Thomas Hobbes visuelle Strategien: Der Leviathan, Urbild des modernen Staates: Werkillustrationen und Portraits*. Berlin: Akademie, 1999.
—. "Thomas Hobbes's Visual Strategies." In *The Cambridge Companion to Hobbes's 'Leviathan,'* ed. Patricia Springborg. Cambridge: Cambridge University Press, 2007, 29–60.
Brink, Brian Vanden. *Ruin: Photographs of a Vanishing America*. Rockport, ME: Down East Books, 2009.
Brink, Cornelia. "Secular Icons: Looking at Photographs from Nazi Concentration Camps." In *History and Memory* 12 (2000): 135–150.
Britton, Karla Cavarra, ed. *Constructing the Ineffable: Contemporary Sacred Architecture*. New Haven: Yale School of Architecture, 2010.
Brockmann, Stephen. *German Literary Culture at the Zero Hour*. Rochester, NY: Camden House, 2004.
Brockmann, Stephen, and Frank Trommler, eds. *Revisiting Zero Hour 1945: The Emergence of Postwar German Culture*. Washington, DC: American Institute for Contemporary German Studies, 1996.
Broszat, Martin, and Michael Dübbe, eds. *Deutschlands Weg in die Diktatur: Internationale Konferenz zur nationalsozialistischen Machtübernahme im Reichstagsgebäude zu Berlin*. Berlin: Siedler, 1983.
Brunner, Dieter. "Kunst am Bau im Heilbronn der 50er Jahre." In *Heilbronn und die Kunst der 50er Jahre: Das Kunstgeschehen der 50er Jahre in Heilbronn*, ed. Andreas Pfeiffer. Heilbronn: Städtische Museen, 1993, 90–105.
Buchinger, Kirstin, Claire Gantet, and Jakob Vogel, eds., *Europäische Erinnerungsräume*. Frankfurt am Main: Campus, 2009.
Buekschmitt, Justus. *Ernst May*. Stuttgart: Verlagsanstalt Alexander Koch, 1963.
Bürgi, Andreas, ed. *Europa Miniature: Die kulturelle Bedeutung des Reliefs, 16.–21. Jahrhundert*. Zürich: Verlag Neue Zürcher Zeitung, 2007.
Buisseret, David. "Modeling Cities in Early Modern Europe." In *Envisioning the City*, ed. D. Buisseret. Chicago: University of Chicago Press, 1998, 125–143.
Burckhardt, Jacob. *The Civilization of the Renaissance in Italy*, trans. S. G. C. Middlemore. London: Penguin Books, 1990.
Burda, Hubert. *Die Ruine in den Bildern Hubert Roberts*. Munich: Fink, 1967.
Buys, Anthea. "*Hiroshima Mon Amour* and the Necessity of Oblivion." In *English Studies in Africa* 52 (2009): 50–60.
Buzard, James. *The Beaten Track: European Tourism, Literature, and the Ways to Culture, 1800–1918*. Oxford: Oxford University Press, 1993.
Camerota, Filippo. "Tribolo e Benvenuto della Volpaia: Il modello ligneo per l'assedio di Firenze." In *Niccolò detto Il Tribolo tra arte, architettura e paesaggio*, ed. Elisabetta Pieri and Luigi Zangheri. Poggio a Caiano: Comune di Poggio a Caiano, 2000, 87–104.
Cancik, Hubert, ed. *Der Neue Pauly: Enzyklopädie der Antike*, vol. 10. Stuttgart: Metzler, 2001.
Canetti, Cecilia, et al. *Vedute di Roma nel 1500*. Rome: Dino Audino, 1990.
Carl Georg, Duke of Mecklenburg, *Garten und Landschaft gestern und heute: Zur Geschichte der Gefühle in der Natur*. Haigerloch: PES-Edition, 1984.

Carroll, Lewis. *Sylvie and Bruno Concluded*. In *The Complete Works*. London: The Nonesuch Library, 1939, 457–674.
Caruth, Mary. *Unclaimed Experience: Trauma, Narrative, and History*. Baltimore: Johns Hopkins Press, 1996.
Casal, Rodrigo Cacho. "The Memory of Ruins: Quevedo's 'Silva' to 'Roma antigua y moderna.'" In *Renaissance Quarterly* 62 (2009): 1167–2003.
Claasen, Hermann. *Gesang im Feuerofen: Köln – Überreste einer alten deutschen Stadt*. Düsseldorf: Schwann, 1947.
Clemens, Paul. *Punching Out: One Year in a Closing Auto Plant*. New York: Doubleday, 2011.
Clément, Gilles. *Le jardin en mouvement*. Paris: Pandora, 1991.
---. *Le jardin en mouvement: De La Vallée au Parc André Citroën*. Paris: Sens et Tonka, 1994.
Coffin, David R. *The English Garden: Meditation and Memorial*. Princeton: Princeton University Press, 1994.
Colonna, Francesco. *Hypnerotomachia Poliphi: The Strife of Love in a Dream*, trans. Joscelyn Godwin. London: Thames & Hudson, 1999.
Confino, Alon. "Memory Studies and Cultural History: Problems of Method." In *American Historical Review* 102 (1997): 1386–1403.
—. *The Nation as a Local Metaphor: Württemberg, Imperial Germany, and National Memory, 1871–1918*. Chapel Hill: The University of North Carolina Press, 1997.
Connors, Joseph. "'Ars tornandi': Baroque Architecture and the Lathe." In *Journal of the Warburg and Courtauld Institutes* 55 (1990): 217–236.
Constructa Bauausstellung 1951 Hannover 3. Juli bis 12. August, ed. Die Verbände und Organisationen der Bauwirtschaft, Bauwissenschaft und Baukunst. Hannover: Deutsche Messe- und Ausstellungs A.G., [s.a.].
Conti, Cinzia. "Il modello ligneo dell'Anfiteatro Flavio di Carlo Lucangeli: Osservazione nel corso del restauro." In *Sangue e Arena*, ed. Adriano La Regina. Milan: Electa, 2001, 117–125.
Cornelißen, Christoph. "Die Nationalität von Erinnerungskulturen als ein gesamteuropäisches Phänomen." In *Geschichte in Wissenschaft und Unterricht* 62 (2011): 5–16.
Cornish, Alison "Embracing the Corpse: Necrophilic Tendencies." In *Dead Lovers: Erotic Bonds and the Study of Premodern Europe*, ed. Basil Dufallo and Peggy McCracken. Ann Arbor: University of Michigan, 2006, 57–70.
Corvisier, André, ed. *Actes du colloque international sur les plans-reliefs au passé et au présent*. Paris: SEDES, 1993.
Cosgrove, Mary. "Narrating German Suffering in the Shadow of Holocaust Victimology: W. G. Sebald, Contemporary Trauma Theory, and Dieter Forte's Air Raids Epic." In *Germans as Victims in the Literary Fiction of the Berlin Republic*, ed. Stuart Taberner and Karina Berger. Rochester, NY: Camden House, 2009, 162–175.
Cramer, Johannes, and Niels Gutschow. *Bauausstellungen: Eine Architekturgeschichte des 20. Jahrhunderts*. Stuttgart: W. Kohlhammer, 1984.
Crew, David. "Building or Bodies? Using Photographs of the Bombing of Dresden, 1945–1975." Talk presented at the German Studies Association, New Orleans, 2003.
Dams, Saskia. *Der Englische Garten im Schwetzinger Schlossgarten: Der Tempel der Botanik und das römische Wasserkastell mit Aquädukt und Obelisk*. Munich: Grin, 2008.
Daston, Lorraine. "Neugierde als Empfindung und Epistemologie in der frühmodernen Wissenschaft." In *Macrocosmos in Microcosmo: Die Welt in der Stube: Zur Geschichte de Sammelns 1450 bis 1800*, ed. Andreas Grote. Opladen: Leske & Budrich, 1994, 35–59.

Daston, Lorraine, and Katharine Park. *Wonders and the Order of Nature 1150- 1750*. New York: Zone, 1998.
Dauer, Hans, and Karl Maury. *Frankfurt baut in die Zukunft*. Frankfurt am Main: Kramer, 1953.
Davis, Mike. *Dead Cities, and Other Tales*. New York: New Press, 2002.
Dekkers, Midas. *The Way of All Flesh: A Celebration of Decay*, trans. Sherry Marx-Macdonald. London: Harvill, 2000.
Demand, Thomas. *Model Studies*. London: Ivorypress, 2012.
Denham, Scott, and Mark McCulloh, eds. *W. G. Sebald: History – Memory – Trauma*. New York: de Gruyter, 2006.
Deriu, Davide. "Transforming Ideas into Pictures: Model Photography and Modern Architecture." In *Camera Constructs: Photography, Architecture and the Modern City*, ed. Andrew Higgott and Timothy Wray. Burlington, VT: Ashgate, 2012, 159–178.
Dettmar, Werner. "Kassel im Luftkrieg." In *Leben in Ruinen: Kassel 1943–1948 im Gedenkjahr der Stadt Kassel zur Erinnerung an ihre Zerstörung am 22. Oktober 1943*, ed. Christina Coers-Dittmar and Alexander Link. Kassel: Jonas Verlag, 1993, 11–22.
Diefendorf, Jeffry M. "America and the Rebuilding of Germany." In *American Policy and the Reconstruction of West Germany, 1945–1955*, ed. Jeffry M. Diefendorf, Axel Frohn, and Hermann-Josef Rupieper. Cambridge: Cambridge University Press, 1993, 331–351.
—. *In the Wake of War: The Reconstruction of German Cities after World War II*. New York: Oxford University Press, 1993.
Diefendorf, Jeffry M., ed. *Rebuilding Europe's Bombed Cities*. Basingstoke: Macmillan Press, 1990.
Diefendorf, Jeffry M., Axel Frohn, and Hermann-Josef Rupieper, eds. *American Policy and the Reconstruction of West Germany, 1945–1955*. Cambridge: Cambridge University Press, 1993.
Diemer, Dorothea. "Giovanni Ambrogio Maggiore und die Anfänge der Kunstdrechselei um 1570." In *Jahrbuch des Zentralinstituts fiir Kunstgeschichte* 1 (1985): 295–342.
Domarus, Max. *Der Untergang des alten Würzburg im Luftkrieg gegen die deutschen Grosstädte*. Gerolzhofen: Franz Teutsch, 1978.
Douglass, Ana, and Thomas A. Vogler. "Introduction." In *Witness and Memory: The Discourse of Trauma*. New York: Routledge, 2003, 1–53.
Douglass, Ana, and Thomas A. Vogler, eds. *Witness and Memory: The Discourse of Trauma*. New York: Routledge, 2003.
Drooker, Arthur, and Christopher Woodward. *American Ruins*. London: Merrell, 2007.
Du Pérac, Etienne. *Le antiche rovine di Roma nei disegni di du Péarc*. Milan: Pizzi, 1990.
—. *I Disegni de le ruine di Roma e come anticamente erono* [1574], ed. Rudolf Wittkower, 2 vols. Milan: Pizzi, 1963.
Dürer, Albrecht. *Etliche vnderricht zu befestigung der Stett / Schlosz / vnd flecken*. Nuremberg: n.p., 1527.
—. *Schriftlicher Nachlaß*, ed. Hans Rupprich, vol. 3. Berlin: Deutscher Verein für Kunstwissenschaft, 1969.
Duras, Marguerite. *Hiroshima mon amour: Scénario et dialogue*. Paris: Gallimard, 1960.
—. *Hiroshima Mon Amour: A Screenplay by M.D.: For the Film by Alain Resnais*, trans. Richard Seaver. New York: Grove Press, 1961.
Durth, Werner, and Niels Gutschow. *Architektur und Städtebau der fünfziger Jahre*. Bonn: Deutsches Nationalkomitee für Denkmalschutz, 1990.
—. *Träume in Trümmern: Planungen zum Wiederaufbau zerstörter Städte im Westen Deutschlands 1940–1950*, vol. 2: *Städte*. Braunschweig: Friedrich Vieweg & Sohn, 1988.

Duttlinger, Carolin. "A Lineage of Destruction? Rethinking Photography in 'Luftkrieg und Literatur.'" In *W. G. Sebald and the Writing of History*, ed. Anne Fuchs and J. J. Long. Würzburg: Königshausen & Neumann, 2007, 163–177.

Eastman, Michael, Douglas Brinkely, and William H. Grass, *Vanishing America: The End of Main Street*. Milan: Rizzoli, 2008.

Ebersold, Günther. "Die Italiensehnsucht des Kurfürsten." In *Lebenslust und Frömmigkeit: Kurfürst Carl Theodor (1724–1799) zwischen Barock und Aufklärung*, ed. Alfried Wieczorek. Regensburg: Pustet, 1997, 231–235.

Echternkamp, Jörg, ed. *Das Deutsche Reich und der Zweite Weltkrieg*, vol. 9/1: *Die Deutsche Kriegsgesellschaft 1939 bis 1945: Politisierung, Vernichtung, Überleben*. Munich: Deutsche Verlags-Anstalt, 2004.

Eco, Umberto. *The Open Work*, trans. Anna Cancogni. Cambridge, Mass.: Harvard University Press, 1989.

Eiche, Sabine. "Francesco Maria II della Rovere's *Delizia* in Urbino: The Giardino di S. Lucia." In *Journal of Garden History* 5 (1985): 154–183.

Eikelmann, Renate. *Bayerisches Nationalmuseum: Handbook of the Art and Cultural History Collections*. Munich: Hirmer, 2002.

Eisold, Norbert. *Das Dessau-Wörlitzer Gartenreich: Der Traum von der Vernunft*. Cologne: DuMont, 1993.

Elkan, Benno, ed. *Römer-Maske: Eine Festschrift phantastischer Satire und satirischer Phantasie*. Frankfurt am Main: Hauser, 1925.

Erben, Dietrich. "Denkmal." In *Handbuch der politischen Ikonographie*, ed. Uwe Fleckner, Martin Warnke, and Hendrik Ziegler, vol. 1. Munich: Beck, 2011, 235–243.

Evans, Jennifer. *Life among the Ruins: Cityscape and Sexuality in Cold War Berlin*. New York: Palgrave Macmillan, 2011.

Fabian, Johannes. *Time and the Other: How Anthropology Makes Its Object*. New York: Columbia University Press, 2002.

Fache, Thomas. "Gegenwartsbewältigungen: Dresdens Gedenken an die alliierten Luftangriffe vor und nach 1989." In *Luftkrieg: Erinnerungen in Deutschland und Europa*, ed. Jörg Arnold, Dietmar Süß, and Malte Thießen. Göttingen: Wallstein, 2009, 221–238.

Falser, Michael S. *Zwischen Identität und Authenzität: Zur politischen Geschichte der Denkmalpflege in Deutschland*. Dresden: Thelem, 2008.

Faucherre, Nicolas, and Antoine de Roux. "Les plans en relief de Louis XIV, des outils de travail pour la construction de la frontière." In *Les plans en relief des places du roy: Actes du colloque international sur les plans-reliefs*, ed. Antoine de Roux, Nicolas Faucherre, and Guillaume Monsaingeon. Paris: A. Biro, 1989, 101–105.

Faust, Ludwig. *Als die Vernichtungsmaschinerie lief ... Bad Dürkheim im Luftkrieg 1939–1945*. Bad Dürkheim: Ludwig Faust, 2005.

Fehrle-Burger, Lili. *Die Welt der Oper in den Schloßgärten von Heidelberg und Schwetzingen*. Karlsruhe: G. Braun, 1977.

Feldman, Martha. *Opera and Sovereignty: Transforming Myths in Eighteenth-Century Italy*. Chicago: University of Chicago Press, 2007.

Felman, Shoshanna. "Education and Crisis, Or the Vicissitudes of Teaching." In *Testimony: Crises of Witnessing in Literature, Psychoanalysis, and History*. New York: Routledge, 1992, 1–56.

Ferero-Mendoza, Sabine. *Le temps des ruines: L'éveil de la conscience historique à la Renaissance*. Seyssel: Champ Vallon, 2002.

Findlen, Paula. "The Museum: Its Classical Etymology and Renaissance Genealogy." In *Museum Studies: An Anthology of Contexts*, ed. Bettina Messias Carbonell. Oxford: Blackwell, 2004, 23–50.

—. "Die Zeit vor dem Laboratorium: Die Museen und der Bereich der Wissenschaft 1550–1750." In *Macrocosmos in Microcosmo: Die Welt in der Stube: Zur Geschichte des Sammelns 1450 bis 1800*, ed. Andreas Grote. Opladen: Leske & Budrich, 1994, 191–207.

Finker, Kurt. *Der Dämon kam über uns: Faschismus und Antifaschismus im Geschichtsbild und in der Geschichtsschreibung Westdeutschlands (1945–1955)*, ed. Friedrich-Martin Balzer. Bonn: Pahl-Rugenstein Nachfolger, 2008.

Fischer, Friedhelm. "German Reconstruction as an International Activity." In *Rebuilding Europe's Bombed Cities*, ed. Jeffry M. Diefendorf. Basingstoke: Macmillan Press, 1990, 131–144.

Fischer, Manfred F. "Heidelberger Schloss." In *Geschichte der Rekonstruktion: Konstruktion der Geschichte*, ed. Winfried Nerdinger. Munich: Prestel, 2010, 339–342.

Fleckner, Uwe, Martin Warnke, and Hendrik Ziegler, eds. *Handbuch der politischen Ikonographie*. Munich: Beck, 2011.

Föll, Werner. *Chronik der Stadt Heilbronn*, vol. 10: *1970–1974*. Heilbronn: Stadtarchiv, 1999.

Frampton, Kenneth, Silvia Kolbowski, and Richard Pommer, eds. *Idea as Model*. New York: Rizzoli, 1981.

Franklin, Ruth. "Rings of Smoke." In *The Emergence of Memory: Conversations with W. G. Sebald*, ed. Lynne Sharon Schwartz. New York: Seven Stories Press, 2007, 119–143.

Frese, Annette. "Bühnengestaltung für die Sommerresidenz: Typologie der 'Decorationes.'" In *Hofoper in Schwetzingen: Musik – Bühnenmusik – Architektur*, ed. Silke Leopold and Bärbel Pelker. Heidelberg: Winter, 2004, 181–246.

—. "Nicolas de Pigage 1723–1796: Leben und Werk." In *Hofoper in Schwetzingen: Musik – Bühnenmusik – Architektur*, ed. Silke Leopold and Bärbel Pelker. Heidelberg: Winter, 2004, 247–250.

Frevert, Ute. "Perspektivenwechsel: Die NS-Vergangenheit in den achtziger Jahren." In *Geschichtsvergessenheit – Geschichtsversessenheit: Vom Umgang mit deutschen Vergangenheiten nach 1945*, ed. Aleida Assmann and Ute Frevert. Stuttgart: Deutsche Verlags-Anstalt, 1999, 258–271.

Friedrich, Jörg. *Der Brand: Deutschland im Bombenkrieg 1940–1945*. Munich: Propyläen, 2002.

—. *The Fire: The Bombing of Germany 1940–1945*, trans. Allison Brown. New York: Columbia University Press, 2006.

Frisch, Max. *Tagebuch 1946–1949*. Frankfurt am Main: Suhrkamp, 1960.

—. *Sketchbook 1946–1949*, trans. Geoffrey Skelton. New York: A Helen and Kurt Wolff Book, 1977.

Fritzsche, Peter. *Stranded in the Present: Modern Time and the Melancholy of History*. Cambridge: Harvard University Press, 2004.

Fuchs, Anne, and J. J. Long, eds. *W. G. Sebald and the Writing of History*. Würzburg: Königshausen & Neumann, 2007.

Fuge, Janina, Rainer Hering, and Harald Schmid, eds. *Das Gedächtnis von Stadt und Region: Geschichtsbilder in Norddeutschland*. Hamburg: Dölling und Galitz, 2010.

Gabriel, Albert. *La cité de Rhodes*. Paris: E. de Boccard, 1921.

Gaddis, John Lewis. *The Landscape of History: How Historians Map the Past*. New York: Oxford University Press, 2002.

Gall, Lothar, ed. *FFM 1200: Traditionen und Perspektiven einer Stadt*. Sigmaringen: Thorbecke, 1994.
Grandin, Greg. "Empire's Ruins: Detroit to the Amazon." In *Imperial Debris: On Ruins and Ruination*, ed. Ann Laura Stoler. Durham: Duke University Press, 2013, 115–128.
Gedächtnisausstellung Karl Knappe, ed. Galerie Günther Franke. Munich: Galerie Günther Franke, 1975.
Gehebe-Gernhardt, Almut. *Architektur der 50er Jahre in Frankfurt am Main – am Beispiel der Architektengemeinschaft Alois Giefer und Hermann Mäckler*. Frankfurt am Main: Waldemar Kramer, 2011.
Geimer, Peter. *Die Vergangenheit der Kunst: Strategien der Nachträglichkeit im 18. Jahrhundert*. Weimar: VDG, 2002.
Gerchow, Jan, and Petra Spona. *Das Frankfurter Altstadtmodell der Brüder Treuner*. Frankfurt am Main: Henrich Editionen, 2011.
Gercke, Peter, et al., *Antike Bauten in Modell und Zeichnung um 1800: Vollständiger Katalog der Korkmodelle und der Sonderausstellung 1986*. Kassel: Staatliche Kunstsammlungen Kassel, 1986.
Gerhardt, Uta. *Soziologie der Stunde Null: Zur Gesellschaftskonzeption des amerikanischen Besatzungsregimes in Deutschland 1944–1945/1946*. Frankfurt am Main: Suhrkamp, 2005.
Gibbon, Edward. *The Autobiography of Edward Gibbon, Esq.* New York: Turner and Hayden, 1846.
—. *The History of the Decline and Fall of the Roman Empire*, ed. David Womersley. London: Penguin, 1994.
—. *Gibbon's Journey from Geneva to Rome: His Journal from 20 April to 2 October 1764*, ed. Georges A. Bonnard. London: Thomas Nelson, 1961.
Giersberg, Hans-Joachim. *Schloss Sanssouci: Die Sommerresidenz Friedrichs des Großen*. Berlin: Nicolai, 2005.
Giles, Geoffry G., ed. *Stunde Null: The End and the Beginning Fifty Years Ago*. Washington, DC: German Historical Institute, 1997.
Ginzburg, Carlo. "The Sword and the Lightbulb: A Reading of *Guernica*." In *Disturbing Remains: Memory, History, and Crisis in the Twentieth Century*, eds. Michael S. Roth and Charles G. Salas. Los Angeles: The Getty Research Institute, 2001, 111–177.
Glaser, Hermann. *Kleine Kulturgeschichte der Bundesrepublik Deutschland 1945–1989*, 2nd ed. Bonn: Bundeszentrale für politische Bildung, 1991.
—. "So viel Anfang war nie." In *So viel Anfang war nie: Deutsche Städte 1945–1949*, eds. Hermann Glaser, Lutz von Pufendorf, and Michael Schöneich. Berlin: Siedler, 1989, 8–23.
Gluck, Carol. "The 'End' of the Postwar: Japan at the Turn of the Millennium." In *States of Memory: Continuities, Conflicts, and Transformations in National Retrospection*, ed. Jeffrey K. Olick. Durham: Duke University Press, 2003, 289–314.
Goebbels, Joseph. *Goebbels-Reden*, vol. 2: *1939–1945*, ed. Helmut Heiber. Düsseldorf: Droste, 1972.
Goebel, Ulrich, and Oskar Reichmann, *Frühneuhochdeutsches Wörterbuch*. Berlin: de Gruyter, 1993ff.
Goethe, Johann Wolfgang. *Italienische Reise*. In *Werke: Hamburger Ausgabe*, vol. 11, ed. Erich Trunz. Munich: Beck, 1988, 7–349.
—. *Italian Journey*, trans. W. H. Auden and Elizabeth Mayer. London: Penguin, 1962.
Gollancz, Victor. *In Darkest Germany*. London: Victor Gollancz, 1947.
Gooch, G. P., et al. *The German Mind and Outlook*. London: Chapman, 1945.

Gottlieb, Gunther, ed. *Geschichte der Stadt Augsburg: 2000 Jahre von der Römerzeit bis zur Gegenwart*. Stuttgart: Konrad Theiss, 1984.
Gowing, Lawrence. "Mantegna." In *Andrea Mantegna*, ed. Jane Martineau. Milan: Electa, 1992, 2–7.
Grafton, Anthony. "The Ancient City Restored: Archaeology, Ecclesiastical History, and Egyptology." In *Bring out Your Dead: The Past as Revelation*. Cambridge, Mass.: Harvard University Press, 2001, 31–61.
Gregor, Neil. *Haunted City: Nuremberg and the Nazi Past*. New Haven: Yale University Press, 2008.
Gregory, Brad S. *The Unintended Reformation: How A Religious Revolution Secularized Society*. Cambridge, Mass.: Harvard UP, 2012.
Griffiths, Alison. "The Revered Gaze: The Medieval Imaginary of Mel Gibson's 'The Passion of the Christ.'" In *Cinema Journal* 46 (2007): 3–39.
Grigsby, Darcy Grimaldo. *Colossal: Engineering the Suez Canal, Statue of Liberty, Eiffel Tower, and Panama Canal: Transcontinental Ambition in France and the United States during the Long Nineteenth Century*. New York: Periscope, 2012.
Groh, Christian. "Remembering the Air War: Public Debate and Remembrance of the Bombing of Pforzheim." Paper presented at the German Studies Association, Pittsburgh, 2006.
—. "'Was Pforzheim angetan wurde!' Erinnerungsorte und Denkmäler zum Luftkrieg." In *Luftkrieg: Erinnerungen in Deutschland und Europa*, eds. Jörg Arnold, Dietmar Süß, and Wolfram Thießen. Göttingen: Wallstein, 2009, 183–199.
Grosshans, Rainald. *Maerten van Heemskerck: Die Gemälde*. Berlin: Boettcher, 1980.
Grote, Andreas, ed. *Macrocosmos in Microcosmo: Die Welt in der Stube: Zur Geschichte des Sammelns 1450 bis 1800*. Opladen: Leske & Budrich, 1994.
Günther, Harri, ed. *Gärten der Goethezeit*. Leipzig: Edition Leipzig, 1993.
Günther, Klaus. "Ein Modell legitimen Scheiterns: Der Kampf um Anerkennung als Opfer." In *Strukturwandel der Anerkennung: Paradoxien sozialer Integration in der Gegenwart*, ed. Axel Honneth, Ophelia Lindemann, and Stephan Voswinkel. Frankfurt am Main: Campus, 2013, 185–247.
Günther, Rosmarie. "Die kurpfälzische Akademie der Wissenschaften." In *Der Pfälzer Apoll: Kurfürst Carl Theodor und die Antike an Rhein und Neckar*, ed. Max Kunze. Ruhpolding: Rutzen, 2007, 39–48.
Guez, Olivier. *L'impossible retour: Une histoire des juifs d'Allemage depuis 1945*. Paris: Flammarion, 2007.
Gutschow, Niels. "Hamburg: The 'Catastrophe' of July 1943." In *Rebuilding Europe's Bombed Cities*, ed. Jeffry M. Diefendorf. Basingstoke: Macmillan Press, 1990, 114–130.
—. "Wiederaufbau, Neubau und Rekonstruktion in Asien: Zur Kontinuität von Objekt und Ritual in Nepal, Indien und Japan." In *Geschichte der Rekonstruktion: Konstruktion der Geschichte*, ed. Winfried Nerdinger. Munich: Prestel, 2010, 36–47.
Habermas, Jürgen. *The Structural Transformation of the Public Sphere: An Inquiry into a Category of Bourgeois Society*, trans. Thomas Burger. Cambridge, Mass.: MIT Press, 1989.
Hahn-Woernle, Birgit. *Die Ebstorfer Weltkarte*. Ebstorf: Kloster Ebstorf, 1987.
Halbwachs, Maurice. *On Collective Memory*, trans. Lewis A. Coser. Chicago: University of Chicago Press, 1992.
Hammel, Heide. *Und neues Leben blüht aus den Ruinen: Der kulturelle Wiederaufbau in Pforzheim 1945–1949*. Heidelberg: Verlag Regionalkultur, 2003.

Handbuch Internationale Gartenbauausstellung Hamburg 1953. Hamburg: Hanseatische Druckanstalt, 1953.

Hansert, Andreas. *Georg Hartmann (1870–1954): Biografie eines Frankfurter Schriftgießers, Bibliophilen und Kunstmäzens*. Vienna: Böhlau, 2009.

Harbison, Robert. *The Built, the Unbuilt and the Unbuildable: In Pursuit of Architectural Meaning*. London: Thames and Hudson, 1991.

Hardenberg-Novalis, Friedrich von. *Das dichterische Werk, Tagebücher und Briefe*, vol. 1, ed. Richard Samuel. Munich: Carl Hanser, 2004.

Hare, Augustus. *Walks in Rome*, 20th ed. London: Paul Kegan, 1913.

Hartmann, Georg, and Fried Lübbecke. *Alt-Frankfurt: Ein Vermächtnis*. Frankfurt am Main: Der Goldene Brunnen, [1950].

Hartmann, Werner. *Halberstadt brennt: Eine Dokumentation über Halberstadt im Luftkrieg insbesondere über die Zerstörung der Stadt am 8. April 1945*. Halberstadt, 1990 [first version published in 1967].

Haskell, Francis, and Nicholas Penny. *Taste and the Antique: The Lure of Classical Sculpture, 1500–1900*. New Haven: Yale University Press, 1981.

Hauschild-Thiessen, Renate, ed. *Die Hamburger Katastrophe vom Sommer 1943 in Augenzeugenberichten*. Hamburg: Verein für Hamburgische Geschichte, 1993.

Heber, Wiltrud. *Die Arbeiten des Nicolas de Pigage in den ehemals kurpfälzischen Residenzen Mannheim und Schwetzingen*. Worms: Wernersche Verlagsgesellschaft, 1986.

Hecker, Hans-Joachim. "Um Glaube und Recht: Die 'fürstliche' Stadt 1505 bis 1561." In *Geschichte der Stadt München*, ed. Richard Bauer. Munich: Beck, 1992, 148–165.

Heckscher, Wilhelm Sebastian [William S. Heckscher]. *Die Romruinen: Die geistigen Voraussetzungen ihrer Wertung im Mittelalter und in der Renaissance*. Ph.D. diss., Hamburg University, 1935 (Würzburg: Richard Mayer, 1936).

Hederich, Benjamin. *Gründliches Mythologisches Lexikon* [1770]. Darmstadt: Wissenschaftliche Buchgesellschaft, 1986.

Hegel, Georg Wilhelm Friedrich. *Vorlesungen über die Philosophie der Weltgeschichte*, ed. Karl Heinz Ilting, Karl Brehmer, and Hoo Nam Seelmann. Hamburg: Felix Meiner, 1996.

Heibel, Jutta. *Vom Hungertuch zum Wohlstandsspeck: Die Ernährungslage in Frankfurt am Main 1939–1955*. Frankfurt am Main: Waldemar Krause, 2002.

Heinemann, Elizabeth. "The Hour of the Woman: Memories of Germany's 'Crisis Years' and West German National Identity." In *American Historical Review* (1996): 354–395.

Heinzelmann, Martin. *Göttingen im Luftkrieg 1935–1945*. Göttingen: Die Werkstatt, 2003.

Hell, Julia. "The Angel's Enigmatic Eyes, or the Gothic Beauty of Catastrophic History in W. G. Sebald's 'Air War and Literature.'" In *Criticism* 46 (2004): 361–392.

Hell, Julia, and Andreas Schoenle, eds. *Ruins of Modernity*. Durham: Duke University Press, 2010.

Helmberger, Werner. "Carl Joseph May (1742–1822): Hofkonditor und Korkbildner." In *Rom über die Alpen tragen: Fürsten sammeln antike Architektur*, ed. W. Helmberger and Valentin Kockel. Landshut: Arcols, 1993, 63–89.

Helmberger, Werner, and Valentin Kockel, eds. *Rom über die Alpen tragen: Fürsten sammeln antike Architektur*. Landshut: Arcols, 1993.

Helmendorfer, Erich. *Frankfurt – Metropole am Main: Geschichte und Zukunft*. Düsseldorf: Econ, 1982.

Helmer, Stephen D. *Hitler's Berlin: The Speer Plans for Reshaping the Central City*. Ann Arbor, MI: UMI Research Press, 1985.

Helmrath, Johannes. "Die Aura der Kaisermünze: Bild-Text-Studien zur Historiographie der Renaissance und zur Entstehung der Numismatik als Wissenschaft." In *Medien und Sprachen humanistischer Geschichtsschreibung*, ed. Johannes Helmrath, Albert Schirrmeister, and Stefan Schlelein. Berlin: de Gruyter, 2009, 99–138.

Helmrath, Johannes, Albert Schirrmeister, and Stefan Schlelein, eds. *Medien und Sprachen humanistischer Geschichtsschreibung*. Berlin: de Gruyter, 2009.

Henderson, Susan Rose. *The Work of Ernst May, 1919–1930*. Ph.D. diss., Columbia University, 1990.

Hennebo, Dieter, and Alfred Hoffmann. *Der architektonische Garten: Renaissance und Barock*. Hamburg: Broschek, 1965.

Herbert, Ulrich, ed. *Deutschland Danach: Postfaschistische Gesellschaft und Nationales Gedächtnis*. Bonn: J. H. W. Dietz, 1999.

Herf, Jeffrey. *Divided Memory: The Nazi Past in the Two Germanys*. Cambridge, Mass.: Harvard University Press, 1997.

—. "Divided Memory, Multiple Restorations: West German Political Reflections on the Nazi Past, 1945–1953." In *Revisiting Zero Hour 1945: The Emergence of Postwar German Culture*, ed. Stephen Brockmann and Frank Trommler. Washington, DC: American Institute for Contemporary German Studies, 1996, 89–102.

—. "Multiple Restorations: German Political Traditions and the Interpretation of Nazism, 1945–1946." In *Central European History* 26 (1993): 21–55.

Herscher, Andrew. *Violence Taking Place: The Architecture of the Kosovo Conflict*. Stanford: Stanford University Press, 2010.

Hersey, John. *Hiroshima*. New York: Knopf, 1946.

Hesse, Michael. "Tempel, Themen, Aquädukte: Antikerezeption in den Schwetzinger Parkbauten." In *Der Pfälzer Apoll: Kurfürst Carl Theodor und die Antike an Rhein und Neckar*, ed. Max Kunze. Ruhpolding: Rutzen, 2007, 175–181.

Heydenreuther, Reinhard. "Der Magistrat als Befehlsempfänger: Die Disziplinierung der Stadtobrigkeit 1579 bis 1651." In *Geschichte der Stadt München*, ed. Richard Bauer. Munich: Beck, 1992, 189–210.

Hirsch, Marianne. *The Generation of Postmemory: Writing and Visual Culture after the Holocaust*. New York: Columbia University Press, 2012.

Hirschfeld, Christian Cay Laurenz. *Theorie der Gartenkunst*. 5 vols. Leipzig: M. G.Weidmanns Erben and Reich, 1779–1785.

—. *Theorie der Gartenkunst*, ed. Franz Ehmke. Stuttgart: Deutsche Verlags-Anstalt, 1990.

—. *Theory of Garden Art*, trans. Linda B. Parshall. Philadelphia: University of Pennsylvania Press, 2001.

Hock, Sabine. "Frankfurt am Main zur Stunde Null 1945: Zwei Briefe von Walter H. Rothschild." In *Archiv für Frankfurts Geschichte und Kunst* 63 (1997): 535–557.

Hoenes, Josch, and Irene Nierhaus, eds. *Landschaft, Gehäuse, Orientierung: Territorialisierungs- und Naturalisierungsprozesse in Städten, Wohnen und Körper*. Berlin: Reimer Verlag, 2010.

Hoffmann, Wilhelm. *Nach der Katastrophe* [1946]. Stuttgart: Lithos-Verlag, 2001.

Hofmann, Fritz, and Peter Schmieder. *Benno Elkan: Ein jüdischer Künstler aus Dortmund*. Essen: Klartext Verlag, 1997.

Hofmann, Karl Ludwig. "Die kurpfälzische Gemäldegalerie in Mannheim – von der Fürstensammlung zur Bildungseinrichtung." In *Lebenslust und Frömmigkeit: Kurfürst Carl Theodor (1724–1799) zwischen Barock und Aufklärung*, ed. Alfried Wieczorek. Regensburg: Pustet, 1997, 239–243.

Hoffmann, Kurt, Rudolf Lodders, and Albrecht Sander. *Die Hochhäuser am Grindelberg*. Stuttgart: Julius Hoffmann, 1959.
Hohrath, Daniel. *Die Kunst des Krieges lernen? Die Entwicklung der Militärwissenschaften zwischen Renaissance und Aufklärung*. Rastatt: Wehrgeschichtliches Museum 2003.
Honneth, Axel, Ophelia Lindemann, and Stephan Voswinkel, eds. *Strukturwandel der Anerkennung: Paradoxien sozialer Integration in der Gegenwart*. Frankfurt am Main: Campus, 2013.
Horbas, Claudia, and Museum für Hamburgische Geschichte, eds. *Es brannte an allen Ecken zugleich: Hamburg 1842*. Heide: Boyens, 2002.
Hull, Isabel V. *Sexuality, State, and Civil Society in Germany, 1700–1815*. Ithaca: Cornell University Press, 1996.
Hunt, Lynn. *Measuring Time, Making History*. Budapest: Central European University Press, 2008.
Huyssen, Andreas. "Air War Legacies: From Dresden to Baghdad." In *Germans as Victims: Remembering the Past in Contemporary Germany*, ed. Bill Niven. New York: Palgrave Macmillan, 2006, 181–193.
Imorde, Joseph. "Atmosphärische Landschaft." In *Landschaft, Gehäuse, Orientierung: Territorialisierungs- und Naturalisierungsprozesse in Städten, Wohnen und Körper*, ed. Josch Hoenes and Irene Nierhaus. Berlin: Reimer Verlag, 2010, 149–159.
Imperial War Museum. London: Imperial War Museum, 2000.
Impey, Oliver, and Arthur MacGregor, eds. *The Origins of Museums: The Cabinet of Curiosities in Sixteenth- and Seventeenth-Century Europe*. Oxford: Clarendon, 1985.
Jacobs, Jane. *The Death and Life of American Cities*. New York: Random House, 1961.
Jarausch, Konrad H. *Die Umkehr: Deutsche Wandlungen 1945–1995*. Munich: Deutsche Verlags-Anstalt, 2004.
Jarausch, Konrad H., and Thomas Lindenberger, eds. *Conflicted Memories: Europeanizing Contemporary Histories*. New York: Berghahn, 2007.
Jaspers, Karl. *Die Schuldfrage*. Heidelberg: Lambert Schneider, 1946.
—. *The Question of Guilt*, trans. E. B. Ashton. New York: Dial Press, 1947.
Jay, Martin. *Downcast Eyes: The Denigration of Vision in Twentieth-Century French Thought*. Berkeley: University of California Press, 1993.
Kagan, Richard L. "*Urbs* and *Civitas* in Sixteenth- and Seventeenth-Century Spain." In *Envisioning the City*, ed. David Buisseret. Chicago: University of Chicago Press, 1998, 75–107.
Kaiser, Josef. *"Gemeinsames Schicksal – gemeinsame Arbeit!" Zur Wiederentstehung des demokratisch-politischen Lebens in Bad Dürkheim nach dem Zweiten Weltkrieg*. Neustadt a.d. Weinstrasse: Neue Pfälzer Post, 1987.
Kansteiner, Wulf. "Finding Meaning in Memory: A Methodological Critique of Collective Memory Studies." In *History & Theory* 41 (2002): 179–197.
—. *In Pursuit of German Memory: History, Television, and Politics after Auschwitz*. Athens, OH: Ohio University Press, 2006.
Kanther, Michael A., and Marc Olejniczak. *Bomben auf Duisburg: Der Luftkrieg und die Stadt 1940 bis 1960*. Duisburg: Mercator-Verlag, 2004.
Kaplan, E. Ann. *Trauma Culture: The Politics of Terror and Loss in Media and Literature*. New Brunswick, N.J.: Rutgers University Press, 2005.
Kaplan, E. Ann, and Wang, Ban, eds. *Trauma and Cinema: Cross-Cultural Explorations*. Hong Kong: Hong Kong University Press, 2004.

Kaplony, Andreas. "Das Zürcher Jerusalem-Modell aus dem Jahr 1846." In *Europa Miniature: Die kulturelle Bedeutung des Reliefs, 16.–21. Jahrhundert*, ed. Andreas Bürgi. Zürich: Verlag Neue Zürcher Zeitung, 2007, 149–164.
Kaschnitz, Marie Luise. "Rückkehr nach Frankfurt." In *Gesammelte Werke*, ed. Christian Büttrich and Norbert Miller, vol. 5. Frankfurt am Main: Insel, 1985, 142–153.
—. *Totentanz und Gedichte zur Zeit*. Hamburg: Claassen & Goverts, 1947.
Keller, Volker. *Mannheim im Bombenkrieg 1940–1945*. Gudensberg-Gleichen: Wartberg, 2003.
Kemfert, Beate. *Hermann Goepfert (1926–1982): Nachkriegskunst in Frankfurt am Main*. Frankfurt am Main: Waldemar Kramer, 1999.
Kempowski, Walter. *Der rote Hahn: Dresden im Februar 1945*. Munich: btb, 2001.
Kennan, George F. *Sketches from a Life*. New York: Pantheon Books, 1989.
Kettenacker, Lothar. *Germany since 1945*. Oxford: Oxford University Press, 1997.
Kettenacker, Lothar, ed. *Ein Volk von Opfern? Die neue Debatte um den Bombenkrieg 1940–1945*. Berlin: Rowohlt, 2003.
King, Ross. *Brunelleschi's Dome: How a Renaissance Genius Reinvented Architecture*. New York: Penguin Books, 2000.
Klemperer, Victor. *Ich will Zeugnis ablegen bis zum letzten: Tagebücher 1942–1945*, ed. Walter Nowojski. Berlin: Aufbau, 1995.
Klessmann, Christoph. "'Das Haus wurde gebaut aus den Steinen, die vorhanden waren': Zur kulturgeschichtlichen Kontinuitätsdiskussion nach 1945." In *Tel Aviver Jahrbuch für deutsche Geschichte* 19 (1990): 159–177.
Klötzer, Wolfgang. "Zur Geschichte der Frankfurter Wahlkapelle." In *Keine liebere Stadt als Frankfurt: Kleine Schriften zur Frankfurter Kulturgeschichte*, vol. 2. Frankfurt am Main: Waldemar Kramer, 2000, 397–408.
Klötzer, Wolfgang, ed. *Die Frankfurter Altstadt: Eine Erinnerung*. Frankfurt am Main: Waldemar Kramer, 1983.
Kloft, Matthias Theodor. *Kaiserdom St. Bartholomäus Frankfurt am Main*, 2nd ed. Regensburg: Schnell & Steiner, 1999.
Kluge, Alexander. "Der Luftangriff auf Halberstadt am 8. April 1945." In *Chronik der Gefühle*, vol. 2: *Lebensläufe*. Frankfurt am Main: Suhrkamp, 2000, 27–82.
—. *Der Luftangriff auf Halberstadt am 8. April 1945*. Frankfurt am Main: Suhrkamp, 2008.
Knappe, Karl. *Das Gesetz heisst Wand – der Ausweg Plastik*. Stuttgart: Verlag KG, 1950.
Knell, Hermann. *To Destroy a City: Strategic Bombing and Its Human Consequences in World War II*. Cambridge, Mass.: Da Capo Press, 2003.
—. *Untergang in Flammen: Strategische Bombenangriffe und ihre Folgen im Zweiten Weltkrieg*. Würzburg: Veröffentlichungen des Stadtarchivs, 2006.
Knocke, Helmut, and Hugo Thieler. *Hannover: Kunst- und Kultur-Lexikon*. Hannover: Schaefer, 1994.
Knox, Dilwyn. *Ironia: Medieval and Renaissance Ideas on Irony*. Leiden: Brill, 1989.
Kockel, Valentin. "Rekonstruktion als Rezeption: Die Rekonstruktion antiker Stadtbilder und ihre Verbreitung." In *Geschichte der Rekonstruktion: Konstruktion der Geschichte*, ed. Winfried Nerdinger. Munich: Prestel, 2010, 96–113.
Köhler, Jörg R. *Städtebau und Stadtpolitik im Wilhelminischen Frankfurt*. Frankfurt am Main: Waldemar Kramer, 1995.
Kos, Wolfgang. *Eigenheim Österreich: Zu Politik, Kultur und Alltag nach 1945*. Vienna: Sonderzahl, 1994.

—. "Die Schau mit dem Hammer." In *Eigenheim Österreich: Zu Politik, Kultur und Alltag nach 1945*. Vienna: Sonderzahl, 1994, 7–58.

—. "'Zukunftsfroh und muskelstark': Zum öffentlichen Menschenbild der Wiederaufbaujahre." In *Eigenheim Österreich: Zu Politik, Kultur und Alltag nach 1945*. Vienna: Sonderzahl, 1994, 59–150.

Korthaus, Johannes. *Die Zerstörung Freiburgs am 27. November: Augenzeugen berichten 1994*, ed. Stadt Freiburg i. Brsg. Freiburg i. Br.: Promo, 1994.

Kostof, Spiro. *The City Assembled: The Elements of Urban Form through History*. Boston: Bullfinch, 1992.

Kracauer, Siegfried. "Calico-World: The UFA City in Neubabelsberg." In *The Mass Ornament: Weimar Essays*, trans. Thomas Y. Levine. Cambridge, Mass.: Harvard University Press, 1995, 281–288.

—. "Die Nichtexistenz der Altstadt: Eine philosophische Deduktion." In *Römer-Maske: Eine Festschrift phantastischer Satire und satirischer Phantasie*, ed. Benno Elkan. Frankfurt am Main: Hauser-Press, 1925.

Kramer, Franz Albert. *Vor den Ruinen Deutschlands: Ein Aufruf zur geschichtlichen Selbstbesinnung*. Berlin: Wedding-Verlag, 1945.

Kramer, Nicole. "Ikone des Wiederaufbaus: Die 'Trümmerfrau' in der bundesdeutschen Erinnerungskultur." In *Luftkrieg: Erinnerungen in Deutschland und Europa*, eds. Jörg Arnold, Dietmar Süß, and Malte Thießen. Göttingen: Wallstein, 2009, 259–276.

Kreidl, John Francis. *Alain Resnais*. Boston: Twayne, 1977.

Kropat, Wolf-Arno. *Frankfurt zwischen Provinizialismus und Nationalismus: Die Eingliederung der "Freien Stadt" in den preußischen Staat*. Frankfurt am Main: Waldemar Kramer, 1971.

—. *Hessen in der Stunde Null 1945–1947: Politik, Wirtschaft und Bildungswesen in Dokumenten*. Wiesbaden: Selbstverlag der Historischen Kommission für Nassau, 1979.

—. ed., *Aufbruch zur Demokratie: Alltag und politischer Neubeginn in Hessen nach 1945*. Exhibition Catalogue. Wiesbaden: Hessisches Hauptstaatsarchiv, 1996.

Kühne, Hans-Jörg. *Zwischen Krieg und Frieden: Bielefeld 1945*, ed. Stadtarchiv, Landesgeschichtliche Bibliothek Bielefeld. Gudensberg-Gleichen: Wartberg, 2004.

Kugler, Hartmut. *Die Vorstellung der Stadt in der deutschen Literatur des Mittelalters*. Munich: Artemis, 1986.

Kulturstiftung Dessau-Wörlitz, ed. *Unendlich schön: Das Gartenreich Dessau-Wörlitz*. Berlin: Nicolai, 2005.

—. *Der Vulkan im Wörlitzer Park*. Berlin: Nicolai, 2005.

La Regina, Adriano, ed. *Sangue e Arena*. Milan: Electa, 2001.

LaCapra, Dominick. *Representing the Holocaust: History, Theory, Trauma*. Ithaca: Cornell University Press, 1994.

—. *Writing History, Writing Trauma*. Baltimore: Johns Hopkins University Press, 2001.

Lachenicht, Susanne. "Mythos Trümmerfrau? Trümmerräumung in Heilbronn 1945–1955." In *Heilbronnica 2: Beiträge zur Stadtgeschichte*. Heilbronn: Stadtarchiv, 2003, 319–360.

Lakerveld, Carry van. *Opkomst en Bloei van het Noordnederlandse Stadsgezicht in de 17de Eeuw: The Dutch Cityscape in the 17th Century and Its Sources*. Amsterdam: Amsterdams Historisch Museum, 1977.

Landesamt für Denkmalpflege Hessen, ed. *Baudenkmale in Hessen: Stadt Kassel I*. Braunschweig: Friedrich Vieweg & Sohn, 1984.

Langenbacher, Eric, Bill Niven, and Ruth Wittlinger, eds. *Dynamics of Memory and Identity in Contemporary Europe*. New York: Berghahn, 2012.
Langley, Batty. *New principles of gardening: or, The laying out and planting parterres, groves, wildernesses, labyrinths, avenues, parks, &c. after a more grand and rural manner, than has been done before ...* London: A. Bettesworth et al., 1728.
Lazardzig, Jan. *Theatermaschine und Festungsbau: Paradoxien der Wissensproduktion im 17. Jahrhundert*. Berlin: Akademie Verlag, 2007.
Lefebvre, Henri. *The Production of Space*, trans. Donald Nicholson-Smith. Oxford: Blackwell, 1991.
Leibniz, Gottfried Wilhelm. "Denkschrift II." In *Leibniz und seine Akademie: Ausgewählte Quellen zur Geschichte der Berliner Sozietät der Wissenschaften, 1697–1716*, ed. Hans-Stephan Brather. Berlin: Akademie der Wissenschaften, 1990, 75–80.
Leibniz, Gottfried Wilhelm. "Examen Religionis Christianae (Systema Theologicum)." In *Sämtliche Schriften und Briefe*, ed. Deutsche Akademie der Wissenschaften Berlin. Series 6: *Philosophische Schriften*, ed. Leibniz-Forschungsstelle der Universität Münster, vol. 4, C. Berlin: Akademie, 1999, 2355–2455.
Leopold, Silke. "Opernrepertoire des Schwetzinger Schloßtheaters." In *Hofoper in Schwetzingen: Musik – Bühnenmusik – Architektur*, ed. Silke Leopold and Bärbel Pelker. Heidelberg: Winter, 2004, 87–154.
Lienhardt, Conrad, ed. *Rudolf Schwarz (1897–1961): Werk, Theorie, Rezeption*. Regensburg: Schnell & Steiner, 1997.
Lifton, Jay. *Death in Life: Survivors of Hiroshima*. New York: Random House, 1967.
Lindemann, Ophelia. "Opfergeschichten: Paradoxien der Anerkennung zwischen Erzählen und Zuhören." In *Strukturwandel der Anerkennung: Paradoxien sozialer Integration in der Gegenwart*, ed. Axel Honneth, Ophelia Lindemann, and Stephan Voswinkel. Frankfurt am Main: Campus, 2013, 249–273.
Lindgren, Uta. "Les plans-reliefs de Bavière au XVIe siècle." In *Actes du colloque international sur les plans-reliefs au passé et au présent*, ed. André Corvisier. Paris: SEDES, 1993, 167–173.
Lipsmeyer, Elizabeth. *The Donor and His Church Model in Medieval Art from Early Christian Times to the Late Romanesque Period*. Ph.D. diss., Rutgers University, 1981.
Lübbe, Hermann. "Der Nationalsozialismus im politischen Bewusstsein der Gegenwart." In *Deutschlands Weg in die Diktatur: Internationale Konferenz zur nationalsozialistischen Machtübernahme im Reichstagsgebäude zu Berlin*, ed. Martin Broszat et al. Berlin: Siedler, 1983, 329–349.
Lübbecke, Fried. "Benno Elkan – Alsbach i.H." In *Deutsche Kunst und Dekoration* 30 (1912): 21–28.
—. "Fried Lübbecke über sich selbst." In *Die Frankfurter Altstadt: Eine Erinnerung*, ed. Wolfgang Klötzer. Frankfurt am Main: Waldemar Kramer, 1983, 427–431.
—. *Die gotische Kölner Plastik*. Strassburg: Heitz, 1910.
—. *Die Plastik des deutschen Mittelalters*. Munich: Piper, 1922.
—. *Treuner's Alt-Frankfurt: Das Altstadtmodell im Historischen Museum*. Frankfurt am Main: Waldemar Kramer, 1960.
Lüdtke, Alf. *Eigen-Sinn: Fabrikalltag, Arbeitererfahrungen und Politik vom Kaiserreich bis in den Faschismus*. Hamburg: Ergebnisse, 1993.
Ludwig, Annette. "Zwischen Krieg und Wirtschaftswunder: Künstlerische Reflexionen in der Nachkriegszeit." In *Heilbronn und die Kunst der 50er Jahre: Das Kunstgeschehen der 50er Jahre in Heilbronn*, ed. Andreas Pfeiffer. Heilbronn: Städtische Museen, 1993, 38–53.

Macaulay, Rose. *Pleasure of Ruins* [1953]. New York: Barnes & Noble, 1996.
MacGregor, Arthur. "Die besonderen Eigenschaften der 'Kunstkammer.'" In *Macrocosmos in Microcosmo: Die Welt in der Stube: Zur Geschichte des Sammelns 1450 bis 1800*. Opladen: Leske & Budrich, 1994, 61–106.
Maclear, Kyo. "The Limits of Vision: 'Hiroshima Mon Amour' and the Subversion of Representation." In *Witness and Memory: The Discourse of Trauma*, ed. Ana Douglass and Thomas A. Vogler. New York: Routledge, 2003, 233–247, 326.
Makarius, Michel. *Ruines*. Paris: Flammarion, 2004.
Mandelkow, Karl Robert, ed. *Goethe im Urteil seiner Kritiker*, vol. 4. Munich: Beck, 1984.
Manno, Antonio. "Rilievi scultorei e plastici di fortezze: Annotazioni e proposte per una storia delle idee di città e della guerra nel patriziato veneziano." In *Europa Miniature: Die kulturelle Bedeutung des Reliefs, 16.–21. Jahrhundert*, ed. Andreas Bürgi, Zürich: Verlag Neue Zürcher Zeitung, 2007, 49–64.
Marino, Angela. "Modelli e storia urbana: Da immagine simbolica a strumento di progetto." In *Europa Miniature: Die kulturelle Bedeutung des Reliefs, 16.–21. Jahrhundert*, ed. Andreas Bürgi. Zürich: Verlag Neue Zürcher Zeitung, 2007, 65–77.
Masey, Jack, and Conway Lloyd Morgan. *Cold War Confrontations: US Exhibitions and Their Role in the Cultural Cold War*. Baden: Lars Müller, 2008.
Marchal, Peter. *Kultur- und Programmgeschichte des öffentlich-rechtlichen Hörfunks in der Bundesrepublik Deutschland: Ein Handbuch*, vol. 1: *Grundlegung und Vorgeschichte*. Munich: kopaed, 2004.
Marchand, Yves, and Romain Meffre. *The Ruins of Detroit*. Göttingen: Gerhard Steidl, 2010.
Margalit, Gilad. *Guilt, Suffering, and Memory: Germany Remembers Its Dead from World War II*, trans. Haim Watzman. Bloomington: Indiana University Press, 2010.
Martin, Andrew John. "Stadtmodelle." In *Das Bild der Stadt in der Neuzeit: 1400–1800*, ed. Wolfgang Behringer and Bernd Roeck. Munich: Beck, 1999, 66–72.
Martin, Sigurd, and Ingo Wintermeyer, eds. *Verschiebebahnhöfe der Erinnerung: Zum Werk W. G. Sebalds*. Würzburg: Königshausen & Neumann, 2007.
Martineau, Jane, ed. *Andrea Mantegna*. Milan: Electa, 1992.
Maseberg, Günter, ed. *100 Jahre Geschichte: 1905–2005: Das Museum – Die Stadt – Die Halberstädter*. Halberstadt: Städtisches Museum, 2005.
Mason, Tony, and Nick Tiratsoo. "People, Politics and Planning: The Reconstruction of Coventry's City Centre, 1940–53." In *Rebuilding Europe's Bombed Cities*, ed. Jeffry M. Diefendorf. Basingstoke: Macmillan Press, 1990, 94–113.
Maurice, Klaus. *Der drechselnde Souverän: Materialien zu einer fürstlichen Maschinenkunst/ Sovereigns as Turners*, trans. Dorothy Ann Schade. Zurich: Ineichen, 1985.
McGowan, Margaret M. *The Vision of Rome in Late Renaissance France*. New Haven: Yale University Press, 2000.
Meier, Bettina. *Goethe in Trümmern: Zur Rezeption eines Klassikers in der Nachkriegszeit*. Wiesbaden: Deutscher Universitätsverlag, 1989.
Meinecke, Friedrich. *Die deutsche Katastrophe: Betrachtungen und Erinnerungen*. Wiesbaden: Brockhaus, 1946.
Meinhardt, Matthias. "Der Mythos vom 'Alten Dresden' als Bauplan: Entwicklung, Ursachen und Folgen einer retrospektiv-eklektizistischen Stadtvorstellung." In *Städte aus Trümmern: Katastrophenbewältigung zwischen Antike und Moderne*, ed. Andreas Ranft and Stephan Selzer. Göttingen: Vandenhoeck & Ruprecht, 2004, 172–200.
Meißner, Günter, ed. *Allgemeines Künstler-Lexikon*, vol. 8. Munich: Saur, 1994.

Melion, Walter S. "Love and Artisanship in Hendrick Goltzius's 'Venus, Bacchus and Ceres' of 1606." In *Art History* 16 (1993): 60–94.

Messerschmidt, Rolf, "' ... in freier, gleicher, offener und furchtloser Weise dem ganzen Volk dienen': Zur Entstehung und Rolle des Hessischen Rundfunks in den ersten Nachkriegsjahren." In *Hr – 50 Jahre Rundfunk für Hessen*, ed. Heiner Boehnke et al. Frankfurt am Main: Insel, 1995, 19–28.

Metken, Günter. *Rudolf Schlichter: Blinde Macht: Eine Allegorie der Zerstörung*. Frankfurt am Main: Fischer, 1990.

Meyer, Jean. "Le concept de plans-reliefs sous Louis XIV." In *Actes du colloque international sur les plans-reliefs au passé et au présent*, ed. André Corvisier. Paris: SEDES, 1993, 11–13.

Middlebrook, Martin. *The Berlin Raids: RAF Bomber Command Winter 1943–44*. London: Viking, 1988.

Minges, Klaus. "Die Sammlung als Medium des Weltbildes." In *Kunstchronik* (April 1994): 229–235.

Mitscherlich, Alexander. *Die Unwirtlichkeit unserer Städte: Anstiftung zum Unfrieden*. Frankfurt am Main: Suhrkamp, 1965.

Moeller, Robert G. "The Bombing War in Germany, 2005–1940: Back to the Future?" *Bombing Civilians: A Twentieth-Century History*, ed. Yuki Tanaka and Marilyn B. Young. New York: The New Press, 2009, 46–76.

—. "The Politics of the Past in the 1950s: Rhetorics of Victimisation in East and West Germany." In *Germans as Victims in the Literary Fiction of the Berlin Republic*, ed. Stuart Taberner and Karina Berger. Rochester: Camden House, 2009, 26–42.

—. "Remembering the War in a Nation of Victims: West German Pasts in the 1950s." In *The Miracle Years: A Cultural History of West Germany, 1949–1968*, ed. Hanna Schissler. Princeton: Princeton University Press, 2001, 83–109.

—. "War Stories: The Search for a Usable Past in the Federal Republic of Germany." In *American Historical Review* 101 (1996): 1008–1048.

—. *War Stories: The Search for a Usable Past in the Federal Republic of Germany*. Berkeley: University of California Press, 2001.

Moessner-Heckner, Ursula. *Pforzheim Code Yellowfin: Eine Analyse der Luftangriffe 1944–1945*. Sigmaringen: Thorbecke, 1991.

Moltke, Johannes von. "Ruin Cinema." In *Ruins of Modernity*, ed. Julia Hell and Andreas Schoenle. Durham: Duke University Press, 2010, 395–417.

Morris, Mark. *Models: Architecture and the Miniature*. Chichester: Wiley-Academy, 2006.

Mosbach, Bettina. *Figurationen der Katastrophe: Ästhetische Verfahren in W. G. Sebalds 'Die Ringe des Saturn' und 'Austerlitz.'* Bielefeld: Aisthesis, 2008.

Mühlhauser, Regina. "Vergewaltigungen in Deutschland 1945: Nationaler Opferdiskurs und individuelles Erinnern." In *Nachkrieg in Deutschland*, ed. Klaus Naumann. Hamburg: Hamburger Edition, 2001, 384–408.

Müller-Raemisch, Hans-Reiner. *Frankfurt am Main: Stadtentwicklung und Planungsgeschichte seit 1945*. Frankfurt am Main: Campus, 1996.

Naumann, Klaus. "Der Bombenkrieg: Deutsche als Opfer – ihrer selbst?" In *Der Krieg als Text: Das Jahr 1945 im kulturellen Gedächtnis der Presse*. Hamburg: Hamburger Edition, 1998, 33–71.

Naumann, Klaus, ed. *Nachkrieg in Deutschland*. Hamburg: Hamburger Edition, 2001.

Necker, Sylvia. *Konstanty Gutschow 1902–1978: Modernes Denken und volksgemeinschaftliche Utopie eines Architekten*. Hamburg: Dölling & Galitz, 2012.

Nerdinger, Wilhelm. *Architektur der Wunderkinder: Aufbruch und Verdrängung in Bayern 1945–1960*. Salzburg: Anton Pustet, 2005.
Nerdinger, Wilhelm, ed. *Geschichte der Rekonstruktion: Konstruktion der Geschichte*. Munich: Prestel, 2010.
Neumann, Klaus. "Lange Wege der Trauer: Erinnerung an die Zerstörung Halberstadts am 8. April 1945." In *Luftkrieg: Erinnerungen in Deutschland und Europa*, ed. Jörg Arnold, Dietmar Süß, and Malte Thießen. Göttingen: Wallstein, 2009, 203–220.
Neumann, Vera. *Nicht der Rede wert: Die Privatisierung der Kriegsfolgen in der frühen Bundesrepublik: Lebensgeschichtliche Erinnerungen*. Münster: Westfälisches Dampfboot, 1999.
Newman, Jane O. *Benjamin's Library: Modernity, Nation, and the Baroque*. Ithaca: Cornell University Press, 2011.
Nicholson, Helen. *The Knights Hospitaller*. Woodbridge: Boydell Press, 2001.
Niehaus, Michael, and Claudia Öhlschläger, eds. *W. G. Sebald: Politische Archäologie und melancholische Bastelei*. Berlin: Erich Schmidt, 2006.
Niethammer, Lutz. "Privat-Wirtschaft: Erinnerungsfragmente einer anderen Umerziehung." In *'Hinterher merkt man, daß es richtig war, daß es schiefgegangen ist': Nachkriegserfahrungen im Ruhrgebiet*, ed. Lutz Niethammer. Berlin/Bonn: J. H. W. Dietz Nachf., 1983, 17–105.
—. "War die bürgerliche Gesellschaft in Deutschland 1945 am Ende oder am Anfang?" In *Deutschland Danach: Postfaschistische Gesellschaft und Nationales Gedächtnis*, ed. Ulrich Herbert et al. Bonn: J. H. W. Dietz, 1999, 18–35.
Niven, Bill. "Introduction: German Victimhood at the Turn of the Millennium." In *Germans as Victims: Remembering the Past in Contemporary Germany*, ed. B. Niven. New York: Palgrave Macmillan, 2006, 1–25.
Niven, Bill, ed. *Germans as Victims: Remembering the Past in Contemporary Germany*. New York: Palgrave Macmillan, 2006.
Niven, Bill, and Chloe Paver, eds. *Memorialization in Germany since 1945*. New York: Palgrave Macmillan, 2010.
Nornes, Abé Mark. "Cherry Trees and Corpses: Representations of Violence from WW II." In *The Japan/America Film Wars: World War II Propaganda and Its Cultural Contexts*, ed. Abé Mark Nornes and Fukushima Yukio. Chur: Harwood, 1994, 147–162.
—. *Forrest of Pressure: Ogawa Shinsuke and Postwar Japanese Documentary*. Minneapolis: University of Minnesota Press, 2007.
—. *Japanese Documentary Film: The Meiji Era through Hiroshima*. Minneapolis: University of Minnesota Press, 2003.
Nossack, Hans-Erich. *The End: Hamburg 1943*, trans. Joel Agee. Chicago: University of Chicago Press, 2004.
Oesterle, Günter, ed. *Erinnerung, Gedächtnis, Wissen: Studien zur kulturwissenschaftlichen Gedächtnisforschung*. Göttingen: Vandenhoeck & Ruprecht, 2005.
Olick, Jeffrey K. *In the House of the Hangman: The Agonies of German Defeat, 1943–1949*. Chicago: University of Chicago Press, 2005.
—. "What Does It Mean to Normalize the Past? Official Memory in German Politics since 1989." In *States of Memory: Continuities, Conflicts, and Transformations In National Retrospection*, ed. J. K. Olick. Durham: Duke University Press, 2003, 258–288.
Olick, Jeffrey K., ed. *States of Memory: Continuities, Conflicts, and Transformations in National Retrospection*. Durham: Duke University Press, 2003.

Olick, Jeffrey K., Vered Vinitzky-Seroussi, and Daniel Levy, eds. *The Collective Memory Reader*. Oxford: Oxford University Press, 2011.

Olmi, Giuseppe. "Die Sammlung – Nutzbarmachung und Funktion." In *Macrocosmos in Microcosmo: Die Welt in der Stube: Zur Geschichte des Sammelns 1450 bis 1800*, ed. Andreas Grote. Opladen: Leske & Budrich, 1994, 169–189.

Oppelt, Hans. *Würzburger Chronik des denkwürdigen Jahres 1945 ... im Auftrag der Stadt Würzburg*. Würzburg: Ferdinand Schöningh, 1947; reprint 1995.

Overy, Richard. *The Bombing War: Europe 1939–1945*. London: Allen Lane, 2013.

Paczkowski, Jörg. *Der Wiederaufbau der Stadt Würzburg nach 1945*, 2nd ed. Würzburg: Ferdinand Schöningh, 1995.

Palm, Rolf, ed. *Heilbronner Kriegs-Opfer 1939–1945*. Neckarsulm: Industrie- und Handelskammer, 1994.

Panofsky, Erwin. "Albrecht Dürer and Classical Antiquity." In *Meaning in the Visual Arts: Papers in and on Art History*. Chicago: University of Chicago, 1955, 236–285.

—. "'Et in Arcadia Ego': Poussin and the Elegiac Tradition." In *Meaning in the Visual Arts: Papers in and on Art History*. Chicago: University of Chicago Press, 1955, 295–320.

Patt, Lise. "Searching for Sebald: What I Know for Sure." In *Searching for Sebald: Photography after W. G. Sebald*, ed. Lise Patt. Los Angeles: The Institute for Cultural Inquiry, 2007, 62–69.

Paul, Jürgen. "Reconstruction of the City Centre of Dresden: Planning and Building during the 1950s." In *Rebuilding Europe's Bombed Cities*, ed. Jeffry M. Diefendorf. Basingstoke: Macmillan, 1990, 170–189.

Pelker, Bärbel. "Sommer in der Campagne – Impressionen aus Schwetzingen." In *Hofoper in Schwetzingen: Musik – Bühnenmusik – Architektur*, ed. Silke Leopold and Bärbel Pelker. Heidelberg: Winter, 2004, 9–37.

—. "W. A. Mozart zu Besuch in der Kurpfalz." In *Theater um Mozart*, ed. Bärbel Pelker Heidelberg: Winter, 2006, 59–82.

Peter, Richard. *Dresden – eine Kamera klagt an*. Dresden: Dresdner Verlagsgesellschaft KG, 1950.

Pfeiffer, Andreas, ed. *Heilbronn und die Kunst der 50er Jahre: Das Kunstgeschehen der 50er Jahre in Heilbronn*. Heilbronn: Städtische Museen, 1993.

Pflicht, Stephan. *Kurfürst Carl Theodor von der Pfalz und seine Bedeutung für die Entwicklung des deutschen Theaters*. Reichling: Ehresmann Verlag, 1976.

Pieri, Elisabetta, and Luigi Zangheri, eds. *Niccolò detto Il Tribolo tra arte, architettura e paesaggio*. Poggio a Caiano: Comune di Poggio a Caiano, 2000.

Porter, David. *Ideographia: The Chinese Cipher in Early Modern Europe*. Stanford: Stanford University Press, 2001.

Potts, Alex. *Flesh and the Ideal: Winckelmann and the Origins of Art History*. New Haven: Yale University Press, 1992.

Pratt, Mary Louise. *Imperial Eyes: Travel Writing and Transculturation*. New York: Routledge, 1992.

Price, David Hotchkiss. *Albrecht Dürer's Renaissance: Humanism, Reformation, and the Art of Faith*. Ann Arbor: University of Michigan Press, 2003.

Puff, Helmut. "The City as Model: Three-Dimensional Representations of Urban Space in Early Modern Europe." In *Topographies of the Early Modern City*, ed. Arthur Groos, Hans-Jochen Schiewer, and Markus Stock. Göttingen: Vandenhoeck & Ruprecht, 2008, 193–217.

—. "Ruins as Models: Displaying Destruction in Postwar Germany." In *Ruins of Modernity*, ed. Julia Hell and Andreas Schönle. Durham: Duke University Press, 2010, 253–269.

—. "Self-Portrait with Ruins: Maerten van Heemskerck, 1553." In *The Germanic Review: Literature, Culture, Theory* 86 (2011): 262–276.
Quattländer, Peter U. *Heilbronn: Planung des Wiederaufbaues der Altstadt: Dokumentation zur Ausstellung des Stadtplanungsamtes 1994*. Heilbronn: Stadtarchiv Heilbronn, 1994.
Rancière, Jacques. *The Future of the Image*, trans. Gregory Elliott. London: Verso, 2007.
Ranft, Andreas, and Stephan Selzer. "Städte aus Trümmern: Einleitende Überlegungen." In *Städte aus Trümmern: Katastrophenbewältigung zwischen Antike und Moderne*, ed. A. Ranft and St. Selzer. Göttingen: Vandenhoeck & Ruprecht, 2004, 9–25.
Ranft, Andreas, and Stephan Selzer, eds. *Städte aus Trümmern: Katastrophenbewältigung zwischen Antike und Moderne*. Göttingen: Vandenhoeck & Ruprecht, 2004.
Reinert, Sophus A. "Lessons on the Rise and Fall of Great Powers: Conquest, Commerce, and Decline in Enlightenment Italy." In *American Historical Review* 115 (2010): 1395–1425.
Reisinger, Claus. *Der Schloßgarten zu Schwetzingen*. Worms: Wernersche Verlagsanstalt, 1987.
Reitzenstein, Alexander Freiherr von. *Die alte bairische Stadt in den Modellen des Drechslermeisters Jakob Sandtner, gefertigt in den Jahren 1568–1574 im Auftrag Herzog Albrechts V. von Bayern*. Munich: Callway, 1967.
Rentschler, Eric. "The Place of Rubble in the *Trümmerfilm*." In *Ruins of Modernity*, ed. Julia Hell and Andreas Schoenle. Durham: Duke University Press, 2010, 418–438.
Renz, Alexander. *Chronik der Stadt Heilbronn*, vol. 6: *1945–1951*. Heilbronn: Stadtarchiv, 1995.
—. *Chronik der Stadt Heilbronn*, vol. 7: *1952–1957*. Heilbronn: Stadtarchiv, 1996.
Riani, Paulo. *Kenzo Tange*. London: Hamlyn, 1969.
Riegert, Willi. *Heimat unter Bomben: Der Luftkrieg im Raum Steinfurt und in Münster und Osnabrück 1939–1945*. Dülmen: Laumann-Verlag, 2003.
Riezler, Sigmund. "Albrecht V." In *Allgemeine Deutsche Biographie*, vol. 1 [1875]. Leipzig: Duncker & Humblot,1967, 234–237.
—. "Wilhelm V." In *Allgemeine Deutsche Biographie*, vol. 42 [1897]. Leipzig: Duncker & Humblot, 1971, 717–723.
Rodenstein, Marianne. "Goethehaus, Frankfurt am Main." In *Geschichte der Rekonstruktion: Konstruktion der Geschichte*, ed. Winfried Nerdinger. Munich: Prestel, 2010, 434–436.
—. "Römer und Römerberg." In *Geschichte der Rekonstruktion: Konstruktion der Geschichte*, ed. Winfried Nerdinger. Munich: Prestel, 2010, 314f.
Romanelli, Giandomenico, Susanna Biadene, and Camillo Tonini, eds. *'A volo d'uccello': Jacopo de' Barbari e le rappresentazioni di città nell'Europa del Rinascimento*. Venice: Arsenale, 1999.
RomanyWG, *Beauty in Decay: The Art of Urban Exploration*. Berkeley: Gingko Press, 2010.
Ross, Stephanie. *What Gardens Mean*. Chicago: University of Chicago Press, 1998.
Roth, Harriet, ed. *Der Anfang der Museumslehre in Deutschland: Das Traktat 'Inscriptiones vel Tituli Theatri Amplissimi' von Samuel Quiccheberg*. Berlin: Akademie, 2000.
Roth, Michael S. *Irresistible Decay: Ruins Reclaimed*. Los Angeles: The Getty Research Center, 1997.
—. *Memory, Trauma, and History: Essays on Living with the Past*. New York: Columbia University Press, 2012.
Roth, Michael S., and Charles G. Salas, eds. *Disturbing Remains: Memory, History, and Crisis in the Twentieth Century*. Los Angeles: The Getty Research Institute, 2001.
Roux, Antoine de, Nicolas Faucherre, and Guillaume Monsaingeon, eds. *Les plans en relief des places du roy: Actes du colloque international sur les plans-reliefs*. Paris: A. Biro, 1989.

Rumpf, Hans. *Das war der Bombenkrieg: Deutsche Städte im Feuersturm: Ein Dokumentarbericht*. Oldenburg/Hamburg: Gerhard Stalling, 1961.

—. "Luftkrieg über Deutschland." In *Bilanz des Zweiten Weltkrieges: Erkenntnisse und Verpflichtungen für die Zukunft*. Oldenburg/Hamburg: Gerhard Stalling, 1958, 159–175.

Sander, August. *Die Zerstörung Kölns: Photographien 1945–46*. Munich: Schirmer-Mosel, 1985.

Sandl, Marcus. "Historizität der Erinnerung/Reflexivität des Historischen: Die Herausforderung der Geschichtswissenschaft durch die kulturwissenschaftliche Gedächtnisforschung." In *Erinnerung, Gedächtnis, Wissen: Studien zur kulturwissenschaftlichen Gedächtnisforschung*, ed. Günter Oesterle. Göttingen: Vandenhoeck & Ruprecht, 2005, 89–119

Sangallo, Giuliano da. *Il Libro di Giuliano da Sangallo: Codice Vaticano Barberiniano Latino 4424*, ed. Christian Hülsen. Leipzig: O. Harrassowitz, 1910.

Schedel, Hartmann. *Weltchronik: Kolorierte Gesamtausgabe von 1493*, ed. Stephan Füssel. Cologne: Taschen, 2001.

Scherff, Klaus. *Trümmerbahnen*. Stuttgart: transpress, 2002.

Schiermeier, Franz. *"Relief der Haupt- und Residenzstadt München": Das Stadtmodell von Johann Baptist Seitz 1841–1863*, ed. Renate Eikelmann. Munich: Bayerisches Nationalmuseum, 2000.

Schissler, Hanna, ed. *The Miracle Years: A Cultural History of West Germany, 1949–1968*. Princeton: Princeton University Press, 2001.

Schingo, Cianluca. "I modelli del Colosseo." In *Sangue e Arena*, ed. Adriano La Regina. Milan: Electa, 2001, 105–115.

Schmalacker-Wyrich, Esther, ed. *Pforzheim 23. Februar 1945: Der Untergang einer Stadt in Bildern und Augenzeugenberichten*. Pforzheim: J. Eßlinger, 1980.

Schmid, Armin. *Frankfurt im Feuersturm: Die Geschichte der Stadt im Zweiten Weltkrieg*. Frankfurt am Main: Frankfurter Bücher, 1965. 2nd ed., Frankfurt am Main: Societätsverlag, 1984.

Schmidt, Friedrich. *Geschichte der Erziehung der Bayerischen Wittelsbacher*. Berlin: Hofmann, 1892.

Schnatz, Helmut. *Tiefflieger über Dresden: Legenden und Wirklichkeit*. Vienna: Böhlau, 2003.

Schoell-Glass, Charlotte, and Elizabeth Sears. "'Amerika kennt keine Ruinen': Horst W. Jansons Amerikabild." In *Zeitschrift für Ideengeschichte* 3 (2009): 97–114.

—. *Verzetteln als Methode: Der humanistische Ikonologe William S. Heckscher*. Berlin: Akademie, 2008.

Schoenle, Andreas. *Architecture of Oblivion: Ruins and Historical Consciousness in Modern Russia*. DeKalb, Ill.: Northern Illinois University Press, 2011.

Scholderer, Hans-Joachim. "Bühne und Maschinerie des Schwetzinger Schloßtheaters." In *Hofoper in Schwetzingen: Musik – Bühnenmusik – Architektur*, ed. Silke Leopold and Bärbel Pelker. Heidelberg: Winter, 2004, 155–176.

Scholl, Monika. "Bretterbude? Neue Erkenntnisse zur Baugeschichte des Theaters." In *Hofoper in Schwetzingen: Musik – Bühnenmusik – Architektur*, ed. Silke Leopold and Bärbel Pelker. Heidelberg: Winter, 2004, 251–303.

—. "Das Schwetzinger Schloßtheater – Der Idealtypus eines Sprech- und Musiktheaters des 18. Jahrhunderts." In *Theater um Mozart*, ed. Bärbel Pelker. Heidelberg: Winter, 2006, 83–101.

Schreiber, Franz. *Augsburg: Die Bombennacht im Februar 1944*. Gudensberg-Gleichen: Wartberg, 2004.

Schwab, Ingo. "Zeiten der Teuerung: Versorgungsprobleme in der zweiten Hälfte des 16. Jahrhunderts." In *Geschichte der Stadt München*, ed. Richard Bauer. Munich: Beck, 1992, 166–188.

Schweikert, Uwe, ed. *Marie Luise Kaschnitz*. Frankfurt am Main: Suhrkamp, 1984.
Sckell, Friedrich Ludwig von. *Beiträge zur bildenden Gartenkunst für angehende Gartenkünstler und Gartenliebhaber*. Reprint of 2nd ed., Munich 1825. Worms: Werner, 1982.
Sebald, W. G. *Luftkrieg und Literatur: Mit einem Essay zu Alfred Andersch*. Munich: Hanser, 1999.
—. *On the Natural History of Destruction: With Essays on Alfred Andersch, Jean Améry and Peter Weiss*, trans. Anthea Bell. London: Hamish Hamilton, 2003.
—. *Die Ringe des Saturn*. Frankfurt am Main: Fischer, 1997.
—. *The Rings of Saturn*, trans. Michael Hulse. New York: New Directions, 1999.
Seberich, Franz. *Das Stadtmodell 'Würzburg um 1525' im Mainfränkischen Museum*. Würzburg: Freunde Mainfränkischer Kunst und Geschichte, 1968.
Sedlmayr, Hans. *Verlust der Mitte: Die bildende Kunst des 19. und 20. Jahrhunderts als Symbol der Zeit*. Salzburg: Otto Mueller, 1948.
Seelig, Lorenz. "The Munich *Kunstkammer*, 1565–1807." In *The Origins of Museums: The Cabinet of Curiosities in Sixteenth- and Seventeenth-Century Europe*, eds. Oliver Impey and Arthur MacGregor. Oxford: Clarendon, 1985, 76–89.
Seng, Eva-Maria. *Stadt – Idee und Planung: Neue Ansätze im Städtebau des 16. und 17. Jahrhunderts*. Munich: Deutscher Kunstverlag, 2003.
Senge, Joachim. *Goethe-Enthusiasmus und Bürgersinn: Das Freie Deutsche Hochstift – Goethemuseum, 1859–1960*. Göttingen: Wallstein, 2009.
Siedler, Wolf Jobst, and Elisabeth Niggemeyer. *Die gemordete Stadt: Abgesang auf Putte und Straße, Platz und Baum* [1961]. Berlin: Siedler, 1993.
Siegmund, Andrea. *Die romantische Ruine im Landschaftsgarten: Ein Beitrag zum Verhältnis der Romantik zu Barock und Klassik*. Würzburg: Königshausen & Neumann, 2002.
Sigg, Otto. "Das 17. Jahrhundert." In *Geschichte des Kantons Zürich*. Zurich: Werd-Verlag, 1996, 282–363.
Simmel, Georg. "Die Ruine." In *Philosophische Kultur: Gesammelte Essays*, 2nd ed. Leipzig: Alfred Kröner, 1919, 125–133.
—. "The Ruin." In *Essays in Sociology, Philosophy and Aesthetics*, ed. Kurt H. Wolff. New York: Harper and Row, 1965, 259–266.
Simon, Ulrich. "Der Provokateur als Literaturhistoriker: Anmerkungen zu Literaturbegriff und Argumentationsverfahren in W. G. Sebalds essayistischen Schriften." In *Sebald: Lektüren*, eds. Marcel Atze and Franz Loquai. Eggingen: Edition Isele, 2005, 78–104.
Simpfendörfer, Siegfried. "Nah und fern – das Thema der Landschaft in der Kunst der 50er Jahre: Eine Collage." In *Heilbronn und die Kunst der 50er Jahre: Das Kunstgeschehen der 50er Jahre in Heilbronn*, ed. Andreas Pfeiffer. Heilbronn: Städtische Museen, 1993, 54–67.
Sindram, Dirk, and Antje Scherner, eds. *Princely Splendor: The Dresden Court 1580–1620*. Milan: The Metropolitan Museum of Art/Staatliche Kunstsammlungen Dresden, 2004.
Skrdla, Harry. *Ghostly Ruins: America's Forgotten Architecture*. Princeton: Princeton Architectural Press, 2006.
Smail, Daniel Lord. "History and the Telescoping of Time: A Disciplinary Forum." In *French Historical Studies* 34 (2011): 1–6.
Smith, Pamela. *The Body of the Artisan: Art and Experience in the Scientific Revolution*. Chicago: University of Chicago Press, 2004.
Smith, William, ed. *A Dictionary of Greek and Roman Biography and Mythology* [1880]. London: Tauris, 2007.

Solms, Reinhard Graf zu. *Ein kürtzer Aufzug vnnd überschlag / Einen Baw anzustellen / vnd in ein Regiment vnd Ordenung zupringen / mit denen so darauff mit aller arbeit seyn wurden.* Cologne: Erben Arnold Birckman, 1556; Düsseldorf: Jacob Baethen, 1556.
Sontag, Susan. *Regarding the Pain of Others.* New York: Farrar, Straus, and Giroux, 2003.
Sorge, Dorothee. *Baukunst als Formung des eigenen Schicksals: Das Architekturverständnis von Rudolf Schwarz.* Cologne: Kunsthistorisches Institut der Universität, Abt. Architekturgeschichte, 2008.
Spannagel, Martin. "Carl Theodor als pfälzischer Apoll, der Palatin und die arkadische Vorgeschichte Roms." In *Der Pfälzer Apoll: Kurfürst Carl Theodor und die Antike an Rhein und Neckar,* ed. Max Kunze. Ruhpolding: Rutzen, 2007, 159–168.
Specklin, Daniel. *Architectvra von Vestungen / Wie die zu vnsern zeiten / an Stätten / Schlössern vnd Claussen / zu Wasser / Land / Bery und Thal / mit jhren Bollwercken / Caualiren / Streichen / Gräben vnd Läuffen mögen erbawet ... werden Jetzt aber auffs new ubersehen.* Strassburg: Lazarus Zetzner, 1608.
Speer, Albert. *Inside the Third Reich: Memoirs,* trans. Richard and Clara Winston. New York: Macmillan, 1970.
Spender, Stephen. *Journals 1939–1983,* ed. John Goldsmith. London: Faber and Faber, 1985.
Spindler, Max, ed. *Handbuch der bayerischen Geschichte,* vol. 2. Munich: Beck, 1967.
Stadtverwaltung Bad Dürkheim, ed. *Der 18. März 1945 in Bad Dürkheim: Zeitzeugen berichten über die Bombardierung der Stadt.* Horb am Neckar: Geiger-Verlag, 2006.
Stafford, Barbara Maria. *Artful Science: Enlightenment Entertainment and the Eclipse of Visual Education.* Cambridge, Mass.: MIT Press, 1994.
Starobinski, Jean. *The Invention of Liberty: 1700–17l89,* trans. Bernard C. Swift. Geneva: Skira, 1964.
Steinweg, Wolfgang. *Das Rathaus Hannover,* ed. Fremdenverkehrsverein, 3rd ed. Hannover: Benatzky, 2003.
Stendhal. *Promenades dans Rome.* Nendeln: Kraus Reprint, 1968.
—. *A Roman Journal,* trans. Haakon Chevalier. New York: Orion Press, 1957.
Stengel, Stephan von. *Der Kurfürst Karl Theodor in Rom: Tagebuch seiner zweiten Romreise,* ed. Günther Ebersold. Mannheim: Palatium, 1997.
Stewart, David B. *The Making of a Modern Japanese Architecture: From the Founders to Shinohara and Isozaki,* 2nd ed. Tokyo: Kodansha International, 2002.
Stewart, Susan. *On Longing: Narratives of the Miniature, the Gigantic, the Souvenir, the Collection.* Durham: Duke University Press, 1993.
Stobbe, Urte. *Kassel-Wilhelmshöhe: Ein hochadeliger Lustgarten im 18. Jahrhundert.* Berlin: Deutscher Kunstverlag, 2009.
Stoler, Ann Laura. "Imperial Debris: Reflections on Ruins and Ruination." In *Cultural Anthropology* 23 (2008): 191–219.
Stoler, Ann Laura, ed. *Imperial Debris: On Ruins and Ruination.* Durham: Duke University Press, 2013.
Stonard, John-Paul. *Fault Lines: Art in Germany 1945–1955.* London: Ridinghouse, 2007.
Stoppard, Tom. *Plays Five: Arcadia, The Real Thing, Night & Day, Indian Ink, Hapgood.* London: Faber and Faber, 1999.
Strasser, Ulrike. *State of Virginity: Gender, Religion, and Politics in an Early Modern Catholic State.* Ann Arbor: University of Michigan Press, 2004.

Stupperich, Reinhard. "Carl Theodors Romreisen 1774/1775 und 1783." In *Der Pfäzer Apoll: Kurfürst Carl Theodor und die Antike an Rhein und Neckar*, ed. Max Kunze. Ruhpolding: Rutzen, 2007, 17–24.
Süß, Dietmar. "Review Article: Memories of the Air War." In *Journal of Contemporary History* 43 (2002): 333–342.
Svoboda, Karl J. *Eine kurfürstliche Winterreise nach Italien: Die Reise des Grafen von Veldenz alias des Kurfürsten Carl Theodor von der Pfalz von Mannheim nach Rom im Jahre 1774/75.* Ubstadt-Weiher: Verlag Regionalkultur, 1998.
Szymczyk-Eggert, Elisabeth. "' ... sogar wäre es mir lieb, wenn Ihr Schwetzingen besuchtet.'" In *Gärten der Goethezeit*, ed. Harri Günther. Leipzig: Edition Leipzig, 1993, 148–159.
Taberner, Stuart, and Karina Berger, eds. *Germans as Victims in the Literary Fiction of the Berlin Republic*. Rochester: Camden House, 2009.
Tanaka, Yuki, and Marilyn B. Young, eds. *Bombing Civilians: A Twentieth-Century History*. New York: The New Press, 2009.
Tange, Kenzo. *Architecture and Urban Design 1946–1949*, ed. Udo Kultermann. New York: Praeger Publishers, 1970.
—. *Katsura: Tradition and Creation in Japanese Architecture*. New Haven: Yale University Press, 1972.
Tauber, Alon. *Zwischen Kontinuität und Neuanfang: Die Entstehung der jüdischen Nachkriegsgemeinde in Frankfurt am Main 1945–1949*. Wiesbaden: Kommission für die Geschichte der Juden in Hessen, 2008.
Taylor, Frederick. *Dresden: Tuesday, February 13, 1945*. New York: HarperCollins, 2004.
Thießen, Malte. *Eingebrannt ins Gedächtnis: Hamburgs Gedenken an Luftkrieg und Kriegsende 1943 bis 2005*. Hamburg: Dölling und Galitz, 2007.
—. "Das kollektive als lokales Gedächtnis: Plädoyer für eine Lokalisierung von Geschichtspolitik." In *Geschichtspolitik und kollektives Gedächtnis: Erinnerungskulturen in Theorie und Praxis*, ed. Harald Schmid. Göttingen: V&R unipress, 2009, 159–180.
—. "Die 'Katastrophe' als symbolischer Bezugspunkt: Städtisches Gedenken an den Luftkrieg in der BRD und der DDR." In *Die Weltkriege als symbolische Bezugspunkte: Polen, die Tschechoslowakei und Deutschland nach dem Ersten und Zweiten Weltkrieg*, ed. Natali Stegmann. Prague: Masarykův ústav a Archiv, 2009, 91–108.
Thomas, Julia A. "Photography, National Identity, and the 'Cataract of Times': Wartime Images and the Case of Japan." In *American Historical Review* 103 (1998): 1475–1501.
Timpe, Stefan. "Denkmalgestaltung als Prozess: Zur jüngsten Restaurierung der Fassaden des Frankfurter Römers." In *Denkmalpflege und Kulturgeschichte* 1 (2005): 2–8.
Toews, John Edward. *Becoming Historical: Cultural Reformation and Public Memory in Early Nineteenth-Century Berlin*. Cambridge: Cambridge University Press, 2004.
Triolet, Elsa. "Der Prozeß tanzt" [7. Juni 1946]. In *Der Nürnberger Lernprozess: Von Kriegsverbrechern und Starreportern*, ed. Steffen Radlmaier. Frankfurt am Main: Eichborn, 2001, 251–267.
Triolet, Elsa. *L'inspecteur des ruines*. Paris: La bibliothèque française, 1948.
—. *The Inspector of Ruins*, trans. Norman Cameron. New York: Roy Publishers, [1953].
Trouillot, Michel-Rolph. *Silencing the Past: Power and the Production of History*. Boston: Beacon Press, 1995.
Vagt, Kristina. *Politik durch die Blume: Gartenbauausstellungen in Hamburg und Erfurt im Kalten Krieg (1950–1974)*. Hamburg: Dölling & Galitz, 2013.
Van Rensbergen, Henk. *Abandoned Places*. Tielt: Lannoo, 2007.

—. *Abandoned Places 2*. Tielt: Lannoo, 2010.
Varchi, Benedetto. *Storia fiorentina*. Florence: Salani, 1963.
Vasari, Giorgio. *Le vite de' più eccellenti pittori scultori e architettori*, vol. 5. Novara: Istituto Geografico de Agostini, 1967.
—. *Lives of the Painters, Sculptors and Architects*, trans. Gaston du C. de Vere. London: Random House, 1996.
Vees-Gulani, Susanne. "The Experience of Destruction: W. G. Sebald, the Airwar, and Literature." In *W. G. Sebald: History – Memory – Trauma*, ed. Scott Denham and Mark McCulloh. New York: de Gruyter, 2006, 335–349.
—. "'Phantomschmerzen': Durs Grünbeins 'Porzellan' und neue Wege in der Literatur über den Luftkrieg." In *Luftkrieg: Erinnerungen in Deutschland und Europa*. Göttingen: Wallstein Verlag, 2009, 277–296.
—. *Trauma and Guilt: Literature of Wartime Bombing in Germany*. Berlin: Walter de Gruyter, 2003.
Vergara, Camilo José. *American Ruins*. New York: Monacelli Press, 1999.
Vigano, Marino. "La fortezza in casa: Modelli di piazzeforti tra guerra e conoscenza del territorio (XVI–XIX secolo)." In *Europa Miniature: Die kulturelle Bedeutung des Reliefs, 16.–21. Jahrhundert*, ed. Andreas Bürgi. Zürich: Verlag Neue Zürcher Zeitung, 2007, 79–90.
Vivian, Bradford. *Public Forgetting: The Rhetoric and Politics of Beginning Again*. University Park, PA: Pennsylvania State University Press, 2010.
Vogel, Hans. *Die Ruine in der Darstellung der abendländischen Kunst*. Kassel: Karl Winter, 1948.
Vogt-Spira, Gregor. "Senses, Imagination, and Literature: Some Epistemological Considerations." In *Rethinking the Medieval Senses: Heritage, Fascinations, Frames*, eds. Stephen G. Nichols, Andreas Kablitz, and Alison Calhoun. Baltimore: The Johns Hopkins University Press, 2008, 51–72.
Wagner, Monika. "Gips." In *Lexikon des künstlerischen Materials: Werkstoffe der modernen Kunst von Abfall bis Zinn*, ed. M. Wagner. Munich: Beck, 2002, 106–113.
Wagner, Ralf Richard. "Arkadien auch in Schwetzingen?" In *Hofoper in Schwetzingen: Musik – Bühnenmusik – Architektur*, ed. Silke Leopold and Bärbel Pelker. Heidelberg: Winter, 2004, 39–54.
Warmoes, Isabelle. "La collection des plans-reliefs français et la question de la représentation du relief chez les ingénieurs militaires (XVIIe–XIXe siècle)." In *Europa Miniature: Die kulturelle Bedeutung des Reliefs, 16.–21. Jahrhundert*, ed. Andreas Bürgi. Zürich: Verlag Neue Zürcher Zeitung, 2007, 115–126.
—. *Musée des Plans-Relief: Historic Models of Fortified Towns*. Paris: Patrimoine, 1999.
Watanabe-O'Kelly, Helen. "The Management of Knowledge at the Electoral Court of Saxony in Dresden." In *Ways of Knowing: Ten Interdisciplinary Essays*, ed. Mary Lindemann. Boston: Brill, 2004, 53–65.
Weber, Alfred. "Haben Wir Deutsche seit 1945 Versagt?" [1949] In *Politik im Nachkriegsdeutschland*. Alfred-Weber-Gesamtausgabe, vol. 9, ed. Eberhard Demm. Marburg: Metropolis, 2001, 91–107.
Weckel, Ulrike. *Beschämende Bilder: Deutsche Reaktionen auf alliierte Dokumentarfilme über befreite Konzentrationslager*. Stuttgart: Franz Steiner, 2012.
Weiss, Roberto. *The Renaissance Discovery of Classical Antiquity*. Oxford: Basil Blackwell, 1969.
Welzbacher, Christian. "Der Wiederaufbau des Frankfurter Goethehauses: Altstadtsanierung – Schöpferische Rekonstruktion – Kulturpessimismus – Symbolpolitik." In *Die Alte Stadt* 33 (2006), 317–330.

Welzer, Harald. "Krieg der Generationen: Zur Tradierung von NS-Vergangenheit und Krieg in deutschen Familien." In *Nachkrieg in Deutschland*, ed. Klaus Naumann. Hamburg: Hamburger Edition, 2001, 552–571.

Wendler, Reinhard. *Das Modell zwischen Kunst und Wissenschaft*. Munich: Fink, 2013.

—. *Die Rolle der Modelle in Werk- und Erkenntnisprozessen*. Ph.D. diss, Humboldt University, Berlin, 2008.

Werner, Ferdinand. "Der Garten der kurfürstlichen Sommerresidenz Schwetzingen." In *Lebenslust und Frömmigkeit: Kurfürst Carl Theodor (1724–1799) zwischen Barock und Aufklärung*, ed. Alfried Wieczorek. Regensburg: Pustet, 1997, 63–72.

Whately, Thomas. *Observations on Modern Gardening, Illustrated by Descriptions*. London: Payne, 1770.

White, Hayden. "The Irrational and the Problem of Historical Knowledge in the Enlightenment." In *Irrationalism in the Eighteenth Century*, ed. Harold E. Pagliaro. Cleveland, OH: Press of Case Western Reserve University, 1972, 303–321.

—. *Irrationalism in the Eighteenth Century*. Cleveland, OH: Press of Case Western Reserve University, 1972.

—. *Metahistory: The Historical Imagination in Nineteenth-Century Europe*. Baltimore: The Johns Hopkins University Press, 1973.

Wieczorek, Alfred, ed. *Lebenslust und Frömmigkeit: Kurfürst Carl Theodor (1724–1799) zwischen Barock und Aufklärung*. Regensburg: Pustet, 1997.

Wiegand, Hermann. "Zwei geistige Antipoden am Hof Carl Theodors – Voltaire und Desbillons." In *Lebenslust und Frömmigkeit: Kurfürst Carl Theodor (1724–1799) zwischen Barock und Aufklärung*, ed. Alfried Wieczorek. Regensburg: Pustet, 1997, 159–168.

Wierling, Dorothee. "Generations as Narrative Communities: Some Private Sources of Public Memory in Postwar Germany." In *Histories of the Aftermath: The Legacies of the Second World War in Europe*, ed. Frank Biess and Robert G. Moeller. New York: Berghahn, 2010, 102–120.

Wilms, Wilfried. "Speak no Evil, Write no Evil: In Search of a Usable Language of Destruction." In *W. G. Sebald: History – Memory – Trauma*, ed. Scott Denham and Mark McCulloh. New York: de Gruyter, 2006, 183–204.

Wilson, Catherine. *The Invisible World: Early Modern Philosophy and the Invention of the Microscope*. Princeton: Princeton University Press, 1995.

Wilton-Ely, John. *Piranesi, Paestum & Soane*. London: Azimuth, 2001.

Wintermeyer, Ingo. "'... kaum eine Schmerzensspur hinterlassen ... '? Luftkrieg, Literatur und der 'cordon sanitaire.'" In *Verschiebebahnhöfe der Erinnerung: Zum Werk W. G. Sebalds*, ed. Sigurd Martin and Ingo Wintermeyer. Würzburg: Königshausen & Neumann, 2007, 137–161.

Wolff, Paul, and Fried Lübbecke. *Alt-Frankfurt* [in 3 Folgen]. Frankfurt: Englert & Schlosser, 1923–1926.

Woodward, Christopher. *In Ruins*. New York: Pantheon, 2001.

Yates, Frances A. *Theatre of the World*. Chicago: University of Chicago Press, 1969.

Zeyher, Johann Michael, and G. Roemer. *Beschreibung der Gartenanlagen zu Schwetzingen: Mit 8 Kupfern und einem Plane des Gartens*. Mannheim: Benderische Buchhandlung, 1809.

Zeyher, Johann Michael, and J. G. Rieger. *Schwezingen und seine Garten-Anlagen*. Mannheim: Schwan und Götz [1826].

Zimmermann, Max Georg. *Die bildenden Künste am Hof Herzog Albrecht's V. von Bayern*. Strasbourg: Heitz, 1895.

Zimmermann, Reinhard. *Hortus Palatinus: Die Entwürfe zum Heidelberger Schlossgarten von Salomon de Caus, 1620*. Worms: Wernersche Verlagsgesellschaft, 1986.
—. *Künstliche Ruinen: Studien zu ihrer Bedeutung und Form*. Wiesbaden: Reichert, 1989.
—. "Ruin." In *The Dictionary of Art*, vol. 27. London: Macmillan, 1996, 323–324.
Zuckmayer, Carl. *Deutschlandbericht für das Kriegsministerium der Vereinigten Staaten von Amerika*, ed. Gunther Nickel, Johanna Schrön, and Hans Wagener. Frankfurt am Main: Fischer, 2007.
Zürcher, Gustav. "'Vom elenden, herrlichen Leben': Die Nachkriegsgedichte von Marie Luise Kaschnitz." In *Marie Luise Kaschnitz*, ed. Uwe Schweikert. Frankfurt am Main: Suhrkamp, 1984, 193–208.
Zupko, Ronald Edward. *Italian Weights and Measures: From the Middle Ages to the Nineteenth Century*. Philadelphia: American Philosophical Society, 1981.

Movies

Demenok, Artem, dir. *Welthauptstadt Germania*. Documentary, 52 min., ARTE/RBB. Germany 2004.
The Effects of the Atomic Bomb on Hiroshima and Nagasaki. Documentary, Japan [1946]. Tokyo: Nichiei Eizō [2010].
Ophuls, Max, dir. *Lola Montès* [1955]. DVD. Criterion Collection, 2010.
Resnais, Alain, dir. *Hiroshima mon amour* [1959]. DVD. Criterion Collection, 2003.
Resnais, Alain, dir. *Nuit et bruillard* [1955]. DVD. Criterion Collection, 2003.
Riefenstahl, Leni von, dir. *Triumph des Willens* [1935]. DVD. Synapse Films, 2006.
Wilder, Billy, dir. *A Foreign Affair* [1948]. Universal Pictures.

Online Sources

Abschlussbericht der Historikerkommission zu den Luftangriffen auf Dresden zwischen dem 13. und 15. Februar 1945 (Dresden: Landeshauptstadt Dresden, 2010) <http://www.dresden.de/media/pdf/infoblaetter/Historikerkommission_Dresden1945_Abschlussbericht_V1_14a.pd>.
Arnold, Jörg. "Sammelrez: Bombenkrieg." In H-Soz-u-Kult, June 28, 2004 <http://hsozkult.geschichte.hu-berlin.de/rezensionen/2004-2-062>.
Blank, Ralf. "Review of Jörg Friedrich's *Brandstätten: Der Anblick des Bombenkriegs* (2003)." In H-Soz-u-Kult, October 22, 2003 <http://hsozkult.geschichte.hu-berlin.de/rezensionen/2003-4-044>.
Ference, Ian. "On 'Ruin Porn.'" In *Huffingtonpost*, posted January 31, 2011 <http://www.huffingtonpost.com/ian-ference/on-ruin-porn_b_816593.html>.
Leary, John Patrick. "Detroitism." In *Guernica*, January 15, 2011 <http://www.guernicamag.com/spotlight/2281/leary_1_15_11/>.
Morton, Thomas. "Something, Something, Something, Detroit: Lazy Journalists Love Pictures of Abandoned Stuff." In *Vice* [2009] <http://www.viceland.com/int/v16n8/htdocs/something-something-something-detroit-994.php?page=1>.

Pecker, James E. "Italo Gismondi and Pierino Di Carlo: 'Virtualizing' Imperial Rome for 20th C. Italy." In *American Journal of Archeology* 112 (2008) <http://www.ajaonline.org/sites/default/files/01_Packer%20RvArt.pdf>.
Vergara, Camilo José. *Invincible Cities* <http://invinciblecities.camden.rutgers.edu/intro.html>.
Virtuelle Altstadt [Frankfurt am Main] <http://www.virtuelle-altstadt.de/das-altstadtmodell.html>

Index